S0-EAP-866

WITHDRAWN
UTSA LIBRARIES

DRY MESSIAH

The Life of Bishop Cannon

Virginius Dabney

DRY MESSIAH

THE LIFE
OF BISHOP CANNON

GREENWOOD PRESS, PUBLISHERS
WESTPORT, CONNECTICUT

Copyright 1949 by Virginius Dabney

Reprinted with the permission
of Alfred A. Knopf, Inc., New York

Reprinted from an original copy in the collections
of the Brooklyn Public Library

First Greenwood Reprinting 1970

Library of Congress Catalogue Card Number 73-110825

SBN 8371-3225-8

Printed in the United States of America

He belonged to that class of eminent ecclesiastics — and it is by no means a small class — who have been distinguished less for saintliness and learning than for practical ability. Had he lived in the Middle Ages he would certainly have been neither a Francis nor an Aquinas, but he might have been an Innocent. . . . And in any case, by what odd chances, by what shifts and struggles, what combinations of circumstance and character had this old man come to be where he was? Such questions are easier to ask than to answer; but it may be instructive, and even amusing, to look a little more closely into the complexities of so curious a story.

— "Cardinal Manning"
by Lytton Strachey

Foreword

BISHOP JAMES CANNON, JR., one of the most extraordinary personalities of his time, was an American type who needs to be studied and understood. A man of colossal energy, vast shrewdness, and consummate ability, he was one of the country's salient figures in the era when ecclesiastical edicts were being widely translated into statutory enactments, and even into organic law.

The furious zeal that he brought to his crusade for prohibition and the almost superhuman will that spurred him on were as characteristic of him as was his willingness to use questionable means if they promised to be effective.

The career of no other personage in the prohibition movement affords quite so broad and inclusive an insight into Anti-Saloon League strategy and tactics on the local, the state, the national, and the world level. Bishop Cannon was a leader for nearly half a century in league work, and he was conspicuous in all four of the above-mentioned areas of prohibitionist agitation. Not only so, but after achieving his goal in three of them, he founded the World League Against Alcoholism, and sought to bring in the millennium on a global scale.

Not much is left today of the structure of legalized morality he helped to create; yet there are signs that strong and aggressive prohibitionist movements are under way in various parts of the country. Dry leaders not only express a determination to bring prohibition back on a state-by-state basis to the nation as a whole, but certain spokesmen for the brewers and the distillers say there is real danger that the effort will succeed. Several nonpartisan publicists have scanned the political and social horizon of late and have concluded that we may well be faced in the fairly near future with another fierce prohibitionist onslaught. The setbacks sustained by the drys in November 1948, notably in Kansas, are regarded by their strategists merely as incentives to a redoubled effort.

If and when that effort brings the long-awaited drive for the revival of prohibition, the career of Bishop Cannon should afford instructive warnings to everyone concerned.

The drys, viewing the fate that finally overtook both the Bishop and prohibition, can hardly fail to recognize that the adverse reaction to Cannon's methods in this and other fields was highly significant in bringing about the Eighteenth Amendment's downfall. Those methods, as shown in the pages that follow, were used effectively in his local-option campaigns in Virginia and in his state-wide campaign there. They were transferred to the national stage, and were employed in some degree in the world movement. Although temporarily successful, they proved a boomerang in the end.

Such techniques were unworthy of the millions of sincere men and women who prayed, worked, and sacrificed for prohibition, in the firm conviction that theirs was a righteous cause. Yet these methods were typical of a certain coterie of professional drys, who seemed more concerned with ends than with means.

Above all, Cannon's story should be a warning to the army of Americans who oppose any return to the lawlessness, hypocrisy, and fraud that are synonymous with prohibition. It should put them on guard against the sharp practices that Cannon used in the early years of the century to usher in the dry dispensation, and should make them wary of future dry messiahs who lull them to sleep with soothing soporifics and pious pronouncements.

James Cannon, Jr., has been termed "the most powerful ecclesiastic ever heard of in America." One of his doughtiest adversaries conceded that he had "the best brain in America, no one excepted."

Certainly he was one of the most significant and most ominous figures of his time, a man whose tempestuous career holds lessons for us all.

Richmond, Virginia

CONTENTS

ILLUSTRATIONS

DRY MESSIAH

The Life of Bishop Cannon

CHAPTER *i*

Genesis of a Moral Leader

SHERMAN was blasting his way through Georgia, and Lee was entrenched for his last desperate stand in front of Petersburg, when a dyspeptic youth, who made it a practice never to swear or to touch tobacco or alcohol, confided to his diary as he lay encamped with a unit of the Federal Army in Florida:

> Again tempted and found wanting. Sin, sin. Oh how much peace and happiness is sacrificed on thy altar. Seemed as though Devil had full sway over me today, went right into temptation, and then, Oh such love, Jesus snatched it away out of my reach.

Some time later the young man wrote that he "spent part of day foolishly as I look back, read a Novel part through." Then four days afterward, on November 13, 1864, he recorded:

> Rev. Mr. Lewis came on boat and preached to us . . . plain simple his words, yet by aid of Holy Spirit was spoken with power. Warmed my soul with Holy love and fired it with greater hatred for sin. The Blessings of this day — O how precious.

The author of these elevating lines was Anthony Comstock, who was to boast half a century later that in his forty-one years with the New York Society for the Suppression of Vice he had "convicted enough persons to fill a passenger train of sixty-one coaches, sixty coaches containing sixty passengers each, and the sixty-first almost full."

And on the same November 13, 1864, another incipient smiter of evildoers was coming into the world. At Salisbury, on Maryland's Eastern Shore, a squealing infant arrived in the family of James Cannon, a prominent local merchant. The baby was named for his father. It was fitting that Anthony Comstock, whom James, Jr., was to praise publicly on various occasions in future years, should have recorded his aversion to iniquity on James's natal day.

The family into which this mewling mite had been born was one of considerable substance. James Cannon, Sr., was of pre-Revolutionary English stock, and his wife, Lydia Primrose, was Scotch in her antecedents. One of the early Cannons in this country was James, professor of mathematics in Benjamin Franklin's College of Philadelphia. This Cannon was one of the leaders in the Pennsylvania State Convention that met in 1776, just across the hall from the Continental Congress.

Another prominent Cannon was William, Governor of Delaware from 1863 to 1865. Governor Cannon was a brother of James Cannon, father of the man who was later to become Bishop Cannon. James Cannon, Sr., was living in Bridgeville, in the southern part of the state, when the Civil War began. His sympathies were so strongly with the Confederacy and he proclaimed them so loudly that he finally was forced to flee in order to escape arrest. His brother, the Governor, aided him in his flight.

Cannon and his wife, together with their two young children, a son and a daughter, settled in the town of Salisbury, Maryland, where the father purchased a large house at the corner of Main and St. Peter streets. He opened a men's furnishings and shoe business in the same building. It was there that James Cannon, Jr., was born late in 1864. The site is now occupied by a drugstore.

It is significant that the Cannon family has a long record of antipathy to intoxicants, and that in Sussex County, Delaware, where Bridgeville is situated, the first grocer who refused to sell alcoholic beverages was a Cannon.

The atmosphere in which young James grew up was one of extreme piety and inherited hatred of saloons. His parents attended the Methodist Church in Salisbury until the close of the war, but the pastor persisted in making such offensive references to the Confederacy and its sympathizers that the Cannons and

4

others withdrew in 1866 and formed Trinity Methodist Episcopal Church, South. The elder Cannon and his wife were among its most zealous and devoted members throughout their residence in Salisbury. Cannon was superintendent of the Sunday school for many years, as well as chairman of the Board of Stewards. Daily family prayers, Wednesday-night prayer meeting, and Friday-night class meeting were on the unvarying agenda of the Cannons, together with the usual Sunday school and Sabbath preaching service. Nothing was permitted to interfere with these rites.

It is a curious fact, however, in view of his subsequent career, that young James did not become a full-fledged member of the church until he went to college. Exhorted more than once by evangelists to "come to Jesus," he declined.[1] It was not until he was converted at a revival while a student at Randolph-Macon College that he affiliated formally with the church.

Jim or Jimmie Cannon, as he was called, seems to have led a fairly normal existence during his youth in Salisbury. He was a delicate boy, but not sickly. He took part in such sports as baseball, but there is no record that he developed any particular virtuosity in this sphere. He had a riding horse and attended to it himself. Those who knew him at this period say he was not so austere as he later became, and that he seemed to be endowed with something closely resembling a sense of humor. He made an excellent record as a student in the local grammar and high schools, and was graduated from the latter, the Wicomico High School, at the age of only fifteen. Instead of entering college the following autumn, he took graduate work at the school for another session. During his years in high school he did a good deal of outside reading.

His parents were among the most prominent and respected of Salisbury's citizens. Then, as now, the towns of rural Maryland were predominantly pietistic and Sabbatarian in their attitudes, and James and Lydia Cannon found the atmosphere congenial. Mrs. Cannon was active in temperance work, and it was while accompanying her on her rounds among the poor that her son obtained his first glimpse of the dire effects of excessive drink. There were twelve saloons in Salisbury, which was the center of the liquor trade on the lower part of the Eastern Shore peninsula.

Dry Messiah

Mrs. Cannon organized the local Woman's Christian Temperance Union. It had only two other members at the outset, but her zeal was great, and she continued to fight for the elimination of the saloon. Her efforts were finally successful, but not until two years after her death, which occurred in 1902. Mrs. Cannon was buried with the pin of the White Ribbon on her breast, the only jewelry she had ever worn.

Young Jim was a frequent attendant at the temperance meetings held in the seventies and eighties, when the nation-wide movement was getting up steam. The primary aim at these gatherings was to persuade those present to "sign the pledge." This commitment to aridity usually read: "I hereby pledge myself, God being my helper, to abstain from the use of intoxicating liquors (including wine and cider), except in cases of necessity." Of course, the final clause provided a Gargantuan loophole for snide fellows with elastic consciences. Perhaps it was for this reason that Frances E. Willard, whose election as national president of the W.C.T.U. in 1879 gave a powerful fillip to the temperance movement, composed the following rhymed pledge for children:

> I promise not to buy, sell or give
> Alcoholic liquors while I live;
> From all tobacco I'll abstain
> And never take God's name in vain.

If a young blade at a temperance meeting seemed reluctant to sign on the dotted line, attendant W.C.T.U.'s taxed his powers of resistance by chanting:

> Young man why will you not sign the pledge,
> And stand with the true and the brave?
> How dare you lean over the dangerous ledge,
> Above the inebriate's grave?

Such procedures were works of supererogation in the case of Jim Cannon. He not only signed the pledge, but at the age of twelve promised his mother to aid her in her fight on the whisky business. He kept his promise and was doubtless among the youthful members of the Loyal Temperance Legion, whose ominous slogan was: "Tremble, King Alcohol, we shall grow up!"

6

They grew up in time to outlaw His Majesty for a period of nearly thirteen years. There is no reason to believe that Jim Cannon ever patronized the saloons of Salisbury. In fact, it may be taken for granted that he did not.

In the fall of 1881, following a year of graduate work in the local high school, Cannon was matriculated in Randolph-Macon College, situated in the village of Ashland, Virginia, fifteen miles north of Richmond on the Richmond-Washington highway. Randolph-Macon, founded in 1830, is the oldest incorporated Methodist college in the United States and is one of the superior Southern denominational institutions. It was named for John Randolph of Roanoke and Nathaniel Macon of North Carolina, for no other reason, apparently, than that they were prominent in public affairs a century or more ago. Neither was a Methodist and, as the college historian sadly records, neither was even a "professed Christian." "Nor did either," the historian goes on, "ever manifest any interest in the college by making a contribution to it or otherwise." Indeed, William Cabell Bruce tells us in his biography of Randolph that when that waspish gentleman was asked if he would consent to have this institution for the education of young Methodists named for him, he was said to have replied: "Yes, you may use my name, for when educated they will cease to be Methodists."

It was in this institution of slightly more than one hundred students, with its rather bucolic atmosphere, that James Cannon, Jr., was enrolled. Half a dozen buildings, some of brick and others of frame construction, surrounded the little campus on three sides. Tall trees shaded the walks that connected the class-rooms, the dormitories, and the chapel.

There were two literary societies at Randolph-Macon in 1881, the Washington and the Franklin. Cannon promptly joined the Washington Society and was chosen second vice-president at the first meeting of the session. He could not have been known to many of the members until a week or two before, and his election indicates that he was regarded as something of a leader, even at the age of sixteen. During the succeeding four years he served in almost every office of the society from president down. At each weekly meeting there were orators, declaimers, debaters, and essayists, and Cannon was often active in one or another of these roles. The minutes show that even in his first session he made a decided impression as a debater, for the secretary, in describing the ability with which he upheld the affirmative of the question: Should the Sexes be Educated in the Same Room? declares: "We were all amazed to see the speaker so eloquent." This was in January 1882, when Cannon was seventeen. Such references to the eloquence of members are rare in the minutes of the society.

Usually the themes discussed were of a serious nature, but occasionally there were such sophomoric performances as debates on "Resolved, that the looking glass is more beneficial to the ladies than the hairbrush," or "Resolved, that the calico ticket is beneficial to students." Cannon proclaimed the virtues of the looking glass as against those of the hairbrush, but did not participate in the discussion concerning the "calico ticket," a late nineteenth-century synonym for "the ladies." This despite the fact that he was something of a savant in the field, for at the time he was wooing Miss Lura Virginia Bennett, daughter of Dr. W. W. Bennett, president of the college. They were married some years later.

The Washington Literary Society conducted its meetings under strict parliamentary rules, and fines were imposed upon members who violated those rules. There were also fines for such offenses as eating in the hall, failing to be prepared for debate or declamation when called on, "shooting a marble across the floor," and so on. In one instance Jim was fined a dollar. The minutes give no clue to the nature of the offense that brought down this severe penalty upon him. Usually the fines ranged from ten to fifty cents.

The society elected Cannon "first commencement orator" in 1884, and "society medalist" in 1885. It also chose him in 1883 as one of the six representatives on the board of directors of the *Randolph-Macon Monthly.*

Thus there appears to be little doubt that Jim was admired by a fair number of his fellow students. On the other hand, some of these insist that he was on the whole "very unpopular." They describe him as having been excessively solemn and serious, dyspeptic in appearance, and puritanical in his ideas — in short, "a Cromwellian." These college-mates declare that Cannon kept strictly in the paths of rectitude and virtue, and that he also sought to dissuade his friends from moral lapses. One Randolph-Macon graduate reports that, in discussing a student who frequently interlarded his talk with the something less than sulphurous expletive "By gravy!" Cannon declared that nearly every other word of this man was an oath. Obviously, Jim was regarded by some as an exemplar of the *unco guid.*

Cannon's hatred of liquor increased during his years at Randolph-Macon, for he seems to have had difficulties with some of his acquaintances. Years later he described his experiences in the following language:

> I saw my fellow-students led off into back rooms and supplied with drink from "regulated" licensed saloons, and have helped to carry them to their rooms and put them to bed, foolishly drunk, noisily drunk, stupidly drunk, disgustingly drunk, crazily drunk. I have sat beside them and held their heads when their stomachs revolted against the poison which had been poured into them. I have helped to hold them in bed when, crazy with the poison, they have struggled to get up and fight somebody. I have tried to get them in shape for work the next day, so that they might not be called up and expelled.

At about the time that Cannon entered the college, Dr. Bennett, its president, founded the *Southern Crusader,* a temperance paper, and began a vigorous movement for the passage of a local option law by the Virginia legislature. The whisky business in the state was then operating almost without restrictions of any kind, and it was the aim of Dr. Bennett, and of Dr. W. W. Smith, later president of Randolph-Macon Woman's College, to bring about the adoption of legislation permitting each community to decide whether it would be "wet" or "dry." Cannon was one of several young people who aided in the work by folding and addressing the *Crusader* for the mail. Partly as a result of this campaign, both the principal political parties promised in their platforms to favor a local option law, and such a law was passed in 1886 by a large majority.

The immense energy which Cannon revealed in later years

was made partially manifest at Randolph-Macon. In addition to his constant preoccupation with the work of the Washington Literary Society and his mailing of temperance leaflets, he was an occasional participant in campus games of baseball and football, and he belonged to the Sigma Chi fraternity. His wooing of Miss Bennett also was one of his more important extra-curricular activities.

His exceptional record as a student was due in part to his ability and in part to his industry. He revealed uncommon literary capacity and in 1884, the year he was awarded the B.A. degree, he won the Pace Medal for the best essay written by a member of the student body. He took as his subject the Mormon question, which was widely discussed at the period, and was regarded by many as involving a "moral issue." After winning his degree he returned the following year and took a number of graduate courses.

In March 1885 he caught a severe cold standing in the rain at the inauguration of Grover Cleveland and it settled in his lungs. The illness almost killed him, but he pulled through. When he recovered, he spent six months tramping through the mountains of western North Carolina, and he never had any further lung trouble. This was fortunate, as his brother and sister both died of tuberculosis at a fairly early age.

Cannon was one of the most zealous of Randolph-Macon alumni, and for several years in the early 1900's he served as president of the Randolph-Macon College Alumni Society. In 1903 the college conferred on him the honorary degree of Doctor of Divinity.

Restored in health by his tramp through the North Carolina mountains, Jim Cannon was matriculated at Princeton Theological Seminary in the autumn of 1885. Princeton Seminary was a Presbyterian institution and he was the only Methodist on its rolls when he entered. With characteristic determination he not only enrolled for the regular three-year course but decided that during the same period he would take an M.A. at Princeton College.

Owing to the proximity of New York City, the young ministerial student spent frequent week-ends there. The colossal thieveries of Tammany Hall under the Tweed Ring had been unveiled some years before, but the Tiger had largely recovered from these revelations and was once more dominant on Manhattan, thanks to the gracious collaboration of the saloon- and brothel-keepers and the proprietors of gambling hells. Such a gaudy sociological picture was attractive in more ways than one to Cannon's inquiring mind. He seems to have passed most of his New York week-ends at the Bowery and Water Street missions, where the human wreckage spewed up from the Tammany sewers presented some intriguing case histories for an aspiring theologue.

He completed his courses at the seminary and the college successfully, and at the end of three years was awarded the B.D. degree by the former and the M.A. by the latter. At the college he passed graduate work in ethics, philosophy, history, and Assyriology. Thus in 1888, at the age of twenty-three, James Cannon, Jr., was ready for the Methodist ministry and far better equipped than most of his colleagues in that calling.

His first business venture of consequence came in his senior year at the seminary. He and John L. Lee, afterward a prominent Presbyterian clergyman, were elected by the class as book agents. This entitled them to a room free of rent, where they kept current volumes on sale. The students got a discount on the books of from twenty-five to thirty-three per cent, and the agents a profit of from ten to fifteen per cent. The two men planned to earn enough money to enable each to marry and to go to Scotland for a year of study; but after a couple of months Lee decided that the agency consumed too much of his time and asked Cannon to take it over. The latter, with typical energy and indefatigability, assumed the whole burden and even added one or two sidelines in the shape of encyclopedias, dictionaries, and so on. He made a profit for the year of about three thousand dollars, including a thousand dollars' worth of books. It was a sample of the extremely shrewd business judgment he was to show thenceforth.

As matters turned out, Cannon did not go to Scotland for a year of study. He and Lura Bennett were married on August 1, 1888, in Louisa County, Virginia, where her family had removed following her father's retirement as president of Randolph-Macon. Instead of journeying to Niagara Falls or some other equally fashionable retreat for those dwelling in newly acquired hymeneal bliss, they went to the Chautauqua Assembly at Chautauqua, New York, and spent three weeks "taking the Bible course and attending the lectures and concerts, and enjoying the good fellowship."

Then on November 13 of that year, his twenty-fourth birthday, the Rev. James Cannon, Jr., formally joined the Virginia Conference of the Methodist Episcopal Church, South, at Portsmouth, bought a horse and buggy, and began the career of a Methodist circuit rider.

CHAPTER *ii*

Pastor and Pedagogue

THE FIRST charge entrusted to the young pastor by the conference consisted of six small churches in Charlotte County, one
of the tobacco counties in Southside Virginia near the North
Carolina line. The Civil War had ended only twenty-three years
before and, like the rest of the South, Charlotte had not emerged
from the shadow of defeat. Then, as now, the county was almost
wholly rural, for there was no town inside its borders with more
than a few hundred inhabitants.

Cannon and his bride boarded at Keysville and also for a time
at Charlotte Courthouse. With one or the other of these small
villages as his headquarters, the fledgling cleric covered the circuit in his buggy. The distance from one end of it to the other
was twenty miles, and over the roads of that era it was sometimes difficult to keep engagements. Cannon often drove his
horse furiously, and the equipage careened crazily from side
to side as it tore over the ruts and "thank-you-ma'ams," raising
clouds of dust or slithering through the mud.

Cannon does not appear to have become involved in any sort
of controversy or to have incurred any notable antagonisms during his year on the Charlotte circuit, but, whereas most of his
predecessors and successors on the circuit were regarded with
affection by their parishioners, few, if any, ever spoke affectionately of him. All conceded his capacity for achievement and his
great kinetic force, but even his admirers confessed that he was
not a lovable, or even a companionable, person. It was impossible
to "feel close to him," one of his chief defenders admitted.

13

Lura, a daughter, the first of the Cannons' nine children, was born while they were in Charlotte. Not long afterward, at the end of twelve months on that circuit, Cannon was transferred to the seaport town of Newport News, situated on Virginia's great landlocked harbor, Hampton Roads. In that urban atmosphere his latent propensity for speculative business ventures burgeoned handsomely. He bought lots in various sections of the city, took stock in land companies, and joined with friends in the erection of a block of tenement houses, which he held as an investment for some time.[1] In 1891, after two years in Newport News, he was transferred to a considerably better charge, the church at Farmville. This shift took him back into the tobacco belt once more, to one of its most prosperous towns. In addition to looking after his pastoral duties there, Cannon purchased lots in various places, as well as bank stock.[2] If it is deemed astonishing that a man who apparently had only the most limited financial resources, and who had merely held a small rural circuit for one year, could have embarked upon such extensive business ventures, the fact is that he nevertheless did so. He had an unquestioned penchant for such matters, and he was to make the most of his talent from that time forward.

While he was at Farmville, a group of Methodists in that area secured a charter from the Virginia legislature incorporating the Blackstone Female Institute at Blackstone, Nottoway County, another tobacco town. After obtaining the charter in 1892, they began erecting a building, but were unable to complete it because of insufficient funds. The board of trustees owed $11,000, the unfinished building contained no furniture, they could borrow no more money, and they could not guarantee any salary for principal or teachers. After trying unsuccessfully to persuade various persons to take charge of the institute, they finally turned to Cannon, then twenty-nine years of age. At first he laughed at the idea. All but one of his friends advised him to decline the offer. He told the trustees that he would not take the position if they could get anyone else, but he finally gave in and in 1894 became principal of the hollow shell known as the Blackstone Female Institute.

How hard he had to work in order to establish the institute

as a going concern is shown by the fact that he grew a beard solely because he could not spare ten minutes a day for shaving. He was to drive himself at virtually the same terrific pace for the next quarter of a century and to remain unshaven throughout the entire period. In 1908 he wrote concerning his labors in building up the institute:

> For the first seven years Mr. Cannon was at Blackstone, he averaged 19 hours per day of hard work. He drove his buggy time and again over well nigh every part of Eastern Virginia, he preached three times nearly every Sunday, driving from thirty to sixty miles; he was stable boy, drayman, trainman, steward, bookkeeper, canvassing agent, professor and principal. He put the ordinary work of fourteen years into seven. For the last seven years Mr. Cannon has worked on the average of 18 hours a day. He has been obliged, owing to the size of the school, to give up his position as stable boy, drayman and trainman, and to divide the work of canvassing, but he has continued to be steward, bookkeeper, assistant canvasser, professor and principal. He risked all his money and pledged all his credit to build up the Blackstone Institute.

In 1929 Cannon said that in order to enable parents to send their children to the institute he "bought and sold horses, cattle, hogs, wheat, corn, timber, stumpage — anything which had property value — and wherever possible I tried to make a fair profit, and I usually did." Apparently these various commodities were accepted in lieu of cash from parents who were unable to pay tuition for their daughters in any other way.

When Cannon became principal at Blackstone, a lofty moral note was struck at the outset, for he provided the institution with the motto: "Thorough Instruction Under Positive Christian Influences at Lowest Possible Cost." In the catalogue one finds the following elucidation of the school's *raison d'être:*

> In estimating rightly the value of any school as a place for the training of children, Christian parents must take this question into consideration: What place is given to the soul in the work of this school? When tested by this standard, private schools established for the purpose of making money fall short; state schools are under the same condemnation . . . the religious belief of the fac-

ulty of instruction is not a controlling question – they may even be *free thinkers* or *agnostics,* as some of them are. A distinctly Christian school is the only kind which gives to the soul its proper place, and can satisfactorily answer the question of the Christian parent. *Other schools train for earth; the truly Christian school trains for earth and heaven.*

Principal Cannon was especially critical of the State Female Normal School. It offered everything in the way of instruction that was offered at Blackstone, and more besides. At the same time, its rates were as low, if not lower. Situated only about thirty miles away, it was in direct competition with his own institution. His chief criticism was that the normal school was not operated under "positive Christian influences." For instance, under the heading "Teacher's Course" in the Blackstone catalogue, the following statement is made: "This course is specially arranged for those who wish to prepare themselves for teaching, yet do not wish to go to the *State School* [at Farmville], but who wish to be in a *Christian School.*" This statement is repeated under the heading "Pedagogy."

While the presidency at Farmville was occupied, during Cannon's incumbency at Blackstone, by active and zealous church members, there was no requirement that every teacher "must openly declare a belief in the Gospel of our Lord Jesus Christ," such as was invariably stipulated at Blackstone. The courses given conformed to the general pattern of evangelical orthodoxy. The catalogue explained, for example, that the course in "history is taught not simply to cultivate the memory, but to bring clearly to the mind of the student the relation of one age to another, and to show that in all the ages an increasing purpose runs, and that God rules and directs all things." The catalogue also contained this reassuring dictum: "We give the names of the students, but not their postoffices, as the catalogues of schools are frequently sought by godless wretches to send debasing literature to the students." With respect to the relationship between the principal and his charges, it is stated: "No young ladies are wanted as students at the institute who are not willing to accept the guidance of the principal as that of an older friend, who is planning to give them such training as will develop them into helpful and attractive women."

In his management of the Blackstone Institute, as in his other labors in all parts of America and beyond the seas, Cannon revealed the most prodigious energy, the most extraordinary talent for practical accomplishment, and the most astounding ability to turn out a vast deal of work in a short time. It must be remembered that after he had put the institute firmly on its feet — that is, by the early 1900's — he became increasingly active in other spheres, so that his total volume of work was as great as ever. His ability to keep up with the affairs of the school, despite prolonged absences, was a never failing source of wonder to those who observed it. For example, he would return to the institute after several months in Europe and, in the small interval of twenty-four hours before his departure elsewhere, familiarize himself with the grade of work done by each of the four hundred students, in addition to many other matters relating to the institution. His memory was so accurate that, with no opportunity to examine the record of a student except on one of these hurried trips, he found it possible, as much as a year or two afterward, to converse intelligently with her parents concerning her work.

Cannon was principal of the institute from 1894 until 1918, when he was elevated to the episcopacy. After his election to the superintendency of the Virginia Anti-Saloon League in 1909, he concluded that an associate principal was needed, and in May 1910 the Rev. Thomas Rosser Reeves, a Methodist, was chosen by the trustees. During the session of 1910–11, Reeves was the actual head of the institution, but Cannon retained the title. Then in 1911 Cannon was asked to take over the arduous task of establishing the Southern Assembly at Lake Junaluska, North Carolina, and he accepted. He returned to Blackstone as principal in 1914 and remained until he relinquished the post permanently four years later.

Cannon was subjected to heavy verbal shelling from time to time by Methodists who sought to ascertain the amount of his annual compensation from the school. The first important offensive of this sort was launched in 1908, when the Revs. W. W. Lear and J. A. Winn, prominent Methodist ministers, and Richard B. Davis, a leading layman who had served as Assistant Attorney-General of Virginia, made an effort to learn the size of Cannon's salary.[3]

Davis wrote Cannon that he was currently reported to be receiving between $5,000 and $10,000 a year from the Blackstone Female Institute and asked whether this was correct. Cannon denied that he had obtained "an average yearly salary" of as much as $5,000. At about the same time he denied receiving "from $5,000 to $10,000 a year from the Blackstone Female Institute." Whether these denials took account of the amounts he received in the shape of living quarters and board for his large family and tuition for his daughters is not known.

In discussing Cannon's contract with the institute Davis said:

> First, this school assigns and turns over to its principal at 100 cents on the dollar, in part payment of his salary, all of its unpaid accounts, including debts known to be uncollectible. This seems to me a very pernicious practice, as it puts all the debtors of a church school in the hands of an individual and at his mercy.
>
> Second, Mr. Cannon takes all the unpaid accounts and worthless debts of the school at face value, in part payment of his salary. . . .
>
> Third, if Mr. Cannon holds thousands of dollars worth of school debts that will never be collected, he certainly holds very strong instruments of obligation against certain debtors that might give him powerful influence with some persons.

In reply Cannon said:

> They raise the cry that Mr. Cannon is insincere because he is making "$5,000 per year." And Mr. Cannon tells them . . . that . . . he would never have done what he has for the past fourteen years for $5,000 per year for any purely business enterprise, and if he had invested in the same amount of money and labor in other ways, he believes that he would easily have made double that which he has received from his contract with the Blackstone Institute. . . .
>
> If Mr. Davis were able to calculate the interest on the money which has been due Mr. Cannon on the books from time to time, and if Mr. Davis could calculate what amount of the debts held

by Mr. Cannon will be collected, he might be able to get an accurate estimate of Mr. Cannon's income from the school. But as this is not easily done, Mr. Davis will have to remain ignorant, as is Mr. Cannon, of Mr. Cannon's average yearly income from the Blackstone Institute. . . .

The fact remains that the trustees . . . are satisfied with their income, and that the Farmville District Conference, under whose supervision and control the institute is conducted . . . declined to request an investigation of the financial affairs of the institute, thus showing implicit confidence in the management of the school.

G. T. Cralle, one of the trustees, entered the controversy at this point to say that there was "nothing to conceal" about Cannon's salary, and that the matter was being brought up at that time in order to embarrass him because of an uncompromising fight he was making in the Virginia Conference to prevent Randolph-Macon Woman's College from being placed under the Carnegie Foundation for the Advancement of Teaching. Cralle added that "we do not pay him half as much as he is worth."

Three years later the salary question was broached again, when E. G. Moseley, associate editor of the *Danville Methodist* and one of the most prominent laymen in the Virginia Conference, said in his paper:

For years it has been whispered abroad that the Rev. James Cannon, Jr., while principal of the Blackstone Female Institute, and especially for the last seven or eight years of his connection with that institution, received very large sums of money from the institute; that he was lining his pockets with the earnings of this church school, and that he was doing so in accordance with the terms of a contract with the trustees.

Cannon replied [4] that he "would greatly rejoice if he could truthfully assert that his compensation had been $5,000, $7,500, or $10,000 per annum. . . . But he really does not know what he will receive." A week previously he had quoted the executive committee of the institute as saying that he "has used his personal credit and private means for the development of our institute when he could borrow no more money, and this he did without security, sometimes advancing for the board as much as $20,000 to carry on the necessary improvements, and waiting for years for repayment, and never taking one dollar of interest for the thousands he has advanced." The committee added that he had "taken the unpaid accounts on our books as part payment of his salary . . . and he holds today thousands of dollars of notes and book accounts which can never be collected. He has insisted upon pursuing this course in order that he might feel himself perfectly free to exercise his own judgment in offering educational opportunities to girls who could not otherwise obtain an education."

This arrangement is widely believed to have placed a substantial number of Methodist preachers in the Virginia Conference under financial obligation to him, and to have been one of the sources of his power in that conference.

Apparently the board itself did not know what Cannon was getting from the institution. A letter written by the Rev. W. Asbury Christian,[5] who succeeded Cannon as principal of the institute in 1918, throws a good deal of light on the extent to which the board was uninformed concerning the annual income of the principal. Dr. Christian said:

> When Cannon was president of the institute, afterwards the college, up to Dr. Reeves' presidency [1910–11] all money received was deposited to the credit of James Cannon, Jr., and all checks were made in his name. No one knew what came in and what went out but Cannon. At the annual meeting of the board he made a kind of general report. His contract with the school was never put on the records. A minor contract was recorded in which he was to have all he collected after paying certain expenses, and no report was to be made by him as to the amount he collected on open accounts.

Christian did not touch upon the terms of the arrangement between Cannon and the board for the period that followed Reeves's presidency. Perhaps he was unfamiliar with it. One surmises that the amount of annual income Cannon derived from the institution will remain an unsolved mystery. Repeated efforts on the part of his adversaries failed to elicit the desired information.

It is highly significant that, whereas his compensation was generally fixed at between $5,000 and $10,000 in the rumors which were bruited about in Methodist circles throughout the state, he reported in his income-tax returns a total income from this and all other sources far below either of these figures. This despite the fact that, in the controversies referred to above, he never intimated that the usufructs of his labors for the school were so infinitesimal. For instance, he said in 1911, as noted above, that he "would greatly rejoice if he could truthfully assert that his compensation had been $5,000, $7,500 or $10,000. . . . But he really does not know what he will receive." There is no hint here that he was getting far less than $5,000, nor is there such a hint in the other statements already cited. But if he was, in fact, being paid on so modest a scale, what possible objection could he have had to saying so, in view of the charges being made in the Methodist press that he was "lining his pockets" and the other assaults made upon him by members of his own denomination?

From 1895 through 1915, state income-tax returns were open to public inspection. If any of Cannon's numerous critics thought of examining his returns, they must have been supremely skeptical as to the accuracy of what they found; for the personal-property books for Nottoway County, Virginia, where he filed his returns, show that the largest total income reported by him from all sources during that entire period was $2,750 for the year 1910. The next highest, $1,900, was reported for 1909, followed by $1,750 for 1908. Between 1895 and 1907 his reported income ranged between $850 and $1,400 yearly. In 1913 and 1914, when the exemption had been raised to $2,000, Cannon swore that his income did not exceed that amount. In 1915, when the exemption was $1,800, with $200 additional for each child under twenty-one years of age, his total exemption could not have exceeded $3,000. He filed no income in excess of that sum.

Yet if we are to believe a written statement he made in 1929,[6] his income prior to his election as Bishop, in May 1918, was much larger than the salary paid to bishops at that time. For in explaining that before his election he had incurred substantial obligations in various places, he said:

> Of course, my election to the episcopacy did not cancel any of these obligations. It was necessary to arrange to meet them, as

well as to support my family and to educate my children, and it was impossible to do these things from my salary as Bishop, *which was much smaller than I had been receiving.* [Italics supplied.]

In 1918 the salary paid to bishops of the Southern Methodist Church was $5,000, with up to $1,200 additional for clerical help or office expenses, together with all traveling expenses while on duty. For the twenty years from 1895 to 1915, then, Cannon never made more than $3,000 in any one year, and most of the time he made far less than that, if his sworn statements to the tax authorities are to be believed. His annual income tax ranged from nothing up to a high of $17.50. Yet he stated in 1929 that prior to 1918 he had made much more than $5,000 per year! He could hardly have meant that he made this only in 1916 and 1917 (for which years his returns were not open to public inspection), because his statement as to the expense of supporting his family and educating his seven living children contains the definite implication that a much longer period was meant. In sum, it is impossible to reconcile Cannon's income-tax returns with his declaration in 1929 concerning his income prior to his election to the episcopacy. The only rational conclusion is that he either falsified his returns or lied about his income.

The size of the Cannon salary was a matter of interest to his neighbors in the town of Blackstone, but they were more largely concerned with his personality and his attitude toward the community. As usual, controversy swirled about his head. The townspeople either liked him very much or disliked him heartily. He and Mrs. Cannon seldom took part in the social life of the neighborhood, and he is said to have discouraged would-be callers from visiting him and his family at the institute. At least one such visitor was informed by Cannon, in what the visitor considered brusque and abrupt language, that he and Mrs. Cannon did not come to Blackstone for social purposes, and that Mrs. Cannon could not take up her time receiving callers. Mrs. Cannon may have wished to ingratiate herself with the neighbors, but from the time of their marriage, six years before, he had dominated her almost completely, and his wishes usually prevailed in the household. Such was to be the case throughout their married life.

The small boys of Blackstone appear to have detested Cannon. The dour, humorless, ascetic-looking man with the black beard, who sought to discipline them for whistling at the girls or being otherwise cantankerous, was regarded by the youngsters as an impossible person. They took great pleasure in bedeviling him. He chased them away from the school scores if not hundreds of times. On one occasion they stretched a wire across his path a short distance from the ground and then began serenading the students. Cannon rushed out of the building, tripped over the wire in the darkness, and fell sprawling, amid the diabolical snickers of his tormentors.

Some of the lads who indulged in these pranks were pupils in the grammar school that he operated at one time for both boys and girls, as a branch of the institute. At recess one day some of these youths pursued a rooster belonging to a woman who lived near by, and succeeded in slaying it with stones. Cannon set out solemnly in quest of the culprit. He held a formal trial, with himself as judge, summoning witnesses and going through the motions of a court hearing. This inquisitorial procedure was regarded as highly ridiculous.

There is reason to believe that Cannon unbent and was much more inclined toward levity in his contacts with the girls at the institute than when he appeared in public. It is unquestionably true that many of the Blackstone students regarded him with unrestrained admiration. He made a determined effort to ingratiate himself with them and he undoubtedly succeeded. Many refused absolutely to credit the charges of various kinds that were hurled at him during his incumbency and after.

The Blackstone trustees seem to have defended Cannon whenever his administration was under attack. Perhaps they felt that criticism of him was, in a measure, aimed at them, because of their responsibility for the proper conduct of their executive officer. It appears likely, however, that most of the board felt Cannon to be a genuinely great man. They were mainly businessmen and merchants from the small towns of southern Virginia, or farmers from that region, and they were undoubtedly awed by Cannon's dominating presence and his truly extraordinary achievement in taking hold of what seemed a hopeless failure and transforming it in a few years into an impressive success. When he retired as principal to become a Bishop, the trustees gave further proof of their esteem by passing fulsome resolutions, which included the declaration that "what Arnold of Rugby was to his boys, Dr. Cannon has been to the Blackstone girls."

When Cannon launched another of his business ventures in 1904 by acquiring control of the *Baltimore and Richmond Christian Advocate,* in partnership with the Rev. J. Sidney Peters, he began agitating at once for the passage of a bill by the General Assembly providing for state aid for high schools and the establishment of a high school in every county in Virginia. At least half of the one hundred counties in the Old Dominion were without accredited public or private high schools. Prominent educators in various sections of the commonwealth sought the adoption of the high-school bill at the session of the legislature that convened in 1904. Cannon, who was the author of the bill and one of its sponsors, was instrumental in securing a hearing before the proper legislative committee and in arranging to have representatives of secular and religious institutions speak in its behalf. The measure passed the House but died in the Senate through lack of time. The effort was renewed at the session of 1906 and the bill became law. A system of county high schools was accordingly established and the state's educational advancement was importantly enhanced. To James Cannon, Jr., should go a substantial share of the credit.

The most long-drawn-out and acrimonious controversy involving educational matters in which Cannon was ever engaged was the bitter fight over the proposal to place Randolph-Macon Woman's College at Lynchburg, Virginia, one of the leading educational institutions in the South, under the Carnegie Foundation for the Advancement of Teaching. The president of the college when the controversy began was Dr. W. W. Smith, its founder, who was also chancellor of the five institutions in the Randolph-Macon System. Chancellor Smith was a man of intellectual force and wide mental horizons who rendered invaluable service to the cause of Southern education. No other Southern college or university for men or women had been accepted by the Carnegie Foundation at that time and he was anxious to have the woman's college placed under it, for the prestige this would give the institution and the pensions that would thus be made available to its retired teachers. Accordingly, in 1906 the college trustees, upon his recommendation, passed the resolutions required by the foundation. These resolutions declared that in the "selection of trustees, officers and teachers, there are no denominational tests." Smith explained that this was no more than the assertion of a fact, since the charter did not prescribe any such tests. The Carnegie officials had said that if the charter was free from such requirements, nothing else was needed to qualify the institution. This should have ended the matter.

But although relations between the two men had been quite cordial, and Dr. Smith had made no secret of his desire to have Cannon, a much younger man, succeed him as president of the woman's college, Cannon said there was a "moral issue" involved in the Carnegie matter, and that he could not agree to the declaration that there were no denominational tests in the selection of the trustees. He stated that "for more than thirty years the trustees had been selected in accordance with a regular method from the ministry and laity of the Baltimore and Virginia conferences, and, by Dr. Smith's own printed declaration, its trustees were representatives of the two conferences." He took the position that, in the passage of the resolutions, the trustees were, in effect, signing away the church's control over the college in return for Carnegie gold. In the pungent words of one of his associates in the fight, the question was whether "Cæsar or Christ should rule." Such loud outcries greeted this caustic pronunciamento that its promulgator amended it to read "Carnegie or Christ."

In 1907, when the storm over the Carnegie matter broke in the Virginia and Baltimore conferences, Cannon was the dominant figure in the former. Southern Methodism was divided into about fifty conferences, and the Virginia Conference was one of the two or three largest. It comprised most of Tidewater and all of Southside and Eastern Shore Virginia, together with small areas of the Eastern Shore of Maryland and southern Delaware.

Face to face with the "moral issue" that he said was presented by the resolutions of President Smith and the board, Cannon at once began an assault upon them in the columns of the *Advocate*. There was a fearful hubbub. The matter was discussed at almost interminable length week after week, month after month, and year after year. The Virginia Conference took it up at several successive sessions, and the General Conference of 1910 adopted a resolution, introduced by Cannon, which declared that the church has a right to a voice in the management of the schools founded by it. Animosities that continued for decades were engendered, particularly in the Virginia Conference; personalities could not be kept out of the statements of the disputants, and while the argument was frequently advanced that this was no way for "Christian men" to deal with one another, it seemed to have little effect. Finally, in 1911, the trustees voted to rescind the resolution they had adopted in 1906, and at the same time agreed that when there were vacancies on their board, they would submit for approval one name for each vacancy to the conference in which the vacancy existed and that, when approval was secured, they would elect. This action satisfied Cannon and his allies in the fight and would have ended the matter. Four of the trustees, however, applied to the courts for an injunction restraining the board and the conferences from putting the plan into effect. This petition was formally dismissed in 1913, thus closing the controversy. The Carnegie Foundation had decided in 1909, in view of certain action taken by the trustees in that year, that Randolph-Macon Woman's College could no longer be carried by it. Neither that institution nor Randolph-Macon College at Ashland has since been placed under the foundation.

President Smith died about a year before the final decision was handed down in the courts. Many are of the opinion that his life was considerably shortened by worry over the Carnegie matter. He was a man of fine sensibilities and he felt greatly humiliated that his motives should have been impugned and his integrity questioned by members of his church. The controversy preyed on his mind and weakened his resistance to disease.

Cannon, on the other hand, was cast in different clay. Controversy was almost the breath of life to him. He asked no quarter and gave none. Charges were hurled at him from one direction or another over a large part of his adult life, but he hurled them back with all the verve and acerbity of which he was capable. It was often said of him by his adversaries that he had "the hide of a rhinoceros," so difficult was it to make him quail under fire. In scores of debates, in controversies in many parts of America and in foreign lands, Cannon remained invariably calm, no matter how blistering the criticism leveled at him. He seems to have emerged from the Carnegie controversy temperamentally and emotionally unscarred, but many of his friends were permanently alienated from him.

CHAPTER *iii*

A Pen Dipped in Vitriol

W‍HEN Cannon assailed Dr. W. W. Smith over the Carnegie matter, it was by no means the first time that he had picked a quarrel with a man nearly twice his age. He began showing these unmistakable propensities in the 1890's. Time and again, then and later, he went out of his way to attack older ministers, even bishops.

Usually in those early days he belabored the opposition in the columns of the *Methodist Recorder,* a monthly whose editorship he assumed in 1894, the year he took over the presidency of the Blackstone Institute. It was agreed that he would receive no editorial salary, but he appears to have found compensations in other directions.

Through a series of assaults in the *Methodist Recorder,* he began undermining the reputation and influence of various older leaders in the Virginia Conference and building up his own. His first victim was the Rev. Dr. John J. Lafferty, editor of the *Richmond Christian Advocate.* Dr. Lafferty had published a pamphlet entitled *Twenty Years an Editor,* in which he made certain statements concerning the Rev. Dr. W. W. Bennett, Cannon's father-in-law, then deceased. There were torrid exchanges between the two Methodist editors in the pages of their respective publications and such a pother arose that the whole matter was investigated at the Virginia Conference of 1895. The committee of inquiry, on the whole, was much more critical of Lafferty than of Cannon and Bennett. The brashness of Cannon's attack on Lafferty angered the latter's friends, but the episode

28

demonstrated various things. One was that Cannon was a tough and resourceful antagonist, cool, calculating, and lucid in his polemical writing and absolutely unruffled under fire.

Having unhorsed his first antagonist, the cocky young controversialist lost little time in loosing a blast against the three most influential older men in the Virginia Conference. These were the Rev. Dr. Paul Whitehead, the Rev. Dr. Powell Garland, and the Rev. Dr. Alexander G. Brown, all of whom had served several successive terms as presiding elders. Cannon proposed to limit the service of presiding elders to four years, a suggestion that Whitehead, Garland, and Brown found distasteful. Another furor was stirred up and there was acrimonious argument. Cannon gave his reasons for urging the change but the opposition was certain that he was primarily concerned with trying to weaken the grip of the three presiding elders and, at the same time, to strengthen his own. Yet such was the ability of this pugnacious thirty-three-year-old parson that he actually carried his point at the Virginia Conference of 1897, which passed a memorial urging his plan upon the General Conference. That body never adopted it, however.

This uproar had barely quieted down when Cannon proceeded to stir up another, more resounding than any in which he had previously been engaged. It had to do with the celebrated "war claim" controversy which shook the church from center to circumference in the late nineties. The facts relative to this matter were briefly as follows:

The Southern Methodist Publishing House at Nashville was wrecked during the Civil War by the Federal armies, and after the close of hostilities the church sought to collect damages from the government. It was not until the nineties that any results were obtained. In 1895 the Rev. Dr. J. D. Barbee and D. M. Smith, book agents for the church, made a contract with E. B. Stahlman, a prominent Methodist, that they would give him thirty-five per cent of whatever amount he could collect from Congress on the claim. They stipulated that "no improper means" were to be used. Stahlman went to work and succeeded in getting through a bill appropriating $288,000 to the church in payment for the damage done during the war. After the measure had passed, however, it was charged that improper methods had been used not only by Stahlman but also by the book agents. At the request of Barbee and Smith, the Committee on Publishing Interests investigated the matter at the General Conference of 1898 at Baltimore and exonerated them of any wrongdoing. Shortly afterward the United States Senate decided to make a full inquiry. The Senate investigating committee reached the conclusion that Stahlman had deliberately deceived the Senate while working to secure the passage of the bill, and that the book agents had "purposely withheld information from certain Senators which the Senate deemed material in procuring the passage of the bill." Stahlman admitted that he had purposely misled the Senate,[1] but Barbee and Smith vehemently denied any intent to deceive anyone. During 1898 and 1899 four regularly constituted church tribunals made separate investigations of the part played in the matter by Barbee, who acted for the book agents throughout, and each of them held unanimously that he had not been guilty of misconduct in office.

But this did not settle the issue in the minds of some members of the church, Cannon among them. Taking the stand, customary with him under such circumstances, that a "moral issue" was involved, Cannon severely condemned the course that had been pursued by the book agents and the book committee, which had supervision over the agents. By means of agitation in the columns of the *Recorder,* he procured the passage by the Virginia Conference of resolutions urging the General Conference of 1902 to condemn the methods employed in the collection of the claim. The charges of misrepresentation made against the agents were based upon the supposition that they had schemed to prevent Congress from finding out that Stahlman was to receive a percentage of the amount collected.

There were tempestuous scenes on the General Conference floor at Dallas, Texas, when the matter came up in 1902. The Committee on Publishing Interests brought in a majority and a minority report. The majority group, numbering thirty-three committee men, held that there was no obligation to return the money and stated that "the church distinctly repudiates all the acts of concealment, misstatement, or unfairness on the part of any and all persons representing the church in the prosecution of this claim before Congress, either intentional or otherwise." The minority group, numbering eighteen and headed by Cannon, brought in a report condemning the book agents and Stahlman in such extreme terms that it was claimed to be libelous by some of the members of the conference. This scathing document recommended the return of the $288,000 to the government.

The most important charge against Barbee and Smith related to a telegram they had sent to a member of the Senate without the knowledge of the Rev. Dr. Collins Denny, chairman of the book committee. This telegram was regarded by many as designed to create the impression that Stahlman was not to receive a percentage of the amount collected. Dr. Denny subsequently declared with much justice that, under the circumstances, "it would have misled anybody." Senator Pasco of Florida, who was pushing the bill calling for the settlement of the war claim, had wired the book agents as follows: "Some malicious persons are circulating a slanderous story about the capitol with evident purpose to obstruct the passage of our bill. It is to the effect that you have made a contract with Mr. Stahlman to pay him 40 per cent of the amount recovered. . . ." Barbee and Smith wired in reply: "The statement is untrue, and you are hereby authorized to deny it." Most of the controversy centered on this telegram. Stahlman, as stated above, was to get thirty-five per cent.

When the controversy reached its crescendo on the conference floor, feeling was intense, but there appears never to have been much doubt of the outcome. The majority report was adopted by a vote of 113 to 79 and Cannon and his allies were defeated. At the same time, almost all the members of the book committee, including Chairman Denny, were re-elected for the succeeding quadrennium. Barbee died two years later. It is widely believed that his death was hastened by the charges brought against him in relation to the "war claim." Like Drs. Lafferty, Whitehead, and Smith, all of whom Cannon attacked fiercely at one time or another, Barbee was Cannon's senior by many years.

In addition to the acrimonious wrangling in which the editor of the *Recorder* engaged on the floor of the Dallas conference, he had an encounter there of a rather different kind. On the closing day, immediately after Bishop Alpheus W. Wilson had pronounced the benediction and as the delegates were rising from their seats to leave the hall, members of the Virginia delegation heard a resounding smack! Sessler Hoss, son of Bishop E. E. Hoss, had rushed over to the delegation and without preliminaries of any sort had slapped Cannon's face. It developed that Cannon had written something in the *Recorder* that young Hoss, a freshman at Vanderbilt University, construed as a reflection on his mother; so, as soon as the closing session of the conference was over, he seized the opportunity to obtain revenge. Eyewitnesses declare that the red-faced Cannon made no effort to strike back at Hoss. E. G. Moseley, of the Virginia delegation, stepped between them after the first blow had been passed, and the encounter was over.

The editorship of the *Methodist Recorder* had given Cannon a rather important audience whenever he chose to express himself with respect to any of the major issues then confronting the church or the country. True, the audience was not particularly large numerically, but it included many strategically placed figures in Virginia Methodism. At the end of a decade of conducting this publication Cannon decided to seek wider fields of editorial activity. Hence in December 1903 he joined with the Rev. J. Sidney Peters in purchasing seventy-five per cent of the stock of the Advocate Publishing Company, publisher of the *Baltimore and Richmond Christian Advocate*. The price paid was $15,000. Cannon became editor of the weekly, which circulated in the Virginia and Baltimore conferences, and Peters co-operated with him as associate editor and business manager. The *Methodist Recorder* was scrapped.

Here was another important business venture for Cannon. He and Peters became sole owners of the *Advocate* two or three years after they acquired control, and in 1911 Cannon bought complete control himself. He kept it until 1918, when he sold it to the Virginia Conference for $16,400.

In carrying on his controversies with the anti-prohibitionist press, in dealing out lusty blows on behalf of various moral objectives, in his extended disputes over the Carnegie matter, his compensation at Blackstone, and similar affairs, Cannon almost invariably stated his position fully in the *Advocate*. And by "fully," something decidedly beyond the ordinary is meant; for it seems safe to say that his controversial manifestoes are among the longest of the kind ever penned. He seldom appeared able to "turn around" in fewer than from two to three thousand words; his statements often ran to the most appalling length, and, while he usually exhausted every aspect of his thesis in a style consistently trenchant, clear, and forceful, he was often unnecessarily repetitious.

During the early years of Cannon's regime as editor, the *Advocate* published almost all varieties of patent-medicine advertising, including "cancer cures" and other equally egregious nostrums. This had been the practice prior to the paper's purchase by Cannon and Peters, and there was no change until 1907. In that year the editor announced that such matter would be thrown out. Thenceforward the *Advocate* contented itself with the frequent publication of remedies for digestive disorders, coughs, colds, croup, freckles, kidney and bladder ailments, corns and bunions, "scraggy hair," "the blues" and "that tired feeling," not forgetting "nasty breath," an infirmity known to fame even in that primitive age.

At the end of the first three years of the Cannon-Peters operation, they announced that they had made nothing whatever over and above expenses. But although Cannon urged the Virginia Conference many times during the period of his ownership to take the paper over, elect an editor, and pay him a fixed salary, it appears that, for at least a part of the time, the paper was making money for him. There is, for example, the statement published in the *Advocate* shortly after Cannon sold it to the conference, signed by "A Steward of Madison Circuit," averring that Cannon took the paper when it "ran in debt every year," but "put it back on a paying basis and turns it over to the conference again in a prosperous condition."

The history of Cannon's editorship of the *Baltimore and Richmond Christian Advocate*, like the history of his editorship of the *Methodist Recorder*, is largely the chronicle of the various campaigns, crusades, disputes, and quarrels in which he was

engaged during the years that he directed its policies. It was
perhaps as an organ of the "moral forces" in their jihad against
the rum demon that the *Advocate* served him most usefully. He
wrote on one occasion that, with the church paper "going into
the homes of Methodist preachers and leading laymen, it was
impossible for the wet papers to destroy the confidence of our
Methodist people by their slanderous attacks upon our workers."
But that is a story for another chapter — indeed, a whole series
of chapters.

CHAPTER *iv*

All Aboard for the New Jerusalem

Those who entertain the notion that the Anti-Saloon League was a mundane body cencerning itself exclusively with the very earthy business that is the liquor traffic should not overlook its importantly pietistic aspects. In the first place, those familiar with the league's history know that its founder, the Rev. Dr. Howard H. Russell, frequently declared that the organization was of divine origin and that he had been ordained by God to "drive the satanic liquor traffic down to its native hell." In the second place, from the time of its establishment in the middle nineties, the league became virtually a branch of the Methodist and Baptist churches, many of whose pastors and lay brethren referred to it as "the church in action." In the third place, the organization's votaries have always termed themselves "the moral and religious forces."

It was natural that James Cannon, Jr., should have been attracted to such a self-appointed symbol of righteousness as the Anti-Saloon League. We have seen that as a lad he was taught by his mother that alcohol was a monumental curse, and that as a college student he aided in the distribution of a temperance paper. Hence, when the league was founded by Dr. Russell in 1895, Cannon's attention was arrested almost from the outset, and in 1901 he was one of the little band of earnest workers who founded the Anti-Saloon League of Virginia at Richmond. From the beginning he was the Virginia league's chief lobbyist and most gifted promoter.

He was familiar with the unholy alliance between the liquor-venders and the politicians in various sections and with the unconscionable greed of many beer, wine, and whisky dealers. He was privy to the facts concerning the saloon, as ruggedly operated in that era of rugged individualism. He saw manufacturers, distributors, and sellers of distilled, malt, and vinous beverages exhibiting a hard-boiled indifference to legitimate complaints from the public. Their customary attitude was "mind your own business and leave ours alone." Some years later, when the trade began reaping the whirlwind, its organs referred bitterly to its failure in earlier days to take cognizance of justifiable criticism. "The liquor business . . . seems incapable of learning any lesson of advancement, or any motive but profit," wailed the *National Liquor Dealer's Journal*. "To perpetuate itself, it has formed alliances with the slums. . . . It deliberately aids the most corrupt political powers."

But it was not only his knowledge of the general situation that strengthened Cannon in his determination to make war on the traffic; he had also had personal experience that impressed upon him the importance of such action. During his pastorate in Newport News, for example, he conducted the funeral of an infant child whose father was a heavy drinker. It devolved upon Cannon to secure clothing and a coffin for the burial; but the besotted father took the clothes and shoes from the little corpse and exchanged them for whisky. When Cannon came to conduct the service, he found the body stripped and the father lying in a drunken stupor on the floor.

During his presidency at Blackstone Institute, Cannon had a narrow escape from death or serious injury at the hands of an intoxicated man. On the train between Richmond and Blackstone a stranger who was in his cups suddenly drew a long knife and brandished it wildly within a few inches of Cannon's throat. If the inebriate had not been promptly overpowered by the train crew, the Cannon epiglottis might have been carved into several parts. On another occasion, when the dry leader was traveling through the slate quarries of Buckingham County, Virginia, the door of a barroom near the roadside opened and several men reeled out, shouting and firing pistols. They apparently were making heroic efforts to puncture the doctor's famous "rhinoc-

eros hide," but they were too much under the influence to draw
a bead on him, so he escaped unharmed.

As early as 1902 Cannon was named to the executive committee of the Anti-Saloon League of America, so that he was one
of the pioneers in the movement.

Cannon pointed to the position of his church on this issue. For
many years the Southern Methodist Discipline had contained the
following provision:

> Let all our preachers and members abstain from the manufac-
> ture or sale of intoxicating liquors to be used as a beverage, from
> signing petitions for such sale, from becoming bondsmen for any
> person as a condition for obtaining a license, and from renting
> property to be used for such sale. If any member shall violate any
> of the provisions of this paragraph, he shall be deemed guilty of
> an immorality.

In addition to citing the stand of his church on the question,
Cannon also invoked the Scriptures. Seeking to prove that Holy
Writ calls down a murrain upon the liquor traffic, he quoted:
"Woe shall be unto him that putteth the bottle to his neighbor's
lips"; and St. Paul's "It is good neither to eat flesh, nor to drink
wine, nor anything whereby thy brother is caused to stumble,
or is offended, or is made weak." He conceded that there is no
"absolute prohibition on the use of wine, as such, in the teaching
of Christ or of the Apostles," but added that "this fact does not
justify the claim that Christ or Paul would approve, or even
tolerate, the covetous, body-and-soul destroying liquor traffic of
the present time."

He somehow failed to mention that Christ not only did not
forbid the use of wine but made wine at the marriage feast at
Cana, drank it at the Last Supper, and urged His disciples to
drink it, and that Paul recommended a little "for thy stomach's
sake and thine often infirmities." Cannon might have said, too,
that in the Old Testament wine is praised much oftener than it
is condemned; that Jehovah required an offering of wine to Himself twice daily in the sacrifice, and that Jehovah, through Moses,
told His servants to buy both wine and "strong drink" and to
enjoy themselves with them. Some have contended that the wine

referred to in these various passages was unfermented grape juice, but the Hebrew word, *yayin,* and the Greek word, οἶνος, have no such connotation. It was *yayin* that Noah consumed on that lamentable occasion so graphically described in Genesis, ix, 20–1, and St. Paul used the word οἶνος in Ephesians, v, 18, when he said: "Be not drunk with οἶνος, wherein is excess." Various other passages might be cited in complete refutation of the theory that either *yayin* or οἶνος was non-intoxicating.

But wholly aside from such esoteric matters as the meaning of certain Hebrew and Greek words, there were manifest evils in the America of 1900 growing out of the liquor business. It was the era when Carry Nation was charging hither and yon, swinging her trusty tomahawk on the glassware of the saloon-keepers, smashing the plate-glass mirrors, breaking into slivers the enticing array of bottles behind the counter, and demolishing the aphrodisiac pictures that lined the walls, while customers and the proprietor fled under a barrage of missiles. Barkeepers accordingly posted manifestoes: "All Nations Welcome except Carry."

The hatchet-wielding amazon from Kansas was a heroine with the nascent Anti-Saloon League. That organization also was becoming increasingly conscious of the invaluable allies it enjoyed in the Methodist and Baptist churches. Without the Methodists and the Baptists it could never have made appreciable headway. President Grant had recognized the puissance of the Methodists years before when he made his famous observation that there were "three political parties" in the United States — the Republican Party, the Democratic Party, "and the Methodist Church."

The importance of these large denominations to the prohibitionists was especially manifest in the rural areas — and the South was overwhelmingly rural. The great cities were usually strongly hostile to restrictive legislation, partly because the Methodists and Baptists were less predominant there. Another factor was the antipathy of long standing between the country and the city, which often tends to make the one combat whatever the other finds attractive. In the small towns and villages and on the farms the belaborers of alcohol found a receptive audience — a fact attributable, in some measure at least, to the incurable itch of dwellers in those regions to inflict some mild form of torture upon denizens of the urban Babylons.

One of the major factors in the growth of the prohibition movement was the great influence wielded by country and small-town pastors over their parishioners. The church has always had a larger place in rural community life than in the life of the city. To thousands of devout Virginians living in the rural districts during the final years of the nineteenth century and the early years of the twentieth, the pastoral visit was an event to be remembered and cherished. The automobile was virtually unknown, and country dwellers found communication among themselves much more troublesome and complicated than it is today. Living, as they did, in comparative isolation, the occasional stopover of the minister seemed to them a pleasant excitement as well as a stimulus to spiritual experience.

The cleric who traveled the roads of eastern Virginia in a buggy forty or fifty years ago passed through flat or gently rolling country, much of it uncultivated and down-at-heel. He observed the effects of an agricultural system not yet adjusted to the dislocations that followed the violent uprooting of slavery and the breakup of many of the antebellum plantations. In the tobacco counties he saw large areas planted in Virginia leaf. There was corn along the alluvial river bottoms, and there were occasional fine tracts of timber. But vast stretches were given over to piny woods and to the desolation of broomsedge and weeds. The trucking areas of Tidewater were rather intensively cultivated, and along the roads one heard the dulcet grunt of porkers fattening on peanuts against the day when their hindquarters would be transmuted into far-famed Smithfield hams. Yet here again the soil was allowed to deteriorate, to suffer erosion and to become crosshatched with gullies.

The pastor who drove his buggy over the dirt roads of eastern Virginia near the turn of the century was likely to find his clothes coated with dust if the season happened to be dry, or his equipage bogged in the soggy loam if rain had fallen. Often he dismounted to open a gate, placed athwart the highway to prevent cattle from straying. Often his horse stopped to drink as they forded a creek or river. Occasionally a grating, scraping sound issued from the woods near the road and he saw a squirrel gnawing a hickory nut almost above his head. Or a furry something darted suddenly into view as a rabbit or a fox streaked before him into the underbrush. In summer, as he lolled in his creaking vehicle, the pastor watched the shifting patterns of sunlight on the dappled floor of the forest, observed the midges as they buzzed lazily in the warm air, or with his whip brushed horseflies from the flanks of his sweat-flecked animal. In winter his carriage frequently sank into the mud or bounced over the frozen ground. Sometimes it startled a covey of partridges and sent them, with heavily drumming wings, into the nearest cover. Sometimes a cardinal flashed its dazzling plumage against the drabness of the naked woods, while far away in the leaden sky a lone buzzard wheeled in ever widening arcs.

Such were the scenes that greeted the rural minister as he visited among his parishioners in eastern Virginia. His influence among them, for reasons already recounted, was great. The fact is important to any student of the prohibition movement, so closely linked with the rural churches of the nation.

The crushing poverty which bore down upon the Southern people for decades after Appomattox made the establishment of adequate public-school systems utterly impossible. The denominational schools were useful stopgaps, but they reached only a limited number of pupils. Millions of whites were left without any but the most meager instruction. The consequence was an excessively high native-white illiteracy rate. This rate was gradually reduced, but even in 1920, immediately following the adoption of the Eighteenth Amendment, it was 6.1 per cent in the Southern states as against 1.1 in the rest of the country.

There is no intention here of blaming the Baptist and the Methodist churches for the excessively large group of unlettered members affiliated with those denominations. Any church enlisting Southerners by the million at this period necessarily incorporated thousands upon thousands of such unfortunate persons. The extent to which this condition must have obtained in the nineties and the early 1900's can be imagined from the formal report made in 1928 by the Rev. Dr. Albert Richmond Bond, a leading Baptist clergyman of Birmingham, following an exhaustive study of native-white illiteracy in the Southern states.[1] Dr. Bond, who was educational secretary of the Education Board of the Southern Baptist Convention from 1920 to 1927, and secretary of the Southern Baptist Education Association from 1915 to 1927, based his findings upon the United States Census for 1920 and the Census Report upon Religious Bodies for 1916. He said that if more recent figures had been available, his conclusions would have been substantially the same.

Dr. Bond discovered that the Methodist and Baptist churches contained far more illiterates than any other churches in the South. He did not attempt to explain the phenomenon, but merely reported his statistical findings. He could have said, in explanation, that these two denominations had made a special effort to enlist the masses, that they put forth no pretense to social exclusiveness, and that they had exhibited a concern for the underprivileged and the downtrodden, facts certainly more creditable to them than otherwise. But, as noted above, Dr. Bond contented himself with a detailed statistical report. That report was so convincing that the Education Board of the Southern Baptist Convention adopted a resolution declaring that "native white illiteracy is a Southern problem and within the South preeminently a Baptist problem." While the board was not formally concerned with the precise degree of responsibility shared by the Methodists, examination of the Bond report leaves no doubt that the Methodists were second only to the Baptists in the number of their illiterate members.

It goes without saying that both these churches include many men and women of sound learning and high cultural attainments. It is also patent that a considerable number of such men and women favored prohibition. At the same time, it cannot be overlooked that the mass support for the dry movement centered in two denominations which — in the South, at least — embraced thousands in every state who were incapable of writing their own names.

There is no evidence that the Northern branches of these same denominations were cursed with illiteracy to a like degree. In fact, there is reason to believe that they were not, since the native-white illiteracy rate in the North has long been much lower than that in the South. At the same time, light is thrown on the personnel of the Methodist and Baptist churches throughout the nation by an article in the *American Mercury* for August 1927. The authors, Ellsworth Huntington and Leon F. Whitney, analyzed the contents of the latest edition then extant of *Who's Who in America*, with a view to ascertaining which religious denominations had the largest number of males listed per 100,000 adherents. Nearly 27,000 persons were included in the volume, of whom about half gave their religious affiliations. The Huntington-Whitney compilation showed the following number of men, per 100,000 adherents, listed in *Who's Who:*

Unitarians, 1,185; Universalists, 390; Episcopalians, 156; Congregationalists, 115; Presbyterians, 62; Christians, 45; Friends, 31; Jews, 20; Methodists, 18; Baptists, 16; Reformed, 13; Mormons, Disciples, and Adventists, 11 each; Lutherans, 8; Roman Catholics and Brethren, 7 each; Evangelicals, 5; and United Brethren, 3.

Eliminating the smaller sects and taking only those with memberships at the time of at least 850,000, it appears that the Presbyterians, Congregationalists, and Episcopalians were furnishing, roughly, from more than three to nearly ten times as many men to *Who's Who* in proportion to their adherents as the Baptists and Methodists. Large denominations making a poorer showing than the two last named were the Disciples, Lutherans, and Catholics. The Lutherans and the Catholics have a considerable percentage of foreign-born.

One important reason why the Methodists made a relatively poor showing in the foregoing tabulation resides in the fact that this church has a rigidly centralized type of organization, which tends to trammel individual initiative. The bishops are well-nigh all-powerful in the denomination, while in each conference great authority is centered in the ruling group, which generally is built around the presiding elders, lately known as district superintendents. Every Methodist church belongs to a district conference as well as to a larger conference, both of which agencies hold annual meetings. The larger conferences, such as the Virginia Conference (with ten districts in Cannon's time), are linked to one or two other conferences of similar size, under a bishop.

All Aboard for the New Jerusalem

A General Conference of the entire denomination is held every four years. (The terminology here is confusing, since the word "conference" can mean either an area of ecclesiastical jurisdiction or a gathering of delegates.)

No other Protestant church in America offered so many opportunities for centralized direction as the Southern Methodist Church before its merger with the Northern church. This type of organization tends to submerge the individual and to make him amenable to the ukases of those who dominate his conference.

At the same time, it enables the ruling coterie to throw the entire denomination almost solidly in this direction or that on a given issue involving religion or morals. That is why the church of James Cannon, Jr., was the most militantly aggressive of all the large American churches in its hostility to the saloon and its advocacy of prohibition. That, too, is why this same denomination was able to make its influence felt so potently in opposition to dancing, the theater, card-playing, and Sunday games. The church was so organized that officially it spoke almost with one voice on such "moral issues" as these.

The fact should not be overlooked that in the latter part of the nineteenth century the Southern Methodists exhibited a considerable social awareness. Their efforts on behalf of justice for the Negro, their vigorous excoriations of lynching, and their exhortations to employers to grant their employees a living wage, stamped them as the Southern denomination that, despite its puritanical predilections, probably did most to further social well-being at the period.

Nor should it be imagined that the average evangelical pastor of this era was a sour-visaged bluenose, wholly lacking in human sympathies. Despite his aversion to forms of amusement now generally deemed innocuous, there were often human juices in him and a warmheartedness that many found engaging. It is true that Cannon, with his glacial personality and general unapproachability, was more of a puritan than an evangelical, more spiritually akin to the men who hanged the "witches" of Salem than to Wesley and Whitefield.

The mood of 1900 was so different from the mood of today

that a glance at some of its major manifestations may not be amiss. Anthony Comstock was approaching the close of his spectacular career. John L. Sullivan, whose mighty right had made him Boston's first citizen, had retired, loaded with diamond belt buckles and other such trophies, and was slowly drinking himself to death in his saloon on Forty-second Street, New York. It was the "trust-busting" era, and feeling against the "money power" was so vigorous that certain commodities were advertised as "not made by a trust." The *Rubáiyát,* lately illustrated by Elihu Vedder, was having a tremendous vogue. Charles Dana Gibson was influencing the dress, habits of thought, and manners of the populace with his "Gibson Girl" and "Gibson Man." Mark Twain and Mr. Dooley were the leading humorists. Edwin Markham's *Man with the Hoe* had just appeared and been hailed as "the battle-cry of the next thousand years." DeWolf Hopper had scaled the heights with his recitation of *Casey at the Bat.* The "shirtwaist vogue" had arrived and sages declared that "the shirtwaist has come to stay." Ardent spirits flowed freely in many parts of the republic, but standards as to what were proper subjects for fictional treatment were far more stringent than at present. For example, during the nineties Hamilton Wright Mabie had held that Stephen Crane's *George's Mother* was "harsh and unnecessarily frank," even after the phrase: "for he had known women of the city's painted legions" had been deleted from chapter iii. At about the same time Richard Watson Gilder had almost bought a tale for the *Century Magazine* but had ended by rejecting it because the author, in describing the shooting of a Negro man, had said: "The bullet had left a little blue mark over the brown nipple." The idea that a woman might smoke in polite society was nowhere entertained. In fact, a woman was arrested for smoking on Fifth Avenue in 1904.

That was also the year when Bishop Henry C. Potter, of the Episcopal diocese of New York, was the principal speaker at the opening of the Subway Tavern, a "model saloon" at Mulberry and Bleecker streets, New York City. The Archbishop of Canterbury, who was in this country at the time, commended the Bishop for his action, but almost everybody else, including even some liquor dealers, criticized him severely. Bishop Potter declared in his dedicatory address that "the effort to bar the saloon is one of the most comic and tragic failures of history."

Even the *Wine and Spirit Gazette* let go with a broadside against the New York prelate.[2] "It is safe to assume," said this organ of the trade, "that Bishop Potter was really in ignorance of the trap that had been set for him, else he would not have consented to figure so prominently as a 'puller-in' for a liquor house. That is the long and short of the peculiar exhibition that Bishop Potter made of himself in invoking divine blessing upon a gin-mill." This same journal went on to say that Hugh Dolan, former president of the Wine, Liquor and Beer Dealers' Association of the state of New York, "hit the nail on the head when he came out in the following interview" against Bishop Potter's rum shop:

> Why did the Bishop want to go down to that saloon? He ain't doin' any good by that. . . . Priests, Bishops, and ministers ought to stay away from saloons. Let 'em preach against saloons if they want to. When they go into them, they lead lots of weak ones with them. I don't want to say anything against the Subway Tavern, but you can get drunk there just as quickly as you can at my bar.

The *Wine and Spirit Gazette* also related that "some novel drinks" were being dispensed at the tavern, including "Doxology Cocktail, Rock of Ages Rickey, Potter Cocktail, Heavenly Highball, High Church Absinthe Frappe and Christian Temperance Pousse Cafe."

Terrence, the head bartender at the Waldorf, offered his customers the "Bishop Potter Cocktail." Latter-day researches have not revealed whether it was identical with the above-mentioned "Potter Cocktail." At any rate, Terrence announced that "when served, the 'Bishop Potter Cocktail' has the opalescent color of a stained glass church window." He added that he had "worked up a great Sunday morning trade on them."

Such behavior as that of Bishop Potter at the Subway Tavern was rare, but occasionally other members of the cloth lent their names to similar causes. There was the Rev. Dr. Morrill, pastor of the People's Church, Minneapolis, who erected a combination church, tavern, and theater, all with a common entrance, on the theory that, if people will drink, they should drink in a righteous cause. Proceeds were to go to charity. There were even preachers who endorsed certain brands of whisky publicly in the press. One of them was the Rev. John C. Orebaugh, of Anderson, Indiana, who, in newspaper advertisements, pronounced Duffy's Pure Malt Whiskey "a God-given medicine." The makers of Duffy's modestly declared that their distillate was "the greatest tonic stimulant and body-builder known to science."

In the early 1900's it was much easier to promulgate such ideas successfully than it has been since. Consider the fact that in 1840 the directors of an English insurance company voted to charge a total abstainer ten per cent more than their usual life-insurance premium, since they regarded him as "thin and watery, and as mentally cranked, in that he repudiated the good creatures of God as found in alcoholic drinks." [3]

A total abstainer in the United States in 1900 had no such uphill road as this, but the president of the National Wholesale Liquor Dealers' Association appears not to have stammered as he solemnly intoned in the early stages of the dry movement:

> Liquor . . . relieves more misery than it causes; it produces more joy than sorrow; it adds to efficiency instead of taking away from it; it is a tonic for the body, a stimulant for the body, producing stronger and healthier minds, which is a great preventive of crime of all kinds, and causes a lesser demand for institutions such as jails and hospitals for the insane, feebleminded, etc. . . . than would be required under prohibition or total abstinence.[4]

In further vindication of the purity of its motives, the liquor dealers' association averred in formal resolutions that it was more deeply interested in the cause of temperance than the Anti-Saloon League, the W.C.T.U., or the Good Templars. Added proof that alcohol is an unadulterated blessing was provided from another source, which pointed out that "the Bartenders' Union is probably the only labor organization which regularly opens and closes its meetings with prayer."

Not to be outdone, the brewers and vintners produced a touching rhapsody celebrating the contributions of beer and wine to civilization. It said, in part:

All Aboard for the New Jerusalem

What would the history of the race have been without the alleviating drop of wine in the cup of human misery? . . . The picture is in truth too dark to contemplate — imagination travels over that dreary sea of man's inhumanity to man and finds no islet of hope or mercy whereon to rest its wing. . . .

One of the most patent and salient facts of history is that the *drinking races*, the liberal consumers of wine and beer and ale, have always been in the vanguard of human progress and have made the greatest sacrifices for liberty. . . .

There is much more in this vein. The natural inference is that a direct relationship existed between the amount of wine and beer consumed by the various peoples and nations since the time of ancient Rome and the vehemence of their yearning after freedom.

The Anti-Saloon League also produced some fancy statements and statistics contemporaneously with the foregoing. It declared, for example, that "nearly 3,000 infants are smothered yearly in bed by drunken parents."

At this period not only were the "moral and religious forces" thoroughly aroused against the venders of alcoholic beverages, but they also envisioned Coca-Cola as a potential scourge of mankind. Consider the resolutions adopted by the Holston conference of the Methodist Church, South, at its 1905 meeting. This conference includes southwestern Virginia, eastern Tennessee, and southern West Virginia. The resolutions, in part, follow:

We call attention to "coca-cola"! While it commenced as an apparently innocent drink, yet it is the coming enemy of our young men, for these reasons: First, it contains chiefly caffeine, or the elements of strong coffee, and therefore keeps awake; second, it stimulates the whole nervous system; and third, it produces a habit almost as strong as the tobacco habit. Keep an average boy awake till two o'clock in the morning, fire and stimulate his whole nervous system, and turn him loose in a town or city full of temptations, and his destruction is almost sure to follow. Mothers all over this land are bewailing the fact that their boys do not come home at night and retire as they used to do, and "coca-cola" is one of the chief causes of this nocturnal revel. We warn our preachers against this subtle enemy.

Dry Messiah

Such was the decidedly psychopathic atmosphere in which the dry movement got well under way, not only in Virginia but in numerous other states. Bizarre claims were emanating from both camps as James Cannon, Jr., joined the executive committee of the Anti-Saloon League of America and prepared to storm the citadel of booze.

CHAPTER *v*

On the Trail of the Rum Demon

F<small>EW</small> persons took the Anti-Saloon League of America seriously at the turn of the century. Its grim-visaged leaders were generally regarded as fanatics. Scarcely anybody thought the organization had a chance of making appreciable progress as it began its determined drives for local-option elections over a wide area of the United States. The counties and cities of the state were allowed to exercise the right of local option under the law passed in 1886, but the temperance forces had made little headway during the decade and a half since that statute's enactment, for they lacked cohesiveness and *élan*. These deficiencies were to be supplied by the Anti-Saloon League.

Operating through a field agent, the Virginia branch of the league began closing saloons by the local-option method with monotonous regularity. After this had been going on for about two years, Cannon mobilized the anti-liquor lobby at Richmond in 1903, and the General Assembly passed the Mann Act, of which he was co-framer with State Senator William Hodges Mann. This rather involved measure provided, with certain exceptions, that licenses for the retail sale of liquor could be issued only in towns with police protection and five hundred or more population. They were issued by the judge of the circuit court, under the act, and in most cases the judge had to certify, before he approved the application, that a majority of the qualified voters of the district or town concerned were in favor of the issuance, and that he did not feel the license would be "injurious to the moral or material interest of the community." In almost every case, the circuit judge could not conscientiously certify to this, with the result that over five hundred saloons were closed almost at one stroke and the barrooms were well-nigh eliminated from the rural districts.

Having aided in achieving this important victory, Cannon resumed his strenuous labors as superintendent of the Blackstone Institute and editor of the denominational organ. At the legislative sessions of 1904 and 1906 he was active on behalf of the high-school bill, but no temperance legislation of importance engaged his attention at that time, although he was president of the Virginia Anti-Saloon League from 1904 to 1906. Then in 1908 he joined with Richard Evelyn Byrd, Speaker of the House of Delegates – and father of Admiral R. E. Byrd and Senator Harry F. Byrd – in framing a bill that specifically forbade the issuance of any liquor license in any community, magisterial district, or town having fewer than five hundred inhabitants. The temperance lobby functioned effectively, under Cannon's leadership, and the bill became a law. This drove the barrooms into the populous areas, chiefly the large cities.

These victories were won with considerable ease, despite the almost unanimous opposition of the daily newspapers of Virginia. During its early years the Anti-Saloon League was largely ignored by the secular press. When it was not ignored, it was criticized. Cannon was the particular target of these journalistic gibes, for he was disliked by a majority of the state's newspapermen, both personally and professionally. The Richmond papers were especially caustic in their attitude.

Soon after the turn of the century the three Richmond dailies were described by Cannon as "wet," "wetter," and "wettest." In 1909, after some years of experience with them, he summed up their attitude toward prohibition and its advocates as follows:

Of all the Richmond newspapers, the *Times-Dispatch* has been most unfair and cowardly in its treatment. The *Journal* has been fussy, flaring, and sensational, but it has given space for replies to its slanders. The *News Leader* has been blatant, denunciatory, frantic, almost insane in its opposition to anything or anybody who proposed that it would be better for men to deny their appetite for strong drink and their lust for money for the sake of others, but the *News Leader* also will usually allow persons to defend themselves against its attacks, or to reply to arguments of the editor; but the *Times-Dispatch* is cowardly and unfair.

In an unguarded moment, the editor of the *Times-Dispatch* enunciated in his editorial columns the dictum that "every man has a right to drink liquor to his comfort." This phrase was pounced upon by Cannon and was reiterated and emphasized by him in his public statements for the next decade. When "personal liberty" arguments on behalf of the saloon were advanced by the wets, Cannon declared that what they really wanted was "the right to drink liquor to their comfort."

In his warfare on alcohol he took the position that the scrupulously clean saloon, with fetching exterior and dignified whitecollar customers, was potentially much more dangerous than the foul-smelling dive with men reeling in and out of the swinging doors. His theory was that gilded sin was more likely to entrap the unwary, since vice in its grosser forms was too revolting to appeal to the novice. "For my own boys," he wrote, "I would fear one of the social clubs of so-called high life, or one of the eminently respectable, splendidly furnished buffets, more than I would fear a hundred dives." He was hitting shrewdly here at the "high society" element — one of his favorite pastimes. That element was almost wholly out of sympathy with his reform program and he was aware that one sure way to arouse the proletarians on behalf of prohibition was to dangle before them the hostility of the social upper crust, whose members were notoriously fond of imbibing mint juleps and other similarly piquant decoctions in their exclusive clubs.

In his agitation against the saloon it was Cannon's habit to argue that thirst and avarice were the sole motives actuating the defenders of the liquor traffic. For example, in discussing the value of an "educational campaign" to be held in the state prior to certain local-option elections, he said that by means of such campaigns "the absolute indefenselessness of the liquor traffic is brought to light, so that the community as a whole is obliged to confess that the only reason why the traffic should not be abated is because certain men wish to gratify their appetites or to make money by the downfall of their fellow-men."

During this period local-option elections were being held throughout Virginia, and Cannon spoke in almost all of them. He threw himself into the fight with the same zeal and fire that he had shown in other spheres. His colossal capacity for work, his ability as a debater and speaker, his ruthless, relentless pursuit of his objective, were qualities that brought results. He was a walking encyclopedia of information concerning the prohibition movement, and he knew the record of every Virginian in public life on the question.

When the executive committee of the Virginia Anti-Saloon League met on March 9, 1909, it elected Cannon league superintendent. The superintendent had active charge of the league work, since the position of president was largely honorary. Cannon accepted the post on condition that he receive no salary, but only his expenses. As he was president of Blackstone Institute and part owner of the *Baltimore and Richmond Christian Advocate,* and since it was at about this time that he began playing the stock market,[1] he was able to support his wife and seven children without any pay from the league. As superintendent, he succeeded the Rev. Dr. R. H. Bennett, his brother-in-law, who announced that he was resigning to devote all his time to his pastorate.

Either of Cannon's other two jobs would have been sufficient to occupy the time of a normal man. Yet he had no hesitation in accepting a third, the most arduous of all. Not only so, but his appointment was admitted by every competent judge to be the best possible. The fact that he was to perform duties incident to the presidency of a girls' school and the editorship of a church paper along with his league superintendency made no difference to anybody who was interested in the dry movement. Cannon was conceded to be the ablest, most resourceful, most indefatigable leader available.

At its annual meeting in February 1909 the league had decided, in accordance with the recommendation of its legislative committee, of which Cannon was chairman, not to press at that time for a state-wide prohibition law. It emphasized that it would do so later, but stated that it did not believe the time was quite ripe for such a movement.

On the Trail of the Rum Demon

At about the same period there was formed in Richmond an organization styling itself the Personal Liberty Association. Its aim was to stem, if possible, the rising tide of dry sentiment in the state. The association claimed a membership of three thousand and on its rolls were many of Richmond's most distinguished citizens. The association employed Edmund Pendleton, ex-editor of the *Evening Journal*, as its secretary, and announced that it was ready for business.

Was Cannon dismayed at the emergence into the political arena of this formidable phalanx of Virginia aristocrats? Far from it. The Personal Liberty Association played directly into his hands by affording him an excellent opportunity to ridicule bibulous "high society" and thus to arouse the masses on behalf of prohibition. In a devastating article entitled "Three Thousand Thirsty Men" the superintendent of the Anti-Saloon League virtually floored the opposition. He quoted from dispatches which declared that the association has "the backing of the liquor element, and will especially look to the defeat of Judge William Hodges Mann (for Governor) and the public chastisement of the Rev. James Cannon, Jr." After a few gibes at these proponents of personal liberty who were out to castigate him publicly, he opined that they were riled because they had been unable to "save the Sunday liquor to the social clubs." Calling them "Knights of the Little Brown Jug," he pointed out that the Anti-Saloon League had secured legislation which "actually stretched forth its impolite and reckless hand and infringed upon the inalienable rights of society folks, of members of fashionable clubs, and has said to them, 'You cannot have your bar-room open on Sunday any more than the rank and file can have theirs.'" He then went on to say:

> And every Sunday since that awful day when the Byrd-Mann law went into effect, denunciation has rolled forth from the dry and thirsty throats of those greatly abused men who have been deprived of their inalienable right to drink liquor to their comfort on Sunday.

This was the first round in the warfare between Cannon and the Personal Liberty Association, and there is little question that the doctor had his opponents on the ropes when it ended. Not only so, but he kept them on the ropes from that time forward. The organization was a vulnerable target for his mockery, and he employed his indubitable talents in this sphere to good advantage.

If the association had appeared on the scene some years previously and had managed matters in such a way as not to invite the imputation that it was an aggregation of tippling aristocrats, it might have been a serious obstacle in Cannon's path, at least for a time. But as things turned out, it probably helped rather than hindered. Certainly there was no visible slackening of the drive to dry up the state. While the word had not been given to launch the movement on behalf of state-wide prohibition, that was sure to come soon. Meanwhile the wets were fighting with their backs to the wall.

In 1905 Cannon had said that the closing of every saloon was simply a matter of dollars and cents, and that if sufficient money was forthcoming to put workers in the field and to distribute literature, there would be no question as to the extermination of the traffic. In 1909 he repeated the assertion, saying that if the drys wanted to drive all the barrooms out of the Old Dominion, they had only to send in adequate contributions to finance the work.

In the summer of 1909 State Senator Mann, author of the act of 1903 whereby the saloons were virtually eliminated from the rural districts, was campaigning for the governorship against Harry St. George Tucker, later a member of Congress, whose record was by no means as dry as Mann's. Cannon was extremely anxious to see Mann nominated, not only for personal reasons, but also because a Tucker victory would have been a severe blow to the Virginia Anti-Saloon League's prestige. Senator Thomas S. Martin, the state's Democratic boss, was also for Mann, but he found himself embarrassed by the fact that many leading members of his organization were "wet."

In view of these circumstances, there is reason to believe that Cannon and Martin made a deal, whereby Martin threw the support of his friends to Mann in return for a promise from Cannon that state-wide prohibition would not be made effective until after the expiration of Mann's term. Numerous prominent Democrats who appeared to be in a position to know asserted that this deal was made. Among them was the late Colonel Joseph Button, then clerk of the state Senate, and subsequently State Commissioner of Insurance for twenty-three years. Colonel Button related that he was present when Cannon called on Martin at the latter's room in a Richmond hotel before the Mann-Tucker campaign. The story of what took place is here told by him for publication for the first time. Colonel Button wrote:

As I recall it, Senator Martin opened the conversation by stating that he was warmly attached to Judge Mann, who had been his loyal friend and supporter. He said, however, that much to his regret, he had never been in a position to aid him in his ambitions; that he would like to see him Governor, and personally would support him, but he was afraid that he could not bring a large element of his adherents to his support because of Judge Mann's well-known temperance views. This element feared that were he made Governor, he would try to have enacted much more radical liquor legislation.

According to my recollection, Dr. Cannon's reply was that there need be no fear on that score, as the temperance people had gotten about all they could ask for until the people could catch up with the advanced position they had already attained; that it was not their intention to ask for more legislation during Governor Mann's term, in the event of his election.

With this statement on Dr. Cannon's part, Senator Martin agreed to go into the fight for Mann's nomination, and to appeal to his "wet" friends to support him, which he did, and with the result that most of the leaders, although disagreeing with Judge Mann in his views, did give him their active support.

Mann defeated Tucker by a majority of 5,078 votes. Since the liquor vote in several cities, notably Norfolk, went to Mann, it seems to have been sufficient to swing the election. Certain Democrats close to Martin and Mann have always denied that there was any deal. They point out that strenuous efforts were made by the drys to secure a referendum on state-wide prohibition during Mann's term, and that if there had been a deal, these efforts would not have been made. The answer of the Tucker adherents to this contention is that one of two things is true: either

Cannon double-crossed Martin on the agreement, or the Anti-Saloon League was putting up a bluff to cover up the deal when it sought a referendum during Mann's term on state-wide prohibition, since it knew that such a referendum would be blocked in the preponderantly wet state Senate. Mann disclaimed all knowledge of any deal and Cannon denied emphatically that there was one between himself and Martin.

It is difficult, however, to disregard the testimony of Colonel Button, who was present when Martin and Cannon discussed the approaching gubernatorial campaign of 1909. A warm friend of Martin, although not of Cannon, the colonel was positive in his recollection that there was a specific agreement. Certainly it is a fact that no important temperance legislation was adopted during Mann's term. It is also a fact that the *entente cordiale* established between the Martin and Cannon machines in 1909 was the beginning of a long period of close co-operation between the two groups. Senator Martin was thereafter to be found almost invariably supporting the measures advocated by Cannon, while Cannon usually saw eye to eye with Martin. Each was shrewd enough to realize the advantage of having the other's support.

When the Virginia Anti-Saloon League finally announced that it would press for a state-wide prohibition law, its leaders, including Cannon, asserted that, from the organization's founding, a state-wide law had been their ultimate goal and their declared purpose. But if this purpose was proclaimed in the early days of the movement, there is a great scarcity of evidence to that effect. On the contrary, a determined effort seems to have been made at that period by the "moral and religious forces" to create the impression that state-wide prohibition was not the league's objective.

Consider, for example, Cannon's assertion in the *Advocate* for August 2, 1906, in the course of a discussion of the results of state-wide prohibition in Maine:

> Personally this writer believes that local option is the best method for Virginia, but he is not prepared to say that it is the best method everywhere. Conditions must always be carefully

studied, and the method which will produce the best permanent results must be followed.

Now, at this time Cannon, according to his own statement, was "the recognized leader of the prohibition forces of Virginia." He makes the flat and unqualified declaration that he "believes local option is the best method for Virginia," as compared with the state-wide prohibition system then in force in Maine. He does not say that he thinks it is best because Virginia is not ready for a state law. Truly, as he said in 1916, the league had been "intensely practical" in the methods by which it had endeavored to "attain its ideal"!

Further, not until the 1908 annual report of the committee on temperance of the Virginia Conference of the Methodist Church, South, does the committee reveal that state-wide prohibition is the goal of the dry forces. The report adopted in the fall of 1907, signed by Cannon as committee chairman, does not indicate that such is the plan.

At its annual convention in February 1908, the Anti-Saloon League of Virginia adopted the following resolution, on the recommendation of the legislative committee, of which Cannon was chairman:

> We favor the principle of local option in carrying on our work of the abolition of the saloon; and if we are given such legislation as will prevent evasion of the law, and as will provide adequate penalties for law violators, and as will give full opportunity for a fair expression of the wishes of the duly qualified electorate, we see no good reason to depart from our present policy. But if we cannot obtain legislation that will protect us in our rights, and give relief to the people from the present controllable evasion and violation of the law, we shall be obliged to change our method and demand the right to vote on statewide prohibition.

Here we have another statement from Cannon that he himself contradicted the following year. At that time, as has been pointed out, he asserted that state-wide prohibition had been contemplated by the league from the very beginning. How could this be, if in 1908 the league favored "the principle of local option"?

Dry Messiah

In this connection it is interesting to examine some rather astounding assertions made in 1908 by the Anti-Saloon League of America. In the Virginia edition of the *American Issue*, the league's official organ, for March 28 of that year, is an editorial entitled "Anti-Saloon, Not Prohibition." This editorial appears in the space reserved for the national organization, not in the Virginia section of the publication; hence it is an official pronouncement of the Anti-Saloon League of America. It says, in part:

> It is the trick of the advocates of the saloon to misrepresent the present movement as an effort of the temperance people to promote total abstinence by law. This is untrue. Prohibition, as the word is used in the United States, means prohibition of the saloon, not of the personal use of alcoholic drinks. . . . It is to the interest of the brewers and distillers and saloonists to deceive the people into the belief that the effort of temperance people is to enforce total abstinence by law. No such issue is involved in any prohibition movement.

The executive committee of the Anti-Saloon League of America stated in 1916, when its plan to "enforce total abstinence by law" had been openly proclaimed, that the league had always favored "the adoption of state and national prohibition" (of the personal use of alcoholic drinks), the very thing the league had denied eight years before.

Surely, in view of the foregoing, few will dispute that the Anti-Saloon League of America, like the Anti-Saloon League of Virginia, had been "intensely practical in the methods by which it has endeavored to attain its ideal"!

CHAPTER *vi*

A Moral Newspaper

WHEN, in accordance with its declared policy of "Pauline opportunism," the Anti-Saloon League of Virginia finally broadcast that its aim was state-wide prohibition — after it had kept that objective carefully concealed for years — Cannon concluded that it would be difficult, if not impossible, to achieve his objective without a newspaper at Richmond to serve as the organ of the "moral and religious forces." He was continually harassed by the three existing Richmond papers, all of which were wet and all of which had been unfair to him at times. So he determined to give rein to his literary and business ability in still another sphere, that of daily journalism. He accordingly persuaded a group of friends to join him in the establishment of the *Richmond Virginian.*

These friends, it seems safe to say, were not attracted by Cannon's personality. They recognized his capacity for achievement in virtually any field that he entered, but it is doubtful if they were drawn to him by anything remotely resembling affection. Even some of his most ardent disciples have confessed that he was personally unattractive to them. He seemed not to be a man of any warmth, although an occasional friend or acquaintance testified to the contrary. A nationally known prohibition worker once described him [1] as "cold as a snake." A leading Virginia prohibitionist said of him publicly in 1918: "He may not be the best beloved, but he is the most feared man in Virginia." Only on the rarest occasions did Cannon display emotion of any kind. A man who had known him for forty years said he had never seen him laugh and seldom had seen him smile.

Dry Messiah

But this very grimness made him all the more formidable as an antagonist. When the first copy of the *Richmond Virginian* came from the presses on January 28, 1910, the public, whether wet, moist, or dry, knew that things were going to happen from that day forward. The paper was published every afternoon except Sunday by a stock company, capitalized at $100,000. Its plans for the future were discussed in the leading editorial of the initial issue, entitled "Salutatory," which said, among other things, that the paper "begins with the largest bona-fide subscription list ever acquired in Virginia by a new paper." It also enunciated the following elevating sentiments relative to news of crime and sporting events:

> Publicity is a valuable moral agency and exposure a real deterrent of crime and wrongdoing, and while the *Virginian* will not carry its readers through the sewers, it will print such reports of crime and evil conduct as are necessary for the protection of society. But all such news will be printed as a warning to evil-doers, and never as an enticement.
>
> Sporting news will be handled with proper discrimination. Genuine recreation and sports have their proper place in the life of the young, and while the *Virginian* will in no way promote any form or species of gambling, prize fighting or sport that is forbidden by law or detrimental to good morals, yet the paper will give special attention and liberal space and illustrations to wholesome sports.

The paper's pronouncements in its opening issue with respect to prohibition were so mild as to set some observers to wondering whether it would be content to advocate local option or whether it would go the whole distance and favor state-wide prohibition. They were not kept in suspense for long, however, for the *Virginian* soon came out militantly for a state-wide law.

It also became an outspoken champion of various moral movements besides prohibition, such as better observance of the Sabbath, more stringent divorce laws, and so on. But, despite the lofty tone of the paper's salutatory editorial and its numerous subsequent expressions of a similar nature, it not infrequently experienced difficulty in living up to the principles it professed. There was, for example, its salutatory promise not to "promote any form or species of . . . prize fighting." Within less than two weeks it was publishing news of the pugilistic world, and it continued to do so throughout its entire existence, at times giving it prominent front-page display, and printing photographs of bruisers pommeling one another in the ring. When Jack Johnson defeated Frank Moran in Paris in 1914, the *Virginian* carried a round-by-round account of the fight in the most prominent position on page one. Before Jack Dempsey met Jess Willard at Toledo in 1919, the paper announced on several successive days: "Four Great Experts to Tell *Virginian* Readers of Fight." The news that Dempsey had knocked out Willard in three rounds was chronicled on the front page under a heavy black headline, and photographs were published later. Yet when a bill was introduced in the Virginia legislature the following year providing for the legalization of prize fighting in the state and the creation of a state athletic commission to supervise and control boxing contests of ten rounds or less, the *Virginian* was a perfect picture of outraged virtue.

"It is inconceivable that it should succeed," said the paper concerning the bill. "The moral forces of the Commonwealth, after many years of hard struggle, have made Virginia a decent place in which respectable people may live in comfort and rear families in comparative safety. Let there be no backward step, no yielding to the clamor for brutal and debasing exhibitions to line the pockets of a coarse crew who wish to exploit the young, the foolish and the depraved."

Yet at the very time that this editorial appeared, the paper was printing prize-fight news, and ten days later it carried a long signed article by Georges Carpentier giving advice on how to succeed as a prizefighter!

As we have seen, the paper also announced in its salutatory editorial that it would "in no way promote any form or species of gambling." The management evidently believed that stock speculation was not a form of gambling, for market news and stock quotations were carried after the first two weeks. In addition, detailed accounts of horse-racing at Jacksonville, Tampa, Juárez, and other points were to be found on the sports page.

The *Richmond Evening Journal* twitted the *Virginian* for these inconsistencies. On its editorial page, the *Journal* carried reproductions of various items from the *Virginian* dealing with horse-racing, card-playing, and prize fighting, with the following legend over all: "Sample Items from the Richmond Virginian Which Appeals to the Godly for Its Support." Underneath was the following:

Rev. James Cannon, D.D., . . . has charged that the wet newspapers, as he chooses to style them, and all papers printing whiskey advertisements, are in the same class, and deserve to be censured, in his estimation, as much as he would censure a barkeeper for dispensing a drink over the counter. . . .

Rev. James Cannon, D.D., is challenged to define the difference between the Rev. James Cannon, D.D., a minister of the Gospel standing in a Methodist pulpit in any church in Virginia, preaching the Gospel and preaching against worldly and frivolous amusements, preaching against prize fighting, preaching against stock gambling — which preaching is in conformity with the tenets of the Methodist Church — and James Cannon, Jr., president and owner of a daily newspaper advertising, day after day, bridge whist and euchre parties played for prizes of value, as well as money; horse racing, prohibited by the laws of the State of Virginia; stock gambling, admitted to be one of the most vicious agencies for the downfall of youth and man, and prize fights. . . .

Cannon, with monumental irrelevance, replied that these statements of the *Journal* were "sheer hypocrisy," because the *Journal* printed news of prize fights, races, the stock market, and so on, and consequently had no right to criticize anyone else for doing the same thing. He also said:

A newspaper . . . may publish reports of a prize fight as a part of the news of the day, but it does not sell its columns to advertise the prize fight. It may describe the betting and gambling in Norfolk, but it does not sell its columns to the bookmakers. . . .

Manifestly, the position of the *Virginian* was a difficult one. For its management realized, of course, that it would have to be made reasonably interesting if it was ever to succeed. The stockholders had put up the money needed to enable the paper to begin operations, but they could not keep on providing funds indefinitely. They saw that it would be impossible to build up a large list of readers if it limited the contents of its news columns to soporific disquisitions on the moral state of the nation. A lively sports department was, among other things, essential, but to report certain kinds of sporting events meant to run counter to the taboos of Methodist and Baptist orthodoxy. Confronted by this state of things, Cannon and his associates evidently concluded that the paramount objective should be to keep the paper alive, owing to what was correctly deemed to be its essential role in the movement for state-wide prohibition. So the horse races and prize fights were duly chronicled.

When the paper switched from the afternoon to the morning field, in July 1911, another question of similar purport arose; namely, should it publish on Sunday? The board of directors decided in the affirmative, and on March 31, 1912 the *Sunday Virginian* made its bow. The readers received the characteristically reassuring dictum that "care will be taken to exclude from the paper such features as are calculated to do harm, rather than prove uplifting."

The amusing part of this was that few persons in Virginia had denounced Sunday newspapers more fiercely than Cannon. In 1905, for example, he had written [2] apropos of the announcement of the *Richmond Times-Dispatch* that it would shortly publish a Sunday edition:

> The Sunday newspapers and the Sunday excursions and freight trains have done more to secularize the Sabbath than all other agencies combined, and the owners of both will have a tremendous and awful account to meet when they come before the Lord of the Sabbath to explain why they not only desecrated the Sabbath themselves, but tempted millions of others to do the same, all for the purpose of temporal gain. . . . It is to be regretted that the *Times-Dispatch* has not sufficient conscience and backbone to withstand the pressure of a temptation to get gain out of the godless people who insist upon having seven secular papers during the week.

The following year Cannon had written [3] concerning Marshall Field, who had died shortly before, that there was "no taint on his money." One reason for this was that he had "positively refused ever to allow his business to be advertised in Sunday newspapers." And in 1907 Cannon had added the following: [4] "Sunday newspapers cannot honestly be classed as a necessity. . . . There is no justification for the Sunday newspaper on the score of necessity, and those who publish them do it because they want to make money."

In view of these harsh judgments, no one would have expected a newspaper in which Cannon was the principal stockholder to publish a Sunday edition. Yet the *Virginian* did so for eight years. It is true that Cannon and the Rev. J. Sidney Peters, another large stockholder, announced,[5] two weeks before the Sunday edition made its initial appearance, that they were retiring "from all official connection with the paper." But they did not say they were taking this action because the management had determined to publish seven days a week. On the contrary, they said they were retiring because they felt that the success of the paper was assured and that the "principal work" they had had in view was accomplished. They added that "the paper will receive our hearty support, and we shall feel the deepest interest in its continued welfare and prosperity."

Evidently Cannon was criticized in some quarters, following publication of this statement in the *Virginian*. At any rate, the Rev. Graham H. Lambeth — who was serving as editor of the *Advocate* and was to do so for nearly four more years at Cannon's invitation — issued an explanation of Cannon's action in that publication.[6] Since Cannon was sole owner and associate editor of the weekly, it seems reasonable to assume that Lambeth's apologia was approved by him in advance, if not actually written by him. It follows:

> For the two years that Dr. Cannon has been influential — perhaps most influential — in determining the policies of the *Virginian*, he has opposed the Sunday issue. He opposes it still. But there are other men interested in the *Virginian* — men of intelligence, judgment and Christian character. They have felt that if the *Virginian* is to succeed and become a permanent factor in the defense and propagation of the high ideals and principles for which it stands, it must enter the Sunday field. Their judgment and conviction have finally prevailed against the desire and over the opposition of Dr. Cannon and Rev. J. S. Peters, and these

gentlemen retire from the directorate of the paper because they cannot consent to become parties to a policy of which they do not approve. . . . Dr. Cannon informed the management that he would never accept a dollar profit from a periodical running a Sunday edition, and gave certain associates upon the *Virginian* a standing option upon his stock whenever they desired to purchase the same.

Here we have an entirely different explanation for the retirement of Cannon and Peters from that which they themselves gave in the columns of the *Virginian*. Lambeth creates the impression that they will have nothing more to do with a paper that publishes on Sunday. They themselves say that in the future the paper will receive their "hearty support." It may be added, too, with regard to Cannon's renunciation of any future profits and his offer to sell his stock, that there never were any profits, and that nobody wanted the stock. Cannon remained the largest stockholder throughout the life of the paper.

What, in fact, was the relation of Cannon and Peters to the *Virginian* after their retirement "from all official connection with the paper"? Cannon remained the dominant factor in the company for a number of years, if not for the remainder of its life. Peters, for a part of the time at least, was constantly in the business office, where he seemingly handled the finances. In addition, Cannon continued to raise funds for the paper. In 1915, for example, he sent out letters to a list of friends, informing them that it was absolutely necessary that fifty thousand dollars' worth of bonds be sold at once or the *Virginian* would have to suspend. One of the letters fell into the hands of the *Richmond News Leader,* which published it on its front page,[7] much to the embarrassment of the *Virginian*. However, some of the latter's supporters supplied the necessary funds.

Not only did Cannon raise money for the paper long after he had retired "from all official connection" with it, but he contributed editorials to it as well, and in 1917 the paper described him as "the best friend the *Virginian* ever had."[8] Furthermore, he wrote in an unguarded moment in 1941 that he had been "closely connected with the editorial policy" of the *Virginian* for ten years, — that is, throughout its entire life.[9] It is true that he was no longer president of the company after 1912, or a member of the board of directors, but he occupied a decidedly strange position, none the less, when one considers the scathing things he had said a few years previously about Sunday newspapers.

Still another matter that must have given the management of the *Virginian* concern was the amount of drinking done by the staff. Several of its reporters in its early years say they never encountered such conditions elsewhere. "I never saw so much drinking on any newspaper in my life; practically all the members of the news and editorial staffs were rummies," says one who has enjoyed unusually wide newspaper experience in various sections of the United States and who was a reporter for the organ of the moral forces for a brief season. "The city room reeked with whiskey," says another. "Dr. Cannon never seemed to mind particularly during the ten months I was there. The boys used to touch him for loans, even when they were in their cups, and then go out and get drunk all over again on the proceeds. I did it myself."

The manager of one of the local barrooms, who had had newspaper training, came down occasionally for a night's work on the Anti-Saloon League sheet. Later he joined the staff as a full-time reporter. The night when he was tapping on his typewriter in a comfortable state of alcoholic exaltation and a pint fell out of his pocket and clattered loudly to the floor is affectionately recalled by at least one of those who witnessed the episode.

It has been hinted by the unregenerate that the bawdy atmosphere of the *Virginian* was in some measure traceable to the fact that its offices at Governor and Ross streets were only a couple of blocks from the red-light district. "You could stand on the front porch and throw a baseball right into the heart of the district," says a former member of the staff. It is sad, but true, that one of the paper's important writers of moral homilies could often be found drunk in the parlor of a near-by bordello both during and after office hours.

After several years in these distinctly inelegant surroundings the *Virginian* moved to the more refined atmosphere of Seventh and Franklin streets. In the new quarters there was plenty of drinking by an assorted variety of inebriates who still composed the majority of the staff, but most of it was done after hours. Surcease from the strain of writing bone-dry editorials and highly edifying news accounts of the benefits of prohibition was usually sought in the neighboring saloons as soon as the paper was put to bed. A clue to the goings-on at such times is afforded in the complaint registered by one of the few abstainers in the office that he was getting very, very tired of opening his desk in the morning and finding it filled with empty whisky bottles.

The *Virginian's* circulation seems never to have mounted beyond 16,000 paid subscribers, but when it was in the midst of a hotly contested campaign involving "moral issues," it is said to have sent out thousands of free copies. Its influence was not measured in mere circulation totals, however, for, while all the other Richmond papers had more readers, the *Virginian* went to the fighting prohibitionists of the state. Hence propaganda in the hostile press was frequently ineffective, owing to the rapidity with which it was answered in the prohibitionist organ. A similar function was performed by the *Advocate*. In fact, many of Cannon's articles dealing with the prohibition question appeared in both journals. Then there was the *Weekly Virginian,* published from 1916 to 1920, devoted almost entirely to reforms of one kind or another. The contributing editors, in addition to Dr. Cannon, were the Rev. Dr. R. H. Pitt, the Rev. Dr. Thomas Semmes, the Rev. Dr. J. H. Light, and the Rev. Dr. E. T. Wellford, all leading prohibitionists. There was also the Virginia edition of the *American Issue,* official Anti-Saloon League publication, edited by Cannon as league superintendent. Articles appearing in this paper were often reprinted in the *Virginian* or the *Advocate,* or vice versa.

In the nature of things, other news was subordinated in the columns of the *Virginian* to news of the prohibition movement, both state and national. Utterances of eminent clergymen on the evils of alcohol were constantly given prominent display, while the sapient pronunciamentos of such moral leaders as the Rev. Billy Sunday, Congressman W. D. Upshaw, and William Jennings Bryan usually landed on the front page. Upshaw was a particular favorite with the paper, which invariably gave him lavish publicity when he came to town. Consider the following:

> Six full speeches in one day, and every one full of "pep" and Georgia wit and eloquence, was the unstinted investment which the "orator on crutches," Congressman Will D. Upshaw, of Georgia, made for the uplift of Richmond audiences yesterday.
>
> The Georgia lawmaker, who came here in the campaign for law enforcement and world prohibition, under the auspices of the Anti-Saloon League of America, spoke first to the Sunday School of Venable Street Baptist Church on "The New Book of Time — 1920" — from there he dashed away to catch the Sunday School at Union Station Methodist Church, addressing the Bates Bible Class on "Christian Manhood," and then the Junior Sunday School on "Pluck and Purpose."
>
> At 11 o'clock the Georgian spoke to a tremendous crowd on "A Stainless Flag and a Sober World," and such an avalanche of ready wit and patriotic fervor Richmond has not heard since Billy Sunday was here.
>
> At 3:30 the Georgia Congressman was driven through a semi-snow storm to speak at R. E. Lee Camp Soldiers Home. . . .
>
> Despite the severe cold, Venable Street Baptist Church was crowded last night to hear the dynamic Georgian's masterful address on "America's Mission to a Staggering World."

This was the same Mr. Upshaw who spoke at an Anti-Saloon League meeting in Washington, D.C., in 1924 and, in reporting the "results" obtained, wrote to M. G. Kelser, field manager, as follows, according to the Report of the Senate Committee on Campaign Expenditures, June 1926:

My dear Mr. Kelser:
> Sing the Doxology and turn a few somersaults if you want to in celebration of our very fine rally at Immanuel Baptist Church last Sunday night. I turned over to Wheeler's office the cards amounting to a little over $1,100 in subscriptions and about $50 in cash and checks. . . .
>
> I think you will have to shell down the corn and admit that your Georgia friend made a pretty good speech on America's greatest battle. . . .

At the side of the letter he wrote:

A Moral Newspaper

Remember this $1,168 collection cost you no advertising — only $1 taxi. In sending check, "let your conscience be your guide."

The communication was signed,

Yours very dry, W. D. Upshaw.

Cannon stated on numerous occasions that he had sunk from $50,000 to $65,000 of his own money in the *Virginian* and had never got a cent of it back. He claimed, too, that the Rev. J. Sidney Peters had donated from $30,000 to $35,000 to the same cause, without any return. As with his assertion that he never received any pay for prohibition work, no one was ever able to disprove his statement with respect to losses in the *Virginian*. On the other hand, neither Cannon nor Peters produced any documentary evidence that what they said was true. Hence a great many persons were always decidedly skeptical, at least as to the size of the supposed losses.

The *Virginian* was never a money-maker, and it seems certain that most of those who bought stock in it lost the full amount subscribed. The longer it ran, the greater were the sums needed to finance its operations. Contributors were said by Cannon to have poured some $350,000 into the enterprise during the ten years of its existence. Cannon said he sold practically all the property he had and used all his credit to keep the *Virginian* afloat. The late John Garland Pollard, Governor of Virginia from 1930 to 1934, and an almost lifelong leader in the dry movement, who heartily despised and distrusted Cannon, stated [10] that Cannon was confident in the early stages that the paper would be highly profitable. Governor Pollard said that when he was asked to subscribe, Cannon and associates expressed the conviction that he would receive large returns on his investment. Others were less optimistic, but they put the savings of a lifetime into the venture, nevertheless, in order to share in the movement to make Virginia dry. Certainly those who subscribed six or eight years after the *Virginian's* establishment must have done so with little or no hope of any monetary return.

The *Virginian* went downhill gradually. At the outset, the local staff, when sober, was able to hold its own with any of its Richmond competitors. In fact, it scored some impressive scoops over the opposition. State news coverage, on the other hand, was never satisfactory, for in the smaller centers the paper relied mainly on preachers and Sunday-school superintendents, who often regarded a W.C.T.U. clambake as far more newsworthy than a double homicide.

The paper was boycotted from the beginning by many advertisers because of its stand against liquor. As finances dwindled, its city staff disintegrated, and its state news grew increasingly vapid. It managed to keep going in its last years only by cutting its force to a skeleton, and it degenerated into a frowsy-looking sheet. Dr. E. H. Cherrington, potentate of the Anti-Saloon League of America, served the paper in an advisory capacity for several years, and heroic efforts were made to save it from collapse. There were various rumors that it would suspend, and on March 4, 1920 it took note of these by printing a denial that it had any such plans.

But ten weeks later, on May 14, the tottering and gasping *Virginian* suddenly yielded up the ghost. It announced that it had sold its subscription list and its good will to the *Evening Journal,* and that it would cease publication on the following day. It was careful to state, however, that the *Journal* had been taken over by a new management and had become "a consistent and helpful supporter of prohibition and of righteousness."

Thus it was with no twinges of conscience that the *Virginian* finally lowered its colors to the *Journal* after their many years of rancorous warfare. The teetotaling newspaper with the whisky-laden breath was no more.

CHAPTER *vii*

The Hosts of Hell are Routed

JAMES CANNON, JR.'s multitudinous tasks made it impossible for him to devote much attention to his large family. Since for decades he did the work of two or three normal men, little time remained for him to be at ease with his wife and children. That condition had obtained since 1894, when he assumed the prodigious job of establishing the Blackstone Institute. His manifold interests, both religious and secular, absorbed him to such a degree that Mrs. Cannon and the nine children born to them in the first seventeen years of their married life were relegated to a secondary place. Seven of the nine grew up.

While some of Cannon's intimates described him as intensely devoted to his family and his home, it cannot be doubted that his work was easily his chief interest. In 1906 he wrote that his favorite form of amusement was "playing tennis and other innocent games with his children." He seems to have indulged in such diversions occasionally, but work alone — bone-crushing work — was this furious crusader's preferred form of recreation.

Just as the fight to make Virginia legally dry was getting well started, there came to Cannon in August 1911 an invitation to become general superintendent of the Southern Assembly at Lake Junaluska, N.C. The Southern Assembly, which today is visited by Methodists from all parts of the South, was then only a name, and the stockholders had decided to offer Cannon the formidable job of creating in the North Carolina mountains this recreational, educational, and religious center for the Southern Methodist Church. They realized that a man of unremitting energy, alert

71

business acumen, and strong executive capacity was essential to the success of the venture, and Cannon filled all these requirements.

Surmising that the Southern Assembly, when established, would become a "great central power house, from which currents of uplifting influence will go out to all the church," Cannon accepted. He plunged into the work with characteristic verve, after reducing his Anti-Saloon League and editorial responsibilities to a minimum. During the four closing months of 1911 he visited no fewer than fourteen annual conferences in all parts of the South. He was even busier in 1912, especially in the fall and early winter. During the latter period he attended fourteen conferences and also made three trips to Virginia in connection with the controversy involving Randolph-Macon and the Carnegie Foundation. In addition he found it necessary to travel to various Eastern cities in the interests of temperance and other matters.

In order to bring the work of the Southern Assembly to a successful termination, Cannon borrowed $150,000 for the assembly in small sums from Virginia country banks, largely on his own personal credit. These loans were finally consolidated in a bond issue, which was floated by a Richmond trust company. Under his supervision, the assembly was established, and the dam, auditorium, service building, roads, and sidewalks were built, while the lake also was developed. In addition, as a business venture of his own, Cannon built the Virginia Lodge, a hotel of one hundred rooms, at Lake Junaluska. He remained its owner until 1921.

It was only for the first few years after his election as general superintendent of the Southern Assembly that he found it necessary to devote a large share of his time to the project. His salary as superintendent was paid him in stock in the enterprise. He continued as head of the assembly until his election as Bishop, although during the last four or five years of his incumbency it was not necessary for him to devote a great deal of attention to the work. The arduous part of the job had been carried out.

But let us return to the prohibition campaign in the Old Dominion. The extraordinary progress that had been made by the

The Hosts of Hell are Routed

Anti-Saloon League of Virginia since its foundation in 1901 was outlined by Superintendent Cannon in April 1910, as follows:

Nine years ago there were about 4,000 liquor establishments of all sorts in the state; now there are about 850. Nine years ago there were nearly 3,000 saloons; now there are about 750. Then there were about 800 distilleries; now there are about 50. Then the country cross-roads bar-room was the neighborhood center for poverty, vice and crime; now there is no cross-roads bar-room. Then the pot-house distilleries were scattered through the country, in many cases worse than saloons. Now the pot-house distillery has followed the cross-roads bar-room. Then the "fake" clubs were in existence, and were rapidly increasing; now there are no "fake" clubs. Then there were no restrictions on the sale of liquor; now saloons must close from midnight till 5 a.m. all over the state, and in many cities they close at an earlier hour. Then in every city in Virginia the saloon had a license to ruin the young men of the state; now Lynchburg, Danville, Charlottesville, Fredericksburg, Winchester, Staunton, Clifton Forge, Radford and Suffolk refuse to license saloons, and in Bristol and Roanoke they exist by a small purchased majority. Nine years ago a majority of the towns had saloons; now 141 out of 162 have no sale of intoxicants in any form. Nine years ago there were no adequate "blind tiger" laws; now there is on the statute books a strong, well-articulated law "with teeth in it."

In view of this record, it required no political prescience or prestidigitation to see that Armageddon was drawing nigh. The Anti-Saloon League was relentlessly, ruthlessly, persistently driving the wets back. In Virginia, as in many other states, it had taken the front-line trenches and the secondary defenses, and it was now massing its forces for a concerted assault on the inner fortifications. At the session of the Virginia legislature that convened in 1910, the Enabling Act, providing for a referendum by the people on the issue of state-wide prohibition, was introduced. Nobody expected it to pass, and this expectation was fulfilled; but the fact that the measure was offered showed that the Anti-Saloon League had at last decided to throw all its resources into the movement for a state-wide law. The thought was far from

Dry Messiah

comforting to the embattled wets, for the league had acquired the reputation for getting what it went after.

With the die definitely cast, relations between Cannon and the anti-prohibitionist newspapers, particularly those at Richmond, grew more acrimonious than ever.

When the Virginia Conference of the Methodist Church met at Richmond in 1910, there was a fearful row over the manner in which the news of the proceedings was handled by the press. The *Evening Journal,* in the course of the editorial exchanges incident to this controversy, said: "Cannon is not a persecuted innocent; he is an alien bluffer, to whose real character even those he has so long fooled are gradually waking up." The same paper also said: "As for the *Journal,* it would believe on oath any reporter who had had experience with Rev. James Cannon, Jr., in preference to Dr. Cannon." To which the South Hill, Virginia, *Enterprise* replied: "Well, what of it? You are not alone." These were strong words and they provoked lusty retorts.

For example, at the state convention of the Anti-Saloon League in 1911, the organization, headed by Cannon, asserted that there was no difference between the paper that made money on liquor advertising and the saloon-keeper who sold the liquor. "Both are doing exactly the same thing for the same thing, namely money," the report said. "Both are making money out of the damnation of their fellow men, and whenever men can bring the consent of their minds to make money in such a business, they will not hesitate to slander, abuse and vilify in every possible way those who are destroying the profits of their business by their efforts to save their fellow men from ruin."

The legislative committee's report also said, and with some justice:

Your legislative committee, in its fight for the Strode Bill [the Enabling Act], were met with the cry that the Strode Bill was contrary to the Democratic doctrine of local option. Such a cry in the mouth of the drunkard makers is pure hypocrisy. They never stand for any principle. Their record is the same in every state in the Union. Whenever in any state there is no local option law, and an effort is made to pass such a law, they oppose it bitterly. They are fighting a local option law today in Pennsylvania

74

and Maryland, where there is no such law, and they are crying out for local option in Texas, and West Virginia, and Virginia and in every other state where statewide prohibition is the issue.

The *Religious Herald,* the leading Baptist publication in the state, spoke of the "extreme and violent language of the legislative committee's report in denunciation of the secular papers" and added: "Bandying epithets, exchanging abuse, and impugning motives will not hasten the settlement of the vexed question." The editor of the paper was the Rev. R. H. Pitt, a leading prohibitionist who afterward served as president of the Virginia Anti-Saloon League.

Perhaps the fiercest retort that appeared in the lay press following the publication of the resolutions emanated from the sanctum of the *Times-Dispatch.* That bellicose journal said:

> Brethren of the Press: Let not your hearts be troubled about the lying accusations made against you in the report of the legislative committee' of the Anti-Saloon League. . . . The charges made against the newspapers of the state are utterly false, and Dr. Cannon knew they were false when he wrote them. Why dignify him with denunciation? He isn't worth it. Why characterize him as a base slanderer? That is the estimate in which he is held by many persons of good moral character and of sound and disposing mind. Why bandy words with him or about him? One would never think of engaging in such controversy with any other blackguard. . . .

Another publication that jousted with Cannon and his committee was the *Danville Methodist,* of which E. G. Moseley, a convinced dry, was associate editor. Moseley said he objected to the legislative committee's statements concerning papers that published whisky advertising. He expressed the view that "the editors of our secular papers are as a rule gentlemen of as high type of character as are to be found in any state, and are far above being placed in the category in which they were placed by the resolutions."

During the same year, 1911, Major J. Calvin Hemphill, editor of the *Times-Dispatch,* was invited by Dr. R. E. Blackwell, president of Randolph-Macon College, to make an address at the college commencement exercises. When the fact became known, Cannon spluttered with rage. "There would have been equal fitness in selecting the editor of the *Wine and Spirit Gazette*," he screamed in the *Advocate*. "It is amazing that the president of Randolph-Macon College should have failed to realize how abhorrent the *Times-Dispatch* is to thousands of Virginia Methodists." Dr. Blackwell replied quietly that he had invited Hemphill because Hemphill was a distinguished man and that he had not intended to affront anybody. But there was such an uproar from the extreme prohibitionist wing of the college alumni that the major concluded not to deliver the address.

A number of local-option elections were being held at this time, and Cannon charged that in some of them the wets were voting Negroes in large numbers. The latter claimed that the drys were doing the same thing. At all events, Cannon seemed to have convincing evidence of the guilt of the anti-prohibitionists.

As 1911 drew to a close, the lines on both sides became taut in anticipation of the conflict that everyone knew would be waged over the Enabling Act when the legislature convened early in the following year. If it was true, as the anti-prohibitionists charged, that a deal had been made in 1909 whereby the Enabling Act would not go through until 1914, the Anti-Saloon League's activities might be explained on the ground that its representatives knew the bill would not pass for at least two more years and that in 1912 they were merely building up sentiment, with 1914 in mind. At any rate, Cannon and the other league workers were much in evidence, and, even if they were bluffing, they succeeded in convincing many people that they were in earnest.

It was generally believed that the bill would pass the House, so that principal interest centered in the Senate, which was newly elected. Heavy pressure had been brought to bear by the Anti-Saloon League in every senatorial district, and it was manifest that the measure would obtain a larger volume of support in the upper branch of the lawmaking body than it had obtained two years before. When the votes were counted there, the bill was found to have lost by 23 to 15, although it had passed the House by 62 to 30. In addition, the Senate was responsible for the downfall of measures designed to strengthen the anti-gambling law and to prevent election frauds. After the session had adjourned, Cannon accused the Senate of having been "openly and insolently defiant of the moral sentiment of the state."

Charges at this time that Cannon was endeavoring to control the appointments of Governor Mann led to the dry leader's publication of a letter he had received from the Governor. This letter set forth that Cannon had written Mann two years before that he did not propose to recommend to Mann any applicants for office. Mann stated that he could recall only one such recommendation from Cannon since he had become Governor, and "that was on moral grounds."

The second successive defeat of the Enabling Act did not dismay the Anti-Saloon League workers. Deal or no deal, it is doubtful if they had thought it possible to get the bill through before 1914. But they did expect its enactment then, and during 1912 and 1913 the league pounded ahead, its throttle wide open. Cannon thanked God that only three or four Methodist churches in the Virginia Conference were unwilling to permit representatives of the league to occupy their pulpits.

It was also during 1913 that he characterized Richmond as a "hopeless" prospect for reformers and contrasted it with Norfolk:

> There are probably as many churches and church members in proportion to population in Richmond as in Norfolk, but fashionable society has a stronger grip upon church organization in Richmond than it has in Norfolk, and where fashionable society dominates, or is strongly influential in the church, it is exceedingly difficult, if not well nigh impossible, to secure any action by the church against the saloon, for fashionable society has its own saloon and its club-houses, and has its champagne and wines at its various functions. . . .

Despite the depravity of Richmond, the directors of the Virginia State Fair Association announced in 1913 that they would invite President Woodrow Wilson to attend the fair in that city and to deliver an address. Cannon thereupon observed in the *Advocate* that if the President was invited, he ought to be informed that saloons would be in operation at the fair grounds. He added that these saloons were kept open "although, strange to relate, some of the directors are members of the Methodist Church, and some perhaps of other churches." Whether President Wilson was advised that if he attended the fair, he would run the risk of placing himself in the proximity of a saloon is not of record. At any rate, he found it impossible to be present.

As the legislative session of 1914 approached, the embattled wets girded up their loins for a last stand. Their only hope of blocking a referendum lay in the Senate, for the House had surrendered long ago. With the enemy on the run and victory almost achieved, the Anti-Saloon League redoubled its efforts. Superintendent Cannon was a veritable cyclone of activity. He worked night and day, holding interviews, checking over the forty senators, putting pressure on this one and that one, keeping his fingers constantly on the senatorial pulse.

Richmond was aware that the crisis in the controversy over whisky had arrived. Old-fashioned Virginia gentlemen, who saw their toddies and their "night-caps" vanishing rapidly over the horizon, drove down to the Capitol to see if something couldn't be done. After listening to the debates, they strolled over to Murphy's Bar or Campbell's Saloon, adjoining the Capitol Square, for a little something to take the chill of January out of their bones. All agreed that the state of things was serious, but, other than to hope fervently that the Senate would save the situation, there was little they could do. They swore thumping oaths at the thought that "this fellow Jim Cannon" might soon be dictating to them what they should drink. Virginia, they said, had come to a pretty pass when a man had to take orders from a Methodist preacher as to whether he could have a cocktail before dinner.

They looked across the street to Capitol Square, with its bronze figure of Stonewall Jackson, "presented by English gentlemen"; at the historic Capitol itself, rich in its associations with the great Virginians of the past, and wondered how many of those men would have tolerated such tyranny. Thomas Jefferson, who designed the structure after the Maison Carrée at Nîmes; Washington, whose statue from life by Houdon stands beneath the

The Hosts of Hell are Routed

dome; John Marshall, who presided in this same Capitol over the trial of Aaron Burr for treason and who later delivered an address there welcoming Lafayette back to Richmond; John Randolph of Roanoke, whose shrill voice, "like the scream of an eagle," rang through the building and out across the square at the State Constitutional Convention of 1829; James Madison and James Monroe, who also took part in that convention. What would these men have done if the Methodist and Baptist preachers had sought to dictate to them concerning their personal habits? There could be but one answer. And yet, here was this Jim Cannon trying to tell their descendants that it was a sin to sit on the veranda in the cool of the evening and to sip a julep from a frosted silver goblet! The mere thought was enough to make an old-fashioned Virginia gentleman tear his mustachios with rage.

In order more effectively to fill the hearts of recalcitrant legislators with awe, the Anti-Saloon League of Virginia held its annual convention at Richmond about a week after the assembly convened. The gathering was proceeding smoothly, and the lawmakers seemed duly impressed, when Dr. Livius Lankford, a prominent Norfolk physician, tossed a bucketful of sand into the rapidly revolving gears. In an address to the league, he said:

> Any member of the General Assembly who votes against the Enabling Act is actuated by one of three reasons — either he is a man with a price, and the goods have been delivered, or he is related to a liquor dealer and has not enough manhood to go home and say he voted against the whiskey interests, or he is the descendant of a weakling.

It need hardly be said that when Lankford's remarks were published in the newspapers next morning, the members of the General Assembly were roused to enormous wrath. On the other hand, Delegate R. F. Leedy, of Page County, one of the most fervent of the wets, said that the utterance was not worthy of consideration. "I do not believe in training our artillery upon a sparrow, a pewee or a buzzard," he declared on the floor. Delegate W. M. Myers, of Richmond, shouted that Lankford "left a trail of venom behind him like the trail of a snake." Both branches of the legislature unanimously adopted resolutions denouncing the Norfolk physician. It was clear that the latter's remarks were having a bad effect and the league hastened to point out that it was not responsible for the statements of speakers who addressed it. Lankford subsequently issued a public apology. He was a sincere and respected man who had been carried away by his feelings.

The excitement induced by his address soon died and the assemblymen got down to the business of voting on the Enabling Act. As in later times, there were plenty of drinking drys in the legislative halls. These servants of the people were frequently to be found in the near-by saloons but, when they came to vote on Anti-Saloon League legislation, they usually managed to reel back to the Capitol and uphold the cause of morality.

Realizing that there was grave danger of the Enabling Act's passage, its opponents resorted to desperate measures. Three separate attempts were made to have Cannon removed from the floor of the House and Senate, on the ground that he had abused his press privileges, but they came to nothing. He had enjoyed such privileges from the time he acquired the *Advocate* in 1904. When the *Virginian* was established, he retained his membership in the press corps as a "special correspondent" of that journal at the Capitol. He was constantly on the floors of both houses at the session of 1914.

When the time came for a showdown on the enabling bill, the Anti-Saloon League carried all before it in the House. The vote there was 64 to 31 in favor of the bill. With this tremendous majority behind them in the lower branch, Cannon and his fellow workers took their fight into the Senate. Up to the final minute the outcome was in doubt. Before the vote was taken, it was learned that one of the dry senators had been carousing extensively the night before, and an emissary was dispatched to drag him out of bed and bring him to the Capitol at all costs. The emissary showed up with him in due course, and the vote of this pillar of prohibition, who was suffering severely from the effects of the usquebaugh he had consumed, enabled the drys to tie the wets, 20 to 20. This put it up to Lieutenant Governor J. Taylor Ellyson, the Senate's presiding officer, who was not personally dry, to cast the deciding ballot. A hush fell over the assemblage as the Lieutenant Governor said: "The chair votes 'aye.'" Cannon and others rushed up to congratulate him. The Enabling Act had passed.

Many persons were and are of the opinion that Ellyson decided on the spur of the moment to vote for the bill, but that was not so. Long before the legislature convened, the shrewd and far-seeing Cannon had anticipated just such a tie in the Senate and had made his preparations.

In accordance with its practice of querying candidates for office, the league had queried Ellyson and all other aspirants for the lieutenant-governorship in 1913 and had asked them what they would do, if elected, in the event of a tie vote in the Senate on the Enabling Act. Each of them had promised to cast his ballot for it. Hence Ellyson's vote was pledged to the Anti-Saloon League from that time forward.

The date for the referendum on statewide prohibition was fixed in the Enabling Act for September 22, 1914, and both wets and drys began febrile preparations for the conflict. Cannon, needless to say, was the generalissimo of the prohibitionist forces in their drive against those whom he termed "the hosts of hell."

The principal organization of the opposition was the Local Self-Government Association of Virginia, headed by Judge George L. Christian, of Richmond, a highly respected jurist and former president of the Virginia State Bar Association. The Personal Liberty Association, organized four years previously, but inactive over a considerable period, was revived. An entire floor of a downtown office building was rented by the anti-prohibitionists. Among the prominent individuals who aided them substantially was Paul Garrett, of Norfolk, chairman of the executive committee of the Brewers, Wine and Spirit Merchants of Virginia.

The *Virginian* lost little time in hanging on the Local Self-Government Association the sobriquet of the "Bold, Brave Boys of the Bottle." The resuscitation of the Personal Liberty Association also was the signal for Cannon to unsheathe his journalistic snickersnee. He made the following incisive observations upon what he conceived to be the true interests of this organization:

Some years ago this association heard that an effort might be made to curtail this precious right — to drink liquor to our comfort — and there was a great clamor. The inalienable rights of free-born Richmond citizens were in danger and the slogan was sounded, "Let Richmond alone; let us drink liquor to our comfort."

But the danger passed by, the Personal Liberty Association became quiescent, and amid all the political and economic changes of the day, nothing has been sufficient to call this liberty-loving association into action. But the Enabling Act has been passed. . . . This has aroused the sleeping giant, and once again he takes the field and begins to fight for — "personal liberty," he calls it — really the right to drink liquor to his comfort.

Personal liberty then has no meaning to this association, except as it relates to intoxicating liquor. The members of the association respond to no other battle-cry. But when this issue is raised, there is indeed a great stir, and all the members fall into line and cry with indignation, "Give us liquor, or give us death!"

Methodist and Baptist churches throughout Virginia were enlisted in the crusade by the Anti-Saloon League. The Baptist State Mission Board donated the services of three secretaries and six evangelists. Sermons exalting prohibition were heard in scores of pulpits each Sunday, and the emotions of the populace were stimulated and kindled by the pastors and other campaigners for the cause. Temperance organizations, such as the W.C.T.U., buckled on their armor.

Like the white plume of Navarre, the swarthy whiskers of Superintendent Cannon were the oriflamme about which pressed the ranks of the prohibitionist myrmidons. It was he who coordinated the activities of the various co-operating bodies. With the assistance of the Rev. J. Sidney Peters, he attended to such practical matters as precinct organization and the appointment of one captain to every ten voters throughout the state. He supervised the distribution of literature and during the closing sixty days of the drive saw that five hundred thousand pages of it were sent out daily. He wrote many editorials for the *Virginian* and delivered countless speeches in all parts of the Old Dominion. He is said to have made as many as seven speaking appearances in one day, and he often spoke three or four times. As important as any of the foregoing was the fact that he borrowed over twenty-five thousand dollars on his own personal credit to help finance the fight.

The anti-prohibitionists experienced difficulty in persuading prominent citizens to espouse their cause openly. Those who did so were savagely assailed by Cannon and his co-workers, so that others who were contemplating joining them in the anti-prohibitionist trenches not infrequently concluded to remain discreetly silent. The *Lynchburg News*, which aided the dry cause throughout the campaign, remarked editorially a few weeks before the referendum:

> We have actually been shocked at the really venomous attacks that have recently been projected upon distinguished Virginians, whose character, standing and exalted civic virtues are absolutely irreproachable, simply because of their views on prohibition. Such methods are as ungenerous as they are unsportsmanlike — in some instances, utterly shameless and cruel. . . .

Relations between the local option papers and the *Virginian* became extremely bitter. The *Virginian* and the *Richmond Evening Journal* tossed especially harsh epithets at each other. Both were guilty of misrepresentation during the campaign. As in his earlier and later controversies over prohibition and kindred matters, Cannon belabored the opposition with such vigorous phrases as "absolutely false," "appetite and covetousness," "I flatly assert," "I positively deny," "I must insist," "infamous liquor traffic," "drunkard-makers," and "these slanderous and venomous attacks." These are the phrases that occur oftenest in his polemical writings. In contrast to the *Journal*, which tilted almost daily with Cannon, the *Times-Dispatch* decided that the way to hurt his feelings was never to mention his name. Consequently, it gave him the "silent treatment" throughout the contest.

On July 31 Judge Christian issued a statement setting forth his position as head of the Local Self-Government Association. It was a calm, dispassionate declaration of his reasons for preferring local option to prohibition, in which he asserted that he had never taken a drink in a Richmond barroom, and that if he thought "prohibition would prohibit," he would certainly vote for it. He made the mistake, however, of not sending a copy of the statement to the *Virginian*. Perhaps he thought that paper would not publish it.

In any event, as soon as the statement appeared in the other papers, the *Virginian* began attacking it. Almost every day a paragraph was singled out and criticized. To judge from the style, these criticisms were written by Cannon. Finally Judge Christian requested the *Virginian* to publish his declaration in full, since he did not think it fair for the paper to comment upon extracts without ever printing the document in its entirety. He added that he regarded many of the deductions made from it by the *Virginian* as "unwarranted and unjust" and called attention to the fact that the paper had printed a letter from a reader charging him with "unfairness." He expressed the opinion that the only way for *Virginian* readers to tell whether he had been unfair was for the paper to publish his full statement. That journal replied that, since Judge Christian had not sent it a copy when the statement was first issued, it would not publish it now, as the pronouncement was no longer news. It declared further that the judge's language had not been "garbled or twisted out of its proper connection" and that the comments that had been made and the conclusions drawn were "neither unwarranted or unjust." Later the *Virginian* abandoned virtually all pretense to fairness by asserting that it would not publish Judge Christian's statement as a paid advertisement if it were asked to do so.

The local-optionists claimed, quite naturally, that the prohibitionist organ was unjust to Judge Christian. They also contended that the wording of the ballot to be used in the approaching election was improper. It read: "For Statewide Prohibition" and "Against Statewide Prohibition," whereas, in their opinion, it should have read "For Statewide Prohibition" and "For Local Option." They were right in believing that if the ballot had been worded as they wished, local option would have stood a better chance of winning. But Cannon had realized this also and had beaten the plan in the House, after the Senate had passed it by a unanimous vote.

The anti-prohibitionists were considerably less effective with their propaganda than their adversaries. They sought by reason and argument to convince the electorate that the proposed step was unwise. Statistics were marshaled to show that the state would lose revenue, and the contention was advanced that prohibition would not, or could not, be enforced. The drys, on the other hand, appealed primarily to the emotions. They stressed the righteousness of their cause and the "moral issue" involved. When, for example, the *Times-Dispatch* published an interview with Mayor James H. Preston of Baltimore, in which he stated that prohibition laws had failed in the Southern states, the *Virginian* retorted with a posed photograph showing a man surrounded by his five young sons, one of whom carried a card on which were inscribed the words: "Saloons destroy one out of five. Which will it be?" The caption over the picture was: "Maybe your boy is next." In response to elaborate and detailed arguments that the law could not be enforced if passed, the *Virginian* retorted with twenty words printed in oversize type: "Don't be fooled by the haggard and decrepit old falsehood that prohibition doesn't prohibit. It does, and they know it." Such sledgehammer tactics were especially effective after the *Virginian* laid hold of a letter mailed by the Brewers, Wine and Spirit Merchants of Virginia marked "confidential to the trade." It urged prompt payment of assessments levied on the members to fight prohibition.

Although one of the news executives on the *Virginian's* staff spent most of his spare time writing campaign literature for the wets, he seems to have lacked the master touch. Instead of reading his relatively uninspired tracts, the public was titillated by the sight of the Anti-Saloon League's exhibit in a showroom on Richmond's Main Street, containing a lurid array of charts and drawings depicting the "effects of alcohol on the human system." Its gruesome nature caused it to be dubbed the "Chamber of Horrors." And whereas the antis imported speakers who kept their feet on the ground and addressed their audiences in dignified fashion, the drys brought in such renowed spellbinders and exhorters as Richmond Pearson Hobson, the hero of Santiago; Evangelist George Stuart, and the Rev. Sam Small.

The Anti-Saloon League was not wholly lacking in statistics, but it subordinated them to the emotional appeal. When the antis declared that prohibition would deprive the state of more than $500,000 a year in liquor revenue, the statistical rejoinder of the prohibitionists was as follows: Liquor accounts for 85 per cent of crime and the state's criminal costs per year, or $527,253.74. It also accounts for 35 per cent of the cost of hospitals and benevolent institutions, or $302,812.05, as well as 47 per cent of poor relief, or $173,021.45. These amounts total $1,003,087.24, and if the liquor revenue of $548,671.87 for 1913 is subtracted, we have a net cost of the liquor traffic to Virginia per year of $454,405.37.

There is reason to believe, however, that the drys relied much more heavily on the evangelistic note than on such unexciting tabulations as the foregoing. A rather typical ebullition was that of the Rev. Carter Ashton Jenkens, of Richmond, when he addressed a Methodist mass meeting on July 4. Said he:

> I had a vision. It was night. A dark cloud lowered like a black flag in an angry sky. . . . I saw in my vision 10,000 saloons flashing with light. Behind green blinds I heard bacchanalian songs and the music of stringed instruments. I heard the clatter of glasses and the thud of nickels on the counter. . . . I saw children crying for shoes . . . I saw poverty, shame, suffering and death caused by strong drink. The town clock struck twelve. I heard revelry and lascivious songs. . . .

Jenkens then described "another vision," which included sunlit skies, homes "vocal with glad songs," happy children, flowers, and similar appurtenances. His vision had it that "the jails were empty; the police station nearly deserted; theft, murder, suicide ceased." Inquiring of the attendant angel concerning the explanation for this startling transmogrification, Jenkens was informed "in the soft cadence of heaven, 'The saloon is gone.'"

The tribute paid the W.C.T.U. by W. M. Bickers in an address at Fonticello on August 13 was in the same rhapsodical genre. "In the forefront of the great battle to make Virginia a safer place for the boys and girls of today," proclaimed the perfervid Mr. Bickers, "unflinchingly and splendidly stands the rare and radiant regiment of the fair from that world-wide crystallization of consecrated womanhood whose banner is unfurled in every clime — the Woman's Christian Temperance Union!"

The German invasion of Belgium and the Battle of the Marne naturally prevented Virginians from concentrating on the approaching referendum to the virtual exclusion of all other matters, but there was tremendous interest in the outcome. From the fringes of lower Tidewater, home of the succulent oyster, to the bobcat-infested thickets of Cumberland Gap, and from the tobacco and cotton fields along the North Carolina line to the lush pastures and apple orchards of the Shenandoah Valley, the commonwealth stood on tiptoe as the drys and the antis galloped down the home stretch.

Election day, September 22, dawned, and with it came the tolling of church bells from one end of Virginia to the other. Prayer meetings were held in many places and hymns were sung. In Richmond the Woman's Prohibition League of America held prayer services at its headquarters from eight to ten a.m. and simultaneously in nineteen Methodist and Baptist churches from ten a.m. to five p.m. Similar arrangements were made throughout the state. That night there was a great throng in front of Anti-Saloon League headquarters, where returns were flashed on a screen outside the building. Hundreds of men, women, and children joined in singing hymns and in cheering riotously, women wept and became hysterical, as the news was received that this or that locality had voted dry. Several clergymen, including Cannon, addressed the gathering, amid fervent and prolonged hallelujahs.

The final count showed 94,251 votes for state-wide prohibition and 63,886 against it, a dry majority of 30,365. Cannon and his fellow crusaders carried 76 counties, lost 23, and tied with the opposition in one. They won in all the cities except Richmond, Norfolk, Alexandria, and Williamsburg. Three days before the election Cannon had predicted that the Anti-Saloon League would carry nine of the ten congressional districts. As matters turned out, it carried eight and came within ten votes of carrying another. Cannon announced that the league had spent $72,500 in the campaign, of which $48,500 was raised prior to the election.

Dry Messiah

(The deficit of $24,000 was made up by the churches during the succeeding four years.) He estimated that the anti-prohibitionists had squandered between $850,000 and $1,150,000 in their futile effort to retain local option. The antis made no public statement on the subject.

The terrific strain of the state-wide campaign broke Cannon's health temporarily and he suffered the first nervous and physical collapse of his life. No evidence had previously been uncovered that there was a limit to the amount of work he could do. The limit thus revealed, however, was so far beyond the capacity of almost all other men that the wonder was not that his health cracked after the election, but that he managed to maintain his furious pace until the votes were counted. During the closing weeks he was evidently physically used up and able to keep driving ahead solely by virtue of his inner compulsions and his reserve of nervous energy. Once the campaign was successfully concluded, the demoniac will that had spurred him to develop the last ounce of force from his none too robust physique was relaxed and the natural reaction followed.

The thirteen-year fight that had begun quietly, if not inauspiciously, in 1901 with the formation of the Anti-Saloon League of Virginia — an event that few persons at the time believed was of any particular importance — had finally culminated in a decisive triumph. In the course of the struggle grave questions arose concerning some of the methods used by the "moral and religious forces," and especially their leader, but certainly those methods were devastatingly effective. Cannon emerged at once as the most potent political force in Virginia, a man before whom the great majority of those in public life rushed incontinently "to crook the pregnant hinges of the knee." The craven obeisance before him of the average Virginia politician during the ensuing years was to prove a most unedifying spectacle.

CHAPTER *viii*

Cannonian Comstockery

W HILE Cannon is recuperating from the collapse that followed the victory achieved under his leadership in the election of 1914, let us orient him a bit more definitely in the excessively decorous milieu of the early twentieth century.

It was the era when Anthony Comstock was the nation's self-appointed mentor of morality. Indeed, between the doctrines Comstock enunciated and those Cannon proclaimed, there was a marked affinity. The period was one of contrasts and antitheses. Its literary and artistic criteria had reached such a level of chaste irreproachability that Comstock, his mutton-chop whiskers bristling, could belabor Bernard Shaw as "this Irish smut-dealer," and a canvas so lacking in piquancy as *September Morn* could almost cause riots in sophisticated Gotham. Yet every large city had its red-light district, reeking with vice of assorted varieties, a more blatant exhibition of officially sanctioned sordidness and depravity than can be found anywhere in America today.

Cannon elected almost invariably to take his stand figuratively by Comstock's side whenever what he termed "moral issues" arose; and there were many such issues in the first decade and a half of this century. He discussed them frequently and at length in the columns of the *Advocate*. Not only were his attitudes largely the same as those of Comstock, but he defended Anthony publicly from the attacks of the unregenerate and the profane.

In 1906, for example, when Comstock had his famous passage-at-arms with the Art Students' League of New York, Cannon pleaded his cause with gusto. Comstock's confiscation of a league pamphlet containing studies of nudes — which pamphlet, it was sadly recorded, was actually to be sent to "girls and unmarried women" — caused Gutzon Borglum, the sculptor, to exclaim: "My God, what are we coming to? . . . Comstock is the one who is lewd." There followed a spate of cartoons in the press, suggesting that Anthony was on the verge of arresting the Venus de Milo and the Apollo Belvedere, and depicting him in a variety of ultra-sanctimonious and ultra-preposterous poses. Whereupon Cannon rushed to his defense in the *Advocate* under the caption: "Anthony Comstock Triumphant." Cannon termed Comstock "one of the real heroes of reform work."

Cannon, like Comstock, was not sensitive to beauty. True, the year after he wrote the foregoing, he pronounced E. V. Valentine's celebrated recumbent statue of Robert E. Lee in Lexington, Virginia, his favorite piece of sculpture. The statue is that of a fully dressed male figure, which may, or may not, be significant. Years later, when he and a party rode from the Italian mainland to Venice in a motor boat belonging to the King of Italy, the fact that there was little æstheticism in his soul became grievously evident. "As we cut through the burnished water," one member of the group wrote afterward, "we could see the domes of Venice looming against a sunset-reddened sky. The only person who did not strain his eyes on this spectacle was Bishop Cannon. He devoted the trip to reading the London *Times*."

Newspapers and magazines seem always to have been the type of reading matter that attracted him most. He was never considered a widely read man, except in that limited sphere. His writings indicate that he was thoroughly conversant with the contents of the Bible, with the history of Methodism, with the entire prohibition movement, especially in Virginia, and with every detail of certain controversies in which he was engaged, but they do not evidence any appreciable familiarity with the world of literature or art. His interest in the latter appears often to have been conditioned by whether a given canvas or bronze was "lewd" or not. As for music, there is nothing to indicate that his concern for it extended beyond the covers of the Methodist hymnal.

It is perhaps natural, in view of Cannon's strenuous life and manifold other activities, that he failed to develop any important æsthetic interests or to familiarize himself with the *chef d'œuvres* of the cultural world. Although he successfully established a school for girls and saw it raised to the level of a college, his duties at Blackstone were so largely administrative that even in his capacity as an educator he remained a man of limited intellectual horizons. If he had cared to expend the same horsepower in making the acquaintance of great writers, poets, painters, musicians, and philosophers that he expended in securing the enactment of prohibition in Virginia and the nation, editing the *Advocate*, establishing and administering the school at Blackstone, and carrying out the various other projects entrusted to him by one agency or another, he could undoubtedly have remedied the very substantial inadequacies in his cultural background. As it was, although he traveled widely, his outlook remained essentially narrow.

One of the numerous phenomena that excited his concern in the early years of the century was the display of the female form on billboards and in other public places. Most of the costumes in which the ladies exhibited themselves in that unctuously righteous era would today be regarded as of wholly excessive amplitude. But Cannon, together with Comstock and others of like kidney, professed great alarm over this state of things, and Cannon wrote in 1905:

> Who dare assert that modesty, decency and virtue are in any way advanced by the pictures which we see all over our land, on billboards, in store windows, on calendars, and advertising cards? The object of these pictures is to appeal to the passions and appetites of the beholders. . . . And these persons who are advertised by these immodest and suggestive pictures, what do they do? They sell their modesty for 25, 50, or 100 cents a look. . . . All such shows are purely physical, are an appeal to the animal nature, are an open door to the house of ill fame, and the young women who consent to exhibit themselves at so much per look become only too often the companions in sin of the young men who have paid to behold the exhibition of their bodies. . . . Let fathers who value the purity and virtue of their daughters cease to issue calendars and advertising cards which are sought

91

after and admired simply because of their immodest exposure of the female person.

Early in the following year, the Cannonian withers were wrung by the thought that Sarah Bernhardt was to present *Camille* in the Ryman Auditorium in Nashville, where a few days before he had attended a student volunteer conference. It made him "shiver," he declared, to think of that auditorium being used for such a purpose. "On Sunday night a host of 5,000 of the best and brightest of our whole nation, packed on the floor and in the galleries," he wrote. "On Thursday night the platform occupied by a French actress, of brilliant powers but unsavory moral ideals, presenting to the public at high rate the life of a fallen, debauched character — Camille! And yet I learned that there were Methodist stewards on the board of trustees!"

It was during this same period that the San Francisco earthquake set many ministers and others to wondering what the explanation for this visitation could be. Cannon was puzzled by the disaster, for while he conceded that San Francisco was "probably one of the most wicked cities in the United States," he could not deny that "many good persons suffered" in the city's destruction. He concluded, therefore, that it would be incorrect to say that "the object of the . . . earthquake was to punish men for their wickedness." Subsequently he enunciated virtually the same thesis concerning the Messina earthquake.

Football, as played in the early 1900's, came in for some lusty bludgeoning from Cannon, who pronounced it "neither manly nor Christian." He was equally pessimistic over the moral status of the professional baseball player and denounced him as "a godless man." Furthermore, after listening to the language of a team of these popular idols on board a train, Cannon wondered how such men could be regarded as "semi-heroes" by "strong, good men and pure, good women." As for prizefighters, he found it incomprehensible that "decent, law-abiding Christian people" were willing to pay money to watch their debasing exhibitions.

Cannon frequently expressed himself strongly concerning Sabbath observance, and during his incumbency as president of the Blackstone Institute the rules there touching upon such observance were unusually stringent. About the year 1900, for example, he took half a dozen girls to a religious conference at Randolph-Macon Woman's College. On Sunday it was raining, and although the faculty and students of the college as well as the other delegates to the conference went to a Lynchburg church on the street car, Cannon declined to use such means of locomotion on the Sabbath, and he and his girls ostentatiously trudged the two miles through the mud and rain. A few years later he stated that he "made it a rule to make no plan or engagement that involves using a train after breakfast Sunday morning, or until after the ordinary hours for service Sunday night." This rule was later abandoned when Cannon's multitudinous duties and interests caused him to travel 150,000 miles annually throughout nearly the whole world. It is interesting to note that during the period when Cannon declined to use street cars on Sunday or to patronize trains except at certain hours, he apparently found it compatible with his religious scruples to drive his horse furiously at any time of the day or night. He evidently felt that, whereas street-car motormen and railway trainmen were entitled to rest on the Sabbath, horses were not.

Cannon was among the moral leaders who remonstrated violently in 1907 when President Roosevelt issued an order directing that the motto "In God We Trust" be omitted from the new ten-dollar gold pieces. Roosevelt expressed the opinion that the use of such a motto on coins "does positive harm, and is in effect irreverence." At the Virginia Conference of 1907 Cannon offered a resolution expressing "great regret" at the President's action, which resolution was unanimously adopted. There was such a wave of protest from the churches of the country that Congress voted overwhelmingly in 1908 to restore the motto.

In 1911, when Madame Curie, the co-discoverer of radium, was venomously attacked by enemies who sought to blacken her character, by means of what now appears to have been pure calumny, Cannon accepted these allegations at their face value. He stated that the celebrated scientist had been disclosed as the "affinity" of a French professor who already had a wife, and that "affinity in Bible language is an adulteress." "She has lost forever her claim to a place among the great men and women of the world," Cannon wrote. "She belongs from now on in the class with Byron and George Eliot and George Sand."

Doubts troubled Cannon over the question whether "a godless singer" has any place in a church service, for he felt that "the value of many a good sermon is greatly damaged, if not destroyed entirely, by an ungodly choir." "Leaders of the music" should be obtained, as far as possible, he said, "from among the Christian members of the home church," and "a genuine Christian man" should lead the singing.

For many years Cannon was savage in his denunciation of dancing. At the Virginia Conference of 1911 he introduced a resolution declaring that "dancing is contrary to the spirit of our Discipline and of the New Testament, and is opposed to the traditions and the teachings of our church." The resolution was adopted by an overwhelming majority. Some six months later, following a visit to Weaverville College, North Carolina, he wrote that he "rejoiced" over the fact that the students "were having their opportunity for training under genuine and positive Christian influences, with no taint of dancing or plays." In 1913 he expressed himself as grievously shocked over the dancing he saw at a "fashionable hotel." The tango and turkey trot impressed him as "shamefully and shamelessly suggestive" — indeed, he pronounced all round dancing "a temptation to the flesh," since "it brings the bodies of men and women in unusual relations to each other." He went on to say: "There may be some persons who can engage in it without any known excitation of the sexual appetites, but there is no question that it is responsible for the downfall of many souls."

Some years later, as further evidence of the dire consequences of dancing, Cannon related an experience in El Paso, where he preached in the church of Dr. Percy Knickerbocker. The latter, Cannon said, announced as his subject for the night sermon: "Hugging, Kissing and Dancing — Three Shotgun Marriages Performed in the Last Three Months." Knickerbocker told the congregation that the three marriages in question "were performed at the demand of the fathers and brothers of girls who had been frequenting the community Dancing House" and that the girls "admitted that the dance was responsible for their downfall."

Cannonian Comstockery

Not only dancing, but the use of tobacco in any form was regarded by Cannon as un-Methodistic. He was in agreement with resolutions on the subject passed at the Holston conference in 1905 and the General Conference in 1906. The former gathering urged the younger members to abstain altogether from smoking. Apropos of this action, Cannon wrote, following adjournment:

The second unusual feature was the discussion of the use and the effects of tobacco, coca-cola, morphine, cocaine, opium, and kindred drugs. . . . None of them are as dangerous to the abstainers of the community as the drink habit, but all of them are claiming their victims by the thousands. . . . The part of the report which seems to have provoked the warmest debate was the discussion of tobacco. Brother Stuart . . . stated that on one occasion a Bishop and his cabinet, which met in regular session in a room of a private house, smoked and chewed so excessively that they left the room in such bad condition that the lady's servants were not willing to clean it up.

In view of the fact that the church harbored such Gargantuan smokers and chewers among its elect, one finds it rather surprising that the General Conference of 1906 adopted resolutions approving the legislative prohibition of the sale of cigarettes and advising all young ministers against the use of tobacco in any form. Cannon stated that only moderate opposition was manifested to either of these officially expressed attitudes. Eight years later, at the General Conference of 1914, the church passed a rule, still in effect, that every applicant for the ministry must promise to abstain from the use of tobacco.

All of which leads one to ruminate upon some curious contradictions and inconsistencies. Cannon himself did not use tobacco, so he was never in the anomalous position of some of his ministerial colleagues who recommended abstinence to young clerics while indulging their own craving. But Cannon's Blackstone Institute was situated in the center of the tobacco belt, and many pillars of that institution and of Virginia Methodism were growers of and dealers in tobacco — a "drug," according to Cannon, comparable to morphine, cocaine, and opium, and claiming "its victims by the thousands." Another item worthy of record is that, at the very time when Cannon was excoriating the secular press for publishing whisky advertising, his own *Advocate* carried a fertilizer advertisement [1] telling how to increase the yield of this "drug," tobacco.

As for the requirement that every applicant for the Southern Methodist pastorate promise to abstain from the use of tobacco, there have been occasional hints that this promise is not always honored. For example, there was the warning issued in 1925 by Bishop W. N. Ainsworth to the North Georgia Conference, meeting in Macon. The Bishop spoke sternly of ministers who "smoke on the sly," saying that they violate their "solemn pact with God" and that they ought to be "arraigned for court trial." At the General Conference of 1938 in Birmingham, the matter came on the floor when S. O. Kimbrough of the North Alabama Conference sought an amendment to the Discipline which would have merely "urged" abstinence from tobacco upon ministerial neophytes, instead of compelling them to promise it. Kimbrough declared that "in various sections of our church they are saying plainly that this demand [that ministers take a pledge to abstain] is making liars out of our preachers." His amendment was defeated by the General Conference.

But bizarre as such phenomena are, this comedy of contradictions probably reached its apogee in the endowments of two of the leading educational institutions of the Southern Methodist Church. We have noted the denunciation leveled at Coca-Cola and tobacco by Cannon and his colleagues in official church resolutions. Coca-Cola, it will be recalled, was termed "the coming enemy to our young men," and tobacco was adjudged by the church as a whole to be of such a nature that no clergyman ordained since 1914 can use it in any form without destroying his fitness for the ministry. Yet the two largest benefactors of the Southern Methodist Church in its history have been Asa G. Candler, who made his millions in Coca-Cola, and James B. Duke, who made his mainly in tobacco. Candler gave $7,000,000 to Emory University; Duke gave some $40,000,000 to Duke University. We find no evidence that Cannon or any of his colleagues, whether clerical or lay, protested against the church's acceptance of this "tainted" money. Certainly if there was a protest of this character from any quarter, it was wholly ineffective.

Cannonian Comstockery

In addition to the amount set aside by James B. Duke for Duke University, a large share of the Duke tobacco fortune was used in establishing an endowment for superannuated Methodist pastors. In other words, the pastors are pledged not to use tobacco, but when they retire from active service their pensions are paid with income from that forbidden weed. Such are the ethical incongruities that occasionally engage our moral leaders and their parishioners.

CHAPTER *ix*

Clinching the Nails

BEFORE the Virginia legislature convened in January 1916, Cannon had recovered from his breakdown of the previous year and had laid plans for a legislative session, at which the lawmakers were to leap to do his bidding more unquestioningly than ever before.

Laying the groundwork for advances in the sphere of legislated morality, Cannon called for "practical idealism — Pauline Opportunism," and added: "We indeed must be in this stage of our history 'as wise as serpents and as harmless as doves.'" His invocation of what he called "Pauline Opportunism" was a frequent phenomenon of his drive to dry up Virginia.

When the General Assembly began its deliberations, it was faced with the duty of stating the precise conditions under which the prohibitionist mandate of 1914 should be carried into effect. The Enabling Act had set forth some of those conditions in unambiguous language. For example, Section 9 provided that under state-wide prohibition it would be legal for persons, firms, or corporations engaged in 1914 in the manufacture of beer or wine to manufacture such beer or wine for sale in states where such sale was lawful. Section 10 provided that under state-wide prohibition the manufacture and sale of 6 per cent cider would be permitted. It is entirely possible that, without these provisions, the Enabling Act would have been defeated by the legislature in 1914, for, as has already been set forth, there was a tie vote in the Senate, which was broken by the Lieutenant Governor. If a single one of the twenty senators who cast their ballots for the bill in 1914 had voted in the negative, it would not have passed. In addition, many persons supported state-wide prohibition in the subsequent referendum on the quite natural assumption that if it carried, beer and wine could still be manufactured for sale outside Virginia, and cider could be made and sold.

These provisions were put into the Enabling Act in 1914 with the consent and approval of Cannon and the Anti-Saloon League. Yet in 1915, after the victory for state-wide prohibition in the referendum, the league decided to repudiate these solemn stipulations. It announced that it would ask the General Assembly for a prohibition law containing no exemptions for wineries or breweries. It likewise declared that it would endeavor to eliminate cider.

When the assembly convened, Cannon sat enthroned as the supreme ruler of Capitol Hill. Armed with the dry majority of 30,000 returned by the voters fifteen months before, and implemented with the greatly augmented prestige that this victory brought him, he was regnant over the legislative destinies of more than 2,000,000 Virginians. He was at the very zenith of his power over the Virginia legislature. This was demonstrated early in the session. When the time came to appoint the committees, it was found that the appointments to a number of them had to be submitted to Cannon for approval. This was so completely unprecedented that Senators Aubrey E. Strode of Amherst and Walter E. Addison of Lynchburg, who had been prohibitionists and league supporters for many years, protested on the Senate floor.[1]

After the session had adjourned, the *Richmond News Leader* published a communication from Senator Strode,[2] in which he reiterated the charges made by himself and Senator Addison. Bishop Cannon admitted years later that these charges were well founded in so far as they pertained to committees handling "moral legislation." In a statement published [3] at the close of the Hoover-Smith presidential campaign of 1928, he declared unconvincingly, apropros of claims that he had been a "dictator" in Virginia a decade or more previously:

Dry Messiah

I was never conscious that I was a dictator. . . . I do not remember that I ever attempted to use my influence with the Legislature except on measures pertaining to education (I was cosponsor with Judge Mann of the first high school bill passed by the Legislature), prohibition, gambling, vice, Sabbath observance, moving pictures, and child labor. . . . I was never any dictator. . . . I did positively insist, as the representative of the prohibition people of the state, that committees of the General Assembly which would be called upon to pass upon matters pertaining to moral legislation should be so constituted that such legislation should not be killed by hostile amendments or by fatal delays in reporting out from committee the various bills. Both branches of the General Assembly understood my reasons for insisting upon such committee assignments. I do not think any man can indicate any interference on my part. [*Sic!*]

Throughout much of the session of 1916 Cannon occupied a seat on the Senate floor in a chair placed adjacent to the desk of Senator G. Walter Mapp of Accomac, Anti-Saloon League spokesman. Other league workers, including the Rev. J. Sidney Peters and the Rev. Howard M. Hoge, also were on the floor at times while the debate on the prohibition bill, known as the Mapp bill, was in progress. Seated next to Senator Mapp, Cannon was able to confer with him at any time concerning legislation and thus to exercise an even greater influence than if he had sat with the other press representatives. The *Times-Dispatch* for February 25 records the following incident, which is illustrative of the close relations between the Senator and the league superintendent: "Senator Mapp rose and read a letter written him during the day by Rev. James Cannon, Jr. . . . in which hope was expressed that the amendment [to the Mapp bill] would be defeated. Dr. Cannon sat just behind Senator Mapp as he read." The same newspaper also said on March 4, relative to the debate on the bill in the House of Delegates:

Superintendent James Cannon, Jr., of the Anti-Saloon League of Virginia, occupied a seat with the legislators, sitting in the place assigned by the House to Speaker Houston in his capacity as delegate from Hampton. As Speaker of the House, he occupies the big chair on the platform, and his floor seat remains vacant throughout the session. In this seat, in the extreme southeast corner of the House, Dr. Cannon industrially [*sic*] took notes on the proceedings, sitting faithfully through the morning and afternoon sessions.

When the fire on the change-of-venue section grew heavy, and Delegate Swift, of Fredericksburg, who was replying to the attacks, became sorely pressed under the stress, Dr. Cannon prompted him several times on the provisions of the bill touching the matter under discussion.

This was a clear violation of the rules of the House, as Cannon had no right to prompt Swift. Nothing, however, seems to have been done about it.

Owing to Cannon's tremendous power over the lawmakers at this session, it was a foregone conclusion that whatever bills he advocated would be passed substantially as introduced. There was no appreciable opposition in either house. A few audacious spirits, such as Senators Strode and Addison, and Senator C. O'Conor Goolrick of Fredericksburg, protested against the action of the league superintendent in dictating committee appointments, but they were almost alone. The House was even more abject in its surrender to the league. Colonel R. F. Leedy, of Page County, was the only member of that branch who managed to make a sustained and vigorous protest against the Mapp bill. Yet despite the fact that Cannon's ascendancy was almost unchallenged, he demonstrated his political acumen by refusing to admit publicly the authoritarian character of his hegemony, lest perchance he foment rebellion. His policy seemed to be to use the knout on the assemblymen with one hand, but to pat them on the back with the other.

As the session drew to a close, it became more and more evident that Cannon would get what he wanted in the way of "moral legislation." When the prohibition bill came to a vote in the Senate, it was passed, 35 to 3. It was then taken over to the House, where Colonel Leedy launched a furious attack against the Anti-Saloon League and the bill, mainly on the ground that it obviously did not carry out the terms agreed upon two years before.

The following day Leedy averred that he had a good many

other things to say, and the House granted him an hour. He then began a terrific and at times hysterical denunciation of Cannon and the league. In accordance with his unvarying methodology when attacked in public, Cannon sat with unchanging expression throughout the entire harangue. After discussing the bill further, describing it as "conceived in sin and born in iniquity," and pronouncing it the product of "a combination, the crookedest and most unholy since the ministerial garb had been injected into politics," the colonel noted in conclusion that he had used only fifty of his allotted sixty minutes. "But," he said, "if I had spoken four hours, you wouldn't understand me in six months." Whereupon he sat down, amid applause.

The net effect of the colonel's speech may be divined from the fact that the House voted on the prohibition bill almost as soon as he concluded, and the count in its favor was 88 to 5. While the measure was ostensibly designed to bring "state-wide prohibition" to Virginia, it permitted every householder to obtain from outside the state one quart of liquor, three gallons of beer, or one gallon of wine per month. This aspect of the legislation does not seem to have engaged the attention of Colonel Leedy, although he could readily have argued that the Enabling Act of 1914 said nothing about allowing every householder a given quantity of whisky, beer, or wine per month, and that those who voted dry in the referendum of that year voted "for Statewide Prohibition." Cannon said, however, that he did not believe the majority of those who voted thus intended to prohibit absolutely the purchase of intoxicants for personal use. He added that, even with the monthly quotas of alcohol allotted to each Virginia householder under the law, it was the most drastic legislation passed up to that time by any state, with the possible exception of West Virginia. He said, further, that the United States Supreme Court had not then passed upon the right of a state to prohibit the shipment of intoxicants from outside its boundaries for the personal use of its citizens.

When it developed that the Maryland distillers would be the chief beneficiaries of the quart-a-month provision of the Mapp Law, there were hints in the wet newspapers that these liquor interests had contributed substantial sums to the Anti-Saloon

Clinching the Nails

League's 1914 pre-referendum war chest. The sum of eighty thousand dollars was mentioned in these vague allegations. No proof was ever adduced that the Marylanders had offered any money to the league, or that the league would have accepted such an offer if made. The matter was guardedly dealt with in a lachrymose ballad with crocodilian overtones by James Taylor Robertson, which appeared in the *Richmond Evening Journal.* Its concluding stanza follows:

> This is Virginia counting the cost,
> Broken faith and double-crossed.
> These are the people, sold and bought,
> Who voted "dry" and get "one quart";
> And here are the drunkards by the score,
> Drunk on that quart from Baltimore;
> Soused by the Baltimore liquor men
> Who stand in a row and say "Amen"
> Whenever they think of that sacred quart
> Which Dr. Cannon thinks each man ought
> To drink each month, although there's naught
> Of it in the great Enabling Act
> By which the temperance people backed
> Up Dr. Cannon, James, D.D.,
> By whose divine and high decree
> Old Booze will still collect his tolls,
> And we can pickle our hides and souls
> In the name of the Anti-Saloon League!

Cannon's decision not to forbid the purchase of all intoxicants for personal use was a characteristic one. He was always cautious lest he get ahead of public sentiment. While he himself would have rejoiced to have forbidden shipment into Virginia of all varieties of alcoholic beverages, he felt that such a step would be inadvisable under the circumstances. Not only was he careful not to proceed with undue haste, but it is the testimony of those who were associated with him in the prohibition fight that he was unusually willing to listen to advice. When he went into a conference over matters relating to prohibition, he generally did so with an open mind as to the best method of attaining the desired end, according to one man who worked with him. "I never saw a strong, brainy man who was as ready to listen to suggestions from others," is the testimony of another associate. Even some of his antagonists in the Virginia campaigns are ready to testify that their relations with him were quite pleasant and that, while he would not compromise on the principal point at issue, he nevertheless was willing to hear their arguments and sometimes to make concessions. Others say, on the contrary, that while this was true of him in the early stages, it was far from true toward the end, and that success made him arrogant and egotistical.

In addition to securing the passage of the Mapp Act, Cannon was instrumental in having the legislature create a standing Committee on Moral Welfare to take charge of all bills that were decreed to impinge upon the field of morality. While the creation of this committee was under consideration, George McD. Blake, of Richmond, stated in an address that he felt such an agency would be superfluous, particularly in so far as Richmond was concerned. Cannon retorted that he would like to cite two recent episodes as evidencing the need for a Committee on Moral Welfare. It appeared that a Methodist steward and Sunday-school superintendent had been asked by a couple of thirsty young ladies in a Richmond restaurant if they might sit with him, so that they might order cocktails, the rule being that unescorted ladies could not be served alcoholic drinks. The shocked white-ribboner replied that he certainly would not accommodate them. In the other case referred to by the Bishop, a young lady "who had walked from the Union Depot to the postoffice . . . had been accosted and insulted by four men." These two occurrences were deemed by Dr. Cannon to be ample evidence that the Committee on Moral Welfare was essential to Richmond.

At this same legislative session of 1916 a judge was elected to the Virginia Supreme Court of Appeals to fill the vacancy created by the retirement of Judge James Keith. Three men were brought forward for the post: Dean William Minor Lile of the University of Virginia Law School, and Judge Frederick W. Sims of Louisa, neither of whom was a prohibitionist, and Judge Edward S. Turner of Warrenton, an upstanding dry. It was naturally assumed, in view of their respective attitudes on the liquor question, that, if Cannon took any part in the contest, he would support Turner, for he admitted that Turner was the only one of the three who was dry. But Senator Martin was behind Sims, and Cannon joined with the boss of the machine to put Sims across by a small margin. Dean Lile was backed by the bar of the entire state by a majority of approximately 9 to 1, but the Martin-Cannon combination was too formidable. After the caucus had been held, a letter that Cannon had written to members of the legislature urging the election of Sims fell into the hands of the *Richmond News Leader,* which published it on page one under the sardonic caption: "Pauline Opportunism."

One of the legislative session's last acts was the selection of a Commissioner of Prohibition, who would be charged with the duty of enforcing the Mapp Act. Long before the assembly had met, the hostile newspapers had published reports that the job would go to the Rev. J. Sidney Peters. They proved to be correct.

With the adjournment of the General Assembly, the temperance forces began preparations ushering in the one-quart era. October 31, 1916 was the date when the Mapp Act was to take effect. When it arrived, elaborate arrangements had been made for celebrating the outlawry of the liquor traffic. Church services were held throughout the commonwealth and there was great jubilation. The *Richmond Virginian* evoked the mood which prevailed among the more fervent drys with the following page-one exordium:

> To the chorus of church chimes ringing, and of factory whistles screaming in loud accord, Virginia freed her domains from the shackles of the saloon with a mighty stroke last night. For the first time since her glorious history was opened to the world, the Mother of States looks across her fertile lands and through her prosperous cities today to see a landscape freed at last from the pestilence of rum. . . .

It was noteworthy that there was a minimum of brawling in the state on the last day before the putative drought descended upon the land. From Norfolk, for instance, there came a dispatch saying that "a few old-timers have been seen on the streets with marked signs of their long battle with John, but no disorders." Unlike the *Virginian,* the *Times-Dispatch* for November 1 managed to retain its sense of humor despite the awful solemnity of the hour. Its account of the heroic measures to which Richmonders resorted on the preceding day is worth quoting:

> All day long express wagons, drays, moving vans and other emergency carriers delivered liquor and wine consignments to addresses in every section of the city. In the rush to tuck the beverages safely away before the new law became effective, many dispatched their purchases by messenger, or took them home themselves, braving the wink and leer of the passers-by, with martyrlike fortitude.
>
> A quart bottle is hard to disguise. It is still harder to conceal the identity of a gallon jug. In an endless procession, in which half of the male constituent was equipped with a package of irregular outline . . . self-consciousness was at a discount. The crowd looked with envy upon the man who pulled a small barroom behind him in a toy express wagon, and stopped to offer congratulations to a rural visitor who stood watch over two healthy-looking jugs at Fifth and Broad Streets until his son came with a mule cart, and took owner and wet goods away.

The *Times-Dispatch* estimated the amount spent in Richmond in storing up supplies of drinkables at from one million to two million dollars. It explained the lack of drunkenness on the preceding night by saying that "those who were laying in a stock had no intention of getting unsteady on their feet, as they wanted to get their precious supply home intact."

Bonfort's Wine and Spirit Circular stated that a liquor dealer shot and killed himself at Ocean View, Virginia, on October 29. About two months later the same publication said:

> Over in Virginia, where the liquor shipments are recorded, considerable excitement has been created by the report that certain ministers are looking into these records with a view to disciplining their members, in case they are purchasing whiskey.

But there seems to have been at least one parson who approached the problem from a slightly different direction, for late in 1917 *Bonfort's* published the following:

> The *Leader,* of Richmond, Va., tells of a preacher by the name of Jacob Jones who has been in the habit of making trips to Wash-

ington every day, except Sunday, and returning with a satchel, which, on examination, was found to be filled with whiskey and gin.

There were not many such enterprising clerics, however, and bootlegging was by no means so prevalent as it later became. The Mapp Act seems to have been satisfactory to the great majority of Virginians, numbers of whom declare today that under it temperance was much more readily discernible than under the Eighteenth Amendment. Even Richmond's three anti-prohibitionist newspapers — the *Times-Dispatch,* the *News Leader,* and the *Evening Journal* — capitulated at the end of a one-year trial of the Mapp quart-a-month law and pronounced it an unqualified success.

Prohibition was by no means a dead issue, however — a fact that immediately became apparent in the gubernatorial primary of 1917. There were three candidates for the Democratic nomination, nomination being equivalent to election. They were Westmoreland Davis of Leesburg, whose attitude was viewed with much skepticism by the Anti-Saloon League; and John Garland Pollard of Richmond, Attorney General of Virginia, and J. Taylor Ellyson of Richmond, Lieutenant Governor, both of whom had prohibitionist records. As the campaign progressed, the opinion was voiced in many quarters that Cannon was preparing to throw the support of the Anti-Saloon League and the *Virginian* to Ellyson, who was backed by Senator Martin. This opinion was strengthened by the fact that Cannon and Pollard were known to be personally antagonistic toward each other.

The primary was set for August 7, but as late as July 19 the *Virginian* had taken no stand for either of the dry candidates. On July 14 it had printed the statement of the headquarters committee of the Anti-Saloon League, of which Cannon was chairman, in which the committee described the public records of Pollard and Ellyson and their replies to league questions as "satisfactory," and those of Davis as "very unsatisfactory." This despite the oft repeated declaration of the league and of Cannon himself that the league's established and unvarying policy was never to "select, nominate, or oppose candidates for political office," but only to give the public the records of such candidates and let the public decide for itself.

On July 19 the *Virginian* gave its first open intimation that it was planning to throw its support to Pollard or Ellyson, when it declared editorially that the drys ought to concentrate on one of these two men or Davis might be elected. Two days later the paper published a letter written to Pollard on July 7 by the Rev. David Hepburn, assistant superintendent of the Anti-Saloon League, in which Hepburn stated that he was transferring his support from Pollard to Ellyson because of criticisms that he claimed Pollard had made of the *Virginian* and those in charge of it. On July 26 the *Virginian* announced that it would support Ellyson, since it had just completed a survey of the state and had concluded that Ellyson was stronger than Pollard.

The *Virginian* threw all its strength behind Ellyson. Publication in its columns of Hepburn's letter withdrawing his support from Pollard on the alleged ground that Pollard had criticized the paper and certain temperance leaders brought from State Senator E. C. Mathews of Norfolk a signed statement that he was present when Pollard was supposed to have uttered these criticisms, and that Pollard had made no attack on temperance leaders, but had simply complained that the *Virginian* had not done his campaign justice in its news columns. The *Virginian* refused to publish the Mathews statement.

On July 27 the *Virginian* published a letter written it under date of July 25, the day before it announced its support of Ellyson, by the Rev. Dr. Graham H. Lambeth, formerly associate editor of the *Advocate* with Cannon, and a leading dry. This communication said, in part:

> For some time I have discerned from the trend of affairs that the Anti-Saloon League and the *Virginian* were preparing to throw their support to Mr. Ellyson. May I state that in my judgment, in this course, the Anti-Saloon League, so far as its executive officers are concerned, are entirely consistent with a long-fixed habit of partiality toward the [Democratic political] "organization," but wholly inconsistent with the emphatic assertion that the league is not in politics. . . .

Clinching the Nails

Published alongside these charges was a stupendous statement, some ten newspaper columns in length, from Cannon. He had composed the entire broadside within a period of twenty-four hours. He pointed out that Pollard had stated that those who controlled the *Virginian* had been "actively campaigning" for Ellyson for months, "using their official positions with the Anti-Saloon League to advance his candidacy, in direct violation of the declared principles of the league." Replying to these charges, Cannon said:

> If in that statement any reference is made to me, I brand it as false. . . . I have not put forth "efforts" to change the vote of a single officer of the Anti-Saloon League. . . . If the Anti-Saloon League of Virginia has been able to perform any service of value to the people of the state, that service has been performed without any active public assistance from Mr. Pollard, except a few modest cash contributions and the speeches he made in the spectacular statewide campaign; indeed, it has performed that service in the face of Mr. Pollard's sarcastic and biting criticisms, and his reflections upon the independence and motives of some of the leaders of the league, including myself.

Cannon then gave other reasons for preferring Ellyson to Pollard, among them that Ellyson had been "an active and efficient" Baptist for nearly fifty years, and that his position with regard to the dry law had been sound. He failed to mention that Pollard was just as "active and efficient" a Baptist as Ellyson, and that he was a lifelong teetotaler, whereas Ellyson was personally "wet."

Such, in brief, was the substance of Cannon's ten-column blast. Three days later he challenged Pollard to produce proof that "for months" he had been campaigning for Ellyson in his official position as superintendent of the Anti-Saloon League. Pollard repeated the charge, but said he did not desire to enter into a controversy with Cannon and advanced no proof.

The next major development was the publication in the *Virginian* on August 2 of a letter from J. W. Hough, of Norfolk, former president of the Anti-Saloon League, to Pollard, withdrawing his support from him. This communication, dated August 1, said:

Dr. Cannon has been slandered by you in the same manner which the wet newspapers and the underworld have been slandering him for the past fifteen years. His character stands pure, unimpeached, and his accomplishments have done more to purify the politics in Virginia than all other organizations combined, and when he succeeds in putting [*sic*] the United States dry, every worthy son of the country should take off their [*sic*] hats to him.

Hough further declared that at a dinner arranged by him for Pollard at Norfolk on April 8, 1916, at which Pollard's gubernatorial candidacy was discussed, Pollard had "proceeded to very unjustly abuse Dr. Cannon and the Anti-Saloon League officials." Hough then quoted from a letter he had written to Pollard about two weeks later, in which he advised him not to attack Cannon in his campaign and told him that if such an attack was made, he would not take any part in the contest, since he "just could not stand by and see Dr. Cannon abused."

Upon the publication of Hough's letter, Pollard immediately communicated with thirteen of those who had attended the dinner referred to, and all of them signed a statement that "Mr. Hough is mistaken in saying that Mr. Pollard abused Dr. Cannon or any of the Anti-Saloon League officials." A number of them said further that Pollard was ill and that he had had practically nothing to say on any subject at the dinner. This denial was not published in the *Virginian*, although the paper carried on August 5 a rejoinder from Hough, in which he referred to the denial and reiterated his previous charge that Pollard had abused Cannon. Thus the columns of the *Virginian* were closed to statements from Pollard or his headquarters. On July 30 the paper had printed the following letter addressed to those headquarters:

We return copy submitted for an advertisement in behalf of the candidacy of Mr. John Garland Pollard for Governor. In view of Mr. Pollard's slanderous attack upon Rev. Dr. James Cannon, Jr., a Christian minister, who has been the best friend the *Virginian* ever had, we do not care to carry further advertisements in behalf of his candidacy.

Hence the paper would not publish, even as a paid advertisement, Senator Mathews's denial of Hepburn's charges, or the denial by thirteen men who attended the Norfolk dinner of Hough's charge that Pollard had abused Cannon on that occasion. Arbitrarily shut out of the *Virginian* and, for that reason, unable to reach thousands of leading prohibitionists with his statements, Pollard lost a large share of his dry support in the closing days of the campaign.

The tactics employed by the paper evoked fervent demurrers from staunch prohibitionists, as is shown from a letter sent to the *Virginian* under date of August 2 by the Rev. John Moncure, pastor of Williamsburg Baptist Church. This communication was not published by the *Virginian*, although it was addressed to that paper. A copy appeared in the *Evening Journal*, however. Moncure said, in part:

> It is not that you [the *Virginian*] are supporting Mr. Ellyson that I resent, but that you are supporting anyone at all, and that you are doing it in a way that out-Herods the most scandalous methods of the booze crowd.

At the same time, the Norfolk Anti-Saloon League, with only one dissenting vote, adopted a resolution protesting against the action of the *Virginian*, "the official organ of the temperance people of the state," in endorsing "one dry candidate as against another." No reference to the passage of the resolution was made in the columns of the *Virginian*, the "Fair, Clean and Accurate" daily.

Finally the rancorous campaign came to an end on August 7. Candidate Davis had devoted a good share of his attention to a dissection of what he termed "clerical kaiserism" and had thereby attracted the anti-prohibitionists to his banner. The dry vote was split between Ellyson and Pollard, with the result that Davis was elected. He polled 39,318 votes to 27,811 for Ellyson and 22,436 for Pollard. The number of drys who switched from Pollard to Ellyson in the closing days, as a result of the methods used by Cannon, the *Virginian*, and the Anti-Saloon League, is indicated by the fact that Pollard claimed to have gathered more than 34,500 written committals in the months preceding the primary, whereas his total vote was less than 22,500.

While Cannon had attempted an exceedingly difficult piece of

political prestidigitation in his effort to throw the dry vote solidly
to Ellyson, and while his failure to do so is readily comprehen-
sible, there is reason to believe that he was staggered by the
outcome. Apparently he thought he controlled a sufficient percentage of the prohibitionists of the state to swing the primary in
any direction he desired, but the result showed the measure of
his miscalculation. It was the first serious political setback he had
received in many years.

The nomination of Davis was greeted with alcoholic ardor in
the publications of the liquor trade, which described it as a great
triumph for "liberalism." Consider the following from *Bonfort's
Wine and Spirit Circular* for September 15, 1917:

> There are signs of revolt against the preacher politician. Vir-
> ginia has by nominating Westmoreland Davis for Governor,
> placed its stamp of disapproval upon the Rev. James Cannon, the
> acknowledged leader of the church political machine in that state.
> Mr. Davis's majority was so substantial that Rev. Cannon's influ-
> ence on Virginia politics will be nil. . . .

These fantastic fabrications were only too typical of the sort of
thing that graced the pages of the whisky gazettes at the period.
Bonfort's failed to mention that Cannon was beaten in a three-
cornered race, and that the two dry candidates' combined vote
was nearly eleven thousand greater than that of the one wet
candidate. Actually the Davis victory was about the only phenomenon on the horizon at that time which could, by any stretch
of the imagination, be construed as a favorable omen by the
liquor boys. As the editor of *Bonfort's* doubtless knew, national
prohibition was on the way.

When the Virginia legislature convened in January 1918, it was
importuned by Cannon to ratify the Eighteenth Amendment first
among the states of the Union. The complaisant members almost
fell over one another in an effort to comply, but Mississippi foiled
their plans. It voted for ratification on January 8, whereas the
Old Dominion did not do so until January 11. The Virginia Senate
approved the amendment by 30 to 8, the House by 84 to 13.

At the same session Cannon sponsored a motion-picture censor-
ship bill. It might have passed if he had not sailed for Europe

before adjournment. This was the first time since he had become personally active in the promotion of reform legislation, some sixteen or seventeen years before, that he had been unable to remain until the end of a session of the assembly.

On his return from Europe about a hundred of his admirers from all parts of Virginia tendered him a dinner in Richmond, at which he was presented with a sterling-silver pitcher and goblets in token of their appreciation of his work as a moral mentor. The inscription spoke of him as

FEARLESS FOE OF EVIL
ABLE ADVOCATE OF RIGHTEOUSNESS.

A man who attended the dinner said afterward that it was one of the two occasions on which he had seen Cannon "trammeled and embarrassed under a great effort to control his feelings." The other occasion when this almost completely unemotional individual succumbed, at least partially, to his emotions was when he participated in a farewell service at Blackstone a few months later, immediately prior to his departure for Texas to take over his episcopal duties.

He had been elected a Bishop in May 1918. This made it necessary for him to resign as superintendent of the Anti-Saloon League of Virginia, and likewise greatly to diminish his participation in Old Dominion politics.

That explains, at least in some measure, why the Virginia Assembly of 1920 exhibited such independence in its disposition of matters having to do with prohibition. There had been complaints from various directions about the methods used by State Prohibition Commissioner Sidney Peters, and the legislature of 1920 ordered an investigation. At the same time strong opposition to Peters's re-election developed, and Harry B. Smith, of Culpeper, announced his candidacy for the post. On the day before the caucus Bishop Cannon suddenly appeared in Richmond, obviously for the purpose of attempting to stem the tide of anti-Peters sentiment. But when the caucus met, it was plain that the incumbent would have heavy going. Senator Mapp, who nominated Peters, charged that his opponents were marshaled "under the black flag of law defiance." Delegate Edwin H. Gibson, of

Culpeper, who nominated Smith, paid his respects to the clerical lobby, saying that if the caucus re-elected Peters, it would "have the old brothers — the political parsons — back here buttonholing and communing" with the members. He also referred to Cannon's presence on the scene, saying that the Bishop had come "to take Peters home, in the event of his defeat, and give him a job." When the vote was taken, Smith was found to have won, 50 to 48. There were loud hosannas from the wets over the downfall of the Cannon candidate. In 1920, however, the wets were thankful for small things. The Eighteenth Amendment had already become effective and, except that the ousting of Peters necessarily brought chagrin to Bishop Cannon, there was little consolation for them in the election of Smith, who was bone dry, personally and politically. Some slight encouragement was warranted by the fact that the appropriation for enforcement was reduced.

It was not a coincidence that the Anti-Saloon League of Virginia found itself unable to dictate to the legislature as soon as James Cannon, Jr., relinquished the superintendency. The election of Westmoreland Davis to the governorship encouraged the anti-prohibitionists to some extent, it is true, while it is also true that in certain quarters a reaction had set in against "clerical kaiserism." But the most compelling reason for the comparative impotence of the league at the session of 1920 is to be found in the fact that it no longer enjoyed the brilliant and indefatigable, if ruthless and slippery leadership that had carried it to victory so often in the past. Ulysses had gone to the Hesperides, and there was no one left in Ithaca who could draw his mighty bow.

CHAPTER X

Prohibition Comes to America

W HEN the "moral and religious forces" finally proclaimed that a Federal prohibition law was their real objective and acknowledged openly that they were trying to promote total abstinence throughout the United States by legislative fiat, the Rev. Dr. Cannon accented his desire for such an enactment by an augmented participation in the national movement.

In the years when this crusade was gathering momentum, Cannon was one of those who declared that the Anti-Saloon League was not "a political organization." He is known to have issued such a disavowal in 1909. Yet following the enactment of the Eighteenth Amendment, the league published an official circular in which it described itself, with something less than humility, as "the strongest political organization in the world."

Irrespective of whether one regards this bellicose agency as "political," it was wielding an increasingly persuasive influence at the period with state legislatures and the national Congress, to say nothing of the voters. Even the organs of "the trade" were becoming conscious of the danger inherent in the league's activities. In 1907, for example, *Bonfort's Wine and Spirit Circular* laid down the following dicta:

> The Anti-Saloon League . . . is not a mob of long-haired fanatics, as some of the writers and speakers connected with our business have declared, but it is a strongly centralized organization, officered by men of unusual ability, financiered by capitalists with very long purses, subscribed to by hundreds of thousands of men, women and children who are solicited by their various

churches, advised by well-paid attorneys of great ability, and it is working with definite ideas to guide it in every state, in every county, in every city, in every precinct. . . .

A few months later the *Wine and Spirit Gazette* sounded similar alarums:

> What are the business interests, impelled by this wave of prohibition, doing to turn back the destructive tide?
> Practically nothing.
> To meet in convention, have a good time, resolve, and go home.
> Run a literary bureau whose literature only reaches the already convinced.
> The wine producer resolves in his interest.
> The distiller resolves in his interest.
> The brewer is for the brewer; and the wholesaler wants the whole thing, and there you are.
> The common interest and the common cause is neglected, while the crisis is here, and destruction impends. . . .
> The anti-license policy is intelligent, concrete, consistent.
> The opposition has no policy, is disintegrated, chaotic.
> The gift of prophecy is not required to declare the result.
> Gentlemen of the trade, what are you going to do about it?

Even the United States Brewers' Association, whose membership was for years impervious to criticism and contemptuous of the Anti-Saloon League, awakened by 1908 to the fact that this mechanism for translating the will of the Methodist and Baptist churches into legislative enactments could no longer be ignored. At their Milwaukee convention in that year the brewers accordingly enunciated the slogan: "Let us clean house; down with the immoral saloon." Unfortunately, they seem to have promulgated this battle-cry with their fingers crossed, for nothing came of it.

The brewers published what they called *A Textbook of True Temperance,* in which they stressed their lofty purposes and marshaled all the pertinent data they could lay their hands on. There was the quotation attributed to Benjamin Franklin: "The only animals created to drink water are those who from their conformation are able to lap it on the surface of the earth; whereas all those who can convey their hands to their mouths were destined to enjoy the juice of the grape." There was the pronouncement of Congressman Boutell of Illinois to the United States Brewers' Association in 1910: "At the time of the nation's need, when three hundred and eighty millions of war revenues were collected, your industry paid over one-third of the total sum required. And I remember hearing it stated in the House of Representatives when the Spanish War Tax was under discussion, that your industry was the only industry that did not protest against the increased tax, but freely offered to aid in raising the amount." The *Textbook* also quoted T. C. Flanagan, "the famous athlete and founder of the Irish-Canadian Club," as saying that "nearly all trainers of note prescribe beer." He added that "every single American athletic record is held by men who follow this principle." Then came a long list of famous track and field athletes and prizefighters who were said to consider beer essential to the maintenance of their pre-eminence in the world of sport.

The *Textbook* contended, too, that the consumption of patent medicines had always been "abnormally larger in prohibition states, a fact which is easily explained by their content of alcohol." It then listed the results of analyses by "the Massachusetts State Board analyst," which gave the following percentages of alcohol by volume for various well-known patent medicines: Lydia Pinkham's Vegetable Compound, 20.6 per cent; Hostetter's Stomach Bitters, 44.3; Peruna, 28.5; Kaufman's Sulphur Bitters, which claimed to contain "no alcohol," 20.5 per cent of alcohol by volume and "no sulphur"; Parker's Tonic, described as "purely vegetable," 41.6 alcohol; and various other "tonics" and "bitters" with alcoholic percentages ranging from 13.5 to 42.6. It is understood that not a few consecrated prohibitionists, wholly unaware that certain of these nostrums contained so much as a single drop of alcohol, became confirmed addicts and found it impossible to forgo their regular drams of this or that "tonic." Meanwhile they proclaimed themselves teetotalers and inveighed loudly against the curse of drink.

When one examines the maps showing the great strides made annually by the Anti-Saloon League in driving out the barrooms, one can readily understand the fear that gripped the manufacturers, the wholesalers, and the retailers of ardent spirits during those years. Like a tidal wave the temperance hosts were sweeping the saloons out of the rural districts from coast to coast. As Cannon expressed it, "the walls of Jericho were falling down before the armies of the Lord."

Reference has been made to the intensity of Methodism's antipathy to the barroom. Many of this generation have perhaps forgotten the storm raised when Vice-President C. W. Fairbanks, prominent Methodist, gave a luncheon to President Theodore Roosevelt in 1907 at which cocktails were served. The affair took place at the Fairbanks home, and Fairbanks failed of election as a delegate from the Indiana Conference to the General Conference of the Northern Methodist Church because of it. The Rev. Dr. Joshua Stanfield, his pastor, subsequently issued an explanation in the *Northwestern Christian Advocate*. He declared that Fairbanks had always been a "total abstainer" and that he "was not personally responsible for, nor did he know of the 'cocktails' until he reached the table, and while some others present took two, he, true to his custom, took none." Cannon said in the *Baltimore and Richmond Christian Advocate* concerning this weighty matter that "it was an unpardonable insult to him [Fairbanks] that the liquor should have been served except by his order." He likewise pronounced it "a remarkable piece of meanness that whoever was responsible for the presence of the cocktails has not come forth and made affidavit to the fact, and cleared the vice-president of blame."

Although Cannon had previously expressed great admiration for President Roosevelt, the Fairbanks party and other episodes led him to alter his appraisal of the presidential character. Whereas in 1906 he had said that "no ruler of the present time has shown himself to be more earnest in his advocacy of great moral and religious subjects than has President Roosevelt," three years later he repudiated T. R. openly. This was chiefly because of the dampness of the celebration at which Roosevelt welcomed the fleet home following its trip around the world.

In addition to noting the enthusiasm with which the President and other officials inhausted cocktails on such occasions as this, Cannon's part in the drive for nation-wide prohibition included a careful jotting down of facts concerning enforcement of local liquor laws as he traveled about. Happening, for instance, to be in Boston at this period, he set out to test the fidelity with which the restaurants observed the eleven-o'clock closing law. Taking his seat at a café table at ten minutes to eleven, he began toying with the wine list.

"Boss," said the Negro waiter, "do you want somethin' to drink?"

"Why, suppose I do?" said the wily Dr. Cannon.

"Why, do you see that clock?" said the waiter. "Only ten minutes to git it in."

"What do you mean?" asked the doctor.

"Why, you can't git nuthin' to drink here after eleven o'clock," was the reply.

Cannon thereupon began stalling for time. As the minutes passed, the Negro became more and more impatient. Finally he said:

"If you don't tell me what you want, I can't git you nuthin'."

Whereupon his customer looked at him gravely and said: "Very well, bring me a glass of Apollinaris Water."

"Ho!" replied the disgusted blackamoor. "You can git dat all night long."

It is a curious fact that, whereas the canons of etiquette then extant apparently did not forbid a young woman to drink a highball in a restaurant with her male escort, they did proscribe her indulgence in a cigarette under similar circumstances. In 1908, for example, when A. Miller, manager of Rector's in New York, was asked if he would permit a woman to smoke in his establishment, he answered: "Decidedly not." The prevailing mores, however, were gradually cracking up under the impact of more modern attitudes. Publication of Elinor Glyn's bawdy potboiler *Three Weeks* signalized the advent of a new genre in the popular novel, and the preoccupation with sex that brought the author such gratifying financial returns from this pioneering excursion was to become increasingly pronounced with her fellow practitioners in the world of fiction. In like manner the emergence of the "turkey trot," the "grizzly bear," and the "bunny hug" carried contemporary terpsichorean divertissements to a rather advanced position, as the Tin Pan Alley of that long-gone era vibrated to the thaumaturgy of twenty-three-year-old Irving Berlin, who lifted ragtime at one bound from the honky-tonks to the swank salons with *Alexander's Ragtime Band.*

These trends engaged the attention of Cannon and his fellow workers, but not to the exclusion of matters pertaining to what they considered the central problem in the sphere of morality — namely, the liquor problem. Unsuccessful efforts had been made for a number of years by the Anti-Saloon League to secure Federal legislation forbidding shipments of liquor into dry states in violation of the laws of those states, and these efforts were renewed. Temperance and prohibition organizations met in Washington, D.C., December 14–15, 1911, and chose a committee, headed by the Rev. Dr. Arthur J. Barton, to draft the desired measure. Cannon was a member of this committee.

The bill, known as the Webb-Kenyon bill, forbade the interstate shipment of liquor in violation of any law. It passed both houses of Congress by large majorities in 1913, but was promptly vetoed by President William H. Taft, on the ground that it was unconstitutional. Congress thereupon passed the measure over his veto. Its constitutionality was subsequently attacked in the courts.

The man upon whom devolved the task of defending the statute from this assault was Wayne B. Wheeler, whose name bulks large in the hagiology of the Anti-Saloon League. America has produced few individuals of greater capacity or more terrific zeal. Justin Steuart, his publicity secretary and biographer, wrote of Wheeler: "He worked. No man could be associated with him and rest. He took vacations only when forced by the threat of premature death from overwork. Home, family, friendships, pleasures, the whole world of art, literature, and music, all these meant nothing to him beside his consuming passion for the cause whose spokesman he had made himself." Steuart went on to say that Wheeler "loved the limelight . . . he loved power," and that he was "an exponent of force" who "preferred threats to persuasion."

When Wheeler undertook the defense of the Webb-Kenyon Law, he did so with considerable trepidation, for in his heart he agreed with President Taft that the legislation was unconstitutional. But regardless of his private views, which were not known to the public, Wheeler fought the case through the courts over a period of several years in opposition to a squadron of distinguished attorneys representing the liquor interests. Finally, in January 1917, the United States Supreme Court ruled in favor of Wheeler. It was the greatest court victory ever won by the Anti-Saloon League.

But long before the constitutionality of this law was upheld, the league had decided that the law could not be enforced and had announced publicly that the solution of the liquor problem lay in nation-wide prohibition. No real opportunity was afforded for a determination of the enforceability of the Webb-Kenyon Act. It was passed, as we have seen, in February 1913, but it was not implemented at that time with an appropriation. Nevertheless, when the Anti-Saloon League held its annual convention at Columbus, Ohio, in November 1913, it suddenly determined to press for a constitutional amendment. In other words, before a cent had been made available for the enforcement of the Webb-Kenyon Law, and when that law had been on the books for only about eight months, the organized drys pronounced it a failure, dropped the mask behind which they had been operating for decades, and declared openly for the first time that nation-wide prohibition was their goal.

Machinery looking toward the achievement of that objective was immediately set in motion. A resolution submitting the proposed amendment to the vote of the states was introduced in both branches of Congress within a few weeks. In December 1914, shortly before the vote was taken in the House, there was much oratorical spouting by members of that body. Congressman Hobson of Alabama, patron of the measure, favored those present with one of his "Great Destroyer" speeches, while Congressman Vollmer of Iowa apostrophized the shades of "George Washington, the brewer; Thomas Jefferson, the distiller; Abraham Lincoln, the saloon keeper; and Jesus of Nazareth, who turned water into wine." When the vote was taken, the count stood 197 for and 190 against. A two-thirds vote was required, and the resolution consequently failed of passage.

This had been anticipated, and the drive for the amendment was intensified. In 1914 Cannon was named chairman of the

Anti-Saloon League's national legislative committee, a key post that he was to hold continuously thereafter. Petitions with over six million signatures were presented to Congress. Additional impetus was given the dry movement when Secretary of the Navy Josephus Daniels, braving the mockery and ridicule of thousands, and ignoring traditions that had been deemed unassailable since the time of John Paul Jones, banned all alcoholic liquors from naval vessels, navy yards, or naval stations, effective July 1, 1914. The quipsters and the cartoonists nearly laughed themselves to death at the thought of a first line of defense that would thereafter be nourished on grape juice, but Daniels stood firm under the withering barrage.

At this period, Cannon enunciated the doctrine that "a man of small influence who will vote right" is preferable to "an exceedingly able man who is opposed to prohibition." This, in general, was the policy of the Anti-Saloon League, and by means of it the league triumphed in the end. Such singleness of purpose was not to be found in the ranks of the opposition. The vast majority of those who opposed nation-wide prohibition permitted other considerations to influence their political decisions. They preferred a man of high character and strong convictions to a weakling who would vote for Anti-Saloon League legislation while drunk. Not so with the orthodox dry. Prohibition to him was the sole issue and he was ready to follow the Anti-Saloon League blindly.

When the brewers, the liquor dealers, and the distillers saw the introduction into Congress of the submission resolution, they quaked with apprehension. Here at last was the dread event that they had anticipated for so many years. True, nobody expected Congress to adopt the resolution at that time, but the mere introduction of the measure was the signal for sleepless nights in Milwaukee and San Francisco, Baltimore and Louisville, and the other centers whence emanated the better brands of lager and claret, bourbon and rye. In desperation, some of the trade journals were resorting to abuse. For example, *Barrels and Bottles* termed the Anti-Saloon League in 1913 "the most arrant organization of canting hypocrites and jesuitical grafters the world has ever known." But, with cold perspiration standing out upon their brows, the more thoughtful leaders in the whisky, wine, and beer business realized that something more effective than billingsgate was needed to save the situation. Some of them concluded that it would be helpful if the saloon could be invested with an aura of respectability. Certainly it was high time. *Bonfort's* declared frankly that the institution "was getting worse instead of better," and that it had been "dragged into the gutter . . . made the cat's paw for other forms of vice . . . succumbed to the viciousness of gambling, and . . . allowed itself to become allied with the social evil."

Various methods of fumigating and deodorizing the reeking grogshop were tried by the trade as it cast about belatedly in search of an antidote for the relentless attack of the reformers. One of the most futile was that seized upon by the National Retail Liquor Dealers' Association at its 1914 convention in Washington, D.C. This organization formally endorsed the work of the Anti-Profanity League of America and recommended that the cards of the league be placed in all barrooms.

But not even the Anti-Profanity League could save the liquor business now. During 1914 the states of Arizona, Colorado, Oregon, Virginia, and Washington all adopted state-wide prohibition; in 1915 and 1916 Alabama, Arkansas, Iowa, Idaho, South Carolina, Montana, South Dakota, Michigan, and Nebraska followed suit. By 1916 there were twenty-three dry states, and in addition the Anti-Saloon League was constantly winning victories in local-option contests. Then came the congressional elections of 1916. In the words of Wayne B. Wheeler, the league "laid down such a barrage as candidates for Congress had never seen before, and such as they will, in all likelihood, not see again for years to come." League headquarters were kept open late election night, and before the national officers went to bed, they knew that the next Congress would vote to submit the Eighteenth Amendment to the states. Reports from all parts of America showed that at least two thirds of both houses would be safely dry.

It was during this period that Louis D. Brandeis was being considered as a possible appointee to the United States Supreme Court. Cannon appeared before the subcommittee of the Senate Judiciary Committee at Washington on March 6, 1916 in opposition to the appointment. The doctor had resurrected from some dusty file the fact that Brandeis had appeared in 1891 before the Massachusetts legislature as counsel for a group of liquor dealers and brewers. "I do not refer merely to his having appeared as counsel for the liquor dealers," Cannon told the senators. "There is not necessarily anything disreputable in that. I wish to call the committee's attention to the sweeping statements Mr. Brandeis made before the legislature on the liquor traffic and its relations to society." He then informed his auditors that Brandeis had said a quarter of century before that "liquor dealing is not wrong" and had appealed to the legislators of the Bay State in the following language: "Remove from the statute book obnoxious and degrading laws. Remove the uncertainties with which you have surrounded the business, which is sure to exist for ages to come. Remove the discredit you have placed on this trade." Cannon then stated that there was nothing to indicate that Mr. Brandeis had ever changed his views, and added: "I do not think it would look well in the biography of a Justice of the United States Supreme Court to record that he had once been employed as a lobbyist for the liquor traffic." Apparently the revelation that Brandeis had expressed sentiments to the Massachusetts legislature in 1891 which were entertained almost universally at that time failed to shock President Wilson, for the man who uttered them was named to the Supreme Court shortly thereafter.

Early in 1917 Senator James A. Reed, of Missouri, offered his "bone-dry amendment," which went far beyond the Webb-Kenyon Act of four years before, since it excluded from the mails all liquor advertisements or solicitations of orders for liquor. The amendment, to the post-office appropriation bill, was presented as a "wet joker," for Reed was as violently averse to the Anti-Saloon League and all its works as any member of Congress. He was trying to embarrass the professional drys, but they finally decided to support the measure, and it passed both branches.

At this time the reformers were concentrating their energies with a view to securing submission of the Eighteenth Amendment to the states. Cannon was a member of the National Prohibition Committee of Nineteen, which had been chosen, July 10, 1915, by the National Conference of Prohibition Forces to confer with dry leaders in Congress relative to the wording of the proposed amendment. He was also named to a subcommittee of that committee which met in Washington March 28–9, 1917 and decided on the form the amendment was to take.

When the newly elected Congress met in extra session in March 1917 for the purpose of declaring war on Germany, the Anti-Saloon League shoguns were ready with their resolution submitting the Eighteenth Amendment to the state legislatures. President Wilson asked, however, that they postpone introduction of the resolution until the war program had been adopted. Cannon, chairman of the legislative committee, and his colleagues promptly acceded to the presidential request. The administration then presented the Lever food-control bill, designed to conserve foodstuffs. Drys in the House amended it in such a way that it forbade the use of any foods, food materials, or feeds for the production of alcoholic beverages, except for governmental, industrial, scientific, medicinal, or sacramental purposes, and authorized the President to commandeer alcohol and distilled spirits for the government. A group of hostile senators announced forthwith that they would filibuster against the entire measure unless exceptions were made of beer and wine.

In order to avoid delay in the passage of the bill, President Wilson summoned Senator Martin of Virginia, Democratic floor leader, who not infrequently served as a link between the White House and the Anti-Saloon League. Wilson urged that the amendments calling for wartime prohibition of beer and wine be stricken from the bill, lest the entire food-conservation program be held up by a filibuster. Martin then returned to his office and sent for the league's legislative committee, headed by Cannon. The committeemen agreed that if the President would ask them in writing to eliminate the provisions relating to beer and wine, they would accede to his request. He did so and they withdrew these particular amendments. They stated, however, that they would "urge the passage of legislation prohibiting the waste of foodstuffs in the manufacture of beer and wine at the earliest possible date, either in the form of a separate bill or in connection with other war legislation."

The Anti-Saloon League claimed that to permit brewing and distilling to go on while the nation was engaged in a death struggle with the Central Powers was an inexcusable waste. Peter Odegard points out, however, in his excellent history of the league, that whereas that organization had previously contended that the liquor business was economically insignificant and that prohibition would not involve any serious disturbance of the country's economic structure, it now reversed its position and declared that to permit the industry to continue meant leaving "a yawning gap in the armor of our national defense."

The drys were quick to take advantage of the strong anti-German prejudices that had arisen as a result of America's entry into the World War. The fact that a large percentage of the brewers were of German descent was emphasized by the league at every opportunity. An inquiry into the political activities of the Pennsylvania brewers had resulted in a grand-jury investigation and indictments against the United States Brewers' Association, the Pennsylvania Brewers' Association, and about a hundred corporations for violations of the conspiracy section of the Federal criminal code. Both associations and almost all the corporations pleaded guilty and were fined amounts aggregating about one hundred thousand dollars. The German-American Alliance likewise had been opposing prohibition with all its resources. A subcommittee of the Senate Judiciary Committee investigated its activities, and the organization's charter was subsequently revoked by the unanimous vote of Congress. The corruption of the brewing interests uncovered through these inquisitorial procedures, coupled with the fact that most of the beer magnates were of solidly Teutonic extraction, came like manna from above to the Anti-Saloon League. In addition, as already hinted, "the trade" could usually be counted on to do the wrong thing at the right time — for the league. Some of the stupidities of the brewers are summarized as follows by Charles Merz in his discerning volume *The Dry Decade:*

> By their own admission the brewers dumped money into various states to win elections for friends who promptly failed them; they financed a dummy chamber of commerce which existed largely for the purpose of fighting liquor legislation; they employed experts to investigate the strategy of the prohibition movement, at a time when the prohibition movement was shouting its

strategy from the housetops; they organized a blacklist system which threatened to withhold trade from a long list of businesses regarded as unfriendly to the brewers' interests.

The Delaware, Lackawanna & Western Railroad was on this list because it had forbidden its employees to drink liquor. The Grasseli Chemical Company of Cleveland was on the list because some of its officials had given their support to a revival meeting staged by Billy Sunday. The Heinz Pickle Company was on the list because its president was an officer of a Sunday-school association which had championed the cause of prohibition.

Cannon played an important role in putting over national wartime prohibition, as well as the Eighteenth Amendment. General supervision over the fight was in the hands of Purley A. Baker, national superintendent of the Anti-Saloon League, while Cannon, Dr. A. J. Barton, and Dr. E. H. Cherrington planned the campaign. Legislative Superintendent Edwin C. Dinwiddie dealt directly with members of Congress. During June 1917 Cannon made a rapid dash through North and South Carolina, Georgia, Florida, Alabama, and Arkansas in the interest of wartime prohibition. He delivered addresses, placed advertisements in the leading dailies setting forth the reasons why he regarded wartime prohibition as desirable, and conferred with prohibition leaders, urging that all possible pressure be brought to bear upon Congress.

Cannon and the league took full advantage of the lack of co-operation and co-ordination between the brewers, the wine merchants, and the distillers. If these groups had been able to formulate a definite program of opposition to the Eighteenth Amendment, its passage might have been delayed, but while the prohibition forces were concentrating their energies upon a single objective, the liquor interests not only were unable to agree among themselves but were indulging in mutual recrimination. Cannon said in 1917 on this subject: "The brewers and the distillers are not having a very happy time together, for the distillers are very suspicious of the brewers and the makers of light wines. The distillers know that the brewers and the wine merchants would not hesitate to make the distillers 'walk the plank' if by doing so they could save themselves." This diagnosis is at least partially borne out by the statement of P. H. Nolan, chairman of a committee of the National Liquor Dealers' Association, who said at about this period: "The average brewer in a mad desire for wealth is careless of public sentiment. He has no respect for law, regulation or public decency. . . . His business is to corrupt public officials that he may thrive. The brewers of the United States are a menace to society." [1]

The fact that Nolan's opinion was shared by millions of Americans, and the further fact that millions regarded Nolan's liquor dealers as no less villainous and corrupt than the brewers he denounced so fervently, were among the principal reasons why the Anti-Saloon League was carrying all before it. In the great cities, where large immigrant groups were schooled in European attitudes and where the "thou shalt not" philosophy of the Protestant evangels had never become deeply rooted, the league was decidedly on the defensive. But in the small towns and villages, in rural America, where the pastors had been actively propagating the prohibitionist gospel for a decade or more and where there was a seemingly irrepressible inclination to regard the cities as Sodoms steeped in sin, the league was usually all-powerful. The great majority of these communities had voted out liquor in local-option elections, and while they contained citizens who drank as freely as their urban brethren, rural America was politically dry. Not only so, but most Americans lived in small towns and hamlets or on farms, a fact that must be constantly borne in mind by every student of the prohibition movement. The census of 1910 showed 54.2 per cent of the population living in places of fewer than 2,500 inhabitants and 61.3 per cent in places of fewer than 8,000 inhabitants. By 1920 these percentages had fallen to 48.6 and 56.2, respectively. In other words, when the movement for nation-wide prohibition was approaching its climax in 1917, the political center of gravity in this country was not in New York or Chicago or San Francisco, with their armies of foreign-born and their vociferous anti-prohibitionist newspapers, nor yet in Denver or Richmond or Atlanta, with their similarly hostile press, but in Junction City and Smith's Store and Brown's Hollow, where community affairs revolved about the local Protestant church or churches, and where the pastor usually spoke *ex cathe-*

dra on "moral issues." And superimposed upon this situation was another, which gave these areas even more influence than their greater aggregate population entitled them to. This added advantage was acquired through the scandalously unfair system of legislative apportionment under which the states were laid off into districts. The rural regions almost uniformly were given more seats in the state legislatures than they were entitled to on a population basis, while the cities received correspondingly fewer. Also, constitutional mandates for periodic redistricting were so often ignored that the fast-growing cities frequently found themselves discriminated against, as time went on, even more flagrantly than in the original apportionment.

Such heavy prohibitionist pressure was exerted from nearly all parts of rural and small-town America, and from some urban areas as well, that the American Medical Association capitulated at its 1917 convention, under the spell of an address by the celebrated Dr. Charles H. Mayo. The association's House of Delegates, by a majority vote, adopted the following resolution:

Whereas, we believe that the use of alcohol is detrimental to the human economy, and
Whereas its use in therapeutics as a tonic and stimulant or for food has no scientific value; therefore be it
Resolved, that the American Medical Association is opposed to the use of alcohol as a beverage; and be it further
Resolved, that the use of alcohol as a therapeutic agent should be further discouraged.

While an aggressive minority objected to the sentiments expressed in this document, and a lively controversy was waged in succeeding months in the medical press, the action was irrevocable, in so far as that convention was concerned. After the adoption of prohibition the A.M.A. was to repudiate its resolution at several annual conventions, but the action of 1917 came at just the right moment to provide a powerful fillip for a movement that already was well-nigh irresistible.

Illustrative of the shift in sentiment that was manifesting itself on such a wide front was the attitude of Mr. Dooley, the hypothetical Hibernian saloon-keeper created by Finley Peter Dunne, whose sapient and witty observations upon current affairs were comparable in their impact upon the public mind to those of Will Rogers a decade or more later. In 1917 Mr. Dooley virtually immolated himself on the Anti-Saloon League altar, in the following words:

> "I used to laugh at th' pro-hybitionists; I used to laugh them to scorn. But I laugh no more; they've got us on th' run. I wudden't be surprised at anny minyit if I had to turn this emporyum [his saloon] into an exchange fr women's wurruck. Whether ye like it or not, in a few years there won't be anny saloons to lure the married man fr'm his home, furnish guests fr our gr-reat asylums an' jails, an' brighten up th' dark streets with their cheerful glow. . . ."
>
> "I don't believe in this here prohybition," said Mr. Hennessy. "Th' man who dhrinks moderately ought to be allowed to have what he wants."
>
> "What is his name?" asked Mr. Dooley. "What novel is he in?"

The fact that an Irish saloon-keeper, albeit an apocryphal one, could talk in this fashion showed the tenor of the times.

When the dry leadership deemed the moment appropriate for submission of the Eighteenth Amendment to the states for ratification, Cannon sought to prevail on Senator Warren G. Harding, of Ohio, to sponsor the move. Harding left the cloakroom and went on the floor to consult his colleagues. He returned with word that they would pass the amendment and propose it to the states if the drys would agree that it must be ratified within seven years. To this Cannon readily assented. Harding thereupon declared with no little satisfaction: "Well, that is the end of prohibition."

"Oh no, Senator," Dr. Cannon replied, "the amendment will be ratified within two years. We know that three fourths of the states are ready to ratify."

"Why, you should have told me that!" said the indignant Harding.

"Now, Senator, wouldn't that have been smart politics?" Cannon answered.

It was too late for the gentleman from Ohio and his confreres to back out of the agreement that had been made, and everything pointed to the inevitability of the Eighteenth Amendment's submission to the states.

The first real test came on August 1, 1917, when the submission resolution went through the Senate by a vote of 65 to 20. It passed the House on December 17 by 282 to 128. Twenty-seven states had by that time adopted prohibition laws of their own. The Anti-Saloon League calculated that these dry commonwealths would vote for ratification of nation-wide prohibition, and that it would be necessary to bring only nine others into line in order to secure the needed thirty-six. Ratification by the states began in January 1918.

Meanwhile the battle for wartime prohibition was being pressed by the league, and the combination of America's military needs with the admitted corruption of the brewers and their Germanic predilections and antecedents was unbeatable. The bill establishing wartime prohibition passed in the later summer of 1918.

While the professional drys were exulting over the approaching extermination of the saloon, the professional wets were gnashing their teeth in impotent wrath. Hugh F. Fox, secretary of the United States Brewers' Association, said in the association's 1918 year-book:

It is little wonder . . . that the soldier returning from overseas should be filled with hot resentment at the betrayal of Democracy in his absence. It is little wonder that the wage earner . . . should raise vehement protest against a situation forced upon him without his consent and against his will. It is little wonder that the statesman, whose memory recalls the dire results of fanatical social experimentation in the past, should shudder at the enormous impetus given the forces of Bolshevism and anarchy by this measure.

Following passage of the Wartime Prohibition Act, Cannon moved with his family from Blackstone to San Antonio, Texas, for he had been elected a Bishop in May 1918 and had been assigned parts of Texas and Mexico. The Cannons made the trip in an automobile belonging to L. B. Musgrove, chairman of the national campaign committee of the Anti-Saloon League, who lent them his car and chauffeur for the purpose. To the deep disgust of the Bishop, one of the tires was severely punctured in Louisiana when the wheel passed over a pint flask in the highway.

Cannon and his colleagues in the drive against liquor calculated that thirty-six states would ratify the Eighteenth Amendment by April or May 1919, but they underestimated their own potency. The Anti-Saloon League had demonstrated such devastating political effectiveness that the vast majority of state legislators hastened incontinently to obey its imperatives. On January 16, 1919, slightly more than one year from the date of initial ratification by Mississippi, the thirty-sixth commonwealth fell into line. The amendment accordingly was to become effective exactly twelve months later. Every state except Rhode Island and Connecticut ultimately ratified Federal prohibition, and more than eighty per cent of the members of the forty-six ratifying legislatures voted in the affirmative. In six states the vote was unanimous in both houses.

On its face, this is a distinctly impressive showing, but actually the case for prohibition suffered from a glaring, albeit not always recognized, infirmity. That infirmity lay in the fact that in 1918 only thirteen states, all of them in the South and West, had adopted bone-dry legislation of the type that the Eighteenth Amendment was to rivet upon the country as a whole. These thirteen states covered more than one third of the country's total area, but they incorporated only about one seventh of its total population. In other words, the Anti-Saloon League, the W.C.T.U., and their allies had rushed national prohibition through before the country was ready for it. By the use of the high-pressure methods that had filled politicians with awe from coast to coast, they had secured preponderant majorities in both branches of Congress and in nearly every state legislature, but they had not waited until a majority of all the people was clearly favorable to the absolute proscription of alcoholic beverages. Most of the states that had adopted prohibition laws of their own allowed their citizens a quart or two of whisky or a gallon or two of wine or beer per month. It will be recalled that Cannon specifically refused in 1916 to cut the citizenry of Virginia off without a drop, one of his reasons being that he did not deem Virginians to be favorably disposed toward such a step at that time. Yet the Anti-Saloon League of America had voted more than two years before to press for a bone-dry constitutional amendment, and the drive for that amendment was actively under way at the very moment when the chairman of the league's National Legislative Committee determined that Virginia was not ready for complete prohibition. It is difficult to understand why Cannon thought it was unwise to separate Virginians completely from their highballs and their steins by state law, but wise to deprive all Americans, including Virginians, of theirs by Federal law. It may be that, as matters turned out, nation-wide prohibition was achieved several years earlier than its sponsors imagined was possible when they began working for it openly in 1913. But whatever the explanation of this seeming inconsistency, the failure of Cannon and his fellows to develop sufficient sentiment throughout the country as a whole for the complete outlawry of every sort of alcoholic potation was perhaps the worst mistake they ever made. Certainly it was one of the major reasons for the subsequent collapse of enforcement.

But the mistake was irremediable when wartime prohibition became effective on July 1, 1919. For all practical purposes the Eighteenth Amendment also became effective on that date, although technically it did not enter the Constitution until January 16 of the following year.

On the night of January 16, 1920, reformers from all parts of the nation gathered at Washington for a watch-night service formally to usher in the new dispensation. These ceremonies were in contrast to those arranged in observance of the same occasion in New York. A New York restaurant put on a dance at which each guest received a miniature casket as a souvenir. A hotel in the same city draped one of its dining-rooms in black, the walls, tablecloths, and clothes of the guests were black, and a casket filled with black bottles occupied the center of the room. At Norfolk, Virginia, the Rev. Billy Sunday staged mock obsequies. The ceremony began at the railroad station, where the "corpse" of John Barleycorn arrived in a coffin twenty feet long on "a special train from Milwaukee." Twenty pall-bearers placed the coffin on a carriage and marched beside it through the streets to Sunday's tabernacle, while His Satanic Majesty trailed behind in deep mourning and anguish. Sunday then preached to more than ten thousand people on the extermination of the saloon.

After prohibition became effective, the charge was frequently made that it had been "put over" on the country while millions of voting males were in France, or at least occupied with military or naval matters on this side of the water to the exclusion of things political. Cannon made the following comment:

> The statement so loudly made in some quarters that prohibition was adopted while millions of soldiers were in France is absolutely false. The resolution was submitted by Congress in December, 1917, when as Marshal Foch's statement shows, there were not 100,000 soldiers in France. All the legislatures voting in 1918 voted affirmatively before there were 300,000 in France, and the large majority of the members of other legislatures had been nominated before 500,000 soldiers had sailed for France.

This astounding pronouncement appears in the Virginia edition of the *American Issue,* official organ of the Anti-Saloon League, for November 27, 1926, and is stated there to have been reprinted from the *Sunday School Magazine* of the Methodist Church, South. It seems logical to assume that the facts, figures, and sentiments contained therein enjoyed the imprimatur of the Anti-Saloon League of Virginia, if not the Anti-Saloon League of America, or the statement would not have appeared in the league's official publication.

What are the facts? "All the legislatures voting in 1918 voted affirmatively before there were 300,000 in France," wrote Cannon. A total of fifteen states ratified the amendment during 1918,[2] the last being Florida, which did so on November 27, more than two weeks after the armistice was signed. General Pershing reported officially that on November 11, 1918, Armistice Day, exactly 2,071,463 American officers and men were in Europe — as compared with Cannon's fewer than 300,000. As a matter of fact, there were 300,000 American soldiers in France by March 30, 1918,[3] and not only Florida but four other states ratified the amendment between that date and the end of the year. The others were Massachusetts (April 2), Arizona (May 24), Georgia (June 26), and Louisiana (August 8). When Georgia ratified, nearly

1,000,000 soldiers had sailed,[4] and when Louisiana did so, far more than that number were abroad.

Let us bear in mind, too, that ratification required thirty-six states, and that the twenty-one legislatures needed to complete this total voted for the amendment between January 2 and January 16, 1919. Moreover, there was such an astonishing scramble by the politicians to get on the band-wagon that, even after twenty-one legislatures had ratified during the fortnight that ended January 16, nine more followed suit between then and March 10. During January some of the more than 2,000,000 men who had been on the other side of the ocean landed in this country. It is a fair assumption, however, that they were not thinking in terms of politics or prohibition.

It may be true, as Cannon contended, that the large majority of the state legislators who voted for ratification in 1919 "had been nominated before 500,000 soldiers sailed for France." It is also true that many were nominated when the country was in a wholly abnormal state, when the war occupied the public mind to the virtual exclusion of the Eighteenth Amendment and all other domestic questions, and when millions of men were in camp on this side of the water, even if fewer than 500,000 had actually sailed for the other side. In short, the final concentration of pressure behind Federal prohibition came at a time when the Anti-Saloon League was bending all its energies toward that objective and using the war as an argument in support of its aims, whereas the average citizen was far more concerned with the departure of the first A.E.F. contingent for France, with the Liberty Loan drives, the fall of Kerensky in Russia, the renewed French offensive at Verdun, and kindred matters. Thus when Cannon characterized as "absolutely false" the statement that "prohibition was adopted while millions of soldiers were in France," he was skating dangerously near the edge of the truth. Close to 2,000,000 soldiers *were* in France when each of thirty state legislatures ratified the Eighteenth Amendment — that is, when the final step which placed the amendment in the Constitution was taken — and other thousands had barely landed in the United States. Perhaps Cannon would argue that the phrase "prohibition was adopted" connoted the entire process that began with the vote by

Dry Messiah

Congress in 1917 to submit the change in the organic law to the states. If so, his contention was, at best, a half-truth, while one of his other declarations, as we have seen, was flagrantly false.

Would prohibition have come if there had been no war? In all likelihood its triumph could not have been delayed for more than a few years under any circumstances, for the pressures behind it were too overwhelming to be resisted by the disorganized group of squabbling distillers, brewers, and vintners who formed the backbone of the opposition. The well-lubricated political artillery of the Anti-Saloon League was detonating with such synchronous perfection by 1917 that its superiority in fire-power over any conceivable counter-barrage would soon have been demonstrated. The war hastened prohibition, but prohibition would have come soon or late anyway, since America was ripe for it.

Obviously the momentum behind the drive was generated by an organized segment of Christianity. Writing some years after the adoption of prohibition, Cannon elucidated this aspect of the matter in the following language:

> In any discussion of "why" the Eighteenth Amendment was ratified, it cannot be too strongly emphasized that the prohibition movement in the United States has been Christian in its inspiration and has been dependent for its persistent vitality and victorious leadership upon the active and, finally, upon the practically undivided support of American Protestantism, with support from some Roman Catholics.

But while there will be general agreement concerning the primary importance of the part played by organized Protestantism, opinion will be less unanimous concerning the methods used by some of its advocates and disciples. Consider, for example, the proud boast of the late William E. ("Pussyfoot") Johnson, long one of the most illustrious prohibitionists in the world. "I had to lie, bribe, and drink to put over prohibition in America," said this "Christian man" in an article he wrote for the May 1926 issue of *Cosmopolitan*. He added that he would do it all over again if necessary to promote the dry movement, and he appeared to be particularly proud of the amount of lying he did for the cause; he said he lied in a way "to make Ananias ashamed of himself."

If drastic disciplinary action had been visited upon Johnson by the other dry leaders of the country as a consequence of this blatant performance, or if they had disavowed the sentiments he expressed, those leaders would stand absolved today of responsibility for his distinctly un-Christian transgressions. But he was not disciplined in any way, in so far as the public was advised, nor was there an audible disavowal. Certainly Johnson continued to exercise his duties as one of the key officials of the World League against Alcoholism and to lecture in many parts of the United States on behalf of prohibition, under Anti-Saloon League auspices.

Prohibition, then, was in the Constitution at last. One can willingly and gladly concede the sincerity and devotion of millions who toiled and prayed for decades, to the end that liquor might be banished from the United States. One finds it more difficult to absolve Cannon and the other leaders of those devoted millions for their tacit acceptance, if not their positive approval, of the shocking rodomontade of "Pussyfoot" Johnson. Has it remained for professional drys to reconcile lying and corruption with Christianity and righteousness?

CHAPTER *xi*

Elevation to the Episcopacy

J AMES CANNON, JR., was elected a Bishop at the General Conference of 1918 in Atlanta over the bitter opposition of influential members of his church, including more than one member of the episcopacy. The long series of violent controversies in which he had engaged and the vigor with which he had assailed revered figures in Methodism made his name anathema to a large bloc of delegates to the conference.

Before the gathering was brought to order, it was generally recognized that he would be one of the most formidable candidates for the six episcopal vacancies to be filled. At the General Conferences of 1902 and 1906 he had received only one or two votes for the office of bishop, but in 1910 he had polled fifty. This was by no means enough to elect him, but it showed that even at so early a date he was coming to be recognized as a leader in Southern Methodism. In 1914 no bishops were chosen.

When the 1918 conference opened, Cannon's numerous enemies at once began strenuous efforts to defeat him. At the same time his friends launched a determined movement in his behalf. When the balloting got under way, Cannon was among the leaders, with 117 votes, or about forty short of the total necessary to elect. The Rev. Dr. John M. Moore, the Rev. Dr. W. F. McMurry, and the Rev. Dr. U. V. W. Darlington were all chosen on the first or second ballot. Cannon's total on the second ballot mounted to 129. But when the third was taken, the coveted prize moved just beyond his reach, for the Rev. Dr. Franklin N. Parker, who had been trailing him, "jumped over" him and was elected, getting

173 votes to his 148. Again Cannon seemed to have the bishopric within his grasp, but on the fourth and last ballot the Rev. Dr. W. N. Ainsworth and the Rev. Dr. H. M. Du Bose, both of whom had polled fewer votes than he on the previous tally, also "jumped over" him and walked off with the two remaining vacancies in the College of Bishops. Six men had been elected and Cannon was not among them. His foes were jubilant. Next day, however, after twenty-four hours of thought and prayer, Dr. Parker declined the office, saying that he did not feel himself qualified. An anti-Cannon delegate then moved that he be asked to reconsider and that if he refused, the episcopal districts be rearranged so as to make the election of another bishop unnecessary. It was the contention of the anti-Cannon element that six bishops had been duly elected and that it would therefore be out of order to choose a seventh. After considerable jockeying back and forth by the friends and the antagonists of Cannon, Bishop J. C. Kilgo, who was presiding, said to the conference:

"Will you vote to elect a seventh bishop?"

This reference to "a seventh bishop" was taken by many members of the conference to mean that Kilgo was hostile to Cannon and that he was trying, in his capacity as presiding officer, to prevent Cannon's election. Delegates who had mildly opposed Cannon became his supporters when they saw the lengths to which Kilgo and others seemed willing to go to defeat him, and there was a decided reaction in his favor. A motion to elect another bishop to replace Parker was made at once and was carried. On the first ballot Cannon was chosen by a wide margin over all other competitors. His most rabid opponents had unwittingly contributed to his success.

It is rather generally agreed that Cannon would probably not have been elevated to the episcopacy except for his record as a temperance leader. His work in the field of prohibition had made him known throughout the nation, and particularly throughout the South. But for this, his enemies inside and outside the Virginia Conference might have succeeded in blocking his path to the bishopric. Another consideration believed to have influenced a good many delegates to support him was the fact that he had advocated the placing of certain restrictions upon the powers of bishops. But whatever the part played by these matters in the ultimate result, it is manifest that it was only by good luck that Cannon was raised to the episcopacy at the conference of 1918.

Dr. Cannon was hailed by Dr. Claudius B. Spencer, editor of the Northern Methodist *Christian Advocate,* Kansas City, in the following words:

> He is . . . the coolest of speakers, the most granite of reformers, the most indifferent to personal consequences. Not a hair's breadth has he swerved in thirty years to win popularity. He does not know there is such a thing as a weather vane. He is four square and adamant.

> And all the time he is a most shrinking of personalities; empty of vanity, never crowding, never seeking the spotlight; a very interesting conversationalist, though his words are few; a man intensely devoted to his family. . . .

The foregoing thumbnail vignette of our newly elected Bishop deserves careful scrutiny. While it is true that Cannon spoke of himself as "a quiet, shrinking man," a sentiment echoed by the eminent Middle Western ecclesiastic quoted, it would seem to be at least open to question whether such a man could have been a center of controversy almost throughout his adult life. And could a man who "never" sought the spotlight have landed there by accident on literally hundreds of occasions? It seems scarcely credible.

A distinguished Southerner who followed Cannon's career closely over a period of several decades, and whose relations with him were such as to afford an excellent opportunity for the formulation of a judicial appraisal of the man, remarked [1] that Cannon seemed almost invariably to do things in the way that would bring him a maximum of publicity. For example, this fair-minded commentator observed that Cannon should have gone to Chancellor W. W. Smith of the Randolph-Macon system in 1907 before taking any public action with respect to the Carnegie matter. He and Smith were friends and they could probably have arrived at a quiet settlement of their differences, this observer believed, for Cannon apparently did not understand the basis on which the chancellor was seeking to have Randolph-Macon Woman's College placed under the Carnegie Foundation. But instead of approaching Smith in this way, Cannon chose to proceed with a maximum of fanfare and to attack Smith openly on the floor of the conference, thus projecting the entire controversy into the newspapers and rendering an adjustment of differences far more difficult. It was also the view of the above-mentioned student of Cannon's techniques that Cannon's preferred method of advancing his own fortunes was by tearing down the influence or reputation of his rivals — a propensity for which a number of examples have been cited in earlier chapters.

Following his election as bishop, his first episcopal assignments included the Northwest Texas and New Mexico conferences, and the Texas Mexican Mission, Mexican Border Mission, and Central Mexican Mission conferences. Discussing the manner in which he presided over his first conference, Dr. Percy R. Knickerbocker wrote in the *Texas Christian Advocate:*

> One of the things that surprised me in his presidency was the wonderful amount of sympathy in his disposition. I had always looked upon Bishop Cannon as a great intellect, logical, precise, fearless, forward-looking, a practical idealist, but I didn't know that he had such a profound development of his sensibilities. I have never known a Bishop to be more tender of the men in his administration.

This is not so startling a pronouncement as some may imagine. It will be noted, in the first place, that Knickerbocker had not expected to find anything resembling sympathy in the Cannon disposition. This is fairly good evidence that Cannon exhibited this characteristic only rarely. In the second place, it should be borne in mind that the Bishop had inspired something very like affection in the bosoms of many Blackstone girls — evidence that, when he cared to do so, he could be measurably human in his attitudes. The assumption seems reasonable that, in presiding over his first episcopal conference, he made a special effort to ingratiate himself with the pastors under his jurisdiction.

It was in 1918, following his election as Bishop, that Cannon shaved off the beard he had worn for nearly a quarter of a century. With the Blackstone Institute firmly established long since, with Virginia dry and the Eighteenth Amendment on the verge of enactment, the Bishop evidently concluded that he could now spare the ten minutes a day needed for shaving — time that since 1894 he had been unable to squeeze out of his crowded schedule. He was to continue furiously busy for decades after 1918, but at least he was able to find ten minutes during the twenty-four hours that he had not been able to find before.

The disappearance of the Cannon beard has a special pertinence for those who would explore the Cannon psyche, for when it vanished there came a well-nigh complete *bouleversement* in the man's facial expression. During the years when he had a beard, his countenance wore a somewhat benign aspect; its removal made his face harder than before. At the same time he acquired a cruel expression about the eyes that had been almost entirely lacking. Even the Bishop's admirers noted the metamorphosis.

For the first year of his episcopal tenure Cannon and his family lived in San Antonio. Northern Mexico, with a population of about 1,750,000, was part of his see, as was the Mexican population of Texas, New Mexico, Arizona, and California, totaling 1,750,000 more. San Antonio was conveniently located for his various conferences in the Southwest, but in 1919 he removed to Nashville, following his election as chairman of the Education Commission of his church. Then in 1920 he placed his headquarters in Birmingham, since the Alabama and North Alabama conferences had been assigned to him, following the death of Bishop McCoy and the release of Bishop Kilgo from active duty. Cannon was relieved of the New Mexico and Northwest Texas conferences when he took over the two Alabama conferences. He and his family lived in Birmingham two years. In 1922 they went to Washington, D.C., where the episcopal residence remained for more than a decade.

In 1921 Cannon was assigned the Congo Mission, and the following year was given the Cuban Mission. Subsequently he was relieved of this work in Mexico and Cuba and was given Brazil. For some years the only areas assigned him were Brazil and the Congo. He never fixed his official residence in any of his foreign conferences, despite the fact that, prior to his own election to the bishopric, he had insisted that no bishop could preside properly over the affairs of a conference in the foreign field unless he made his permanent residence there.² By 1922 he had reversed his position on the point, as evidenced by his report to the General Conference of that year.

If Cannon had fixed his residence in Brazil or the Congo, he would, of course, have been severely handicapped in his activities at Washington and elsewhere in the interest of prohibition and similar reforms. The scope of those activities can be partially grasped if one considers the back-breaking schedule which he carried at the period. Take, for example, the year 1920, chosen at random. In addition to his episcopal duties in Mexico and Texas, he was one of the leading advocates of the unification of Northern and Southern Methodism, and he drafted long and exhaustive reports on the question from time to time. He was chairman of the legislative committee of the Anti-Saloon League of America, and in that capacity was active in seeking to make the Eighteenth Amendment effective. He was also chairman of the executive committee of the World League against Alcoholism, and he went to Europe twice during the year in connection with the work of that organization. He spent several months abroad in the spring and on his second trip made numerous prohibition speeches in Scotland and attended three international religious gatherings in Switzerland. He was named to the committees of arrangements for subsequent meetings by two of them. During the year he likewise carried out his duties as chairman of the Board of Temperance and Social Service of his church. From 1919 to 1922 he served as chairman of the Southern Methodist Educational Campaign Commission, formed to stress the importance of the church's colleges and universities and to raise funds for them. Under his leadership, $20,000,000 was pledged toward the $33,000,000 goal, despite the business depression of 1921. In addition, he was frequently called on for advice and assistance by various other organizations, such as the Virginia Anti-Saloon League and the Southern Assembly at Lake Junaluska, North Carolina, both of which he had served as superintendent some years previously. Small wonder that the *Florida Advocate* spoke of him as "the most prodigious worker we have heard of since the days of John Wesley."

A rather comprehensive idea of the amount of territory Cannon covered during his first decade as Bishop may be obtained from the following statement, made by him in 1928:

> During the past ten years I have averaged 150,000 miles of yearly travel. I am familiar with the cities of the South and Southwest to the Pacific Coast. I have often been for a brief stay in Philadelphia, Pittsburgh, Cincinnati, Cleveland, Detroit, Chicago, Columbus, St. Louis, Kansas City. I have averaged at least two visits monthly to New York. I have frequently visited Cuba and Mexico. I have averaged two trips yearly to Europe for the past nine years. I have been to the countries of the Near East several times. I have visited Egypt, the east and west coast, central and southern Africa, and the east and west coast of South America and the Canal Zone.

It is obvious that Cannon never spared himself in carrying out the duties imposed upon him. Neither did he spare his subordinates. Since he was willing to work night and day when necessary, he naturally expected those under him to do likewise. As head of the Blackstone Institute, it is said that he often took his secretary with him in the buggy to the depot, dictating to her en route and until the arrival of the train in order that no time might be lost. It was also his custom, on occasion, to have her accompany him on the train for an hour or two, and after his correspondence had been cleared up to send her back to Blackstone. He also made this a practice when he was engaged in raising funds for and building the Southern Assembly, for he frequently took a secretary along on the train from Waynesville and dictated to her until Asheville was reached. She then returned to Lake Junaluska, while Cannon went on to Richmond, Washington, or elsewhere.

As Bishop, he found it necessary to resort to similar time-saving devices, and, as in former years, he was careful to utilize almost every minute while traveling. On trains and steamboats he customarily occupied himself in writing or studying. Many of his contributions to the *Baltimore and Richmond Christian Advocate* were written in railroad stations, in Pullman cars, or on transatlantic liners, and they exhibit a remarkable clarity of style, particularly when it is realized that he often had little or no opportunity for revision.

Elevation to the Episcopacy

In his extensive travels he was seldom so unfortunate as to miss a train or a boat, but in 1919, the year after he became a Bishop, he arrived too late for a train at the Broad Street Station in Richmond, after running a couple of hundred yards in an effort to catch it. Panting and breathless on the platform, Cannon encountered a sailor, who likewise was a few seconds too late.

"Did you miss that Goddam train, partner?" asked the loquacious and irate young man from Uncle Sam's fighting forces, evidently unaware that he was addressing a cleric, for Cannon seldom wore clerical clothes.

"Yes," said the Bishop, "I missed it."

"—— . . . !" bawled the sailor, releasing an appalling stream of blasphemy and obscenity. "Aren't those your sentiments, partner?"

"I suppose so," said the weary and unprotesting Bishop, as he sadly mopped his brow.

Cannon's travels took him often to Mexico during the early years of his service in the episcopacy. He was familiar already to some extent with conditions in that country. In 1907 he had made a trip into the interior as far as Mexico City. On that occasion his pocket was picked while he was listening to the preaching of a priest at the shrine of the Virgin of Guadalupe.

But perhaps the most unpleasant experience he ever had in Mexico occurred on Christmas Eve 1922, when, in attempting to get off a moving train in the dark at Jiménez, he missed his footing and was hurled violently to the ground. He fell on his left side parallel to the train and almost rolled under the wheels, but by clinging to the earth with all his strength he was able to avoid getting on the track. Although he was severely shocked and bruised by the fall, he filled a speaking engagement that night at Parral. Next morning, however, he found that his side was extremely stiff, sore, and bruised. He accordingly went to Torreón, where his wife and son kept him in bed for a week. At the end of that period he was able to go on with his work.

Cannon frequently visited Cuba as well as Mexico while it was under his jurisdiction. Brazil was assigned him in 1926, and he went personally to the field several times. As for the remote Congo, he made three trips to it after it was assigned him in 1921.

Dry Messiah

The Congo Mission, situated in the Belgian Congo, covers a rough quadrilateral of from 60,000 to 70,000 square miles, an area about equal to that of Maryland, Delaware, the District of Columbia, and Virginia combined. It is inhabited by the Batetela tribe, numbering from 750,000 to 1,000,000. The mission was established by Bishop W. R. Lambuth in 1914. He had charge of it through 1919, but for a year or two prior to his death he was in the Orient. The College of Bishops requested Bishop Cannon in October 1921, after Bishop Lambuth's death, to visit the mission, provided it was possible for him to return in time for the General Conference the following May. The Congo missionaries were of the opinion that the trip could not possibly be made in that length of time, but Cannon disagreed. He was never a man to balk at obstacles, and he determined to try it. So he sailed in December in the *Olympic,* his favorite liner.

The difficulties that confront a pilgrim to the Congo may be partially visualized in Cannon's description of the journey:

> The ocean travel to the mouth of the Congo is about 8,000 miles, taking about thirty days, then twelve or fifteen days by river steamer, traveling in the company of the hot sun, flies and mosquitoes by day, and tying up at the bank with additional mosquitoes and nameless insects by night, until 1,000 miles have been covered; then by caravan, on foot or in hammock to the mission station. Other missionaries have their trials. These Congo missionaries have, in addition to the usual trials, sand, flies, jiggers, ants of various kinds and sizes, the flies bringing not only physical discomfort, but dangerous diseases. . . .

On New Year's Eve, when the vessel that took Cannon and his fellow travelers to the mouth of the Congo was one week out of Antwerp, a young man named Gantz, an alumnus of Lafayette College, Easton, Pennsylvania, seems to have made himself more or less immortal. Those on board were celebrating the demise of 1921 and the advent of 1922. On the stroke of midnight, some of the demonstrative Frenchmen and Belgians jumped up and kissed one another, while a couple of other men seized two personable young women on the deck and implanted a kiss upon their lips. Not to be outdone, Gantz grabbed Bishop Cannon, yelled: "Happy New Year!" and bestowed a resounding smack on each of his cheeks. "After that salutation," the Bishop said afterward in describing the incident, "I retired promptly to bed."

The ship took the party safely to port and then, after a thousand-mile journey up the Congo, Cannon traveled by various means to Wembo Nyama, situated four degrees south of the equator. This mission station, as well as the one at Tunda, sixty miles distant, is in a region roamed by lions, leopards, elephants, buffaloes, and hippopotamuses. At one mission station not far away, a crocodile was killed, and a woman's arm was found in its stomach, together with enough brass and iron anklets to show that it had eaten twenty-seven persons. After holding the conference at Wembo Nyama, the Bishop journeyed by caravan to Tunda, where he was entertained by Chief Tunda and his sixty wives. He was greeted by the natives as "Owangi Ongenongeno," which apparently means "Bishop Cannon" in their particular Congo dialect. After leaving Tunda, he set out on the long and arduous journey back to the United States and arrived on the return trip in time for the General Conference in May. He had traveled thirty thousand miles by steamer, train, dugout, donkey, hammock, and foot, and had completed the trip as scheduled.

His second journey to the Congo was made in 1927. He sailed from New York in March of that year, landed in England, and then took ship at Marseille through the Suez Canal and the Red Sea to Zanzibar and Dar es Salaam on the east coast of Africa. From Dar es Salaam he traveled westward into the interior. He held the conference at Wembo Nyama, as planned, and sent a long cablegram to the Southern Methodist Board of Missions, which was in session in this country at the time, urging that there be no reduction in the appropriation for the work in Africa.

When the Bishop set out from the Congo for the coast, he took a short cut, against the advice of missionaries, in order to catch a boat that was sailing conveniently. He was trapped in a swamp by floods and would never have emerged alive had it not been for the help of the natives. Then conditions made it necessary for him to spend the night in a native hut. It is believed that he contracted tropical fever there, for when he reached the coast, he was gravely ill. He managed to board his ship at Cape Town, but shortly afterward grew worse and was given up for dead after the vessel sailed.[3] But he wasn't dead. His reserve vitality pulled him through, and when the boat docked in England, he required only four days in the London Hospital for Tropical Diseases. Feeble and emaciated, following his partial convalescence, he returned to the United States.

In spite of his condition, upon his arrival he plunged into a maelstrom of board and committee meetings of various kinds at Nashville, New York, Washington, Lake Junaluska, Detroit, and other points. Realizing that if the Bishop maintained this frenzied pace in his weakened condition, he would probably kill himself, his physician ordered him to rest for six weeks. Admirers proffered a check for five hundred dollars, and he complied with the suggestion that he go to Switzerland. After a month at Lausanne and other Swiss resorts, he returned to this country and threw himself into his work with his accustomed zeal. During the eight days he was in the United States before sailing to Brazil, he attended meetings of committees of the Federal Council of Churches, the World Alliance on the Congo Mission, and the Anti-Saloon League, and conferred with Dr. W. G. Cram, secretary of the Southern Methodist Board of Missions. He then embarked for South America, accompanied by Mrs. Cannon. There he presided over several conferences, and returned to these shores in November. Although the effects of the tropical fever had not worn off, Cannon continued, on his arrival here, to drive his enfeebled physique at a pace that would have been considered excessive by most persons half his age and twice as robust as he. Work was always to him what recreation was to other men.

CHAPTER *xii*

The Bishop in War and Peace

I<small>N</small> the first World War, Dr. Cannon's withers were wrung by the alliance of the United States with the rum-soaked peoples of France, Italy, and Belgium. He was fierce in his denunciation of the Germans, but his soul was seared by the thought that France, our ally, was "the most alcoholized nation in the world," with Italy and Belgium not far behind. Speaking in Richmond in the spring of 1918, after his return from Europe, he said concerning the French:

> We cannot as a nation afford for one moment, no matter how much we may admire the courage and valor of the French men on the battlefield, or their courtesy and politeness, to adopt as the standards for our nation the standards that are largely in vogue in France concerning intoxicants and women.
>
> I was speaking to one of their officials who was very sympathetic. . . . He said: "Why of course we want to do anything we can that America wants done." When I told him what we had done; that in the capital of our nation it was a crime to sell intoxicating liquor or to manufacture intoxicants, he said "Yes, I had heard of that." But when I said that that includes wine, champagne and beer, he threw up his hands and said "Impossible." He could not grasp the viewpoint. He could not see it. Sympathetic as he was, it was difficult for him to grasp the viewpoint.

The Bishop's denunciation of the alcoholized allies of the United States did not lessen his detestation of Germany. "The attack of Prussianism upon the civilization of the world is the natural harvest from the seed sown by the agnostic, faithless German Biblical critics," he declared after this country entered the war in 1917. He added that there had never been "a more convincing demonstration of the evil results of a Christless education."

The "social and moral uplift of the soldiers" became one of Cannon's prime concerns as the great American war machine swung into action. Shortly after our declaration of war, Cannon, as chairman of the legislative committee of the Anti-Saloon League of America, sent a telegram to President Wilson requesting that our fighting men "be protected from the liquor and vice traffic." Legislation such as Cannon recommended was adopted by Congress in December 1917. Shortly thereafter he said in his report to the Anti-Saloon League's annual convention that the regulations ought to be extended to Europe. He feared that members of the American Expeditionary Force might contract an "appetite for strong drink" or return home "shamefully diseased." "While the people of this country are willing to give freely of their money and of their sons for the winning of this war," he declared, "we cannot agree to lay the sobriety and virtue of our young manhood as an offering upon the continental altars of drunkenness and vice."

In addition to passing various regulations, Congress appropriated $500,000 for recreational and other activities for the soldiers and sailors. The amount was fixed originally at $150,000, but Cannon persuaded Senator Martin, chairman of the Senate Appropriations Committee, to raise it to $650,000. The bill passed the Senate in that form, but Cannon said afterward that the "item was fought by the Tammany Catholic, Fitzgerald, of New York, and by the whiskey advocate, of Louisville, in the conference committee, and it was cut down to $500,000."

On the whole, Cannon was pleased with the steps taken for the purpose of shielding our armed forces. He even expressed the view that "never before in the history of the world has a government passed such orders for the protection of its troops from drunkenness and vice," and he added that "there has never been an army of such size gathered together in which the Christian religion has been so magnified."

But while the safeguards provided in this country for the

fighters were considered by Cannon and other "moral leaders" to be adequate, they became disturbed over reports concerning moral conditions overseas. Such episodes as that described in a letter from the Rev. John O. Moss, a Methodist divine stationed at Waverly, Virginia, to the *Baltimore and Richmond Christian Advocate* troubled them no little. Brother Moss quoted from an account in the *Literary Digest* of a stag party held behind the lines in France by four American soldiers and concluded that something certainly ought to be done at once. The feast was described by one of the four revelers as follows: "We had it in the regular dining room after the usual mess was over, and it was a darn good meal, including a nice turkey, caramel custard, and four quarts of champagne for the four of us, besides other good things." Brother Moss commented: "Those who have read French history are not surprised at this letter. It is a nation of large liberties amounting to license."

The Anti-Saloon League became alarmed over this and similar manifestations and determined to dispatch two special representatives to Europe, with a view to finding out whether the things it was hearing could really be true. The organization informed Newton D. Baker, Secretary of War, and Josephus Daniels, Secretary of the Navy, of the plan, and chose Cannon and the Rev. Dr. E. J. Moore, of Ohio, assistant general superintendent of the league, to make the trip. They sailed in February 1918, accompanied by Cannon's third son, Richard M. Cannon, a boy in his teens.

The coming of the reformers from America on what was widely regarded as a "snooping expedition" was not greeted with hallelujahs by the officers and men of the A.E.F. On the contrary, there were imprecations, both resounding and *sotto voce*, when the soldiers were directed to show the Anti-Saloon League representatives about in areas where men back from the front were relaxing in cafés and billets. It is hardly surprising that efforts were made to prevent the visitors from seeing actual conditions.

The late Dr. Hugh H. Young, of Baltimore, related in his autobiography how one night "after a delightful meal" he and other officers were having "a gay time around a great fire" when a lieutenant from division headquarters arrived and begged to announce that Dr. Cannon was about to arrive for the purpose of gathering data concerning the prevalence of inebriety and venereal disease in the A.E.F. Major Young suggested that, under the circumstances, it would be wise to "remove those thirty bottles from the sideboard." So the incriminating vessels were set on the kitchen floor beyond a closed door. "We were then prepared to receive the Bishop appropriately," the distinguished surgeon wrote, "and we sat down to await the jangle of the bell on the front door."

But the carefully laid plan went agley.

"The first thing we heard was a crash of bottles in the kitchen," said Major Young. "When we opened the kitchen door a flood of light from our mess fell upon the gaunt form of the Bishop, who stood there among the bottles, not knowing which way to turn. We led him quickly into the mess and closed the door. Somehow the Bishop had failed to see the ancient handle on our doorbell . . . and had walked into the entrance hall and from there into the kitchen. . . . He said nothing about the bottles, but at once plunged into the questions uppermost in his mind."

"It has been reported in the United States," he said, "that there is no prohibition in the A.E.F., that the soldiers are very dissolute, drunkenness is general, and the forces are riddled with venereal disease." Dr. Young and his associates "had tabulations on hand to disprove his statements," and they were able to show that "the American army was one of the soberest in the world." They also produced "chart after chart" to prove that the "venereal rate in the forces had steadily dropped until there were now only 16 new cases per thousand men per year, less than one-fifth the venereal rate in the standing army of the United States before the war." All this had its effect upon Dr. Cannon, who "was convinced, and even congratulated us on the great work that had been done."

Then he was escorted across the paneled salon into the paved court and out the front door.

As he passed through the gate in the moonlight, the thought occurred to him that he had not cleared up the matter of the glassware over which he had stumbled in the kitchen. Turning to Dr. Young, he said ominously: "Major, what were those bottles that I ran into?" "Bishop, I can't say just what all those bottles were," was the ingenious reply, "but members of the mess drink a great deal of ginger ale, Coca-Cola, and soda." This happened to be not wholly untrue, since large quantities of soda were used for highballs. Dr. Cannon took his leave, apparently happy in the thought that here, indeed, was a sterling and exemplary group of officers.

Not long afterward he was shown around another quiet sector, this time in the vicinity of Neufchâteau, by a young American lieutenant who was detailed to the task. With Dr. Cannon were two of his sons — James III, then overseas with the Y.M.C.A., and the youthful Richard. The doctor and his two sons were mockingly referred to by the troops as "God and his two apostles." [1]

The party of three and their officer escort left Neufchâteau in the forenoon and moved by automobile in the general direction of the German lines. As the peaceful countryside hove into view, Cannon grasped his guide's shoulder and, pointing toward a wooded area, said: "Lieutenant, are the Germans over there?" The Boche was some forty kilometers away, but in the direction indicated, so the lieutenant answered in the affirmative. "At that point Dr. Cannon began visibly to shake, and he asked if we were in any danger," says the lieutenant. He was assured that the enemy lines were so far distant as to constitute a wholly negligible hazard.

The caravan arrived soon thereafter outside the headquarters of Brigadier General Clarence R. Edwards, commanding the Twenty-sixth Division. The lieutenant went inside to advise the general of his convoy. The crusty West Pointer straightway flew into a rage and rushed from the dugout, with his officers at his heels. When he saw Cannon he did not greet him in any way or shake hands. He opened up instantly with a torrent of profanity of the most comprehensive and earthy character, in which few, if any, Army expletives were spared. He asserted flatly that the doctor had canine ancestry and declared that he did not look with favor upon his "underhanded, slimy, treacherous and sneaking effort" to spy on an Army while its heroic men were relaxing behind the lines. General Edwards continued in this sulphurous vein for some ten or fifteen minutes, while Cannon and his two sons listened in silence. When he had finished, Cannon, who had taken off his hat, bowed low and said: "I thank you, sir." The spluttering general thereupon turned on his heel and strode back into his headquarters.

The verbal blitz had failed to shake the doctor's celebrated imperturbability, and he promptly expressed a desire to continue the tour. Accordingly his officer guide conferred with the general's aide concerning the sights to be shown him. A promontory then being used by the Americans as an observation point was under periodic German shelling, and the aide suggested that the eminent divine should by all means be taken to this decidedly unquiet spot. Indeed, when the aide broached the idea to the still fuming general in his dugout, the latter directed that Dr. Cannon be taken to this rather dangerous place without fail.

The party set out, and just as the promontory came into view some distance ahead, the German artillery opened up on it. "The sight must have been quite terrifying to the Bishop," the lieutenant declares, "and he asked me if that was the spot I had in mind." He was answered in the affirmative.

"He took off his helmet and pointed dramatically to his graying hair, and informed me that as a man of God he had no concern for 'these hoary locks'; that he cared nothing for his useless life and wished to make it count only for the good of mankind; that he was, therefore, completely without reluctance to go where we were going *but* (then laying one arm on the shoulders of the younger son and the other around the shoulders of the older son) he declared that he had promised 'this young lad' when he started on this trip that he would not go anywhere that the boy could not be taken, since he did not desire to quench his youthful spirit and make him feel that he had not participated in everything that was going on; and that he would deem it an act of rank cowardice in order to satisfy his own desire for the experience of danger, to subject 'this youth to the chance of having his young life prematurely ended.'"

So the party went no nearer the promontory, and Cannon inquired of the lieutenant if there was not some place where he could observe life in the front lines without exposing the boy to unnecessary peril. The lieutenant accordingly took him to a spot near Toul, some sixty kilometers behind the lines, where the

French Army had constructed an elaborate system of trenches for training purposes, with simulated dugouts, fire steps, and parapets. These had long since fallen into decay. Dr. Cannon got down into the trenches and looked about, mounted the rotting fire step, and leaned over a parapet with an imaginary rifle in his grasp, sighting out over the calm countryside at imaginary Germans.

A simulated dugout had been prepared at one point and Cannon descended into it "with his usual line of comment, asking innumerable questions as to whether the men sat in the dugouts like this and slept like this, and where they would eat their food, and so forth and so on."

"While this was going on," says the lieutenant, "the younger son chanced to run across the top of this thing, and the rotted logs began to give way. There was apparently no serious danger, but a good deal of loose dirt fell through. The speed with which Bishop Cannon left that locality seems to me in my recollection a fine preview of the passage of the modern jet planes. I could readily have played marbles on the flying tails of his frock coat. When I rejoined him he was quite confident that he had been subjected to terrific bombardment."

The tour having ended, it was decided to return to Neufchâteau. The group arrived after all the regular messes had closed, and the lieutenant took the three Cannons to a French officers' club, the Lafayette, all courtesies of which were available to American officers. Realizing that if Cannon arrived unheralded at this emporium, he would undoubtedly catch the thirsty Americans *in flagrante,* the lieutenant cannily suggested that the doctor remain in the car while he sought to prevail upon the chef to provide a supper, despite the lateness of the hour.

"I went into the club," says the lieutenant, "and took the time to interview personally each officer and to inform him in detail who I was about to bring in, and gave them instructions in the name of General Liggett that all drinks of every kind were to be put out of sight during the period within which the Bishop was a guest." The party was then brought into the club, and not a drinking American was anywhere to be seen. In this chaste and rarefied atmosphere the three Cannons consumed a hearty repast and incidentally allowed the long-suffering lieutenant to pay for it out of his own pocket. They then repaired to their respective billets.

After various other experiences in France, Cannon and young Richard rejoined Dr. Moore and went back to England. They sailed from Liverpool. As the ship cleared the harbor, she was fired on by a German U-boat. The torpedo missed the vessel by only forty feet.

Cannon and Moore filed an immensely long report with Secretaries Baker and Daniels when they reached this country. It was apparently drafted by Cannon and contained a number of recommendations, practically all of which seem to have been ignored by the Federal authorities.

The investigators found that our fighters were faced overseas with the "wine-shop and the prostitute . . . at every turn." They also noted the somewhat less than earthshaking fact that on visits to hotels and restaurants there were "wine bottles and glasses at the plates of a very large number of American soldiers and sailors," while at the "tables in front of the cafés, many of them were seen drinking." Consequently they recommended that both soldiers and sailors in Europe be forbidden to buy, possess, or accept as a gift any kind of intoxicating liquor, including light wines and beer. They also urged that officers and men be forbidden to be in the company of a woman of immoral character either inside or outside a house of prostitution. The two clerics feared that failure to act promptly would lead, among other things, to the "formation of wine-drinking habits by American soldiers and sailors, and the purchase of strong liquors under the cloak of the wine bottle." They further urged that the governments of Great Britain and France be requested to prohibit the sale of intoxicants to members of the American fighting forces in uniform.

The arrival of the armistice later in that year induced the reflection on the part of Dr. Cannon that if another war should come, "demanding that sons come from prohibition homes in America to fight in England, France, or other countries, one of the most important factors would be whether the American and English or French governments would cooperate to offer the same protection to the American youth from drink as he received under the American flag."

Bishop Cannon sailed for Europe in December 1918 to represent the Anti-Saloon League of America and the Southern Methodist Board of Temperance and Social Service at the peace conference. The other emissaries of the league were Dr. H. B. Carré and L. B. Musgrove, while those of the board were Dr. Carré and Dr. John C. Granbery. These organizations were especially desirous of promoting the cause of world-wide prohibition at the peace table.

Cannon and his co-workers at Paris succeeded in getting into Article 22 of the Covenant of the League of Nations a provision making it incumbent upon mandatory powers to prohibit in certain mandated territory "such abuses as the slave trade, the arms traffic, and the liquor traffic," and into Article 23 a clause calling for the naming of a committee for the protection of children, which included the alcohol question in its program. Otherwise they were unsuccessful in bringing about the adoption of their plans at the conference.

Cannon took advantage of the international gathering at Paris incidental to the peace negotiations to arrange a world conference on alcoholism in the French capital for April 3–5, 1919. He visited England, Scotland, and Ireland and spent five weeks speaking in the principal cities preliminary to the conference. When the meeting was held, it was attended by forty-five delegates from twelve countries. The Bishop was its central figure throughout. Plans were made for launching a world-wide temperance campaign and for the establishment by the Anti-Saloon League of headquarters in several strategic places in Europe, as well as in other parts of the world. The movement culminated two months later in the organization of the World League against Alcoholism. Cannon was made chairman of the league's executive committee, a position he held continuously thereafter.

Cannon attended every session of the League of Nations for more than a decade, with a view to enlisting the aid of that agency in the world prohibition campaign. Under the direction of the International Temperance Bureau at Lausanne, supported by small subsidies supplied by about a dozen European governments, efforts were made to persuade the League to set up a commission to formulate a program for the League's handling of the alcohol problem, with a permanent bureau for the program's execution. At last, in 1928, the Assembly of the League requested that body's Health Committee to collect full statistical information on the alcohol question, and that information was published regularly in the League's *Statistical Year-Book*. In the same year the Economic Committee was asked to study the conventions relative to the smuggling of liquor and to make a suggestion to the Council. The results of this latter request appear to have been negligible.

The fact that the proposed inquiry into the alcohol problem was fought by European liquor interests was dwelt upon at every opportunity by Cannon and his fellow workers. They contended that the trade's unwillingness to have an "impartial, scientific" compilation of the facts with regard to the liquor traffic was conclusive evidence that the trade feared the truth. It must not be forgotten, however, that the liquor interests of Europe are familiar with the beginnings of the prohibition movement in America.

They know that the requests of the Anti-Saloon League forty to forty-five years ago were exceedingly moderate. That body did not then proclaim that its ultimate objective was nation-wide prohibition. On the contrary, it specifically denied that it had any such plan. The league simply asked that the people of each community be given permission to vote on whether that community should be wet or dry. Then, as dry sentiment gradually increased, the league's program became more and more ambitious, its real goal was made known, all its energy was concentrated in a final drive, and the Eighteenth Amendment was placed in the Consti- . tution.

Can it be doubted that similar policies were being pursued by the World League against Alcoholism under Cannon's leadership? Consider, for example, the statement distributed by the dry leaders to all members of the League of Nations Assembly at its 1926 session. "There are divergencies of opinion on the alcohol question," this statement says. "No one can say, in truth, what is the best means of settling it. What has to be done now is to study the question scientifically and arrive at the best measures to be taken." [2]

In his capacity as chairman of the executive committee of the World League against Alcoholism, Cannon delivered addresses in numerous foreign lands. The first international congress for the study of alcoholism that Cannon ever attended was in Milan, Italy, in 1913. He attended many others thereafter in various parts of Europe and America. He also delivered addresses from time to time in the British Isles in the interest of temperance.

He was notably active there in the Scottish local-option campaign of 1920, held under the local-option bill secured from the Asquith Ministry eight years before. The movement was pushed with vigor in Scotland, where dry sentiment was much more articulate and more prevalent than in England. In 1919, preliminary to the more intensive campaign of the following year, Cannon had spoken a number of times in Edinburgh and Glasgow and neighboring towns and had been well received. The United States was then at the height of its popularity abroad, and when three Edinburghers interrupted Cannon continually during the course of one of his addresses, six other men picked them up unceremoniously by head and heels and heaved them out of the building. Similarly another heckler in Reading was ejected from the hall by the police. But by 1920 the popularity of the United States in Europe had dropped like a plummet, owing to this country's failure to sign the peace treaty, and by the time Cannon returned to Scotland from Geneva, he found that "the trade" had "gone the limit by poster, circulars and speeches, to prejudice the local option movement as 'made in America,' as promoted and carried on by American money and agitation."

The consequence was that hecklers were everywhere. Agents of the liquor business were usually on hand whenever a temperance meeting was held, and they did their best, Cannon said, either to "destroy the effectiveness of the speaker" or to break up the proceedings entirely. During a series of four open-air meetings that he addressed in the mining districts of Fifeshire, Cannon found that in one "the male portion of the crowd was almost entirely hostile," and he was "exhorted in vigorous and somewhat profane and opprobrious language to go back to America and stay there," along with the rest of his "cowardly, money-loving, hypocritical countrymen." He added, however, that "the questions asked had been framed by the trade and were easy to anybody who had been in our American fight." In Dundee he spoke at an open-air meeting on the Albert Square, where some minor interruptions were followed by a series of salvos from a woman who, he subsequently discovered, was the wife of a pub-keeper. Cannon declared later that this woman had the shrillest voice he ever heard and that she demanded his "immediate return to the selfish, cowardly, money-loving, thick-skinned Yankees, whom she declared to have stayed out of the war in order to grab the trade of the world while Great Britain was fighting for liberty." Since "it was practically impossible to speak at all while her shrill voice was shrieking out denunciations," the Bishop was forced to wait for her to cease her interruptions. She began moving gradually out of the crowd, but whenever he resumed his address, she would wheel around and pour forth another stream of strident abuse. She kept this up for two blocks or more, and the shrillness of her voice was such that it carried easily that distance.

The Bishop made a marked impression with his temperance addresses in Scotland. After the elections Sir Robertson Nicoll, editor of the *British Weekly*, said: "Of all the able Americans who came over to speak in the Scotch local option campaign, the ablest seemed to me to be Bishop James Cannon, Jr."

Four years later, Cannon made a prohibition tour through Scandinavia, at the request of Bishop Anton Bast of Copenhagen, who was in charge of the work of the Northern Methodist Church in the Baltic States and who served as his interpreter on the tour.

In 1925 he was a delegate to the Universal Christian Conference on Life and Work at Stockholm, one of the numerous international gatherings of a similar nature that he attended over a period of more than a quarter of a century, beginning with the World Missionary Conference at Edinburgh in 1910. The Stockholm conference addressed itself to the drink traffic in some detail. The issue became particularly acute after Lord Salvesen of Scotland denounced prohibition as practiced in America, and declared that a Shorter Bible had been published there, under the auspices of the Methodists and the Baptists, from which Bible everything unfavorable to prohibition had been excluded. He also asserted that tobacco-smoking had been made a penal offense in one of the States of the American Union. Thirty-four of the American delegates to the gathering, Cannon among them, signed a statement denying the correctness of these extraordinary allegations.

The conference named a special committee to explore the liquor problem. Of the six members, five comforted themselves with drams at intervals during their week-long cogitations upon the evils of drink, in a castle on the shores of the Baltic. Cannon, the sixth, was the only abstainer, and he was taken aback by the conduct of these five "earnest, Christian men"; but at the end of the committee's deliberations, they united in denouncing "the awful results that have come from the traffic . . . the evils so great and manifold and far-reaching in modern times, such as the degradation of social intercourse, the desecration, even the destruction of family life, with its consequent evil effects upon the coming generation, and threatening the welfare of the whole community through the spread of poverty, misery, disease, vice and crime . . . which experience has demonstrated invariably accompany the traffic in drink."

But while Bishop Cannon was pleased that such laudable sentiments should emanate from so seemingly unpromising a committee, another aspect of the Stockholm conference aroused his ire. This was the treatment it received in the press. Although it was "the most representative and important gathering of Christian churches . . . held in over 1,000 years," it failed, in his judgment, to get proper consideration in the newspapers. The reports of the conference not only were "exceedingly meager and inadequate, but were sometimes exceedingly misleading," he said. "The daily reports sent out by the reporter of the Chicago *Tribune* were a disgrace to journalism and an insult to the Christian churches represented at the conference," Cannon went on. "The reporter was remonstrated with by leading Americans, but treated that great conference as though it were a gathering of clowns or ignorant people. Such treatment would never have been given to a gathering of Roman Catholics or Jews."

Perhaps one of the reports that aroused the episcopal wrath

was that sent out by the Associated Press under date of August 25, 1925. It said:

> The benefits and evils of prohibition, with special reference to the United States, were discussed at the session of the Universal Christian Conference today. Bishop James Cannon, of Washington, was so enthusiastic upon the subject that he spoke several minutes beyond the allotted time, and the audience, growing impatient, asked him to stop.

The Stockholm conference was a much larger and more representative gathering than most of the religious conferences that Bishop Cannon attended annually during the late summer and early fall over a long period. Such agencies as the World Conference on Life and Work, the World Conference on Faith and Order, and the World Alliance for Promoting International Friendship through the Churches were wont to hold their sessions each year during August or September in Switzerland or neighboring countries. Since this was also the period when the League of Nations convened, Cannon usually included Geneva in his itinerary.

He was an enthusiastic supporter of the League from its inception, not only because of its potentialities as a mechanism for the promotion of world prohibition, but also because of the opportunities it presented for the abolition of war. As early as 1906 he wrote an article concerning expenditures for armaments, in which he said.

> An international court with the support of the great nations of the earth would compel the respect of all the nations, and its decisions could be enforced by public opinion, and the cost of maintaining a police force to enforce its demands would be almost nothing compared with the present outlay, which drains so unnecessarily by taxation the laboring people all over the world.

In addition to the international activities already mentioned, Cannon had a conspicuous role in the Near East Relief work of the early 1920's. This was the period when Greeks and Turks were locked in a sanguinary struggle in Asia Minor, a struggle in which Cannon visualized the Christian Greeks as innocent victims of the Mohammedan Turks, whom he termed "murderous

cutthroats" and "bloodthirsty outlaws of the centuries." Ignoring
the barbarous atrocities perpetrated by the Greeks, he cabled
Secretary of State Charles E. Hughes from Paris in the fall of
1922, as the representative of American church and relief organizations in the Near East, urging the United States to take steps
to protect the Christians of Anatolia from the Turks.

On his return to this country from Europe in October 1922, the
Bishop made numerous addresses in the interest of Near East Relief. He also continued his efforts to obtain more vigorous action
on the part of the United States government looking to a termination of the savageries of the terrible Turk, but without success.
In 1923 he was chairman of a committee of fifteen denominational
and philanthropic organizations that drafted recommendations
to President Harding with a view to obtaining "a just settlement
of Near Eastern questions." Later in that year he was received
by King George of Greece, who thanked him for his work in
alleviating conditions in the Near East.

The Grecian monarch was by no means the only European
potentate to receive Bishop Cannon. In 1919 he was one of six
Methodist Bishops who were given an audience in Rome by King
Victor Emmanuel and Queen Helena of Italy. In 1920 he visited
Czechoslovakia and Poland as the representative of the Board of
Missions of his church and was received by President Masaryk
and President Pilsudski, who expressed appreciation for the work
done by American relief workers in those countries. In 1923 he
presented to Queen Wilhelmina of Holland, on behalf of the Federal Council of Churches and the Huguenot-Walloon Commission, a greeting in which the Dutch nation was thanked for its
services during several hundred years to the cause of "liberty and
peace," particularly religious liberty.

In carrying out his manifold duties in many parts of the world,
Cannon crossed the ocean half a hundred or more times. Boarding
a liner for Southampton or Antwerp or Rio meant no more to him
than a few hours' journey by train did to many persons. Often his
sojourns abroad lasted only a week or two. He rushed across to
England on the *Olympic* or some equally fast liner, transacted
business relating to the World League against Alcoholism at its
European headquarters, 69 Fleet Street, London; perhaps hur-

ried to Lausanne or Geneva to attend to other matters, and was back in his Washington office before any but his close associates knew that he had been out of the country. During the late 1920's and early 1930's, however, the ship-news reporters kept such a close watch on his movements that his departures and arrivals were frequently heralded in the press.

In his travels beyond the seas two causes were uppermost in the mind of Bishop Cannon: those of Methodist missions and of world prohibition. Wherever the Methodist Church establishes a mission station, there it seeks to create sentiment against the liquor business.

CHAPTER *xiii*

Methodist Union and Baptist Polemics

In the long struggle to achieve unification of the Northern and Southern Methodist churches — sundered in 1845 as the controversy over slavery deepened — Bishop Cannon was a leading proponent of union. He served on the Southern Methodist Unification Commission in 1918, and also as chairman of the ad interim committee of the joint commission of Northern and Southern Methodism. Late in 1919 the latter agency drew up the plan that, with a few modifications, was subsequently presented to the two branches of the church for approval or rejection. Thus he was strongly in favor of that plan when it was divulged to the special session of the Southern Methodist General Conference at Chattanooga in July 1924.

But opponents of the scheme claimed that it embodied features to which the Bishop had strongly objected several years before. In support of their contention they resurrected an article he had published in the *Baltimore and Richmond Christian Advocate* in the fall of 1917 in which he had declared that "it would be a great mistake for our church to agree to a plan of union which retained as part of the united church, in the same relation it now holds, the present Negro membership of the Northern Methodist Church." Yet under the 1924 plan the Negro bishops of the Northern church and the 350,000 Negro members of that church were to become bishops and members of the united church "without further action." Apparently Cannon had changed his mind on the point.

When the General Conference convened at Chattanooga, feeling was running high between the opponents and the proponents of the plan. This was not evident to the general public, but it was readily discernible to those who attended the committee hearings. And while there were many sincere opponents of unification who objected to it on relatively unassailable grounds, others who professed to oppose it on the same grounds were actually motivated by feelings of sectionalism, religious fundamentalism, or race prejudice. They regarded reunion with the "Yankees" as undesirable per se, they felt that the Northern church was too "rationalistic" in its thinking, or they objected to the relationship between the whites and the Negroes that the plan provided. To Bishop Cannon's credit be it said that he regarded these attitudes as obscurantist and unworthy.

As was anticipated, the conference voted overwhelmingly for unification under the conditions prescribed, the final tally being 298 to 74. It was beginning to seem probable that Bishop Cannon and his allies would be able to make the projected merger a reality. All that remained was for three fourths of the delegates to the annual conferences to vote affirmatively.

Bishop Cannon took charge of pro-unification headquarters, while Bishop Candler directed the fight for the antis. Cannon embarked on an intensive campaign, which not only covered various sections of Virginia, but also extended to a number of other Southern states.

Whereas the unificationists appeared to have the upper hand when the General Conference adjourned in July 1924, the tide began to turn shortly afterward. Before the last of the annual conferences had been held, it was seen that the plan had failed.

But the advocates of a merger for the three branches of the church were not to be denied. They kept the plan alive, and slightly more than a decade later the movement culminated in a successful unificationist drive.

Bishop Cannon was still an advocate of union, although by no means so active in its behalf as formerly. The possibility remained that a few die-hards, such as Seals Aiken of Atlanta — who declared that "you can't merge Robert E. Lee and William Tecumseh Sherman" — would throw the issue into the secular courts. These fears did not materialize, however, and in April 1939 the three branches of Methodism consummated their union at Kansas City, healing a breach that had yawned in this great denomination for ninety-four years. To James Cannon, Jr., it was a gratifying denouement.

In addition to the part Cannon played during the war and the postwar years in the unification controversy, in the furtherance of national and world prohibition, with international religious conferences of various kinds, Near East Relief, the Education Commission of his church, and a variety of other matters, he also made a study of industrial conditions, especially in the South, and was conspicuous in his efforts to bring about improvements in those conditions. Describing the opportunities he had enjoyed for observation in this sphere, he pointed out in 1928 that as superintendent of the Southern Assembly he had visited one hundred Southern towns and cities, and that as chairman of the Near East Relief Advisory Committee he had visited one hundred and forty. Continuing, he said:

I have been down in the coal mines of Virginia, West Virginia, Kentucky and Alabama. I have been in the iron and steel mills of Alabama. I have been in oyster, shrimp, vegetable and fruit packing houses. I have studied labor in tobacco, cotton and truck fields. I have been in tobacco factories of all kinds; I have visited cotton mill towns for the past twenty-five years from Virginia to Alabama. I have met and studied sympathetically many of the industrial leaders of the South, and I have counted some of them as among my best friends.

Moreover I have studied industrial conditions in other sections of the country. When the report of the Committee on the Steel Strike of 1919 had been written — the testimony, the conclusions and the recommendations — the question of its publication was referred to a committee of three, consisting of Chief Warren P. Stone, of the Brotherhood of Locomotive Engineers, Dr. H. C. Herring, secretary of the National Council of the Congregational Churches of the United States, and myself. Mr. Stone finally for good reasons declined to serve. After careful conscientious study for many days, Dr. Herring and myself decided that the report should be published. It was published, and that was the end of the twelve-hour day in the United States Steel Company, which has not only not been damaged by the diminution of hours, but has had an ever-increasing prosperity, and have [*sic*] healthier and happier employees. The study of that report emphasized the evils of long hours, low wages, and the unusual distribution of the profits of industry, and of the consequent enjoyment of the good things of life.

The Bishop then went on, in the same address, to discuss the proposed Federal Child Labor Amendment. "I was obliged to oppose its ratification by the states," he said, "as I could not favor such sweeping Federal control of the labor of children (whether for pay or for the family). I have used what influence I have to defeat the present amendment." His aversion to "sweeping Federal control" of child labor evidently did not extend to "sweeping Federal control" of the traffic in intoxicants.

Cannon maintained a liberal attitude toward organized labor over a period of more than a quarter of a century, in which respect he was well in advance of his generation. As early as 1910, for example, he wrote in the *Advocate* that "labor should be organized." He also praised "the great work that has been done by labor organizations in securing the betterment of the condition of laboring men." Shorter hours likewise were urged by him, to the end that workers might have "that amount of leisure that is necessary for a normal and well-rounded life," while "the highest possible wages" similarly enlisted his enthusiasm.

It was natural, in view of the foregoing, that Bishop Cannon should have become aroused by sweatshop methods in Southern industry, particularly in the textile mills. He accordingly had an important part in drafting the "Appeal to Industrial Leaders of the South," which was signed by forty-one prominent Southern clergymen, including ten bishops, and appeared in the press on March 27, 1927. Cannon's name headed the list of signers. The appeal was a rather mild indictment of industrial conditions below the Potomac, especially in the cotton mills. But in 1927 the facts concerning Southern industry had not been widely publicized, and there was a great outburst of wrath from certain Southern businessmen and newspapers. These worthies professed to regard the appeal as an unwarranted interference by the clergy in matters with which they had no proper concern and of which they knew little or nothing. Certainly the appeal of the forty-one

Methodist Union and Baptist Polemics

Southern clergymen embodied a well-tempered and accurate statement of the facts. If its accuracy was doubted in 1927, doubt is impossible today, in so far as its major theses are concerned.

The gist of the "Appeal to Industrial Leaders of the South" is contained in the following paragraphs:

> We bring before you with . . . confidence . . . the necessity for the improvement of certain social and economic conditions, especially in the textile industry, but existing also in other industries. These are, to speak briefly: The isolation of population in the mill village: the long working week, extending in many industries even to 55 and 60 hours; a certain amount of the seven-day week which still exists in some industries; the employment of women and of children between 14 and 16, at over-long periods of labor; low standards of living; the general absence of labor representation in our factories.
>
> Life in a mill village under company control, while an advance of status in the beginning, is not the best training ground for citizenship, in that it does not train residents for participation in government. It has generally proved in recent years, however it may have been at first, to be unfavorable to education, to religion, and to understanding and sympathy between the citizens of the mill village and those of the larger community. . . . We are convinced that these villages should be merged as rapidly as is consistent with safety into the larger community. . . .

Soon after its publication, the appeal and its signers were verbally belabored by various organizations and individuals, including the *Manufacturer's Record,* the *Southern Textile Bulletin,* the Columbia, S.C., *State,* the Charlotte, N.C., *Observer,* the *Atlanta Constitution,* the Commission on Industry of the Upper South Carolina Conference of the Southern Methodist Church, and John E. Edgerton, president of the National Association of Manufacturers. On the other hand, a large percentage of the press was commendatory.

The arch-conservative *Manufacturer's Record* of Baltimore, the leading publication devoted to business conditions in the South, was especially harsh in its criticism. In addition to extended comment of its own, the *Record* published an article from Edgerton, whom it described as "one of the foremost Methodist laymen of the South." Concerning Edgerton's woolen mill in Tennessee, it said: "He maintains a chapel where his employes meet every morning for religious service before entering upon their day's labor. About 90 per cent of his employes, we have understood, are Christians."

After several searing blasts had appeared in the *Record*, Cannon forwarded to Richard H. Edmonds, the editor, a characteristically verbose reply, sufficient to fill four and a half double-column pages of the magazine, and asked that it be printed in full. Edmonds answered that it was too long and that one thousand words "would be abundant." But the Bishop insisted that his complete statement be carried. In a letter to Edmonds, which was published by him, the Bishop pointed out that the appeal had been discussed in the *Manufacturer's Record* on April 21 and 28 and May 12, 1927, and that these articles were reproduced in pamphlet form and distributed widely. He then said:

> You speak of the "appeal" as a "scheme foisted upon Bishop Cannon and upon other Southern ministers by an outsider in an organization which is more or less identified with many Socialistic, Communistic, and Bolshevistic teachings in this country" [the Federal Council of Churches]. You declared that it was "written by a rank outsider, foisted upon a number of Bishops and other ministers." You slanderously attacked those who prepared the "appeal" and circulated it, by attributing the "motives of those who pull the strings for some ulterior purpose of their own." Every one of these statements is absolutely false, not intentionally so, but nevertheless absolutely false, and they are unbrotherly and unworthy of a Christian man. If you did not know that I was a man of independence and some intelligence, you should have made some inquiry. . . . Furthermore, your attack upon the Federal Council of the Churches of Christ in America is unbrotherly and as narrow as the narrowest of the Hard Shell Baptists would be guilty of. . . .
> You say: "But perhaps no action taken by any group of ministers for many years is as absolutely unjustified, untrue and misleading as the statement issued by Bishop Cannon and others in regard to cotton mill villages in the South." This, again, I flatly deny, and denounce as unjustified slander on your part. . . .
> I suppose that I should not be surprised at your refusal to print

Methodist Union and Baptist Polemics

five or six pages in answer to your sixteen pages, in view of these unbrotherly, unwarranted, slanderous and denunciatory criticisms which you have made of Christian men and women.

A thrust from the Bishop that "Mr. Edmonds should know that the church and the ministry do not exist simply to please manufacturers and employers" brought from the latter the following riposte: "For years I have vigorously and aggressively fought on behalf of the betterment of humanity in general, without regard to manufacturers or employers." By now these polemics were being pursued in a mood of extreme Christian ferocity. Edmonds decided, at long last, to publish Cannon's statement in his issue of February 16, 1928, but the concession was vitiated by the fact that the communiqué was displayed under the caption: "Much Space Wasted to Accommodate Bishop Cannon," and was preceded by the following statement:

> Bishop Cannon, who, in connection with Dr. Worth Tippy, of the Federal Council of Churches, was one of the parties responsible for sending out "An Appeal to the Industrial Leaders of the South" last year, after many months of absence from this country, has issued a statement which he insists upon the *Manufacturer's Record* publishing, as he says, in justice to him and others who signed that unwise appeal. For Bishop Cannon's sake, we regret to comply with his request. The spirit of the letters which have passed from him to the editor of the *Manufacturer's Record*, and the spirit of his lengthy communication, in our opinion, do not breathe the Christian thought which should pervade such work. . . . He charged us with having slandered him, when as a matter of fact, if any slander has been committed, it is surely expressed in some of the Bishop's letters. . . . In the whole correspondence [he] has displayed a spirit which indicates very clearly that by temperament he was hardly fitted to make any suggestions about how the industrial interests of the South should be managed. . . . Our request to the Bishop to condense his article was not only for the purpose of saving space, but for the purpose of saving the Bishop from making an exposé of his temperament. . . .

Cannon's long statement followed. In it he took another slap at Edmonds, speaking of him as "that worthy gentleman, Mr.

171

Richard H. Edmonds, who publicly exults that his church — the Southern Baptist — has no connection with the Federal Council; and probably also rejoices that his church also refuses to co-operate in the work of the American Bible Society, the Universal Christian Conference on Life and Work, the World Conference on Faith and Order, or even to agree to any plan of cooperative effort in the cities of the South and in the most pagan mission fields."

He then addressed himself to his own qualifications for passing judgment upon industrial conditions in the South, and cited many facts and figures to show that those conditions were badly in need of correction. It is unnecessary to quote his argument. Subsequent events have shown the justice of his contentions. If the manifest evils complained of by him had been attacked forthrightly in 1927, it is probable that the subsequent riots and strikes in the textile area either would not have occurred or would have been far less serious.

In April 1928, a year after the "Appeal" was made public, Cannon suggested that Southern employers and employees, as well as other interested parties, hold a conference during the summer of that year with a view to working out a plan for doing away with long hours, low wages, and unsatisfactory living conditions in Southern industry. No conference was held. He renewed the proposal in October 1929 as America stood on the brink of the dark abyss into which it was plunged a few days later, and from which it did not emerge for years. The mental climate of the Great Depression was not conducive to reform in the spheres of industry and labor.

At all events, Cannon's attitude on this issue was one of uncommon enlightenment and understanding, well beyond the relatively narrow vision of many contemporaries.

CHAPTER *xiv*

The Bishop and the Brown Derby

THE SUZERAINTY of the Anti-Saloon League over Congress and nearly all the state legislatures was complete until the late 1920's. Except in the large cities and half a dozen states that are highly industrialized and predominantly urban in character, or heavily populated with the foreign-born, the Methodist-Baptist hegemony was supreme. Indeed, some of those most loudly opposed to prohibition prior to its enactment reversed themselves subsequently and, temporarily at least, advocated its acceptance.

For example, Governor Westmoreland Davis of Virginia, who had been elected over Cannon's bitter opposition and with antagonism to "clerical kaiserism" as a leading plank in his platform, recommended to the General Assembly of 1922 that a constitutional provision be adopted requiring all public officials to take an oath not to violate the prohibition law. The *Richmond Times-Dispatch*, long Cannon's savage foe, executed a complete somersault and placed its imprimatur upon this oath as a test of eligibility for public office. Two years later this once sopping wet newspaper actually declared that "all of us ought to be prohibitionists now" and described "the white ribbon" as "the badge of the good citizen."

During these early years of the dry regime there was, none the less, considerable opposition to prohibition. Normally lawabiding elements of society showed an unwonted propensity for disregarding the statutory *verbotens*. Additional time, however, was needed to establish moonshining, bootlegging, alcohol racketeering, and whisky and beer gangsterism on the colossal scale they

173

attained afterward, when the prohibition law came to be more universally broken than any criminal statute in our history.

But the dry regime soon began to put forth its more curious manifestations. As early as 1921 Izzy Einstein and Moe Smith achieved something like immortality with their antics as Federal enforcement agents. For four years this ingenious pair kept New York on edge as they gyrated from one amazing disguise to another. As automobile-cleaners, milk-wagon drivers, gravediggers, football players, actors, icemen, and churchgoers, they popped up at the most unexpected spots. Almost invariably they brought home the violators and the corpus delicti.

The *agent provocateur* made his appearance in the middle twenties. Federal agents deliberately entrapped citizens into violating the law and then arrested them. This practice reached its apogee in the opening by the government of a large speakeasy in New York City that sold liquor to all comers for a period of six months. These methods provoked such a reaction that they were subsequently abandoned.

Some of the state laws passed in response to the nation's passionate predilection for legislated morality were the Indiana law making it illegal for jewelers to display pocket flasks or cocktail shakers in their windows; the Alabama law proscribing the possession or sale of anything that "tastes like, foams like, smells like or looks like beer," or the possession of a bottle that in shape bore any resemblance to a beer bottle or a whisky flask; the Vermont law, that provided a prison term for anyone arrested for drunkenness who failed to reveal the source of his ardent spirits; and the Georgia law that not only placed near-beer on the official *index expurgatorius*, but also made illegal the possession of even non-alcoholic beverages or drinks "made in imitation of or as a substitute for beer, ale, wine or whisky or other alcoholic or spirited vinous or malt liquors."

Killings of fleeing bootleggers and moonshiners by enforcement officers were becoming increasingly numerous. The amphibious statesmen who regularly voted dry in accordance with the edicts of the Anti-Saloon League, while staggering about in private with whisky-laden breath, were growing more and more numerous. Church deacons who openly avowed their faith in prohibition were all too often privy to the ways of the bathtub-gin trade. Even Mrs. Mabel Walker Willebrandt, who served for some years as Assistant Attorney General of the United States in charge of prohibition cases, admitted in 1929 that, while she still believed enforcement was possible, liquor could then be obtained "at almost any hour of the day or night, either in rural districts, the smaller towns, or the cities." [1] She added that "bootleggers infest the halls of Congress and ply their trade there." [2]

Although there were constant jeremiads from the anti-prohibitionists that huge sums were being wasted by the government in the futile effort to enforce the Eighteenth Amendment, the amounts expended from the Federal Treasury for that purpose seem unimpressive when viewed in the light of the well-nigh astronomical outlays of later years for diverse governmental objectives under President Franklin D. Roosevelt. From 1920 through 1933, the maximum Federal appropriation to the Prohibition Bureau in any one year was only $12,401,620, and in most years the total was well below that figure. Licensed Beverage Industries, Inc., has estimated that the Federal Government spent as much as $39,000,000 in three different years for enforcement. It arrived at this figure by adding to the appropriation for the Prohibition Bureau amounts spent on the Coast Guard, plus the cost of criminal prosecutions under the National Prohibition Act, less fines and penalties collected. The same agency put the total over-all cost of enforcing the dry law from 1920 through 1933 at approximately $363,000,000 from the Federal treasury. These figures take no account of state or local outlays. Dr. James M. Doran, Commissioner of Prohibition, estimated in 1928 that a $300,000,000 Federal expenditure annually would be required to enforce the dry law in all parts of the United States, if the national government were to take over all the responsibilities that the states were neglecting.

During the latter half of the century's third decade anti-prohibitionist sentiment became much more vocal. Groups that had been stunned into silence by the magnitude of the Anti-Saloon League avalanche found their voices. The big-city newspapers, almost all of which had been opposed to the Eighteenth Amendment, but some of which were no longer articulate or had even reversed themselves, began vigorously belaboring the dry regime. Bar associations and executives of big business joined with the American Federation of Labor in attacking prohibition. Several nation-wide groups of "antis" came into being — namely, the Women's Committee for Modification of the Volstead Act, the Association against the Prohibition Amendment, and the Moderation League. Whereas prior to 1918 the American Federation of Labor had been almost the only disinterested agency of consequence that had fought prohibition, impressive opposition from business and the professions manifested itself as the decade waned.

Such was the atmosphere in which the political star of Alfred E. Smith neared its zenith. When Smith was elected Governor of New York for the fourth time in 1926, he became almost immediately the most talked-of candidate for the presidential nomination by the Democratic Party two years later. His state had voted overwhelmingly in 1926 to memorialize Congress on behalf of modification of the Volstead Act, the act by which Congress provided for the Eighteenth Amendment's enforcement, and he was recognized as the country's premier modificationist. It happened that the two other leading aspirants for the Democratic nomination for the presidency in 1928 were likewise militant wets — Governor Albert C. Ritchie, of Maryland, and Senator James A. Reed, of Missouri.

Realizing as much as a year before the Democratic National Convention of 1928 that the Democrats were likely to select an anti-prohibitionist as their standard-bearer, the Anti-Saloon League began mobilizing its forces well in advance, with a view to forestalling the movement. Solemn warnings that retribution would overtake any politician who trafficked with the enemy emanated from league headquarters. Once again Bishop Cannon scented a "great moral issue" and once again he girded up his loins and laid about him vigorously.

As the Democratic convention at Houston, Texas, drew near, it became more and more manifest that Al Smith was to be the nominee. The drys were strong enough in the South to stifle Smith sentiment in almost all political circles, but in the rest of the country hardly anyone but Smith was in the running.

The Bishop and the Brown Derby

Cannon said in an address delivered at a prohibition conference held in Washington, D.C., on February 28 of that year:

> We must, in all sincerity and good conscience declare that we can not, that we will not, support any man for the presidency who may be nominated on a platform including a prohibition-enforcement plank inserted to secure dry votes, but who, owing to his wet or doubtful record, it is hoped can secure also the votes of wet sections of the country, which sections would favor him solely because of his non-enforcement record, or his advocacy of State determination of the alcoholic content of intoxicants, or because of his critical, hostile attitude toward prohibition workers and the prohibition law.

And in a communication published in the *Richmond News Leader* less than two weeks before the Houston convention,[3] Cannon said: "Platform declarations will be useless if Governor Smith is the nominee. If faced with such a nomination, very many life-long Democrats will decide that Democracy will be better served by the defeat of the wet Tammany sachem, Alfred E. Smith, rather than by his election, and will act accordingly."

At about the same time Governor Smith was asked by a New York newspaper if he had changed his views with regard to the Eighteenth Amendment. He replied that he had not. Thus on the eve of the convention he reiterated publicly his stand for modification of the prohibition law.

When the convention opened at Houston on June 26, Cannon was present as the representative of thirty-one dry organizations. It was the third Democratic National Convention he had attended in a similar capacity. He had been on hand at San Francisco in 1920 and had opposed the adoption of a wet plank, and he had done the same at Madison Square Garden in 1924. At both San Francisco and New York he had favored a law-enforcement plank rather than a dry plank, and his objective was the same at Houston.

With the preliminaries out of the way, the convention got down to the business of adopting a platform. It happened that the law-enforcement plank asked by the Bishop was satisfactory to the Smith forces, who were in control of the convention, so it went through without difficulty. During Cannon's statement to the platform committee he was interrupted several times by Senator Millard E. Tydings, of Maryland, who resented certain allusions he made to Maryland's failure to pass a state enforcement act. Although Tydings repeatedly interjected that this or that declaration of the Bishop was "false," the speaker, as usual, remained absolutely unruffled.

After the adoption of the platform the convention proceeded to the choice of a nominee. The combined pressure of the thirty-one prohibitionist organizations was of no avail in the face of the overwhelming wave of Smith sentiment that swept over almost the entire country with the exception of the South, and the New Yorker was named on the first ballot. The prohibition plank on which he was to make the race, and which enjoyed the specific imprimatur of Bishop Cannon, was this:

> Speaking for the National Democracy, this convention pledges the party and its nominees to an honest effort to enforce the Eighteenth Amendment and all other provisions of the Federal Constitution and all laws enacted pursuant thereto.

Following Smith's nomination and that of Senator Joseph T. Robinson, of Arkansas, as his running-mate, the presidential nominee sent a telegram of acceptance from New York, in which he agreed to stand firmly upon the platform adopted, but declared that he thought the Volstead Act should be amended to give the states more power. This was simply a reiteration of his oft-expressed views. There was no reason why anyone should have been surprised, least of all Bishop Cannon. We have seen that the Bishop stated positively before the convention opened that he would not support any wet running on a law-enforcement platform, and that if Smith was the nominee, platform declarations would be useless. We have also seen that Smith said only ten days before the convention opened that he had not changed his mind about the need for modification. Yet the Bishop declared that he and other dry leaders were "stunned" by Smith's telegram. He described it as "a shameless proposition of political double-dealing" and as "an action of brazen, political effrontery." Smith had bolted the platform, he said, because the platform committee had de-

Photo by Foster Studio, Richmond, Va.

CANNON, IN THE EARLY 1900's,

with the beard he wore for twenty-five years because his terrific workday left
no time for shaving.

Wide World Photo

CANNON BEFORE U. S. SENATE LOBBY COMMITTEE

on June 5, 1930. He walked out later, the first time a senatorial committee
had been thus defied.

cided not to adopt a wet plank but had determined upon a law-enforcement plank.

Smith's nomination galvanized Cannon into instant action. He was in poor health at the time, still suffering markedly from the effects of the tropical fever of the year before. Indeed, he was almost too feeble to climb an ordinary flight of steps and was from twenty to thirty pounds under weight. In addition, Mrs. Cannon was seriously ill. But neither his own condition nor that of his wife deterred him. Like a war horse sniffing the battle, he was impatient for the fray, and he made immediate plans for participation in the campaign on a full-time basis. The prospect of smashing the "solid South" seemed to electrify his frail physique and to uncover hidden springs of energy, deriving their strength from some inner source of power.

Cannon knew that millions of dry Protestant Democrats in the South were seething with indignation at the selection by their party of an ultra-wet Roman Catholic. He knew that there was much latent feeling against Catholicism in the South, some of which already had been kindled by the Ku Klux Klan, then at the height of its prestige and power. He knew, too, that the intensity of this anti-Catholic sentiment was usually in inverse ratio to the number of Catholics in a given region. In a state such as Louisiana, for example, where a large percentage of the population owed allegiance to Rome, the Protestants were relatively tolerant. But Cannon was aware that the other Southern states were preponderantly Protestant and rural and that thousands of their citizens had never so much as seen a Catholic, much less learned to know one. On the farms and in the small towns, where Catholics were regarded as strange beings from some remote planet, the possibilities for a campaign addressed to the prejudices of the mob were practically unlimited. As the Asheville conference drew near, it became increasingly plain that the greatest handicap Governor Smith would have to surmount in the South was his religious faith.

When the conference met, a "declaration of principles" was drawn up, setting forth the plans of the anti-Smith Democrats. This pronouncement made no reference to Governor Smith's re-

ligion. Apparently Cannon and Barton felt that it would be bad
strategy to raise this issue openly so early in the campaign. But
the late J. Fred Essary, head of the *Baltimore Sun's* Washington
bureau and one of the few prominent newspapermen at the national capital who looked upon prohibition with a sympathetic
eye, wrote from Asheville that four fifths of the delegates freely
admitted in private that they were fighting Smith mainly because
of his religion and only secondarily because of his antipathy to
the Eighteenth Amendment.

Essary also reported that Cannon told him at Asheville that the
anti-Smith Democrats would welcome contributions from the Republican National Committee. Nearly two weeks after the publication of Essary's dispatch the Bishop stated that he had been
misquoted; he declared that he had merely said his organization
would accept contributions from individual Republicans. Essary,
one of the most distinguished and reliable journalists in America,
thereupon expressed himself as completely confident that he had
quoted the Bishop correctly.

Following the conclave of the "moral forces" at Asheville, the
anti-Smith campaign got under way with a vengeance. Cannon took entire charge and opened headquarters in Richmond,
whence he directed the movement in the fourteen Southern and
border states. Such physical qualms as he had felt shortly before
were vanishing rapidly and he plunged into the contest with all
the terrific energy that had so amazed those who followed his
career in earlier years. He not only gave virtually his entire time
to the campaign, but also made liberal personal loans to the anti-
Smith war chest.

No one could have rightly criticized Bishop Cannon for fighting Smith's candidacy on the ground that Smith was against prohibition. Cannon had battled the whisky traffic for forty years,
and although he called himself a Democrat, he was first of all a
prohibitionist. Nor could he have been justly blamed for opposing the New Yorker because of his long-time affiliation with
Tammany, or for his appointment of a soaking wet Republican,
John J. Raskob, as his campaign manager. But Cannon did not
confine himself to these issues. He hauled in the religious issue,

and he emphasized it, played upon it, and reiterated it until this political campaign throughout the Southern states was transformed into what was almost tantamount to a religious war.

It is true that Cannon denied over and over again that he was opposing Smith on religious grounds. It is true that he charged Smith and Raskob with injecting the religious issue into the contest, for the purpose of creating sympathy for the Democratic candidate. But for twenty years prior to the Smith-Hoover campaign Cannon had uttered the most scathing criticisms of Roman Catholicism. He had actually termed the Catholic Church the "Mother of ignorance, superstition, intolerance and sin." [4]

The *Advocate*, of which he was the sole owner, gleefully recorded from time to time the growth in circulation of the *Menace*, a notorious and scurrilous anti-Catholic sheet published in Missouri, which was succeeded by the *New Menace*. In 1913 the *Advocate* said: [5]

> The *Menace* . . . is proving to be the needed instrument for enlightening the people as to the encroachments of the Roman Catholic hierarchy. . . . This paper has among its supporters men and women of powerful influence throughout the United States. It should receive the support and approval of every Christian minister, every voter and citizen, and every lover of the American principles of free education, purity, freedom of worship, freedom of speech and press, all the rights a free people reserve to themselves. Remember papal bans and curses are against all these!

It is plain from the foregoing that Cannon did not regard the Catholic Church as Christian. In fact, he expressed this opinion on at least one other occasion.

So much for Cannon's attitude toward the church of which Alfred E. Smith was a devoted communicant. But it was his contention that he did not "inject" the religious issue into the Smith-Hoover campaign. This was done by Raskob, he said, when Raskob charged Cannon with using prohibition as a cloak for his bigotry, and by Smith when he declared in his Oklahoma City speech that a large part of the opposition to him was due to his religious faith. Let us examine the validity of these contentions.

Dry Messiah

More than a year before the Houston convention Cannon began harping on the important role the religious issue would have in the campaign if Smith were chosen by the Democrats as their presidential nominee. Several times during 1927 he virtually declared that Governor Smith's religion should bar him from the White House. An address he delivered at Washington, D.C., entitled "The Conflict between Romanism and the Mexican Government," caught the fancy of Senator J. Thomas Heflin, of Alabama, so completely that this notorious Catholic-baiter had the entire speech reproduced in the *Congressional Record*. Thus the Bishop was publicly attacking Governor Smith's religious faith over twelve months before he was nominated. In view of this, it is impossible to see how the nominee and his campaign manager could be justly charged with "injecting" the issue into the campaign for political purposes.

Certainly the religious issue became paramount in the states in which Bishop Cannon operated, with the result that it was the bitterest and most vitriolic presidential contest held in the area since the Reconstruction era. In addition to the printed matter distributed by the Klan and kindred organizations, there was a "whispering campaign" against the private character, personal habits, and religious convictions of the Democratic nominee that probably surpassed anything of the kind in the history of the country. Similar tactics were employed throughout the nation, but they were especially virulent in the South. The fact that Governor Smith enjoyed in New York a reputation for courage, ability, and integrity meant nothing to his detractors, many of whom fired at him only from ambush.

Fairly early in the campaign Bishops Warren A. Candler and Collins Denny of the Southern Methodist Church issued a statement deploring the entry of bishops and ministers of their church into the contest. In reply Bishops Cannon, John M. Moore, Edwin D. Mouzon, Horace M. Du Bose, and W. N. Ainsworth declared:

> It would be an unthinkable repudiation of our personal responsibility as Christian citizens, and a base betrayal of those who have a right to look to us for moral leadership, to retire from the field at this critical juncture. . . .

The Bishop and the Brown Derby

Bishop Cannon left the country in August for Europe and the sessions of the League of Nations and other international gatherings, but he was back the following month and at once began an intensive speaking campaign in Virginia. When on September 20 Governor Smith delivered his Oklahoma City speech, in which he denounced the intolerance of those who opposed him on religious grounds, the Bishop determined to tour the South at once.

"The idea of calling Protestant churches intolerant is a new thing in history," Bishop Cannon retorted. "The determination of the Democrats to force the religious issue to the front in this campaign is the most significant new development. In doing this they have dragged some dynamite into this fight. We did not inject the religious issue into the campaign. They have done it by deliberately branding every man opposed to Mr. Smith as a bigot. Mr. Raskob had the effrontery to declare that I was using prohibition as a cloak for my bigotry, notwithstanding my forty years' record as a prohibitionist."

Cannon announced that he would leave the following week on a speaking tour through Texas, Tennessee, Mississippi, Alabama, Georgia, Oklahoma, and Arkansas. He was mounting the stump daily in Virginia, and his itinerary on his projected trip called for several addresses a day, with frequent jumps of hundreds of miles. He was offered an airplane, but was afraid that this mode of travel would upset him and declined. He made the whirlwind tour by train, covering a large segment of the Southern and border states in an extraordinarily short time.

One of the arguments the Bishop advanced frequently against Governor Smith was that he drank "from four to eight cocktails a day." John Garland Pollard, who was campaigning in Virginia for Smith, despite his own lifelong adherence to the dry cause, took occasion to declare that, whereas the Bishop was assailing the Democratic nominee because of his supposed personal habits, "many of Cannon's most ardent supporters in the [Virginia] General Assembly were drunk while they were enacting 'dry' legislation."

The Smith-Hoover campaign brought large numbers of the clergy back into politics throughout the South. The gentlemen of the cloth had been relatively inactive in political matters since the adoption of the Eighteenth Amendment in 1919, but "Al's" nomination was too much for them, and they rushed into the fray once more. The brunt of the battle was borne by the Baptists and Methodists. While the total number of clergymen who denounced Smith from their pulpits was smaller than was generally supposed, many of those who did not actually preach against him made it plain that they were praying for his defeat, so the result was substantially the same. At virtually every anti-Smith meeting there were ministers on the platform. Generally the program opened and closed with prayer, and not infrequently the prayer was for a Hoover victory. Throughout the principal address ejaculations of "amen" or "amen, brother," were to be heard from the clergy on the platform or from the faithful in the audience. Often a hymn or two was sung. By such methods all the emotionalism of the prohibition campaigns of former years was revived, while at the same time the feverish activity of the electorate, and particularly of the women, was further stimulated by means of the uproar over Catholicism.

Dr. Arthur J. Barton, who had co-operated with Bishop Cannon in sending out the call for the Asheville conference, stated frankly in a Birmingham address that the religious issue was more important than the prohibition issue.[6]

"Elect Al Smith to the presidency," said Dr. Barton, "and it means that the floodgates of immigration will be opened, and that ours will be turned into a civilization like that of continental Europe. Elect Al Smith and you will turn this country over to the domination of a foreign religious sect, which I could name, and Church and State will once again be united."

The Rev. Bob Jones, who spoke from the same platform, had the following to say on this subject: "I'll tell you, brother, that the big issue we've got to face ain't the liquor question. I'd rather see a saloon on every corner in the South than see the foreigners elect Al Smith President!"

As election day neared, the campaign grew increasingly frenzied, and hundreds of speakers harangued the populace throughout the South. Although Cannon's wife had been gravely ill for months with high blood pressure and was at death's door, he continued to speak in all parts of Virginia, sometimes making two

or three addresses in one day. He still maintained that anyone
who charged him with opposing Governor Smith on religious
grounds was guilty of "a malicious political falsehood," but he referred regularly to Raskob as "this wet Roman Catholic Knight
of Columbus and chamberlain of the Pope of Rome." Shortly before the election he composed a terrific broadcast against the
Catholic Church. This fierce assault on the Pope and all his works
was entitled: "Is Southern Protestantism More Intolerant than
Romanism?" The Bishop explained that he had written it "in reply
to the baseless and unjustified accusations of bigotry and intolerance made against him [Cannon] first by John Jacob Raskob and
later by Governor Alfred E. Smith."

Bishop Cannon fired this six-column howitzer so late in the
campaign that there was little or no opportunity for reply. It was
published as a paid advertisement in numerous newspapers and
was printed in leaflet form and distributed widely. Many papers
refused to publish it, even as an advertisement, so flagrantly
anti-Catholic were its contents. At least four and probably more
Virginia dailies declined to carry it, but it appeared in various
weeklies in the last issue before the election, when there was no
opportunity for an answer. The effect upon the dwellers in the
rural districts who had never seen a Catholic can readily be
imagined.

The Bishop opened this blast by characterizing as "deliberate,
malicious, political falsehoods" the charges that he was opposed
to Smith because Smith was a Catholic. He expressed the belief
that millions of Catholics "will be saved by their faith in Christ"
and declared that the Catholic Church is intolerant because Pope
Pius XI had said that non-Catholics "are strangers to the hope of
life and salvation." He then went on to quote from encyclicals
and other pronouncements issued by the popes at various times.
One Pope was quoted as denouncing the Masons, another the
Bible societies and the Y.M.C.A. He cited papal utterances in
opposition to the separation of church and state, as well as interpretations by Dr. John A. Ryan, director of the department of
social action, National Catholic Welfare Conference, of the Catholic position on this and other questions. Concerning the attitude
of Catholicism toward Protestant marriages, Bishop Cannon said:

"Is it intolerant or bigoted to refuse to agree that Romanism has no [*sic*] right to pass judgment upon the validity of marriages performed by Protestant ministers or by the State, and thus brand as adulterers those who have contracted marriages made without the sanction of Romanism, and as a consequence brands children of such marriages as bastards?"

He then quoted from the *Missionary*, "official national organ of the Catholic Missionary Union," published in Washington, which declared that "all Catholic lovers of Christ are feverishly praying for Governor Smith's success," and that "America is going to become pro-Catholic all at once." He also quoted from the *Union and Times*, official organ of the Catholic diocese of Buffalo, which said that "the Protestant Church in the United States has existed upon the unestablished fact that this is a Protestant country," and that "were a Catholic elected tomorrow . . . the Protestant Church would quickly sink from view." Both these publications were described by Bishop Cannon as "official organs of the Roman Catholic Church." He then declared that those who preferred for various reasons not to vote for a Catholic for President did not do so in "violation of either the letter or the spirit of the Constitution," since "the Constitution forbids the passage of any law prohibiting the election of any man because of the religious views which he may hold," but "the Constitution does not forbid any man from voting against any other man because of his religious views."

Replying to these and other assertions made by Bishop Cannon in this article, Dr. John A. Ryan, from whom he had quoted at considerable length, said in *Current History* for December 1928:

The greater part of this article was either completely untrue or gravely misleading. Among the untruths were the following assertions: That according to the Catholic Church, no Protestant can be saved; that according to Dr. Ryan, the Government of the United States is morally obligated to profess and promote the Catholic religion; that a Catholic's religious belief "compels him not to follow his conscience, no matter what it may dictate"; that the Catholic "brands all non-Catholic marriages as adulterous, and the children of such marriages as illegitimate"; that Pope Pius IX pronounced education outside of the Catholic Church, including

The Bishop and the Brown Derby

our public school system, "a damnable heresy." The misleading statements included references to Masonry, Bible Societies, the Y.M.C.A, the reception of the Papal Legate by Mayor Walker and Governor Smith, misused quotations from a chapter contributed by me to the volume *The State and the Church,* and characterization of two Catholic papers from which quotations were made as "official organs of the Roman Catholic Church." Just how Bishop Cannon could reconcile statements and actions of this sort with his sense of justice and decency, I am unable to imagine. . . .

Since the foregoing was not published until December, it appeared a month or more after the poison had been broadcast and the ballots had been counted.

The Bishop was still denying vigorously that he was opposed on religious grounds to the Democratic nominee for the presidency when election day arrived. Governor Smith, with his insouciant and salty personality, his East Side accent, his brown derby, and his cigar, had toured the country to the tune of *The Sidewalks of New York.* Herbert Hoover, known throughout the world for his humanitarian work, and recognized as an able Cabinet member, had read a few dull speeches and made one or two trips in which he demonstrated his ineptitude as a political campaigner. Nevertheless he swept the country. The campaign Bishop Cannon had waged proved remarkably effective, for the erstwhile "solid" South was smashed into fragments. Of the fourteen states in which the anti-Smith Democrats had operated, Hoover carried eight. Seven of the eight had gone Democratic in 1920 or 1924, or both, and four had been Democratic since Reconstruction.

The Bishop lost no time in elucidating the outcome for the benefit of all concerned. Said he:

> The unprecedented defeat of Governor Smith, the wet, Tammany candidate, for the presidency, is an indignant, overwhelming repudiation of the proposal by the people of our country to place the national government in the hands of the wet sidewalks of our cities, aided and abetted by a selfish, so-called liberal element of high society life. This insolent challenge of a sordid, unpatriotic Tammanyism and its self-indulgent allied forces has met with a response which has shown the world the genuine, idealistic, truly progressive Americanism of our people. . . . The pro-

hibition referendum so long desired by the wets has been held, and the enemies of the Eighteenth Amendment have been ignominiously routed.

The Bishop's caustic references during the campaign to persons of Catholic and Jewish faith and to immigrants from southern and eastern Europe, on the supposed ground that they were supporters of Governor Smith, naturally aroused the ire of those elements. He was quoted in the *Baltimore Sun* as having said at Cambridge, Maryland, for example:

> Governor Smith wants the Italians, the Sicilians, the Poles and the Russian Jews. That kind has given us a stomachache. We have been unable to assimilate such people in our national life, so we shut the door to them. But Smith says, "give me that kind of people." He wants the kind of dirty people that you find today on the sidewalks of New York.

This brought a reply from Jacob Billikopf, of Philadelphia, nationally known humanitarian and social worker, and a Russian Jew. "How excruciatingly painful such words are to those of us — be we Italians, Poles or Russian Jews — who have striven to lead useful lives and who are aiming constantly to make this a better and a greater country!" wrote Dr. Billikopf; and he went on to say:

> Were the Prophet of Nazareth to come back to earth, and were He to apply for admission to this country, the Bishop would deny Him such admission because He did not belong to the superior [?] Nordics, who, as is well known, are an anthropological fiction, invented in Germany, and there used as a basis for propaganda during the World War. And were the Apostles to land at Ellis Island, the Bishop would demand their immediate expulsion, both because they were Asiatics and because they could not qualify under the quota law!

During the weeks that followed the election Mrs. Cannon, who had been confined to her bed in Washington, grew worse. On the night of November 25 she suffered a paralytic stroke. The Bishop spoke in New York next day before the New York Methodist Preachers' Association on the outcome of the campaign. On November 27 he was back at her bedside, after experiences in

The Bishop and the Brown Derby

Gotham allegedly involving another woman which were to be the subject of controversies and lawsuits for years to come, and which will be dealt with in detail in another chapter. Mrs. Cannon died that night.

Six weeks later the *Christian Herald,* of New York, made the remarkable announcement that it had unanimously awarded Bishop Cannon a trip to the Holy Land "as the American who during 1928 made the most significant contribution to religious progress." Stanley High, editor of the paper, explained that the Bishop had been chosen because of his "long and distinguished Christian leadership, and in particular because of his campaign in the South on behalf of prohibition before the last national election."

"The wets reviled him," said Mr. High, "and the wet press made him the brunt of its caricatures. But he never flinched, and now in victory he asks no reward for himself."

It was generally agreed that this avatar of righteousness would wield great influence with the incoming Hoover administration. H. L. Mencken, to whom the Bishop referred in 1927 as "the idol of the sensuous, profane and lawless elements of our country," wrote following the election:

"Bishop Cannon will be far more influential at Washington after March 4th than ever the Hon. Harry Micajah Daugherty was in the days of Harding. The course of legislation will be determined to a large extent by his prayers, which are powerful and long. He knows what he wants, and his episcopal blood is steaming."

CHAPTER *XV*

Idyll in a Bucketshop

THE DEFEAT of Governor Smith and the breaking of the once solid South rocketed Bishop Cannon into a position of prestige and influence never before equaled by a cleric in the history of the United States. Mencken rightly described him as "the most powerful ecclesiastic ever heard of in America."

The Bishop lost little time in displaying his new-found puissance. Secretary of the Treasury Andrew W. Mellon had expressed opposition to appropriating an additional $25,000,000 for prohibition enforcement, on the ground that such a trebling of the amount allotted for this purpose could not be carried out "wisely and effectively" until a survey was made to determine just how the money was to be used. Bishop Cannon promptly sent a telegram to Mellon saying:

> It will be difficult for the average citizen to believe that there is much zeal and eagerness on the part of the Secretary of the Treasury to secure adequate enforcement, if he refuses this opportunity to develop and carry out an adequate program. . . .

The message also was signed by Bishop Thomas Nicholson, president of the Anti-Saloon League, and Dr. E. L. Crawford, secretary of the Southern Methodist Board of Temperance and Social Service. But Dr. Clarence True Wilson, secretary of the Northern Methodist Board of Temperance, Prohibition and Public Morals, disagreed with the attitude expressed and supported Secretary Mellon. With the temperance forces divided on the issue, the additional appropriation was cut to $1,719,654.

Idyll in a Bucketshop

Bishop Cannon sailed for the Holy Land in February, as the guest of the *Christian Herald*, which, as previously noted, had awarded him its accolade for his superlative "contribution to religious progress" during the religious war on Al Smith. With him, as his "secretary," went one Mrs. Helen Hawley McCallum, whom we shall meet again in subsequent chapters.

The pair dropped out of the public eye until they sailed back from Southampton on the *Olympic* in April. While crossing the Atlantic from England the Bishop received a radiogram from the unregenerate Representative Fiorello H. LaGuardia, of New York, puckishly demanding to know why he had chosen "a wet ship instead of a dry one." Bishop Cannon replied solemnly, after landing, that "other matters besides 'wet' and 'dry' enter into the choice of a ship," but that "all things being equal, certainly I should select a dry ship." Commenting on the sale of liquor by westward-bound vessels of the United States Lines, he expressed himself as favoring a law to prevent "such cowardly, contemptible methods."

President Hoover was about to appoint his famous Law Enforcement Commission, one of whose functions would be to scrutinize the "experiment" which he had termed "noble in motive and far reaching in purpose." The Bishop had sent a cable from Cairo during his pilgrimage to Palestine suggesting to the White House that the commission include at least one ardent prohibitionist conversant with the entire prohibition movement for the previous quarter of a century, as well as "an honest, outstanding opponent of the prohibition law," and a woman. Hoover's announcement of the commission's personnel in May showed that he had followed the Bishop's advice in all three particulars. Two months later, when George W. Wickersham, chairman of the commission, declared publicly that if the states would lend better co-operation in the enforcement of the prohibition statutes, both "national and state laws might be modified so as to become reasonably enforceable," his assertion was attacked by Bishop Cannon as "premature and defeatist." It was the Bishop's view that Chairman Wickersham should not have voiced such an opinion before his commission had much more than begun its study of the law-enforcement problem.

Cannon declared, during the late spring, that the daily press was a major barrier in the way of adequate enforcement of the prohibition law. It appeared that the editors of the country were mulishly refusing to recognize the law's transcendent benefits.

While this discussion was going forward, preparations were under way for what J. Fred Essary, of the *Baltimore Sun,* termed "the bitterest political struggle in the nation." This was the approaching election of a governor of Virginia. The Old Dominion was the only state to choose a governor in 1929, and it had been carried by Herbert Hoover the preceding year. Both national political organizations considered the Virginia election of prime importance, for if this long-time Democratic stronghold could be carried again by the Republicans, and in a state contest, the phenomenon would have extraordinary significance. It was even reported that President Hoover would take a hand in the canvass.

The embattled anti-Smith Democrats of Virginia who had voted for Hoover in 1928 held a meeting in February 1929 at Lynchburg and urged the faithful to stay out of the Democratic primary the following August, since participants in Virginia primaries are regarded as morally bound to support the nominees in the succeeding November election. Furthermore, the "Hoovercrats," as they had been sarcastically dubbed by Senator Carter Glass the preceding year, announced their intention of holding a convention in the summer, at which, "if it deemed such a course proper," a ticket for state offices would be named.

Bishop Cannon did not attend the Lynchburg conclave, but he sent a long statement that was read to the assembled delegates. It appeared from this document that the Bishop's head had been turned by the immense power that had come to him. His pronunciamento not only included his customary denunciation of Messrs. Smith and Raskob, but actually demanded a public apology from the Democratic leaders of Virginia for the things they had said about him and the other anti-Smith Democrats during the campaign of 1928. He had offered no apologies for the objurgations he had hurled at them, but they must nevertheless immolate themselves before him, or he would not enter the primary!

"Will these leaders," said the Bishop, "frankly and publicly agree that holding the views they did, the Anti-Smith Democrats were conscientious and were justified in their active opposition to . . . Smith, and will they withdraw their denunciations of the Anti-Smith Democrats as 'traitors and intolerant bigots'? . . . Can these leaders who thoroughly misunderstood the situation and so fiercely and unjustifiably denounced men for following their moral convictions, be accepted again as leaders, with confidence and without loss of self-respect, unless they frankly and publicly admit their mistakes?"

The Bishop also laid down a further condition to be met by Governor Harry F. Byrd, Senator Glass, and the other Democratic leaders if they wanted him back in the party: they must "openly and actively" call for the retirement of the Smith-Raskob leadership.

When Bishop Cannon struck this megalomaniac pose, the Democratic leadership of Virginia not only did not apologize to him; it had no word to say in opposition to Smith and Raskob. Had the Bishop been conciliatory, Governor Byrd, Senator Glass, and the rest might have moved against Raskob's retention of the party reins, but now they saw clearly that any move in that direction would be construed as having been made in obedience to ecclesiastical orders.

During the spring three Democrats announced their candidacies for the Governorship, subject to the August primary. They were John Garland Pollard, who had been a candidate in the three-cornered race of 1917, when Dr. Cannon threw his support to J. Taylor Ellyson, and Westmoreland Davis was nominated; G. Walter Mapp, spokesman for the Anti-Saloon League of Virginia in the General Assembly for a decade, who had run for governor in 1925, with Bishop Cannon's support, but had been defeated by Byrd; and Rosewell Page, a brother of Thomas Nelson Page, and for many years a state official. All three had supported Smith for President with varying degrees of intensity.

Before these candidacies were made known, great pressure had been put upon Governor Byrd, the leader of the state Democratic machine, to support someone as his successor in the gubernatorial chair who was *persona grata* to Bishop Cannon. A substantial element of the machine favored this course as the only means of avoiding an outright defeat in the primary or the election. But Byrd was adamant against any such move. Although personally and politically dry, he preferred to go down fighting rather than surrender to Cannon. So he prevailed upon the machine to back Pollard, likewise personally and politically dry, and one of the leading Baptists of the state, a dean at the College of William and Mary, who was as distasteful to Cannon as anybody in Virginia.

Since Cannon had been closely associated with Mapp when the latter was a member of the state Senate, it was generally assumed that he would support Mapp in the primary. Mapp was a man of much more tolerance and personal magnetism than some Anti-Saloon League spokesmen, and while he had made one or two speeches for Smith the previous autumn, he had said nothing to offend the "Hoovercrats." Besides, the Bishop had stated on more than one occasion during the Smith-Hoover campaign that he would cast his vote in that contest for Senator Claude A. Swanson and Congressman P. H. Drewry, both Smith supporters. In addition, the "declaration of principles" adopted by the anti-Smith Democrats at Asheville had said:

> We specifically assert and emphasize the prime necessity for the maintenance in unimpaired vigor of the Democratic Party in every Southern State. We favor and shall work for the election of dry Democratic candidates for the Senate and House of Representatives of the United States. We shall vigorously oppose any effort which may be made by the Republican party to take advantage of differences among Southern Democrats concerning the presidential nominee to elect in any Southern state Republican nominees for the United States Senate, for the national House of Representatives or for any state offices. We believe that the best interests, not only of the Southern states, but of the nation, demand the maintenance of Democratic control of all local government in the Southern states. . . .

In view of the foregoing, and Cannon's support in 1928 of men who voted and worked for Smith, Virginians blinked their eyes when the Bishop issued a statement on June 1 in which he said he would not cast his ballot for any man who had voted for Smith, that he would not enter the August primary, and that all other anti-Smith Democrats should do likewise. He went on to declare that "up to this good hour, no retraction has been made by those Virginia State Democratic leaders who so loudly and persistently attacked Anti-Smith Democrats as 'traitors and intolerant bigots,' etc., nor has there been any open declaration or repudiation of the Smith-Raskob national leadership for its betrayal of Southern prohibition Democrats." He added that there was no reason to suppose that any of the three Democratic gubernatorial candidates would, in the event of his election, refuse in 1932 to support Alfred E. Smith or a man holding his views on prohibition, if such a man were to be nominated.

So much for Bishop Cannon's manifesto of June 1. It laid down dicta completely at variance with the unequivocal declarations he had made during the presidential contest the year before, but it was of great political significance, for it meant that the Democratic nominee for governor would be opposed in November by a coalition candidate backed by the same combination that had carried the state for Hoover twelve months previously. On June 18 the anti-Smiths held their convention in Roanoke, Virginia, and nominated Dr. William Moseley Brown, a thirty-five-year-old professor of psychology at Washington and Lee University, to be their standard-bearer. Shortly afterward the Republicans met in Richmond and likewise nominated Dr. Brown. The fight was on. Bishop Cannon had crawled into bed with the G.O.P. all over again and was engaged in an open effort to throw the state into the Republican column for the second time within a year. More, there was a distinct possibility that he would succeed. With his prestige enormously enhanced by the defeat administered to Smith the year before in Virginia and other Southern states, Democratic leaders felt that they were in for a hard struggle.

But, at this critical juncture, when the Bishop was seemingly riding the crest, when he was fast establishing himself as the undisputed dry leader of the country and apparently was so recognized by President Hoover, who had him to lunch at the White House and consulted him from time to time, his foot slipped. The morning papers of June 20 carried the well-nigh incredible news that this Bishop of the Southern Methodist Church, this consecrated leader of the "moral forces," had been for eight months during 1927 and 1928 a patron of Kable and Company, a New York bucketshop, then bankrupt and in the hands of the authorities. Not only had he been a patron of the concern; his ledger account proved that he had been one of its largest customers. The books showed that during the eight-month period in question the firm had bought for him stocks worth $477,000 and had sold them for approximately $486,000, all for the unbelievably small total payment by the Bishop of $2,500.

When these amazing revelations burst in the public prints, Dr. Cannon issued an explanation, which said, in part:

> For forty years I have engaged in business transactions of various kinds. I have openly bought and sold houses and lots, timber and stumpage, coal, cotton and bank stock and stocks and bonds listed on the New York Stock Exchange, first in Richmond from my personal acquaintances, Col. John P. Branch and Mr. Langbourne M. Williams, both Christian gentlemen, at the head of Richmond stock exchange houses.
>
> I learned of the monthly instalment purchase plan of Kable & Company. I thought the firm to be a reputable firm, and bought and sold some stock through it.

He also declared in another statement:

> I thought I was buying stocks for investment, buying on the partial payment plan, as any man may. I did not know there was any gambling by the company. . . . I do not feel that I did anything wrong in buying stocks on the partial payment plan, and I certainly did not intend to gamble.

He explained further that shortly before the close of the 1928 presidential campaign, the *New York Evening World* had informed him that it had affidavits relating to his dealings with Kable and Company, the partners of which were then under indictment for using the mails to defraud, and had offered to publish any explanation he desired to make. He replied that the *Evening World* had no right to ask him for an explanation, that he had "bought and sold stocks and bonds and any other kind of property," and that this inquiry into his private business affairs was "a contemptible Tammany trick." The newspaper withheld publication of the affidavits. It was not until some eight months later, when the bankruptcy hearings in the case were about to begin in New York, that the press of that city published the facts regarding Bishop Cannon's speculative dealings.

When the hearings got under way, Charles W. Kable, member of the firm, testified that Bishop Cannon's account "must have been speculative, in view of the amount and volume of the transactions." Harry L. Goldhurst, the other partner, and the actual head of the concern, testified that the Bishop had never bought a share of stock outright, and except for the purchase of two hundred shares of Hudson Motors on the partial-payment plan, he "speculated exclusively" in his dealings with Kable and Company. Goldhurst said, however, that Dr. Cannon's transactions were "on the partial payment plan," rather than marginal — whatever that may have meant.

Goldhurst also testified that he had been connected with the firm of Ebel and Company before he organized Kable and Company and that, while there, he had consummated stock transactions for Bishop Cannon. On March 17, 1927 Ebel and Company had been attacked as a "bucketshop" in the state courts by Attorney General Albert Ottinger. The firm was subsequently enjoined from doing business, and William J. Ebel, its head, was indicted on a charge of using the mails to defraud.

Publication of these titillating revelations rocked Methodism from stem to stern. The repercussions were severe enough in the cities, but at least in these relatively worldly and sophisticated centers of population the very idea of dealing in stocks was not something hideously wicked. In the country districts, however, the brethren, as they put on their black Sunday suits and scraped the mud from their shoes preparatory to climbing into their buggies or their Fords to attend church, were bewildered. After service they stood about in the summer heat under the trees, swapping ideas with their fellow parishioners, and wondered in bewildered fashion what it all could mean. They knew that the General Conference of the Southern Methodist Church in 1922 had unanimously adopted a resolution denouncing "all forms of gambling"; but here was a Bishop of that church, their own church, openly admitting that he had bought stocks through concerns that had been pronounced disreputable by the New York authorities. For many years these rural Methodists had regarded buying stocks as plain gambling, for their pastors had told them it was so.

Some of them recalled that Dr. Cannon himself had lashed out savagely at gambling. For example, he had been instrumental, with two other Methodist ministers, in breaking up the operation of gaming devices at the Virginia State Fair of 1908. Boxes of candy, canary birds, watches, and other articles, including money, were being won or lost on the turn of a wheel or by means of some other device. Cannon and his fellow clerics protested to the officers and directors of the fair and these practices were discontinued. The following year he wrote: "If any persons ought to be punished for . . . gambling operations, the very first ones should be the members of the churches."

Remembering the Bishop's long record of open hostility to games of chance, many Methodists and others refused to believe that he had knowingly been a plunger in the stock market. They took it for granted, too, that he had not dealt consciously with bucketshops, and they readily accepted his declaration that much of the criticism coming to him was stimulated by the "wet" and the "Roman Catholic influenced secular press."

The Southern Methodist Board of Temperance and Social Service, of which he was chairman, passed resolutions expressing confidence in his leadership after he had appeared before it and explained his dealings in stocks. The resolutions said that the "attacks on Bishop Cannon, in which the entire 'wet' press is engaged with evident unanimity, have been instigated by enemies of prohibition with the sole purpose of discrediting a great and influential leader of the prohibition forces of the nation." The board pledged him its "confidence, gratitude and affection."

The *Christian Century*, a foremost Protestant organ without denominational affiliations, published in Chicago, came to his defense. Two of Bishop Cannon's associates in the Southern Methodist episcopacy also defended him publicly. Bishop Hiram A. Boaz said he had "no sympathy with the effort by some of the newspapers and the criminal liquor gang to besmirch the good name and lessen the influence of one of the greatest citizens of this country." Bishop John M. Moore intimated strongly that the

wets were solely responsible for the charges made against Bishop
Cannon of "gambling in a bucketshop."

The *Wall Street Journal,* on the other hand, said in a front-
page editorial published June 25 and headed "A Question of
Veracity":

> He [Bishop Cannon] must have known after a few transactions
> that he was not investing or even speculating; he was betting on
> the turn of the market. . . . If this sort of thing can be de-
> scribed as "buying stock for investment on the instalment plan"
> then drawing one card to an inside straight is conservative invest-
> ment. A man of truer principle would have offered no excuse.
> Legislation against gambling is almost as useless as legislation
> against drinking. . . .

The Rev. John Thompson, pastor of the largest Methodist
church in Chicago, the skyscraper Chicago Temple, said in a
sermon early in July:

> Bishop Cannon has brought reproach on the church of Christ
> and the cause so dear to Him and to all lovers of temperance and
> prohibition. He has given the enemy a good chance to scoff at all
> of us. The Church of which he is the Bishop cannot afford to ig-
> nore this. The Bishop's speculation raised the whole question of
> whether Jesus' way of life and the New Testament standards
> should be taken as seriously in relation to money matters as to
> prohibition.

These are only a few of the scores of published comments from
individuals, newspapers, magazines, and organizations throughout the country upon Bishop Cannon's ill-starred adventure with
the stock ticker. Few episodes of the kind in the history of American churches have aroused such widespread and furious controversy. In July the Bishop sent communications to the various
Christian Advocates declaring that he had "not violated any civil
or moral law" and that "at the proper time" he would ask his
church to make a full investigation of all the charges.

Hardly had he done so when the *New York World* and the
Chicago Tribune, both wringing-wet newspapers, published on
July 19 the fact that R. W. Boyden, chief enforcement officer for
the United States Food Administration, had rendered an official

opinion in 1918 which held that Dr. Cannon was a wartime flour-hoarder. The opinion was in response to a request for a ruling from Senator Carter Glass, then a member of the House.

Glass had learned on June 1, 1918 that Cannon had purchased 650 barrels of flour shortly before the Food Administration Law became effective on August 10, 1917, and the Virginia Representative had asked Boyden for a ruling on the "legal and moral" aspects of the transaction. Without giving Boyden Cannon's name or that of Blackstone College, he had placed before the Federal official Cannon's own written explanation that he had bought the flour "to protect Blackstone College from a possible rise in the cost of provisions for the next school year, and held it until I was satisfied that the price to be secured would amply protect us." Cannon went on to say that he then "sold the flour, and all the proceeds were turned into the treasury of Blackstone College."

"Clearly a hoarder" was Boyden's conclusion after a study of the case. His opinion, forwarded to Representative Glass by Food Administrator Herbert Hoover, said, in part:

> The man is clearly a hoarder under the terms of Sections VI and VII of the Food Act, because he held flour "in a quantity in excess of his reasonable requirements for use or consumption by himself and dependents for a reasonable time." Even if we assume that he really bought the flour for the benefit of the college, he is still a hoarder, for he held enough for three years' supply for the college.
>
> He is, by so doing, depriving some portion of the community of its fair share of a scarce food product. The better educated a man is, the more clearly he ought to see this moral principle. I am unable to persuade myself that a college has any special claim to consideration.

Since the purchase of the flour was made just before the Food Law became effective, no effort was made to prosecute Bishop Cannon. The law provided a penalty of two years in jail and a five-thousand-dollar fine for hoarders.

Following publication of these facts in the summer of 1929, the Bishop denied the correctness of Boyden's statement that he had bought three years' supply of flour for the college. He said he purchased the 650 barrels in April 1917; that the college was then using over forty barrels a month, and that he bought the flour on the assumption that 425 of the 650 barrels would last the college until June 1918. He said further that the files for this period had been destroyed by fire, but that he held the bulk of the flour only eighteen days and had then sold it at a profit of not more than $1,300, as far as he could ascertain from available records. The Bishop also produced a statement signed by the executive committee of the Blackstone board of trustees. This had been drawn up during the fall of 1928, at which time it had begun to look as though the "flour profiteering" story would get into the papers. The committee said:

> During the war, in order to make absolutely certain that the college should not suffer, even though the war should continue for two or three years, he [Cannon] made contracts for flour on the basis of his own credit, with the distinct understanding that, if there should be a loss on the contract, he would bear the loss; and that if there should be a profit, it would go toward the payment of obligations which he had assumed for the college. . . . We are satisfied that these reports which are being circulated to destroy his influence in this political campaign are without any foundation.

The *Lynchburg News,* published by Senator Glass, promptly countered by saying editorially: "The *News* is advised that the case is worse even than Bishop Cannon admits and that Bishop Cannon's statement about turning the proceeds of his flour speculation into the Blackstone treasury is not true." Senator Glass then wrote letters to a number of women's colleges asking them for data concerning their flour consumption, with a view to comparing it with the amount of flour claimed as necessary for Blackstone. With their replies before him, he summed up:

> Blackstone, in 1917, had a dining clientele of 385, eating [according to Bishop Cannon] 425 barrels of flour, while Randolph-Macon Woman's College at Lynchburg, with a clientele of 806 persons last year used but 175 barrels of flour; Sweet Briar College, Va., fed 600 persons with 183 barrels; Bryn Mawr, Pa., fed 607 persons with 116 barrels; Hood College, Frederick, Md., fed 475 with 117 barrels; Hollins College, Va., fed 480 with 126 barrels; Mills College, California, fed 723 persons with 119 barrels.

Thus the truly ravenous young women at Blackstone are seen to have eaten 309 loaves of bread apiece per year, if the Bishop's computation is to be accepted, as against an average of 68 loaves for the students at the other six colleges listed!

Boyden had charged Dr. Cannon with buying three years' supply of flour for Blackstone College at a time when profiteering in foodstuffs had become a national scandal, and when President Wilson had appealed to the patriotism of the people not to hoard. Cannon had replied that he purchased approximately a year and a half's supply. It is clear from the flour-consumption figures of other women's colleges that Boyden did not exaggerate, and that Cannon's statement was untrue.

While the Bishop was in the middle of the bucketshop and flour-hoarding controversies, two other charges were hurled at him. The first came from the Rev. Dr. Rembert G. Smith, a Methodist clergyman of Washington, Georgia, and the second from Representative George H. Tinkham, of Massachusetts, a Republican with a famous set of whiskers who was noted both as a foe of prohibition and as an African lion-hunter.

Dr. Smith charged in a letter to the *Lynchburg News* that the Southern Methodist Board of Temperance and Social Service had exceeded its authority during the Smith-Hoover contest of the year before when it lent some of its funds to its chairman, Bishop Cannon, for use in the campaign, and that it had also exceeded its authority in taking note of the bucketshop charges against the Bishop and expressing confidence in his integrity. Bishop Cannon replied that as an individual he had borrowed sufficient of the board's funds the previous summer to pay for typing and mailing the call for the Asheville conference, and that, when the conference was held, money was collected and the loan was repaid. In answer to Dr. Smith's contention that no general board of the church had the right to pass upon the character of a bishop, he said that the "public can determine whether when the chairman of a board is attacked it is proper for the board to declare 'its confidence in the leadership of said chairman.'"

He went on to say that Dr. Smith's communication had been republished in three Washington and Baltimore papers, "in which papers the amazing and absolutely false statement is also made that 'the records show that Bishop Cannon made two loans of $5,000 each to the Anti-Smith Democrats of Virginia.' These papers have been informed that 'the records' must be produced or full retraction made."

The declaration was inaccurate, but only as to details, and the vehemence of Cannon's denial is difficult to understand. He had lent the anti-Smith Democrats large sums. Representative Tinkham was one of many who considered the statement to be justified, for he seized upon the Bishop's denial as an opportunity to cite facts that he said were contained in the campaign expense returns filed by the anti-Smith Democrats of Virginia with the clerk of the House of Representatives. He declared that, according to these records, advances of more than $27,000 had been made by Bishop Cannon to the anti-Smith Democrats. He asked whether certain "unidentified loans in the returns" were made by the Bishop and, if not, by whom they were made. He also inquired whether the loans credited to the Bishop were his own personal funds and, if not, whose funds they were.

Cannon's reply, which seemed a tacit admission of the substantial accuracy of reports he had shortly before branded as "amazing and absolutely false," follows: "All loans to the headquarters committee of the Anti-Smith Democrats of Virginia in connection with the campaign of 1928 were made by James Cannon, Jr., personally, which loans were repaid to him from time to time as contributions were received for the work of the headquarters committee of the Anti-Smith Democrats of Virginia."

Upon receipt of this statement Tinkham suggested that the Department of Justice investigate Cannon's financial transactions during the campaign with a view to determining whether they came within the purview of the Federal Corrupt Practices Act. The Bishop retorted that he had written Attorney General Mitchell offering him access to any information he desired concerning his own activities and those of the Southern Methodist Board of Temperance and Social Service in the presidential campaign of 1928. He also took occasion to say, characteristically, that "Tinkham's attack upon me is simply one of his periodic attacks upon the South, prohibition and Methodism to convince his wet Roman Catholic Boston constituency that he should be retained as their Representative in Congress, which many of them seemed seriously to doubt in the last election."

For the moment, questions having to do with the Bishop's relationship to the Federal Corrupt Practices Act were not pursued further, but this issue was to be a lively one for years thereafter and was to drag almost interminably through congressional investigations and the courts.

Assailed and harassed more ferociously and from more different directions than perhaps any other bishop or minister in American history, Cannon concluded to issue an all-inclusive pronouncement in reply to what he termed the "sweeping slanderous attacks" made upon him by "wet and Roman Catholic and other newspapers throughout the country." This Niagara of words appeared on August 3, captioned "Unspotted from the World," the title of an editorial concerning his stock-market misadventures that had appeared in the *Richmond News Leader.* The manifesto's purpose, among other things, was to demonstrate that a bishop may engage in the kind of business dealings in which he had participated for forty years and still keep himself "unspotted from the world." Of all the many verbose pronouncements that had come from Cannon's pen, this was the pre-eminent example. Running to some eighteen thousand words, or roughly twenty newspaper columns, it discusses in considerable detail his entire business career; the "positively venomous" attacks made on him by Roman Catholic papers and the "intolerance and bigotry" of Roman Catholics; the stock-gambling charges, the flour-hoarding charges, the charges that he had misused funds of the Southern Methodist Board of Temperance and Social Service in the 1928 campaign, the conduct of the "Roman Catholic influenced secular press," the Smith-Hoover campaign, the Virginia gubernatorial campaign then in progress, and other matters too numerous to mention.

"Unspotted from the World" was given to the press, and it was also printed in leaflet form. The first fifty thousand copies of the leaflet were distributed gratis by the Bishop, at a cost to him of two thousand dollars, after which he announced that they could be procured at the rate of three for ten cents, ten for thirty cents, and forty for one dollar.

Idyll in a Bucketshop

Among the most arresting sections of the document was that which related to trading in stocks. Cannon discussed this question *in extenso,* developing his theories as to why there was no impropriety in a Methodist bishop's participation in such un-Methodistic activities.

"I had been brought up with the general idea of country and small town people that all trading in Wall Street stocks was gambling," he wrote, "but I was compelled to face the question in practical fashion as visualized in business men of reputation and standing, not only in the community, but in the churches." He concluded that "there was very much latent hypocrisy in the attitude of very many persons on this subject," and he went on to say:

> Gambling is difficult to define, wholly and completely. The throwing of dice, shooting of craps, the purchase of lottery tickets are all clearly gambling, for there is no element of skill or intelligence involved, nothing but pure chance. Chance and skill enter in card playing; chance and knowledge into horse-racing. . . . I think there should be an end of the hypocritical attitude which insists upon differentiating between the trading in stocks and in other property values, for if such trading in stocks and bonds is immoral, then trading in lots, wheat, and other commodities is immoral, for both represent trading in actual business values. . . .

The above-quoted reference to "country and small town people" was widely regarded as a slur upon the citizens of the village and rural districts, the very people who had rallied in well-nigh solid phalanxes behind the Bishop in many a hard-fought struggle on behalf of morality and the higher life. Furthermore, Cannon's differentiation of crap-shooting and dice-throwing from card-playing and horseracing was interpreted by some as signifying that poker and pari-mutuels had received his apostolic benediction. The latter view was expressed, in substance, by H. L. Mencken in the *Baltimore Evening Sun* for September 2, when he said:

> I cannot go into his ideas at length, for his discussion of them . . . runs to many thousands of words, but their essence may be

briefly stated. It is this: That gambling is immoral only when it is based upon pure chance. The instant skill or judgment enters into it, however defective that skill or judgment may be, it becomes as completely moral as any other business transaction. This is the test: Does the gambler think he has an edge on the other fellow? If the answer is no, he is a sinner and doomed to Hell. But if it is yes, he is as innocent as a Y.M.C.A. secretary slapping a back. . . .

The Bishop declared that his church evidently did not feel that his business activities had affected his spirituality, since the General Conference had elected him a Bishop in the full knowledge that he was at the time "a school teacher, an editor, an Assembly Superintendent, a reform official, a part owner of a daily newspaper, and the owner of a summer resort hotel." But the climax of his "bull *Immaculatum . . . ab hoc sæculo*," as Mencken termed it, was reached at about the halfway mark, or some nine thousand words from the beginning, where he said:

> The readers of this statement are left to judge for themselves how it happened that *this stock trading story, followed by the flour profiteering story, followed by the Smith charge of loaning church funds for political purposes, after slumbering for seven months, all came to life once more after my letter of June 1st to the Anti-Smith Democratic Convention. Were these things accidental, or were they the answer to Raskobism in the Virginia State election? Is not this method of attack eminently characteristic of Tammanyism?*

And bursting into capitals for the only time during the entire eighteen thousand words, the Bishop shouted:

IS NOT THIS A CONCERTED DESPERATE EFFORT OF RASKOBISM TO DESTROY MY INFLUENCE WITH THE PEOPLE OF VIRGINIA IN THE APPROACHING ELECTION? WILL THE PEOPLE OF VIRGINIA APPROVE OR DISAPPROVE OF THESE ATTACKS UPON MY REPUTATION AND INFLUENCE BY THESE POLITICAL ASSASSINS?

Such, in substance, was Bishop Cannon's manifesto, "Unspotted from the World." Comment upon it ranged from fulsome eulogy to scathing criticism. The *Christian Century* came to Cannon's

Idyll in a Bucketshop

defense again with the statement: "Every specific charge against the Bishop breaks down. He had neither profiteered by hoarding food in wartime, nor misused church funds, nor gambled, nor neglected his work to make money." The *Outlook and Independent* said, on the other hand: "No one else could have painted a harsher picture of him than he paints of himself between the lines of this casuistical apologia. The outline he draws of himself is not that of a man of the cloth, but that of a shrewd trader and hard-bitten politician. The details are filled in with unconscious savagery." The *Wall Street Journal* commented: "If, as he says, he has been speculating in stocks for twenty years, he must have known that he was trading in a bucketshop and, therefore, not speculating in stocks, but merely betting on the price movement. His transactions were on a par with betting on a horse race or at a roulette table."

The net effect of Bishop Cannon's broadside seems to have been unfavorable. The Bishop distributed enough leaflets to disillusion large numbers of his admirers. They had completely discounted the stories in the "wet" and the "Roman Catholic" press as slanderous attacks on a great and good man, but when Cannon himself admitted in "Unspotted from the World" that he had been trading in stocks for twenty years and argued that his conduct was entirely proper, their disillusionment was extreme. It was a bit too much for "country and small town people" to digest all at once. Their idol had feet of clay after all.

They would have been shocked still further had they been informed that despite the Bishop's extensive trading in the market during 1927 and 1928, the personal-property books of Nottoway County, Virginia, where he filed his tax returns, showed ownership of not one single share in either year. Stocks in foreign corporations were taxable, whether bought "on the partial payment plan" or not. Having concealed much of his income from the tax authorities over a long period, he sought to hide his wild stock speculation from the public, and at the same time evaded payment to the state of taxes on these securities which were rightfully due it. The facts as to Cannon's falsification of his tax returns, for both income and personal property, are being published here for the first time.

An intriguing item appeared in the press at this period. It was the news that a Washington residence that Bishop Cannon's admirers had bought for him in 1926 had just been condemned by the Federal government. The structure overlooked the Capitol grounds, and the government needed the site for the new Supreme Court Building. The strange thing about this was that it had been considered certain for years that the site in question would be taken over by the Federal government. The *New York Times* for August 7, 1929 said so, and it added that on November 17, 1926, (only a few weeks before the distribution of a circular asking Cannon's friends for contributions toward a home), "the Public Buildings Committee announced its approval of the plans for the Supreme Court building and authorized condemnation proceedings against the property" on which the subsequently purchased house was located.

The circular, sent out in December 1926, said:

> In the critical days in the Virginia [prohibition] fight he [Cannon] contributed approximately $60,000 (all that he had), to insure the success of the movement. . . . Chiefly because of this fact, Bishop Cannon has not been able to buy a home for his family, for at the critical time when money was absolutely necessary to clinch the nails already driven and to press the work to a successful conclusion, he said to his personal friends, "I have been saving money to buy a home, but it is better to save the boys of our State and nation from the saloon than for my single family to have a home."

Funds adequate to the desired purpose were not forthcoming, according to James P. Jones, of Richmond, a leader on the committee that solicited contributions. Whereas it was stated in the newspapers that $12,500 had been raised, at least half of this was put up by the Bishop himself, Jones said.[1] The committee proceeded to acquire a "home" for Cannon, which Cannon selected,[2] but which was sure to be condemned in a short time. The American Issue Publishing Company, the publishing concern of the Anti-Saloon League, with headquarters near by, was owner of the property and had bought it for $11,000 in 1921. Is it conceivable that this organization, with which Bishop Cannon was in close touch, did not know that the Supreme Court Building was to be placed there, as had been announced a few weeks previously by the Public Buildings Committee?

At all events, the Bishop expressed a desire for the property, and the company sold it to him for $12,500. Cannon never lived in it and said he was surprised to learn, soon after it was presented to him, that the Federal authorities proposed to acquire it. When the proceedings took place, in 1929, the Bishop said he thought the place was worth at least $20,000.³ The government refused to pay that amount and condemned the house and lot for $16,000. Cannon then declared that, "as a loyal citizen," he agreed "that the government has a right to acquire property for the general welfare." Asked by a newspaper whether he planned to reinvest the $16,000 in another "home," he replied that he never discussed his private affairs.

As a matter of fact, Cannon waited nine years, until 1938, during which time he had use of the full $16,000. He then bought a house at 24 North Allen Avenue, Richmond, for $4,800.⁴ He and his second wife lived there until his death six years later. This seems to have been the only thing properly describable as a "home" that the Cannons inhabited for any appreciable length of time. It will readily be seen that the difference between the $4,800 this place cost in 1938 and the $16,000 Cannon received for the Washington property in 1929 is $11,200. If the Bishop himself put up $6,500 of the original $12,500 — and Jones believes that this was the approximate figure — he made $3,500 on the deal, plus the $6,000 raised by his admirers. Not a bad piece of business for the Bishop. Jones states that those who contributed the $6,000 had no objection to his using the money for any purpose he saw fit. They were, he says, not at all irked by his making a profit, or by his waiting nine years to buy the home to which they had subscribed.

But what of the febrile political campaign in Virginia? It will be recalled that there were three candidates for the Democratic gubernatorial nomination in the August primary, and that the Republicans and anti-Smiths had chosen Dr. William Moseley Brown in June as their nominee. Bishop Cannon's "Unspotted from the World," which appeared just before the primary, urged the anti-Smiths to stay out of it, since by remaining aloof they would be free to support Dr. Brown in November. When the primary vote was counted a few days later, it was found that Dr. John Garland Pollard, the Bishop's arch-enemy for many years, had been nominated by a huge majority. This merely increased Bishop Cannon's desire to elect Dr. Brown.

But the Bishop was confronted with the grievous fact that he had no issue upon which to rouse the Methodists and Baptists. Thousands of these had battled beside him the year before when the twin specters of usquebaugh and the Vatican stirred the brethren to holy zeal. But with Dr. Pollard, a pillar of the Baptists and a lifelong personal and political dry, running for governor on a platform calling for the continuation of the state program so ably launched by Governor Byrd, there was precious little opportunity to work the electorate up into another sweat over the Pope and Tammany Hall. The Bishop sought to do so by making furious attacks on Smith and Raskob, but his clamorous assertions that they were the principal issues in this state contest left many of his former allies cold. They had "detoured Al" the year before, but now that he had been beaten, they were coming back into the Democratic Party as they had promised to do. The Bishop, on the other hand, had repudiated his own Asheville "declaration of principles" by supporting the Republican nominee.

A few days after the primary Bishop Cannon sailed for Europe, to be gone five weeks. It soon became plain that, in addition to the fact that he had no issue worthy of the name, his political influence had been undermined by the bucketshop and flour-hoarding charges. Throughout the nation people were laughing at him, and nothing is more fatal to a moral leader than to be laughed at. Quips about him began appearing in the public prints; the "Bishop Cannon cocktail," a potent concoction of vermouth and gin, made its appearance; and the Southern Club of Columbia University put on a skit that presented "Bishop Shotgun" speculating feverishly in Wall Street. All this had its inevitable effect on the Bishop's prestige, both in Virginia and throughout the nation.

Idyll in a Bucketshop

But his bellicosity was unaffected, for upon landing in New York on his return from Europe in the middle of September he delivered himself of an interview in which he declared that City Police Commissioner Grover A. Whalen should be removed from office and District Attorney Joab H. Banton impeached for their failure to act against the thirty-two thousand speakeasies reported to be operating in New York City. Breathing lava and brimstone, the Bishop then proceeded to Virginia.

There the Pollard-Brown campaign was in full swing, and many were speculating whether Bishop Cannon would take the stump in Dr. Brown's behalf, as he had done so intensively the year before on behalf of Hoover. Some expressed the view that he knew Brown was beaten and that he would not risk his prestige in a losing cause. Others thought he would plunge into the contest and actively support the coalition candidate. Weeks passed and no word came from him. Early in October he announced that the Volstead Act ought to be amended to make the buyer of intoxicants equally guilty with the seller, a suggestion that did not evoke anything like unanimous approval from the other dry leaders in Washington. But still he remained mum as to the Virginia campaign. Finally on October 8 he turned loose nearly six newspaper columns on the issues of the contest. Yet he said little or nothing that he had not said before. He reviewed the contest of 1928 in immense detail, duly castigated Raskob as a "Roman Catholic Knight of Columbus and chamberlain of the Pope's household," noted that the Democratic leaders of Virginia had not apologized for their conduct the previous year, denounced Pollard, and extolled Brown. He did not indicate what further part, if any, he would take in the campaign during the month that remained before the election.

Three days after the appearance of this statement Bishop Cannon suddenly announced that he was sailing at once for his see in Brazil, to preside over his episcopal conferences there. He expressed surprise that the public had been unaware that he would have to leave for South America in the middle of the campaign and pointed out that his conference dates had been published in the church press. Hardly anyone had noticed that they had ap-

211

peared in the *Nashville Christian Advocate* on September 13 and in subsequent issues. They were not published in the *Richmond Christian Advocate* until the issue of October 11, the day he sailed. Besides, the Bishop had not presided over this Brazilian conference the year before, and some persons doubtless concluded that he might not do so again.

At all events, he departed abruptly on October 11, to be absent until December. Although he could have voted by mail, he said most incomprehensibly before sailing that he was sorry he "would not be able to be present and vote in November for Dr. William M. Brown." Thus, while he was urging everyone else to vote for Brown, he did not do so himself.[5] He also stated in the same interview that he was "exceedingly optimistic" over Brown's prospects, but his manner of leaving was widely interpreted to mean that, as a matter of fact, he saw his candidate was beaten. Certainly his "optimism" was without foundation, for when the votes were counted less than a month later, it was found that Dr. Pollard had won in a landslide. His majority of 70,000 was the second largest received by any gubernatorial candidate in the history of the state.

This triumph for his enemy of many years' standing must have been a bitter pill for the Bishop. His signal failure to persuade the electorate to follow him into the coalition camp of the candidate whose motley backing of prohibitionists and Republicans was depicted by cartoonists as a "camelephant" was sufficiently distressing; but when the man who sent Cannon reeling back in defeat was as personally distasteful to him as John Garland Pollard, the dose cannot have been other than gall and wormwood. A few days after the election he filed a cable from Montevideo, Uruguay, expressing regret at the outcome and reiterating that "Raskobian liberalism versus Southern Democracy still remains the outstanding Democratic party issue."

The fact was that he had long given a slashing repudiation by the people of the state in which he was supposed to be most influential. True, he had had practically nothing in the way of "moral issues" with which to rouse the populace, but if he had played his cards differently, he might have retained a large share of his former prestige, despite the bucketshops and the hoarded flour. If, immediately following the presidential election of 1928, he had issued a conciliatory statement to the Democrats who had supported Smith, giving them credit for having been conscientious in the course they pursued and declaring that he would return to the party at once, he might have had the Democratic leadership of Virginia eating out of his hand. Indeed, despite his truculent attitude, some of the most influential of the politicians wished to compromise by agreeing on a candidate satisfactory to him. Had it not been for Governor Byrd, who flatly refused to consent to such a course, the scheme would almost certainly have been carried out.

It must be borne in mind that, for months following the Smith-Hoover election, the Democratic leaders in Virginia and the rest of the South were simply paralyzed. They did not know what to do or where to turn. If Bishop Cannon had promptly come back to the fold, he might have held the balance of power in almost every Southern state. But he misjudged the situation. He blundered the day after the election by issuing his statement terming the Smith candidacy "this insolent challenge of a sordid, unpatriotic Tammanyism, and its self-indulgent allied forces," and he blundered again three months later when he informed the Democratic leadership that it would have to put on sackcloth in order to receive his episcopal absolution. He overestimated the power he wielded and believed that he could repeat his victory of 1928. For almost the first time in his life his political judgment had proved worthless.

Meanwhile it had become certain that the Bishop's dealings with shady brokerage houses would be scrutinized when the General Conference of his church met at Dallas, Texas, in May 1930. Harry Goldhurst and Charles W. Kable had been indicted when Kable and Company, the Bishop's principal bucketshop, failed, and examination of the company's affairs had shown that Cannon had had extensive dealings with the firm. Then Goldhurst and Kable pleaded guilty in October 1929 to charges of conspiracy and fraudulent sales of stocks through the mails. Goldhurst got five years in Atlanta and Kable received a suspended sentence.

Dry Messiah

Many Methodist ministers and laymen were greatly embarrassed by the unprecedented situation in which they thus found themselves. One of their bishops had admitted substantial business transactions with two men who had confessed to criminal offenses, and one of those men had gone to the Federal penitentiary. It seemed highly important that something be done to purge the church of any responsibility for this state of things. A score of leading laymen consequently began framing charges for presentation to the Dallas conference, charges that Cannon was guilty of conduct unbecoming a bishop. Foremost among those who instituted this grave action were former Secretary of the Navy Josephus Daniels, G. T. Fitzhugh, ex-owner of the *Memphis Commercial Appeal,* and former Representative James P. Woods, of Roanoke, Virginia. These influential Methodists sought a formal trial for Cannon, and the opinion was widely expressed that a trial was a certainty.

The conference met in the First Methodist Church of Dallas. When the foregoing charges were formally lodged, they were referred to the Committee on Episcopacy. To this body, with some ninety members, was delegated the duty of hearing testimony and deciding whether a trial would be necessary. Bishop Cannon, supporting himself on a crutch, entered the closed committee hearing with a packed briefcase under his arm and leaning on his son. He said he found a crutch necessary because he had twisted his ankle in Chicago several months previously.

For three hours the ecclesiastic defended himself before the committee. There was one clear pane in the otherwise frosted-glass doors, and W. A. S. Douglas, staff correspondent of the *Baltimore Sun,* noted through this aperture that Cannon seemed to be answering a great many questions. When the Bishop emerged at the end of the three-hour session, he remarked to an associate: "I'm tired, fearfully tired." Nevertheless, he returned for another hour with the committee that night.

Next day Correspondent Douglas reported that "high authorities, representing both factions of the fight being waged here around Bishop Cannon, admitted today that the Committee on Episcopacy had concluded to bring the Bishop to trial on charges

of actions unbecoming one of his rank." The Baltimore newspaperman said: "the only person in Dallas who, apparently, still
thinks there will be no trial is the Bishop himself."

But twenty-four hours later this same observer stated that "the
publicity given in the press today to the secret 2-to-1 decision of
the Committee on Episcopacy to bring Bishop Cannon to trial
on the subject of his stock-gambling activities, has turned out to
be a life-belt thrown to the accused." For Cannon's admirers had
been quick to buttonhole other delegates in hotel lobbies and
on street corners and to offer such arguments as: "The wet press
is out to crucify this noble man"; "Is Cannon to be tried and convicted by the newspaper reporters?" "Can fairness be expected
from committee members who have broken their oath of secrecy?" These grievous irrelevancies brought from a good many
of the committeemen who had voted for a trial a promise to reconsider.

Two days passed and Sunday came. The Sabbath was used intensively for political maneuvering by both sides, especially those
who were seeking to prevent a trial of the Bishop. This was the
transcendent issue before the conference, and black-coated ministers and laymen were feverishly active in hotel elevators, behind potted palms, and in smoke-filled rooms. Josephus Daniels
and his allies acknowledged that Cannon was gaining ground,
and the argument that "the wet interests," "the Pope," and "Al
Smith" were persecuting this great leader of Protestantism and
morality was having its effect. Finally it was reported that the
Bishop had written a strategic letter of apology to the committee,
following its vote of 56 to 28 for a trial.[6]

Next day, May 19, matters came rapidly to a climax. It developed that Cannon had indeed written the letter of apology
on May 13, immediately after the committee voted to have him
tried. During the intervening six days the committee had been
subjected to an intensive and continuous barrage of warnings
and wheedlings. In the afternoon Messrs. Daniels, Fitzhugh, and
their associates succeeded after great effort in getting another
hearing before the committee for the purpose of presenting
newly discovered evidence bearing directly upon Cannon's rela-

tions with the two New York bucketshops. But even this evidence failed to halt the pro-Cannon trend that had set in. The committee reversed its stand completely and voted 54 to 11 that a trial was not necessary.

On the following day the Bishop hobbled to the conference platform and read the letter that had led to the committee's reversal. There were diametrically opposing accounts of his demeanor from eyewitnesses. The Associated Press correspondent declared that "his eyes filled with tears as he spoke, and when he had finished and returned to his chair, for a long time his face was hidden from the audience." On the other hand, the sapient W. A. S. Douglas wrote: "The Bishop was cool and self-possessed, as usual. There were people present who, in discussing the proceedings afterward, declared that his voice broke on occasion. Impressionable young women reporters insisted that he wept a tear or two. He did neither. He might, for all outward appearances, have been making just a prosaic church announcement instead of a public humbling of himself — made necessary in order to avoid the trial decided as the proper procedure last Wednesday night." Bishop Cannon himself denied later that he had wept in presenting his apologia.

The text of the document follows:

I have made oral statement to the committee on episcopacy in reply to charges filed against me and replied to questions by members of the committee. In order that my attitude may be clearly understood, I am sending this written statement to the committee.

With reference to my transactions with Kable and Company, of New York, on which said transactions the complaint is based, permit me to say that at the time same transpired I thought them to be legitimate business transactions and in no way contrary to the standards of propriety under our church rules.

In looking back over the situation I now realize that in such transactions, as I now understand them, I made a mistake, which shall never occur again and which I deeply deplore.

While my motives are not subject to the construction placed upon them in said complaint, I now realize the impropriety of such transactions and am sorely grieved that my actions have in any wise brought pain and embarrassment to any part of the min-

istry and membership of my beloved church, to which I have
given my life.

Yours sincerely,
James Cannon, Jr.

Fitzhugh, of Memphis, and Daniels, of Raleigh, two of the
leaders in the effort to have the Bishop tried, were quick to point
out that Cannon acknowledged no wrongdoing until he was advised that a trial had been ordered, whereupon he reversed his
position and apologized. Woods, of Roanoke, another anti-Cannon
leader, called the policy successfully pursued by the Bishop's
friends in finally getting him off "skulduggery" and "conniving."
Fitzhugh announced that he would bring additional charges,
based upon records of Kable and Company which had just been
unsealed.

The decision not to try the Bishop was greeted with incredu-
lous amazement in many quarters. Referring to Cannon's success
in escaping trial by means of a belated confession and apology,
the *New York Herald Tribune* observed: "If this was repentance
in the Christian meaning of the word, then a hangover is the
avenue to sainthood."

The inimitable Will Rogers commented in his syndicated newspaper column: "See where the church freed Bishop Cannon for
plunging in Wall Street. They figured that a man's losses were
punishment enough. Imagine a preacher having to wait till the
deacons come in with the collection box to see if he could buy
United States Steel or just Blue Jay Corn Plasters. The church
has asked him and any others to stop it. You can't save souls and
margins too. During the crisis last fall the Bishop might have had
one eye on the text, but I bet the other was on a ticker."

The *Norfolk Virginian-Pilot* recalled that the Bishop had told
the Committee on Episcopacy that he had fallen into the hands
of a "bunch of sharpers" and that he canceled his contracts with
Kable and Company as soon as he learned that it was not a
"proper" investment company. The Norfolk paper pointed out
that this was not what he had said the preceding year in his vast
manifesto, "Unspotted from the World," wherein he deposed: "I
was surprised at the failure of Kable and Company, and greatly
regretted it, but after I was given the facts I thought it to be an

honest failure in which the greatest loser had been Mr. Gold-hurst, and the members of his immediate family, who had advanced large sums to prevent the failure, if possible." The *Virginian-Pilot* concluded: "It is, then, not a fact that Bishop Cannon closed out his account because he discovered that his trusted investment bankers were 'sharpers.' He considered them honest brokers long after his account had been wound up."

On the other hand, the *Christian Century*, as it had done several times before, leaped to the Bishop's defense. It declared that no evidence had been presented to show that Cannon "knowingly patronized a bucketshop, or willingly allowed himself to be used as a decoy duck to bring in other patrons to Kable and Company, or did anything that can fairly be called gambling." The religious weekly said there was nothing surprising in the verdict since "no other was possible on the evidence."

Having found that a trial was not necessary the General Conference proceeded, strangely enough, to adopt a sizzling resolution against stock-market gambling, "which has proven so destructive to the economic, social and religious life of those participating therein." It warned "all Methodists, bishops, preachers and laymen alike," and declared that the "best evidence of a bona fide transaction in stock is that the certificate of stock is actually purchased and issued in the name of the purchaser and actually delivered." Since Cannon, operating through Kable and Company, had bought stocks worth $477,000, and sold them for $486,000, all on a total outlay of $2,500, and apparently without ever seeing a stock certificate, it is clear that his was precisely the type of transaction that was not "bona fide," under the terms of the conference resolution. Dr. Forrest J. Prettyman, long chaplain of the United States Senate, contended on the conference floor that the resolution was "the most supreme expression of hypocrisy that I have ever heard read in a public body."

Fitzhugh, of Memphis, issued a formal protest against Cannon's exoneration, saying that the Bishop's confession "made a trial more than ever imperative," and that the church had put itself in the position of "condemning stock market transactions in the abstract, and condoning them in the concrete."

Yet N. B. Thompson, of North Carolina, declared amid cheers

from the Cannonites that the Bishop would not have been attacked at all for his dealings in stocks had he not taken the leading part in carrying four Southern states against Al Smith. This contention was heard frequently, and it was noted that several of the leaders in the effort to bring Cannon to trial had supported Smith. The rebuttal was that hundreds of Southern Methodist bishops and ministers had opposed the New Yorker, but that Cannon was the only one against whom charges had been preferred.

Bishop Warren A. Candler, of Georgia, interrupted the debate over the motives of those who had instituted proceedings against Cannon to declare: "A majority of the Bishops have requested me to say that they do not buy stocks and bonds. The only stock I've ever had is a cow and pony."

Bishop Cannon's stocks, of a very different genus, had not caused him to be brought to trial, and he was now to win several more victories before the conference adjourned. The first came on his election to the Southern Methodist Board of Temperance and Social Service. Dr. Alexander Copeland Millar, editor of the *Arkansas Methodist,* spoke for Cannon's supporters when he said: "We cannot go back on the greatest prohibition leader in the world, for if we did, the devils in hell would shout with glee and the angels in heaven would weep."

Cries of "Tammany" and "wet" were heard as the issue of the Bishop's re-election to the temperance board was debated, and two leading prohibitionists who opposed Cannon accordingly rose to points of personal privilege. They were Charles M. Hay, of St. Louis, Democratic nominee for the United States Senate in 1928, and Josephus Daniels. Both had supported Al Smith in 1928, which seemed to be regarded by many delegates as prima-facie evidence that they were on the payroll of the bartenders or the brewers. Rev. R. P. (Bob) Shuler, sensational Los Angeles evangelist, lately released from jail, where he had been serving a sentence for contempt of court, expressed the view of many Cannon supporters when he said: "We must take some recognition of the most iniquitous conspiracy in the history of the church. Tammany and the 'wets' do not care whether a man gambles on the stock market. They are veiling their fight on Bishop Cannon." Although the notion that Charles Hay and Josephus Daniels would under any conceivable circumstances pull chestnuts out of the fire for the New York sachems or the liquor interests was fantastic to any unbiased mind, that was the sort of argument which carried weight at Dallas. By a vote of 257 to 124 the conference defeated a move to substitute Bishop A. Frank Smith, of Houston, on the Board of Temperance and Social Service. Next day the board re-elected Cannon chairman.

As if all this were not sufficient, the conference sided with Cannon on another issue before adjournment. A proposal to require each bishop to reside within the boundaries of his district, which would have taken Cannon away to dwell among the heathen in Brazil or the Congo, was voted down. It had been brought forward by his enemies for the purpose of forcing him to leave the United States. This final triumph gave the Bishop victory in every contest in which he had been involved before the conference.

With adjournment there came another rash of statements in the press from friends and foes of the man who by then had come to be widely known as the "Bucketshop Bishop." A solid phalanx of his worshippers continued to defend him against such aspersions, but in the nation were millions who viewed him with profound skepticism and distrust.

Rev. Dr. John E. White, president of the Georgia Baptist Convention, termed the action of the conference in not bringing Cannon to trial "a wound keenly felt by all evangelical Christians" and "an especially heavy blow to the cause of prohibition, for which Baptists and Methodists in the South stand together in close sympathy." He said the conference "passed resolutions condemning all sorts of gambling, but it whitewashed the gambler," and he declared that it would "go down in history as the General Conference of the Southern Methodist Church which whitewashed a gambling Bishop." [7]

Rev. Dr. Bascom Anthony, of Macon, Georgia, a leading Methodist minister, defended Dr. White's position. In a letter to the *Macon Telegraph* [8] he said:

Unfortunately the Hoover-Smith wet dry question that seemed to overreach all else in the daily press also seemed to have controlled the general conference. The real issue has never been passed on its merits. A few of us are determined that it shall be if

it is humanly possible and I for one believe it is. . . . Some have
thought that it was a Methodist affair and that Dr. White . . .
ought not to have expressed opinions about it. From this I would
like to dissent. . . . We have expelled from the South Georgia
Conference in the last fifty years some twelve or fifteen preachers
for adultery, and with two exceptions they have all entered the
Baptist ministry. If that great church were connectional, I would
not hesitate in all these cases, except one, to criticize them for it,
but as each congregation is supreme, fairness does not allow that
the whole church be blamed for it. But the Methodist Church is
connectional, and the doings of our representatives become the
acts of us all and are subject to criticism.

G. T. Fitzhugh, of Memphis, prepared a long statement for the
press reviewing the effort he and his associates had made at
Dallas to have the Bishop brought to trial. This pronouncement
occupied more than five columns, much of it small type, in the
Memphis Commercial Appeal for May 25. Fitzhugh declared
therein that, prior to the vote by the Committee on Episcopacy
in favor of a trial, Cannon showed no regret or remorse for his
dealing with bucketshops, and, when asked if he was sorry he
had engaged in these transactions, his reply was: "I am sorry I
lost my $2,500." Yet after a trial was voted, he expressed great
contrition. Fitzhugh said, furthermore, that when "facts were developed, not by the 'Pope or wet enemies' of Bishop Cannon, but
in a bankruptcy proceeding in the United States District Court of
New York, instead of expressing any regret for engaging in such
transactions, he made a statement over his own signature which
was not in accord with the truth, claiming that he had merely
been engaged in purchasing stocks on the monthly partial payment investment plan."

The Memphian went on to assert that Cannon's correspondence
with Kable and Company and with "one Ebel, both notorious
bucketshop operators in New York . . . had, as the result of
powerful influence brought to bear by someone interested in sup-
pressing it, been sealed up in the office of the United States District Attorney in New York." The substance of this correspondence, but not the complete text, had been obtained in the closing
days of the Dallas conference by Fitzhugh, Daniels, and their

fellows, and they had presented the raw material to the Committee on Episcopacy. But in the words of Fitzhugh:

> To our astonishment we afterwards learned that during the hour we were kept out of the committee room the majority of the committee over the protest of several of the members, had voted to rescind the action of the committee in deciding that a trial was necessary, and thus without any information of this being imparted to us we were allowed to engage in the farce of making a long presentation of facts and arguments to prevent action which the committee knew it had already taken.

The summary of the unsealed correspondence that they had put before the committee at that time included the following:

> In one of his letters to Goldhurst he [Cannon] warned him not to address him at Washington, but at Richmond, as wires to the former address were embarrassing, while they would be understood by Miss Burroughs [his secretary] at Richmond, and he also warned Goldhurst by cable not to wire him at the Methodist missions in South America but in care of the cable company, showing an absolute consciousness of wrongdoing at the very time he was engaged in these transactions, for if they were legitimate investments there would have been no reason on his part for trying to conceal their nature. Besides, the correspondence manifested great anxiety about the outcome of criminal proceedings against Ebel. If Ebel was a violator of the law, why should he, if engaged in legitimate transactions, be concerned about this pernicious law violator? [Ebel never went to prison, although he was indicted.] The affidavits presented [to the committee] also showed that Bishop Cannon left his address so that he could receive information at every port of call as to his stock transactions while he was on his missionary tour.

Cannon's critics told the committee further, the Fitzhugh statement set forth, that the committee's action would be taken in future to mean that "any Bishop hereafter accused of any kind of immorality may, after his character has been arrested and a trial ordered, confess wrong doing which he had theretofore denied, repent as a matter of expediency, escape trial, and continue to be a general superintendent of the church."

Fitzhugh summed up the committee's action in the following

words: "Bishop Cannon is not acquitted of the charges, because he has not been tried at all. The Committee on Episcopacy is not a trial committee and only a trial bars a trial. The charges not only stand against him, but he can be brought to trial on these very charges, which may be presented by any three traveling elders."

A few weeks after the foregoing declaration was published, the full text of the Bishop's correspondence with Kable and Company appeared suddenly in the press. Publication of the documents showed that the Committee on Episcopacy's decision not to have a trial was based on a completely erroneous assumption concerning the nature of Cannon's transactions with Kable and Company. For, whereas Cannon contended in his letter of apology that he had been engaged in what he took to be "legitimate business transactions . . . in no way contrary to the standards of propriety under our church rules," the text of his correspondence made it impossible for any unbiased person to believe this. Furthermore, it was clear that, although the summary of this correspondence presented to the Committee on Episcopacy at Dallas by his accusers was accurate as far as it went, it was a distinct understatement.

When Cannon's letters, telegrams, and cablegrams to his New York bucketshop burst in the newspapers somewhat fatefully on Friday, June 13,[9] many of those who had previously stood by him saw that the transactions with which the correspondence was concerned had only slight relationship, if any, to the innocent investment of money "on the partial payment plan" that the Bishop had been at such pains to describe. It was obvious from these documents, covering the period from October 1927 to May 1928, that Cannon was frantically speculating on the market and avidly seeking unearned gain. Not only so, but he got an advance on his episcopal salary to cover losses; received almost daily cabled market closing quotations from Goldhurst while supposedly engaged upon the Lord's business in South America; continued to deal with Kable and Company after a Richmond bank had strongly indicated to him that the firm was not reliable; signed letters to Goldhurst in terms of affection; showed clearly in several messages that his adventures in the stock market were making him tense and jumpy; and sent at least five separate communications on Sunday to the bucketshop, some of them as he toured the foreign mission field.

Almost simultaneously with the appearance in the press of this damning correspondence with Kable and Company, the *Christian Herald*, of New York, which had given the Bishop its accolade the preceding year for his unparalleled contributions to "religious progress," published an article by him in which he declared that he had been warned that his reputation would be destroyed unless he stopped his fight on the "Smith-Raskob-wet-Tammany-Roman Catholic domination of the Democratic party." He added that "these same politicians" had had detectives following him since 1928 in an effort to "frame" him and asserted: "I have been vilified and slandered by the wet-Tammany-Roman Catholic press in every possible way."

Soon the Bishop announced that his attorneys were examining "wet and Catholic papers" with a view to filing suits against any that had libeled him. He quoted his lawyers as having told him that the *Catholic Union and Times,* official paper of the Buffalo diocese, had done so, and that he intended to sue that journal. Whereupon the *Union and Times* retorted in the following blistering editorial:

> . . . If Bishop Cannon is prepared for a libel suit, we are similarly prepared to answer it. In fact we would welcome it as an opportunity to uncover certain facts that a Senate investigating committee was unable to accomplish.[10] It is now time for someone to call the bluff of an individual who has used his high station in the Methodist Church to play the game of politics and to openly insult American citizens. . . .
>
> Bishop James Cannon, Jr., has threatened the American press. . . . If this fails he will call out the militia, declare martial law and demand the citizenry of this country to play the flunkey before a Methodist divine.
>
> But not the *Catholic Union and Times* under its present editorship. Senators may quake before his refusal to answer pertinent questions; Washington may do the bidding of this clerical mountebank, but so long as God leaves breath in our body James Cannon, Jr., who employs gall for godliness and has confused bile for benevolence, will find us at 85 Erie Street, Buffalo, New York,

ready to face a libel suit and prepared to accept the findings of American courts of justice. We will not walk out and bring contempt upon a dignified and honorable institution whether it be a Senate committee or a village judge sitting at a crossroads. We have nothing to hide, nothing to suppress, nothing to cover from the view of our fellow-citizens. . . . We still believe that an individual by the name of Cannon will be brought to justice.

This was the most direct and forthright challenge the Bishop had received from the Catholic press. He ran away from it. No suit was ever filed by him against the *Catholic Union and Times*. Nor did he ever bring suit against any other Catholic newspaper or magazine.[11] He was constantly complaining that these journals were slandering him and he sued any number of secular newspapers (without, it is true, ever bringing most of these actions to trial), but he shrank from taking even the first step against the Catholic press. One can only conclude that the countless "slanders" which he claimed had appeared in that press were either vastly exaggerated or nonexistent.

Nevertheless, with much of his following he could still explain away almost any criticism by proclaiming that it had been published in the "Roman Catholic" or the "wet" press. The case was otherwise, of course, when he was attacked in a nationally respected organ of dry Protestantism. Such an attack was now to appear in the *Christian Century*, which, as we have seen, had defended the Bishop both before and after his Dallas trial and had never conceded any wrongdoing whatever on his part. The *Christian Century* suddenly reversed its position. Publication of Cannon's complete correspondence with Kable and Company was too much for that estimable journal. In its issue of June 25 it delivered a broadside that carried a triple sting for the Bishop, since it came from a source that had always defended him. Captioned "The Lost Leader," this terrific editorial said:

> . . . There is still no evidence that his operations were not within the law, or that he consciously chose a company of bucketshop swindlers as the agents for his financial transactions. But the picture of an innocent and rather indifferent investor placing in the hands of an old friend a few hundred or a few thousand dollars for investment while he went about his Father's business with

an untroubled mind, has entirely faded out. Instead we see a feverishly anxious speculator haunting the telegraph office, exchanging frequent, sometimes daily, cablegrams from Brazil and elsewhere with his brokers, cautioning them against wiring him at certain addresses where the receipt of such messages might cause "unpleasant complications," scrambling for funds with which to cover margins or to act upon market tips, directing by wire the purchase or sale of this or that stock, "on edge and fearful of flop," scolding his brokers for their failure to carry out his orders, and clamoring for statements of his account. . . .

The *Christian Century* here lifts its voice in solemn and earnest protest against the occupancy of a high place of leadership for moral and spiritual ends in the name of the church by a personality so lacking in moral sensitiveness as to be capable of engaging in such a mad scramble for unearned gain as that in which Bishop Cannon was engaged. . . .

The church itself and those organizations which, like the Anti-Saloon League, profess to represent it in militant activities for the suppression of anti-social institutions, need to disentangle themselves from the reputations and the leadership of persons who are not above the general level in their ethical idealism. We cannot subscribe to the doctrine that if a dry leader is dry enough, nothing else matters. With no desire to be censorious, we cannot do other than express the judgment that Bishop Cannon's speculative transactions, the true nature of which was not revealed by his confession to the Methodist Conference, but which came to light through malicious and wholly unjustifiable publication of his private correspondence, disclose characteristics incompatible with the position which he has occupied.

No useful end would be served by hair-splitting distinctions between gambling and speculation in this case. Call it speculation. But what is it that makes gambling harmful? Is it not that it both expresses and intensifies the desire for profit without service; that it creates an anxious mind, feverishly waiting for a lucky turn to bring fortune, while fearing that an unlucky one will bring disaster; that, not content with the element of chance which is present in some degree in all enterprises, it multiplies chances and deals in artificial situations in which there is no element but chance; that it involves no sense of participation in a socially useful enterprise, but only the hope of personal gain as the outcome of a happy issue of unpredictable events? Every one of these factors was as clearly present in Bishop Cannon's relations with Kable and Company as they would have been at a roulette wheel or a poker table. . . . .

The *Christian Herald* says that the "wets are determined, at whatever cost, and by whatever tactics, however foul, to 'get' Bishop Cannon." Doubtless they are. More's the pity that he should put into their hands weapons of his own forging so much more deadly to his usefulness and reputation than any they could make for themselves. . . . Neither the church nor the Anti-Saloon League can expect the world to take seriously their claims to clear moral vision and a passion for righteousness if they are willing to accept administrative efficiency and executive energy as a substitute for more structural qualities of character.

Bishop Cannon is a lost leader.

This was perhaps the most devastating of all the analyses made of Bishop Cannon's bucketshop adventures, because it came from so unimpeachable a source. In view of the manner in which the *Christian Century* awoke to the true nature of the Bishop's stock-market adventures, as soon as it read his correspondence with Kable and Company, one can only surmise what the result would have been at Dallas, if the Conference Committee on Episcopacy had had the same documents before it.

But those documents had been put under seal in New York through some mysterious influence until after the Dallas conference adjourned. Even during the Goldhurst trial they had not been brought into the open. The papers were finally unsealed by the Caraway Lobby Committee of the United States Senate, with the permission of the United States Department of Justice, but the Senate committee's representative was not allowed to take them to Washington, and the published portions were from short-hand notes made by him in New York.

As a result of their publication Cannon had been convicted in the public mind of bucketshop gambling, but he had not been convicted by his church. Many devout Methodists were wholly dissatisfied with the failure of the conference committee at Dallas to order a trial. They refused to regard the issue as closed, and they sought earnestly for means of reopening the case. They were soon to find four ministers willing to brave the fury of an aroused

Bishop Cannon, made doubly dangerous by virtue of the sweeping power wielded by Methodist bishops over their clergy. Undeterred by these considerations, the four pastors began preparing their case with a view to preferring formal charges of immorality against a bishop — for the first time in the long history of the Southern Methodist Church.

CHAPTER *xvi*

Cherchez La Femme

Pᴜʙʟɪᴄᴀᴛɪᴏɴ of the full and lurid story of Bishop Cannon's misadventures in the bucketshops of Manhattan sent many moral and religious leaders to the wailing wall. Hands folded behind them under the tails of their black jimswinger coats, and Adam's apples waggling above their gates-ajar collars, they shook their heads sadly. The Bishop's complete correspondence with Kable and Company was bad enough, but word had now reached them that four Methodist ministers were preparing to reinstitute charges of gambling against him, with a view to securing a trial by the General Conference of 1934. This seemed to mean that the sacred cause of prohibition, of which he was easily the foremost exemplar, was about to be thrown on the defensive again.

But revelations even more piquant than those having to do with the Bishop's unfortunate contretemps with the ticker tape now exploded in the press. They concerned Cannon's relations with Mrs. Helen Hawley McCallum, who had gone with him to the Holy Land the preceding year as his "secretary."

First came the seemingly innocuous tidings from London, England, that the Bishop had suddenly married Mrs. McCallum. The knot was tied quietly at Christ Church, Mayfair, on July 15, 1930, but the news had somehow been bottled up for six days, for it was not until July 21 that the Associated Press was able to flash the story to the world. By that time, the sixty-five-year-old father of nine and the forty-to-forty-five-year-old widow were en route as bride and groom to Madeira, on board the steamship *Arlanza*. Proceeding thence to Brazil, the Bishop would address

229

himself there to matters ecclesiastical. Mrs. McCallum had not
been well, and they had sailed for England expecting that she
would remain there until his return from South America, at which
time they planned to be married. But on arriving in London they
had decided to wed at once and to give Mrs. Cannon the benefit
of the sea voyage.

Word of the nuptials took most of the Bishop's friends in the
United States completely by surprise. Dr. E. L. Crawford, secretary of the Board of Temperance and Social Service of the Methodist Episcopal Church, South, who shared an office with Cannon
in Washington, said he had no intimation when the Bishop left
that he was planning marriage. On the other hand, Jake F.
Newell, Charlotte, North Carolina, attorney, who had been on
the tour of the Holy Land the year before with the Bishop and
Mrs. McCallum, confessed that he had suspected then that they
would ultimately marry. Noting that news dispatches described
Mrs. Cannon as between forty and forty-five, Newell said: "She
doesn't look a day over 30. She is good looking, tall and blonde."
He also described her as "very intellectual" and as "an extremely
alert woman, with a splendid wit."

The day after the foregoing appeared throughout the United
States, the *Philadelphia Record* astounded even Cannon's sever-
est critics with its publication of a New York dispatch describing
details of the Bishop's courtship and quoting from letters he had
written to Mrs. McCallum. This dispatch, which appeared on
July 23, was as follows:

Special to The Record

New York, July 22 — More details of the courtship of Bishop
James Cannon, Jr., and Mrs. Helen McCallum became known
today.

Several new letters written by the Southern Methodist churchman to the comely widow he married last Tuesday in London
came out today.

And at the same time it was learned that the Bishop first met
Mrs. McCallum under an assumed name.

Bishop Cannon first introduced himself to Mrs. McCallum in
the lobby of the Hotel McAlpin about two years ago. He told
Mrs. McCallum and her friend, Mrs. Joan Chapman, that he was

Cherchez La Femme

Stephen Trent, a writer, before offering to take them in his car to Mrs. Chapman's apartment.

And that same night he gave Mrs. McCallum $20 to help her out of financial difficulties.

A little later the Bishop gave Mrs. McCallum $100 to tide her over another temporary financial distress.

Whether the widow knew her admirer's real name when she took the $100 was not revealed today. She must have known it, however, when she and the Bishop returned from the Holy Land, whither she accompanied him as his secretary.

At that time he settled on her an allowance of $200 a month. This money was used for the upkeep of Mrs. McCallum's apartment at 159 West 85th Street.

From that time on he visited Mrs. McCallum's apartment every time he came to New York City, including the occasions when he returned from mission inspection tours in Africa. Just before leaving for the Congo early this year, the Bishop gave Mrs. McCallum $600 to cover the cost of her cables to him and her expenses while he was abroad.

On the night before his wife died about two years ago Bishop Cannon visited Mrs. McCallum at her apartment. From there he remained in telephonic communication with his sons, who were at their Mother's bedside in Washington.

When he learned his wife's condition was critical, he took the next train home.

A few days after the funeral he returned to Mrs. McCallum for consolation.

The progress of the romance may be traced through some of the missives the churchman indited to Mrs. McCallum from foreign places on his numerous trips to Europe and Africa. . . .

Most of these letters were prosaic in the extreme. They contained few endearments. One rebuked Mrs. McCallum for writing so seldom. Once or twice her aging suitor referred to his hope that she would marry him, and at rare intervals he used terms of love and affection.

Much the same material appeared in the Hearst newspaper chain, either on the day the foregoing was published in the *Philadelphia Record* or a few days thereafter. There was no statement in any of the papers concerning the source of the data, nor was there any explanation of how or where the Bishop's correspondence was secured. An explanation would be forthcoming the following year, but for the present the public was completely in the dark.

The happy pair was on the high seas when the above-mentioned segment of the press carried the foregoing dispatches. Bishop Cannon did not learn that these matters had got into the newspapers until he arrived in Brazil. Asked to comment there on the articles concerning his courtship and on the publication of his correspondence, he said: "I'll enter into no controversy, newspaper or otherwise, concerning my marriage." He added that he and Mrs. Cannon probably would not return to the United States until after the November congressional elections.

But the Bishop changed his plans abruptly in September, when four Methodist ministers filed formal charges of immorality, bucketshop gambling, and flour-hoarding against him with Bishop W. N. Ainsworth, chairman of the College of Bishops. The four ministers cabled Cannon in advance that such was their intention. On September 20 the press carried the announcement that the charges had been filed, and on the following day it was revealed in dispatches from Brazil that the Cannons had sailed for the United States.

Signers of the communication to Bishop Ainsworth were the Rev. Drs. Forrest J. Prettyman, of Baltimore, who had been chaplain of the United States Senate for eight years; J. T. Mastin, a venerable and beloved citizen of Richmond who had been a pioneer in the field of public-welfare work; Costen J. Harrell, of Richmond, pastor of one of the leading churches in the Virginia Conference, now a Bishop; and I. P. Martin, of Abingdon, Virginia, a well-regarded minister.

They requested that Bishop Ainsworth summon a committee of investigation and lay before it charges against the "character and conduct of Bishop James Cannon, Jr." The charges included immorality, bucketshop gambling, flour-hoarding, lying, and "gross moral turpitude and disregard for the first principles of Christian ethics." The ministers reserved the right to bring additional charges and shortly thereafter they did so. The additional allegation read: "We charge Bishop Cannon, Jr., with adultery, and in particular in his relations with Mrs. Helen McCallum."

Cherchez La Femme

While the word "adultery" did not appear in any of the published accounts of the action taken by the four elders against the Bishop, the press carried the declaration that he was to be arraigned on "moral grounds" as well as for bucketshop gambling and for actions related to his political activities.

One of the Southern Methodist bishops who had defended Bishop Cannon regularly in his previous embroilments with his foes was Bishop Horace M. Du Bose. Yet it developed almost simultaneously with publication of the foregoing charges that Bishop Du Bose had written Cannon while the latter was in Brazil suggesting that he make "the supreme personal sacrifice" and resign from the Methodist Episcopal Church, South.[1] Bishop Du Bose explained to inquirers that he had brought forward the suggestion on the basis of Cannon's stock-market activities and his failure to answer questions put to him in the United States senatorial investigation — of which more anon. The Du Bose letter said, in part:

> I can only feel that you are unadvised of the bitter resentment against you on the part of thousands of our best laymen and hundreds of our loyal pastors. I feel that I should be lacking in loyalty to you, the episcopacy and the church if I should fail to so apprise you.

This exhortation was without effect. There was never any appreciable likelihood that a man of Cannon's temperament would resign from the church because he was being criticized, however sharp and widespread the criticism might be. He was not the type to resign under fire. When the formal charges of moral turpitude and other unepiscopal behavior were filed, that ended all chance of his voluntary retirement.

Bishop Cannon did withdraw shortly afterward, however, from an agency over which he had presided since 1918 — namely, the board of trustees of Blackstone College for Girls. In his letter of resignation he declared that "since 1928 there has been a division of sentiment among the people in the territory from which the college naturally draws its support," and he added that "a number . . . have disagreed with my views and my activities during the past two years." Since an effort was under way, the

Bishop went on, to increase the patronage and endowment of the college, he felt that it would be well for him to sever all connection with the board, so that "those who have given my connection with the college as a reason for their failure to give their support" would no longer have this excuse. Cannon said he was resigning from the board "without any suggestion from any person or any committee of the college." Although he had founded the institution and had headed it for twenty-four years except for a brief interval, and then had presided over its board for twelve more years, the board accepted his resignation unanimously. There could hardly have been more complete proof that Bishop Du Bose had correctly described the feeling against Cannon in the ranks of his own church and among many of the very people who so often and so loyally had defended him in the past.

Meanwhile Bishop Ainsworth was moving toward appointment of the twelve Methodist "traveling elders," or ministers, who were to hear the grave charges against Bishop Cannon. En route from Brazil, Cannon had issued a statement to the Associated Press in which he claimed that the action taken against him by the four elders had not been in accordance with the Methodist Discipline. Dr. Prettyman promptly replied that the paragraph of the Discipline quoted by Cannon had been amended in 1894, and that the Bishop evidently had got hold of the long-outmoded document. Since Bishop Ainsworth proceeded with preparations for the inquiry, he evidently agreed with the four ministers that Cannon's contention was without merit.

On his arrival in the United States, the Bishop and his bride were besieged by reporters and photographers. The explosion of flashlight bulbs on the ship and the dock made Mrs. Cannon "hysterical," in the words of the ship's first officer, who requested the cameramen to leave the vessel.

After reaching Washington and taking a careful look at the charges filed against him, the Bishop declared that his first impulse was to issue a "clear, full, sweeping statement in denial," but he explained that the case ought not to be tried in the press. He accordingly asked suspension of judgment "until these complaints have been properly adjudicated in accordance with the procedure prescribed by the church." The Bishop expressed thanks for "the confidence and loyalty of my friends as indicated by letters and telegrams received daily which nullify the abuse, bitterness and scurrility of other communications, usually unsigned, and from wet or Roman Catholic writers."

One of the testimonials of esteem which came to him at this time emanated from the good ladies of the Bristol, Va.-Tenn., W.C.T.U. who attended the Holston conference of the Southern Methodist Church in that city. Although Bishop Du Bose, who had asked Bishop Cannon shortly before to resign from the church, was presiding over the Holston conference, and the Rev. I. P. Martin, one of the four ministers who had preferred formal charges of immorality and bucketshop gambling, was attending the sessions, the W.C.T.U. staged a demonstration in Cannon's behalf. Automobiles with banners proclaiming firm support of the harassed moral leader arrived at the church where the conference was being held. The trusting ladies also placed on a wall, in full view of the conference delegates and visitors, a large banner with the strange device: "W.C.T.U. White Ribboners Stand for the Honor and Purity of Bishop Cannon."

The following week Bishop Cannon filed suit for five million dollars against William Randolph Hearst, claiming that articles published in the Hearst newspapers concerning his courtship and marriage were maliciously libelous, as well as false, scandalous, and defamatory.[2] Among the grounds cited was the statement in the *New York Evening Journal* that he had been in Mrs. McCallum's apartment the night before his wife died, and that when he learned that her condition was critical, he took the next train home. There was the similar declaration in the *Los Angeles Examiner*, albeit somewhat more insinuating in its language: "Their friendship was temporarily interrupted one night when Bishop Cannon, in Mrs. McCallum's apartment, received word of the serious illness of his wife, the former Lura Virginia Bennett. The Bishop rushed to her bedside." There were also objectionable allegations in the Hearst papers that Cannon had employed C. Bascom Slemp, his former political confederate in the holy war against Al Smith, as attorney to defend Goldhurst, the Bishop's pet bucketshop operator. The Bishop denied that he had employed Slemp to defend Goldhurst, and also that he was in Mrs.

McCallum's apartment in New York the night before his wife died in Washington. He admitted having taken Mrs. McCallum to lunch at a restaurant on the day in question.

In explanation of his suit against Hearst, distributed in printed form to delegates attending the Virginia Methodist Conference at Norfolk,[3] Cannon quoted what he described as the full text of confidential messages exchanged between Hearst and his editors. In one of these the publisher was represented as declaring, in a long letter to George Young, editor of the *Los Angeles Examiner,* that, next to fighting the World Court, the Hearst newspapers could do no greater service than to work for the "destruction of the influence of the group which Bishop Cannon represents and controls, and that this could be done by constant, though careful, assaults" upon the Bishop. Hearst added somewhat sadly:

> I have come to the conclusion that it will be next to impossible to directly pin anything to Bishop Cannon. I am sincere in saying that I consider him to have the best brain in America, no one excepted. He has without exception foreseen and prepared for every attack made upon him.[4]

The Bishop also charged that Hearst had received reports from a special agent or agents during 1930 concerning the movements of himself and his son Richard M. Cannon. Bishop Cannon published a brochure and distributed it to newspapers, giving the text of the confidential messages that he said Hearst had sent his editors, and also fourteen "special reports" on Richard M. Cannon's movements filed with Hearst between April 2 and September 27, 1930 by someone who appeared to be a private detective. These reports had to do with young Cannon's activities in California as the head of schools he had opened there. If these documents were genuine, the detective told Hearst that on one occasion, when he was trying to listen in on a conversation between Richard Cannon and another man, "I could overhear little as it is impossible to get near the front of the house without being seen." Another of the detective's "reports" says: "Subject's desk examined but no information of value. No time to go over file." The Bishop quoted a letter of Hearst in which he declared that "our play is to wait until the school is forced to the wall, then let go with all we have to connect Bishop Cannon with the organization."

Although Richard Cannon was in difficulties with the California courts for some eighteen months from late 1929 until early 1931, the damage to the Bishop by virtue of this fact appears to have been slight. We find Dr. Cannon in December 1929 having a lively brush with newspaper photographers at Montrose, a Los Angeles suburb, where court hearings were being held in connection with charges of unsanitary conditions and unpaid wages at the military academy operated by Richard and his wife. The Bishop grappled with a photographer who was snapping him as he emerged from the courtroom, but when he saw that other cameramen were getting action photos of the melee, he quickly consented to pose. Asked by a reporter concerning the recent revelations of his dealings with New York bucketshops, the Bishop retorted: "That's my business, and I certainly consider it a very indelicate question, quite without the province of a newspaper reporter's scope." Whereupon he returned at once to the courtroom.

Bad-check charges were filed against Richard Cannon in several California counties during 1930. He also was charged with nonpayment of wages in two instances. Early in 1931 he got ninety days in the county jail from a Pasadena jury on a charge of failing to pay thirty-three dollars in salary to a teacher in the El Monte boys' school, of which he had been manager. This conviction was reversed some months later by the Appellate Department of the Superior Court, on the ground that the elements of the alleged offense had not been sufficiently proved. There were hung juries in connection with two other similar charges. Nine other charges against him of nonpayment of wages or salaries were dismissed when it was announced that an agreement had been reached on these claims.

The extent to which Bishop Cannon helped his son out of these difficulties is not clear. The news accounts do not refer to the Bishop's presence at any of the court proceedings except the first one. He apparently aided Richard financially, perhaps to a considerable extent, since he reproduced without comment the following statement of a supposed Hearst detective in one of his "special reports": "Found opportunity to examine files. Found set of papers for filing bankruptcy by subject Richard M. Cannon, wife, and Robert E. Lee Military Academy. List Bishop Cannon as one of largest creditors. . . . Total will approximate $25,000, though did not have time to add up. No date on papers as yet. . . . May have longer opportunity for examination later as office is not locked."

Bishop Cannon offered no explanation of the means by which he came into possession of such messages as the foregoing, supposedly exchanged between Hearst and a detective, or the letter which he declared that Hearst had written concerning him to the editor of the *Los Angeles Examiner*. Nor did he speculate openly as to how the Hearst papers and the *Philadelphia Record* secured his own correspondence with his bride-to-be.

Although the *Philadelphia Record*, as noted above, published much of the material concerning the Bishop and Mrs. McCallum that appeared in the Hearst press, Cannon did not file suit against the *Record* until July 21, 1931, the day before the statute of limitations expired. The amount asked was $500,000. The suit was never pressed, although attorneys for the *Record* sought confidently on various occasions to bring it to trial, since they believed they were in a strong position. The case was finally adjudged "non pros." in 1937, after counsel for Cannon conceded at last that it would never be tried. Yet the charges made against the Bishop in the *Record* were altogether similar to some of those which appeared in the Hearst press. The final disposition of the Hearst suits, which were to total $7,500,000, will be noted hereafter.

As the uproar over Bishop Cannon reached a climax, the subject of this monumental tumult entered Sibley Hospital in Washington for treatment of acute neuritis and inflammatory arthritis, complicated by nervous disorders. The latter were brought on, in the opinion of his doctors, by the strain and pressure of the charges that had been filed against him in recent months. He had been using a crutch for some time, because of his arthritis, the Associated Press declared, although he had been quoted as saying at the Dallas conference in the spring that his crutch was due to a twisted ankle. At all events, he was to use a crutch on numerous occasions thereafter.

Bishop Cannon's physician, Dr. R. Lyman Sexton, stated when he first entered the hospital that his arthritis was not chronic. A few days later he said that painful inflammatory arthritis had spread from the Bishop's right foot to his right hand and left foot and knee, "giving cause for some concern." Some ten days later Dr. Sexton announced that the patient was "weaker due to continued pain," but less than a fortnight afterward he pronounced him "out of danger." Cannon subsequently went to Marlin, Texas, where, in a quiet and restful atmosphere, he regained his health sufficiently to appear before the tribunal of his church on the unprecedented charges that had been filed against him.

This hearing was to have opened on November 12, 1930, but the accused was in the hospital at that time, so it had to be postponed until he had returned from his convalescence. Early in February 1931, to the accompaniment of a vast amount of speculation and discussion by the public, the hearing began in Mount Vernon Place Methodist Church, Washington. Great secrecy enveloped the proceedings. Police patrolled the building, and a detective sergeant guarded the locked doors. Nothing was given to the press while the inquiry was going on. The Bishop hobbled to and from the church on the arm of his son, Professor James Cannon, III, of the Duke University faculty, an ordained Methodist minister. The names of the twelve elders who were sitting in judgment upon him were not made known in advance or while the proceedings were in progress.[5] A few witnesses were called by the prosecution, but Cannon summoned none. He conducted his own defense, assisted by his son and the Rev. J. Sidney Peters, his lifelong friend and co-worker.

While many details leaked out after the tribunal had rendered its finding, there was until that time a total lack of news. The country was aware that the hearing had got under way on February 3, but it had no means of ascertaining what progress was being made. The press reported the labored comings and goings of the Bishop, as he limped up and down the church steps on the arm of his son, but once the portals of the building closed behind him, it could not be learned whether his case was going well or badly. Bishop Ainsworth told the twelve ministers who were hearing the evidence that they were on their honor not to talk to anyone about the case, and they hurried from the morning, afternoon, and evening sessions by different doors. As for Bishop Cannon's accusers, they too were unwilling to talk during the proceedings.

After five days of hearings, and some two hours of deliberation by the twelve men who constituted the jury, the verdict was reached. Bishop Ainsworth stood on the church steps in the rain and announced the conclusion of the elders. It was that there was no need to try Bishop Cannon. The full text of his statement follows:

> A committee of investigation in the case of Bishop James Cannon, Jr., concluded its hearing in Washington today. The committee found no trial necessary.

Bishop Cannon was not present when the announcement was made. He had gone to Sibley Hospital and was in bed there. James Cannon, III, who heard Bishop Ainsworth read the finding, rushed to a telephone and told his father of the outcome. Asked subsequently for comment, the Bishop said he had "no statement to make now on any subject."

Thus the nation was confronted with the extraordinary fact that twelve Methodist ministers from all parts of the South had solemnly concluded that a Bishop of their church who had manifestly gambled on an extensive scale in bucketshops, hoarded flour during a world war, and conducted himself in a flagrantly unepiscopal manner with a woman who was not his wife should not even be brought to trial. The Dallas verdict as to the gambling charges had shocked many detached observers both inside and outside the Southern Methodist Church, but at least it could be said that the most damning part of the evidence concerning the Bishop's dealings in bucketshops was not available at Dallas. As soon as that evidence was unsealed and it became generally available through the publication of Cannon's correspondence with Goldhurst, many staunch admirers saw at once that they had been grossly deceived as to the nature of the Bishop's relations with Kable and Company. The forthright admission of the *Christian Century* that it had been mistaken, and its editorial description of Cannon as "a lost leader," were typical of this group. But all such considerations were regarded as unconvincing by the twelve ministers who sat in judgment upon the Bishop. Their action had the effect of clearing Cannon entirely, in so far as his official standing with the church was concerned. For, while it would have been theoretically possible for the men who brought the charges to have renewed them before the quadrennial General Conference in 1934, they made it clear during the Washington hearings that they had no such intention.

The first public comment on the findings came from Dr. Costen J. Harrell, one of the four who had instituted the inquiry. He displayed extreme surprise when advised of the investigating committee's conclusions, and said:

> My co-signers and myself filed charges against Bishop Cannon after very careful investigation. We did this for the cause of righteousness and for the church. We were sure at that time that we were right.
>
> After we heard the evidence in Washington this week, including some very astonishing admissions by Bishop Cannon, we were doubly sure that we were right. The committee did not vote with us, but time will doubtless reveal their blunder.

A similar statement was subsequently made by Dr. Forrest J. Prettyman, who said:

> At the close of the case the elders who brought the charges had not the slightest doubt as to the truth of them; but were only doubly convinced by the admissions on the part of the defendant of every fact which we considered important as substantiating the charges.
>
> It may further be stated that Bishop Cannon endeavored by every means to prevent the facts from coming to light.

How did the Bishop manage to obtain a verdict of "no trial necessary" in the face of his own admissions and the provable facts that were presented to those who sat in judgment upon him?

One is reminded here of the case of Henry Ward Beecher,

whose admirers were unwilling to believe him guilty of adultery even upon the presentation of overwhelming proof. When the tremendous uproar over the Beecher-Tilton case was at its height in the seventies of the last century, the prevailing attitude on the part of the famous divine's followers, according to Paxton Hibben, his biographer, was: "If Beecher is guilty, I don't want to know it; he is too great a man to fall; he has too many interests involved in his position and success."

Similarly, when Cannon was accused of adultery, bucketshop gambling, and flour-hoarding by ministers of his own church who were risking their careers to do so, numerous believers in Methodism and prohibition were unwilling to entertain the notion that a man who stood for so many noble causes could be guilty of such derelictions. They considered the Methodist Church and the Eighteenth Amendment to be more important than any individual, and they rationalized their unwillingness to condemn so symbolic a figure as Cannon, fearing the harm that such a conviction would do to the church and to the dry movement.

There was the further fact that certain non-Methodist elements of the population, who were thoroughly unconvinced of prohibition's beneficent effects, were unquestionably anxious to "get" the Bishop. The twelve Methodist preachers who heard the evidence against Cannon in Washington, all convinced drys, knew this, and they must have found it impossible to divorce the case of Cannon the individual from the case of Cannon the symbol of the Eighteenth Amendment and of Methodism's long fight against alcohol. Cannon was careful also to keep the specter of the Vatican hovering low over the chamber where testimony was being heard against him. While he could not adduce any relationship between his four accusers and the Roman Catholic Church, of course, nor pretend that these four Methodist clergymen were trying to damage the cause of prohibition, he could argue that the men who had preferred charges against him were the unwitting tools of antisocial elements who were seeking to secure repeal and were hostile to organized Protestantism.

A few weeks after the verdict was made known, Dr. Prettyman wrote a long letter concerning the case to Albert H. Dudley, manager of the Baltimore branch of the Federal Reserve Bank of

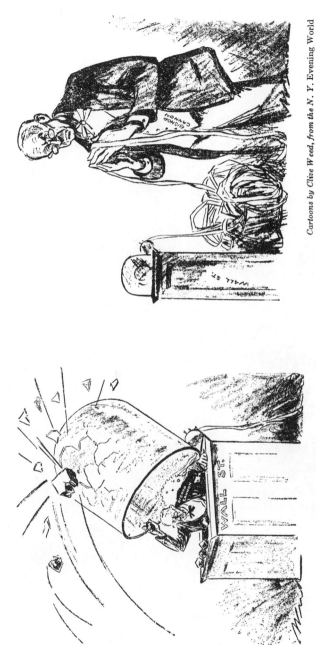

A CARTOONIST VIEWS CANNON'S BUCKETSHOP ADVENTURES

Left, "People Who Live in Glass Houses"; right, "Let Us Pray!"

Cartoons by Clive Weed, from the N. Y. Evening World

Wide World Photo

CANNON LEAVES COURT,

following acquittal on Corrupt Practices charges on April 27, 1934. Next him, his second wife, Helen Hawley Cannon. Far right, Miss Ada L. Burroughs, acquitted with him.

Richmond, which he mimeographed and distributed to interested persons. Portions of this communication were published in the press.

Prettyman pronounced the whole proceeding in Washington a "farce and an absurdity." To begin with, said Prettyman, Cannon tried by all possible means to prevent any hearing. First he claimed, when en route home from Brazil, as noted above, that the charges had not been brought in accordance with the Methodist Discipline. Although confident that Cannon had no basis for this claim, Prettyman agreed to meet him and hear any statement he cared to make. "We did meet him in Richmond," wrote Prettyman, "but found him in such a state of maudlin intoxication from some drug that it was impossible to conduct any satisfactory investigation." No one has ever been able to explain this episode, although the accuracy of the foregoing description has been fully attested. What the "drug" was, and why Cannon was under its influence, remain a mystery.

After this episode, the letter goes on, Cannon advanced the contention to Bishop Ainsworth that the whole of Paragraph 261, which provides for the investigation and trial of a bishop, was unconstitutional. He was again overruled. Hence he failed to prevent the hearing. On the other hand, said Prettyman, he succeeded in "locking up the evidence and keeping it from the eyes of the church and the public." On this point Prettyman wrote:

> To a large extent the case is still under cover and, by action of the committee itself, even the important affidavits offered by Bishop Cannon in his defense are sealed in the records of the case, and not even the accusers were permitted to have copies of them or to make, for themselves and for their own defense, extended notes from them. This is all the more surprising, since Bishop Cannon was allowed to take original documents, filed in the case, to his own room and to have his typist to make copies of them; but when I undertook to make notes from his evidence during the session, and in the room where the hearing was being held, I was enjoined by one of the members of the committee and warned that I would not be permitted to take even my private notes from the room. I appealed to the committee on the ground that we who had brought the charges were on trial, and that the church was

on trial, and that we simply wanted to be in possession of the facts in the case. The committee would not allow us to have any copy of the evidence.

It remained, therefore, a closed, star-chamber proceeding and the church is still kept in the dark as to what were the charges or the character of the evidence, or even the procedure in the investigation. It may be said that those of us who brought the charges were not permitted to make any argument or to offer any rebuttal, or to organize and present the evidence as a whole after it was all in. We felt that it was impossible for the committee to properly weigh the merits of evidence presented after hearing long and complicated statements, all ex parte in character, read but once. We felt that the only outcome of the case, under the circumstances, would be the jumping at conclusions on the basis of preconceived prejudice.

One of Bishop Cannon's admirers argued in a letter to the press that, since the inquiry was in the nature of a grand-jury proceeding, it was proper not to make the charges public, unless and until a true bill was found. "No fairminded persons wish a hurtful rumor or charge to be made public until honorable investigators find them so well founded in facts that they deem it wise and best to make them public," he wrote. "And they are the ones to judge what is wise and just, and not the ones who bring the accusations." This apologist for the Bishop also contended that the latter naturally was allowed to copy all the documents, or he would not have been able to answer the charges they contained.

But nobody produced any valid justification for the refusal to allow Dr. Prettyman and his associates to make notes for their own use on what Bishop Cannon was saying in long and detailed documents that were read only once. Nor is it readily understood why Cannon was allowed "three days with three sessions a day to argue his case without any restriction as to method or time," whereas his accusers were not permitted to "make any argument or to offer any rebuttal."

Dr. Prettyman implied strongly that the atmosphere of the investigating-room was one of hostility, for he declared that when he told of having gone to New York to interview the witnesses in the case, "Rev. Mr. Duran . . . asked why I had not taken some respectable person along with me." Prettyman commented: "Of course the answer was that in seeking the facts connected with the infamous career of Bishop Cannon I had to come in contact with those with whom he had established intimate relations for years." He added that "the insult went unrebuked by any member of the investigation."

The charge of adultery filed against the Bishop by the four ministers of his church revolved mainly about two documents. One of these was an affidavit that Mrs. McCallum was claimed to have signed on April 12, 1930,[6] and the other was an affidavit signed by her friend Mrs. Joan Chapman on September 12, 1930.[7] Both documents were said by Dr. Prettyman to have been presented at the investigation in Mt. Vernon Place Methodist Church, Washington.

The affidavit said to have been signed by Mrs. McCallum bore the same date (April 12) as United Press dispatches from Huntsville, Alabama, and St. Louis, Missouri, reporting that Bishop Cannon had married Mrs. Mary Moore McCoy, of Athens, Alabama, widow of Bishop McCoy. The Huntsville dispatch quoted Mrs. William H. Moore, of St. Augustine, Florida, as saying that she had received "indirect word of the wedding of her sister-in-law," Mrs. McCoy, to Bishop Cannon. Cannon had denied reports of this marriage several weeks previously in Berlin, following his arrival there from North Africa. But Mrs. McCoy was known to be on a trip around the world, and here was the report cropping up again. Furthermore, and this seemed doubly convincing, the dispatch from St. Louis quoted a niece of Mrs. McCoy as saying: "The whole family knows that my aunt and Bishop Cannon are married." She said she understood the knot had been tied in Europe "about two weeks ago." While there was no truth in the reports, and this was definitely established a short time later, there may well have been a direct connection between these articles in the press and Mrs. McCallum's seeming willingness to sign a statement that subsequently was used against the Bishop at the Washington inquiry. A woman who has been visited frequently in her apartment by her cavalier is hardly to be blamed for a feeling of deep resentment and anger if the press

Dry Messiah

carries apparently authentic reports that he has suddenly married another without informing her of the fact.

Yet even this is no full and complete explanation of the McCallum "affidavit." The document's origin needs to be elucidated further. Dr. Prettyman tells us in his statement concerning the Washington investigation that the "confession" was dictated by Mrs. McCallum in her apartment in the presence of three reporters for the *New York Evening Journal:* Austin O'Malley, Sidney Livingston, and John Weissberger; that one of the three typed it, and that she signed it. Dr. Prettyman also declares:

> It was admitted that this woman two days later went in a cab from her apartment in the company of reporter O'Malley to the bank in New York City [where she kept her correspondence with Cannon in a lock-box]. She got out of the cab, walked across the street alone, went into the bank alone and brought out from her lock-box various letters that had been written to her by Bishop Cannon and gave them voluntarily to reporter O'Malley.

Cannon's critics have suggested no motive for her action other than a desire to hit back at the Bishop because of his supposed marriage to Mrs. McCoy. No claim was made at the Washington inquiry that the *New York Evening Journal* or the wets paid Mrs. McCallum anything for the affidavit or the letters. The newspaper made no use of the affidavit in its columns. The document evidently was felt to be too dangerous for publication, and the text has never been published. The *Evening Journal* did carry extracts from the letters, as did other Hearst papers and the *Philadelphia Record*.

At the Washington hearing Bishop Cannon countered the affidavit attributed to Mrs. McCallum with another that she had signed, but which he apparently had written. It was dated April 21, nine days after the other, and was thrown together just before Mrs. McCallum had an abdominal operation in Sibley Hospital, Washington. Dr. Prettyman was forbidden to have a copy of this second affidavit, which was, he said, eight or ten pages long and closely written. He made full notes while it was being read, but was then forbidden to keep the notes, so that he had to rely on his memory for the contents. He said he was competent to give the substance from memory.

Cherchez La Femme

Mrs. McCallum, according to this affidavit, which Prettyman said "was written by Bishop Cannon himself," claimed that "on the 11th of April, 1930, at about 10 o'clock P.M., there was a knock at her door, and someone in the hall announced a 'telegram.'" (Apparently Prettyman erred here as to the date, since at two other points he speaks of the affidavit as being dated April 12, and the document presented at the hearing does, in fact, bear that date.) His account continues:

> She threw on her wrapper and went to the door, and three men entered. They told her that they were going to arrest her for larceny. She said she did not know what "larceny" meant (this is the literary secretary of Bishop James Cannon, Jr.!) They told her that "larceny" meant theft, and that she had not paid her bills. She replied that she would try to pay her bills — that she would get somebody to help her. Then they told her they were not going to arrest her for larceny but for prostitution and that the papers would announce that the secretary of Bishop James Cannon, Jr., was arrested for prostitution. In her excitement, to prevent the newspapers from publishing that the secretary of Bishop James Cannon, Jr., was a prostitute, she dictated at their demand a paper giving the story of her introduction and relation to Bishop Cannon and admitting her unlawful relation to him.

If the foregoing is an accurate description of what happened, it is most extraordinary that neither Cannon nor his wife filed suit for enormous damages against the *Evening Journal*. The Bishop, as we have seen, sued the Hearst newspapers for a total of no less than $7,500,000, all told. Yet he let this episode pass unnoticed, in so far as his extensive litigation was concerned. Prettyman declared that Cannon admitted at the Washington inquiry, in response to a question from him, that he had not made any complaint to the civil authorities or to anyone else against these men for their savage behavior. Small wonder that Prettyman asked subsequently: "Can anyone who knows the character of Bishop Cannon suppose for a moment that he would let go in absolute silence such conduct on the part of these men if he believed for a moment the truth of Mrs. McCallum's later statement?" He pointed out, further, that O'Malley had made oath before a notary that Mrs. McCallum dictated and signed the incriminating paper freely and voluntarily, and added: "In the next place, the fact was proven that, two days after, the woman voluntarily went to her lock-box with one of these men and gave to him letters that had been written to her by Bishop Cannon."

Another aspect of the matter which was stressed by Dr. Prettyman in his analysis, following the conclusion of the hearings, was the failure of Bishop Cannon to present any evidence during the investigation tending to show that Mrs. McCallum had a good reputation in New York or that she had made any convincing social, business, or religious contacts during her eight or nine years' residence in that city. "No one undertook, either in person or by affidavit, to testify that she had any relation to any institution of the city that would fortify her under the implications of this case," Prettyman declared.

Prettyman seemingly did not place great emphasis at the hearing upon the long affidavit from Mrs. Joan Chapman which was presented there. This document, as noted above, was dated September 12, 1930, and went into great detail concerning the relations between Bishop Cannon and Mrs. McCallum, beginning with the episode at the Hotel McAlpin, when Mrs. Chapman was present. In his exhaustive letter to Albert H. Dudley concerning the events of the hearing, Dr. Prettyman devoted only one paragraph to this affidavit and declared that "it was not valuable except as corroborating other established facts," since "most of it was hearsay evidence." Much of this material apparently was deemed too potentially libellous for publication, but the Hearst papers did carry some of it — the milder portions. Mrs. Chapman said in the affidavit that she had first met Mrs. McCallum about nine years previously when the latter first came to New York, after leaving her husband, a Detroit automobile salesman. Mrs. McCallum had been married to him for about five years, Mrs. Chapman said. He died later of tuberculosis.

Some of the reasons why the twelve elders found "no trial necessary," despite the evidence accumulated by Dr. Prettyman and his associates, have been mentioned. There were others. The prosecution decided to introduce a private detective as a witness. This individual was not to have testified against the Bishop directly, but only with respect to an allegation that the Bishop's Washington office had been used from time to time by someone else as a place of assignation. The private detective was to have given certain testimony in the matter that was expected to be damaging to Cannon, although no one claimed that he himself had used his office suite for immoral purposes. But to the astonishment of those who had summoned the detective, his testimony was precisely contrary to their expectations. Of course, this witness should never have been brought into the case unless those responsible for summoning him knew precisely what they were doing. As it was, the thing boomeranged badly and created a highly unfavorable impression upon the twelve elders. Indeed, it is understood to have prejudiced the case of the accusers more than any other single development of the hearing. This grievous mistake on the part of Cannon's accusers gave those who were seeking an excuse to exonerate him the very opening they were looking for.

The intervention of the Hearst press likewise is believed to have influenced the jury in Cannon's favor. This chain of sensational, scandal-mongering, soaking wet newspapers provided the Bishop with precisely the sort of issue that he knew best how to use. There was the fact that Hearst himself was said to have given written instructions to his editors to launch a determined and carefully calculated series of assaults on Cannon, with a view to undermining his influence and weakening the prohibitionist cause. The damaging affidavit attributed to Mrs. McCallum had been signed in her apartment at the behest of three Hearst reporters. There was a sharp divergence between the testimony given at the Washington hearing by Austin O'Malley, one of the three, and that of Cannon himself, as to how and why the affidavit was secured, and the Methodist jury preferred to believe Cannon's version, despite its manifest implausibilities. O'Malley was an employee of the *New York Evening Journal,* a Hearst paper. More, he was obviously a Roman Catholic. That was about all the Bishop needed. The leader of the moral forces had been proved guilty of bucketshop gambling and flour-hoarding before the inquiry so much as opened, but the introduction of such elements as the private detective and a Catholic Hearst reporter seems to have made the elders forget all this as completely as though they had never heard of it.

Did Cannon introduce himself to Mrs. McCallum in the Mc-Alpin Hotel lobby as "Stephen Trent, an author"? Prettyman gave the following version of testimony presented at the hearing:

> The facts brought out in this case which were admitted by him were that he met this woman without introduction in company with another woman in the lobby of the McAlpin Hotel, introducing himself as Stephen Trent, an author. He claimed in his testimony that he had spoken that day before a Methodist ministers' meeting at which time he had prophesied that if the Democrats nominated "Al" Smith, the South would not vote for him. This woman came up to him and shook hands with him and expressed her interest in the anti-Smith movement. That same night, he said, he met her in the lobby of the McAlpin Hotel in company with another woman, and he spoke to her and told her that he sometimes went by the name of Stephen Trent. He took them that night in a cab to the apartment of one of the women, remaining there some time and gave to the woman in question $20.

There are at least three extraordinary things about the foregoing. First, if the lady was, in truth, attending a Methodist ministers' meeting when Bishop Cannon addressed it earlier in the day (and the Bishop makes reference to this as a fact in a letter to her that appeared later in the *New York American*), nobody has explained how she happened to be present at such a gathering. Second, how could Mrs. McCallum have heard him speak without knowing that he was Bishop James Cannon, Jr., the widely heralded moral mentor to a large segment of America? And third, how could Cannon justify his having told her that he was an author and that he sometimes went by the name of Stephen Trent when this was not true?

Such was Cannon's less than convincing version of his first meeting with the woman who later became his bride. Yet this and other equally questionable and dubious declarations in answer to the charges preferred against him were considered satisfactory by the twelve elders.

For reasons best known to himself, the accused cleric never

consented to the publication of his defense against the allegation of adultery. Both he and his wife were entirely innocent of the grave charge, but they were not willing for proof of that innocence to be made known. A good many sound and well-disposed Methodists have never been able to follow that reasoning. In the pungent words of Dr. Prettyman: "By what process of moral justification may a Bishop, accused of vile misconduct in the public press of the country, evade the vindication of his character by seeking to keep his own answer to the charges from the public?"

The twelve elders found "no trial necessary," but the *Nashville Christian Advocate* spoke for a host of Americans, both inside and outside the Methodist Church, when it declared that the outcome did not exonerate the Bishop.

CHAPTER *xvii*

The Bishop Wins Again

THE FOREGOING inquiry into the workings of the episcopal libido had failed to bring altogether tangible results, but now a thoroughgoing probe into the Bishop's far-flung financial operations in the Hoover-Smith campaign loomed on the congressional agenda. It was suspected in high quarters that those operations had been conducted in violation of the Federal Corrupt Practices Act.

This inquiry had been foreshadowed in 1929, when Representative George H. Tinkham, of Massachusetts, demanded additional data concerning the Bishop's expenditures in the presidential contest of 1928. Cannon had left himself open to such a challenge when he publicly denounced certain newspapers for publishing what he termed the "amazing and absolutely false" declaration that during the campaign he had made two loans of $5,000 each to the anti-Smith Democrats of Virginia. That was in July 1929, and Tinkham leaped upon the denial (as was noted in Chapter xv).

While Cannon had not lent the anti-Smith Democrats $10,000 in two installments of $5,000 each, he had lent them a substantial sum. Tinkham put the total erroneously at in excess of $27,000 and demanded to know where the Bishop got the money. He also suggested to Attorney General William D. Mitchell that the Department of Justice dig into the question whether there had been a violation of the Federal Corrupt Practices Act. Cannon retorted that he had written to Attorney General Mitchell offering him access to any information. He added that there was no mystery about the source of the funds. He declared that Tinkham, if he so desired, could "get a list of Virginia banks with which Bishop Cannon has done business for years and find out whether they think Bishop Cannon would have any difficulty in arranging a credit of ten, fifteen or twenty thousand dollars for a period of six months." Cannon went on to say that he "did not hesitate to use his own money and credit to accomplish his purpose" in the 1928 campaign, and that the loans were "fully repaid."

Representative Tinkham loosed his initial blast at the Bishop in the summer of 1929, just as Tinkham was sailing for Europe. The issue became quiescent for some months, but it erupted in full fury the following spring. The Attorney General had given no evidence, meanwhile, of initiating an inquiry into possible corrupt-practice violations by the Bishop, and the Massachusetts wet was determined to bring the matter into the open. The Senate Lobby Committee, headed by Senator T. H. Caraway, of Arkansas, was about to put Henry H. Curran, president of the Association Against the Prohibition Amendment, on the griddle, and Tinkham resolved that Cannon too should feel the inquisitorial fire. He announced, therefore, that he would demand that the Caraway committee investigate the activities of the Bishop and his Southern Methodist Board of Temperance and Social Service. Cannon thereupon wrote Caraway that he would be glad to appear.

The bearded anti-prohibitionist from the Bay State felt that in Cannon's case he was hot on the trail of a major malefactor. He told the Caraway committee that $65,300 of a $172,000 contribution made by Edwin C. Jameson, New York insurance magnate, to the Hoover campaign fund in 1928 had been paid to Cannon, but that Cannon had reported receiving only $17,000 of the amount. Caraway replied that his committee was not empowered to investigate political contributions, but that it would look into any lobbying by the Bishop or agencies represented by him.

Tinkham said in his appearance before the committee that Cannon had engaged in "offensive and coercive lobbying activities." Unquestionably many members of Congress who had felt the force of his lash agreed, but the Bostonian went to preposterous lengths when he sought to buttress his charges by quoting a letter which he said Cannon wrote to Senator Charles Curtis, of

Kansas, in 1926, asking "whether those in control of legislation in the Senate are willing for Congress to adjourn without passing important prohibition legislation."

This mild, even deferential communiqué was described by the over-vehement Tinkham as "an audacious sectarian appeal with an implied threat of political reprisals." "I submit," he went on, "that it is a letter which no Senator should receive without a feeling of resentment and indignation." Many a member of Congress must have winced and smiled wryly at this attempt to paint the national legislature as having so high a sense of integrity that even the merest suggestion from a lobbying organization would be hotly repudiated.

A few weeks later Jameson, a man of medium height with a black mustache, appeared before the Lobby Committee to answer questions concerning his extremely generous contributions to the Hoover and anti-Smith campaign funds. He confessed that he had not inquired carefully into the uses to which his money would be put, since he was merely concerned with whether it would be spent in support of the Eighteenth Amendment. The election of Al Smith, he felt, would have been a body blow to Federal prohibition.

The Caraway Committee and the large crowd of spectators blinked when the New York capitalist stated that he had made it possible for Bishop Cannon to obtain the entire total of $65,300 in cash at various times, and that the Bishop had requested this. Checks were usually for $5,000 or $10,000, and in almost every instance were made out to "Cash," with Cannon's name appearing nowhere on them. He carried off $10,000 in currency from Jameson's New York office on several different occasions.

It developed also that Cannon sent Jameson a telegram from Lake Wales, Florida, on February 12, 1929, instructing him how to report the above-mentioned contributions. This message was dispatched by Cannon after the Senate Committee Investigating Campaign Funds, headed by Senator Frederick Steiwer, had called on him for an accounting. The text follows:

Tried talk long distance New York, but office closed Lincoln's Birthday. After careful examination records think statement should be: paid Headquarters Committee Anti-Smith Democrats seventeen thousand three hundred; paid Virginia Committee Anti-Smith Democrats forty-eight thousand, making total sixty-five thousand three hundred. This corresponds exactly with our official reports. Call Lincoln two nine four six Washington any time after eight thirty until midnight tonight, when leaving for New York; sailing Thursday.

This message requested Jameson to make a report that did not conform to his own records. The New Yorker had paid the entire sum of $65,300 to Cannon, but he followed the latter's directions in filing his statement.

"You followed the information from Bishop Cannon . . . although it did not correspond with your records at all?" asked Senator Caraway.

"Well it doesn't seem to correspond with them now, does it?" [1] was Jameson's reply.

This financial angel of the "moral forces" went on to reveal that he actually gave Cannon $7,300 in cash a month or two after the campaign ended. In explanation he said:

> Bishop Cannon was in debt and was financially — well, I won't say embarrassed, but I mean to say he was in debt, and seemed to have worked so hard in the campaign, and to have paid his own money for things, probably — I don't know what. Anyway, he was in debt for bills and things, so I helped him. I made him that contribution — I don't mean contribution. I made him that gift — just made him a gift.

The Bishop walked out of Jameson's office with the $7,300 in greenbacks, $4,300 of it in December and $3,000 in January. The trusting philanthropist handed over the money in cash, as requested, upon being told by the dry leader that he needed it. Cannon did not even claim that all these "debts" had been incurred during the campaign, but Jameson understood that there was a "deficit" of some kind, and that his $7,300 would cover it. There was never any accounting to Jameson of what Cannon did with the money. [2]

Senator Caraway, noted for his waspish tongue, was well-nigh speechless over this revelation, but he recovered himself sufficiently to toss in sharp comments at various other points in the proceedings.

It appeared, for example, that C. Bascom Slemp, an extremely practical politician from Virginia, who had served as secretary to former President Calvin Coolidge, was the man who introduced Jameson to Cannon. When Jameson seemed uncertain at the hearing whether it was "Slemp who actually brought Bishop Cannon to my office," Caraway cut in with: "If it wasn't Mr. Slemp it was some other great reformer, no doubt."

The facts as to the large sums contributed by a New York capitalist to carry Virginia and other Southern states for Hoover were especially amusing, in the light of the loud wails from Cannon and his followers during the presidential contest of 1928 that Al Smith had been foisted on the South by Tammany Hall and that funds from New York were being poured into Virginia to carry it for Smith.

At the conclusion of Jameson's testimony before the Caraway committee, its chairman requested Charles H. Tuttle, Federal District Attorney, to permit an agent of the committee to examine all records concerning the transactions of Bishop Cannon with Harry L. Goldhurst and the New York bucketshop of Kable & Company. Tuttle assented, and a representative of the committee left for New York. This was on May 16, the week before Cannon's bucketshop adventures were explored at Dallas, Texas, by delegates to the Southern Methodist General Conference. It will be recalled that the full truth concerning his fantastic bucketshop plunging was not made public until after he had squeaked through the Dallas inquiry without a formal trial.

During this period the Caraway committee uncovered the report of Dr. Clarence True Wilson, made immediately following the campaign of 1928, in which the executive secretary of the (Northern) Methodist Board of Temperance, Prohibition and Public Morals revealed that his agency had given $5,000 to Bishop Cannon with which to pay his "printing bills" during the campaign. Said Dr. Wilson:

> When Bishop Cannon was doing his heroic work and being roundly abused by a set of men whom we think will need the bal-

ance of their lifetime to explain some of their remarks away, we did our best to see if we could not get a little bit of money to help pay his printing bills.

Dr. Wilson "spent a sleepless night over the matter. . . . I worried and I think I prayed," he said. When he opened the mail next morning, he found that it contained $35,000 instead of the $15,000 that had been anticipated. The sum of $5,000 was accordingly rushed to the Bishop — whether by check or in specie, the report does not say.

Incidentally, Cannon made no mention of having received this money when he filed his report with the Federal authorities, although it was admitted that the $5,000 was spent in distributing dry literature to many states.[3] Hence the argument he made as to the $48,000 from Jameson (that it was all spent inside Virginia) could not be advanced in extenuation.

When Cannon returned from Dallas, he was scheduled to go before the Lobby Committee again, this time with Senator Thomas J. Walsh, of Montana, presiding in the absence of Senator Caraway, who was in Arkansas. Walsh, one of the ablest and most respected lawyers in the Senate, was a Roman Catholic, a fact that caused him embarrassment, in view of Cannon's constant reiteration that many of the attacks on him had been inspired by members of that church.

The Bishop issued a statement in which he contended that the Lobby Committee was without jurisdiction to inquire into his expenditures in the 1928 campaign. Senator Walsh replied: "We have not hesitated to question other witnesses concerning political expenditures."

On June 3 Cannon came before the committee, with Senator Walsh in the chair. The Bishop entered the hearing using a crutch, but although his face showed deep lines and he seemed almost ill from the strain of the Dallas hearing, he was vigorous in his replies when Walsh began questioning him.

Early in the proceedings he charged that wet and Roman Catholic interests had tried to discredit him and that the committee's investigation of his affairs was "persecution." Laughter, applause, and hisses greeted this sally. Senator Walsh, a Catholic but a dry, said: "I cannot help but get the implication in that statement." Cannon quickly put in: "I do not charge you, Senator, with persecution."

Senator Caraway was not on hand to participate in these exchanges, but he issued a statement from Little Rock upholding Bishop Cannon's contention that the Lobby Committee had no right to inquire into the Bishop's political activities in 1928. He reiterated that the committee was authorized to deal only with "propaganda and lobbying."

The Caraway declaration was cited by Cannon as proving that the committee was exceeding its authority. He defiantly told Senator Walsh and the other members that it was no business of Congress what he did or what money he spent in his "purely private" work in opposition to Al Smith two years previously. Applause and hisses swept the committee room again as the gray-haired, bespectacled churchman almost shouted that he would not reveal the facts, even though he had been warned that others had gone to jail for refusing to answer senatorial questions. "If this committee, appointed to investigate lobbying, assumes the right to investigate my political activities as an individual in the Anti-Smith campaign, then it can assume the right to investigate the activities of every individual citizen who votes or works in any political campaign pertaining to the election of national officers," Cannon said firmly. He added that this was a matter "too vital to be compromised."

Walsh recalled that the committee had investigated the work of the Southern Tariff League and other organizations concerned with congressional elections. He expressed himself as "entirely satisfied that we were wholly justified in pursuing these inquiries, and it would be indefensible for the committee not to go into your activities." Walsh conceded that he might be wrong as to the limit of "this particular committee," but he said the Senate could order an inquiry broad enough to meet all requirements.

None of this moved the Bishop from his position. Cross-examined at length by Senator John J. Blaine, of Wisconsin, Cannon repeatedly refused to answer. He declined with great emphasis to produce the documents showing how he spent the $48,300 [4] that Jameson had sent to Virginia, and said with vehemence: "You'll never see that account!" He did vouchsafe an explanation for wanting to collect and disburse the Jameson money in cash. "I knew the enemy we were fighting in Virginia," said he, "and I wanted to use cash for our workers." The Bishop meant to say that he felt obliged to protect his workers from reprisals at the hands of Virginia's Democratic machine. If the names of those who received the money were divulged — so his argument ran — they might somehow be punished.

A few hours later Cannon issued to the press a statement giving what he said were total expenditures in Virginia by congressional districts. He repeated his denunciation of the committee's attitude as "a deliberate and intolerable infringement upon the rights of American citizens," and then announced that the $48,300 about which information was being sought was spent as follows:

> General purposes of state work, including speakers, travel, automobiles, postage, etc. (round numbers), $16,000; for county and precinct organization, election day work, etc. — First Congressional District, $2,000; Second, $4,500; Third, $6,500; Fourth, $2,200; Fifth, $4,000; Sixth, $3,000; Seventh, $3,000; Eighth, $2,500; Ninth, $2,100; Tenth, $2,500; total $48,300.

Since there were no possible means by which the committee could trace these "round numbers," giving totals disbursed in cash to unnamed persons, this list of expenditures by congressional districts meant almost less than nothing.

In making known these figures the Bishop also said:

> Having labored nearly forty years for the prohibition cause, and having refused to accept any compensation whatever for my work, when I might have had at least $100,000, and having given all I have ever made to maintain a dry newspaper in Richmond, I do not think persons whose opinions I value will believe that I used any of the $48,300 for my own personal profit, especially in view of the results secured by the expenditure of so small a sum compared with $107,000 reported as expended by the Virginia State Democratic Committee to elect a wet Tammany candidate.

Not even the Bishop's worst enemies were ever able to show that he had received pay for his work as a prohibitionist. It is not true, however, that he could have had "at least $100,000" for that work, since during most of his forty years as a dry Cannon held no paying position with the Anti-Saloon League. He was superintendent of the Anti-Saloon League of Virginia for nine years, and had he been paid the usual salary for such a post, he would have received hardly more than $35,000. True, if Cannon had abandoned his educational and religious work and devoted all his time to the prohibitionist cause for forty years, he could have made $100,000, and more. But he could not have carried on his manifold other activities, which were unrelated to prohibition, and have earned "at least $100,000." His statement on the point is, therefore, a quibble, to put it no more strongly.

Then there is his extraordinary allegation that he had "given all I have ever made" to maintain the *Richmond Virginian*. Precisely how much he did give to keep the *Virginian* afloat, as we have seen in an earlier chapter, is debatable. Certainly it was utterly absurd for him to contend that he gave "all" he had ever made to that cause. If this was true, how could he subsequently gamble in bucketshops? If this was true, how did he pay Mrs. Helen Hawley McCallum various sums?

On the day after Cannon issued the foregoing statement he appeared briefly before the Caraway committee, with the chairman still absent. He read a prepared statement which expressed the belief that the inquiry was "a part of the effort for many months of wet and Roman Catholic elements and those who worship party regularity to prevent a recurrence of the Asheville Conference in 1932." He then added:

> I must respectfully state that having answered all questions addressed to me by the committee on which I volunteered to appear as a witness, I shall now withdraw as a voluntary witness. If the committee desires to subpoena me, that is its right.

After reading the foregoing words at the conclusion of his statement, the Bishop gathered up his crutch and amid loud applause and equally loud hisses started out of the room.

"You take your own course, but we have not excused you," Senator Walsh said. "Senator Blaine wishes to question you."

"I will be at my office if the committee wishes to subpoena me," Cannon called over his shoulder, as he left the chamber.

The Bishop Wins Again

The mildness of the language in the Bishop's prepared statement conveys no true picture of the truly venomous attitude that he assumed toward the committee immediately before and during his departure. In the words of Frank R. Kent, the *Baltimore Sun's* celebrated columnist, his contempt was "not only legal, but physical, mental, moral and spiritual." Kent went on to declare that the Bishop "did everything except stick his tongue out at the committee," and that "he might as well have spit on it."

> He left the stand . . . with a face congested with anger and malignant glances darting from his small eyes. His carriage, his air, his words, his looks and his departure were eloquent of loathing. He squarely turned his back on a member in the middle of a sentence. He left abruptly, discourteously, deliberately. It was supreme contempt.

Cannon behaved in this fashion, Kent went on, although "he had been treated with extreme courtesy by the always courteous Walsh," and the "sneers and jeers that have been the portion of so many witnesses under Mr. Caraway were noticeably absent." The commentator asserted that no one in Washington could recall "as direct and deliberate a slap as this Senate committee got from Mr. Cannon," and he added that the question is "not only can the Bishop get away with it, but will the Senate let him get away with it."

Another able and experienced eyewitness, Paul Y. Anderson, wrote in the *Nation:*

> Writing as one who witnessed both incidents, I can testify that the contempt for which [Harry F.] Sinclair served a jail term was the perfection of deference compared to the Bishop's insolent and calculated challenge. Politely, on advice of counsel, the oil magnate declined to answer four questions. After refusing to answer at least forty, Cannon crowned his defiance by deluging the committee with abuse, and walking out of the room in contempt of an order to remain on the witness stand. It was the most complete, direct and deliberate affront ever administered to a body of Congress. It was planned in advance, carried out with deliberation, and delivered with a degree of rank insult perhaps unequaled in Congressional history.

Dry Messiah

Anderson's assertion that the Bishop was guilty of "deluging the committee with abuse" was a serious exaggeration, but the facts were bad enough. It was widely felt that the Senate would have to deal firmly with Cannon or forfeit its own self-respect and the respect of the public. Senator Walsh promptly told the press that he considered the ecclesiastic to be "in plain contempt of the Senate." He stated that although the Bishop had appeared voluntarily, he had thereby placed himself under the committee's jurisdiction, and hence could not withdraw unless and until he was excused.

The stir was tremendous, and the *Baltimore Evening Sun* compared Bishop Cannon to Cardinal Richelieu, "the historical personage he most resembles." Both men were possessed of "inflexibility" and "incredible audacity," said the paper's editorial, which was captioned "Richelieu Returns."

It was the first time in the history of the Senate that a witness had flouted the authority and dignity of a senatorial committee by leaving the witness stand without permission. The Bishop's enemies were exultant, for they felt that here, at last, was a slip that could not be rectified or explained away, and that Cannon would surely suffer condign punishment and be publicly humiliated.

But on the very day that Cannon walked out on the Senate Lobby Committee, Washington correspondents were saying that the committee was "at a loss" concerning the course it ought to pursue, and that "doubt prevailed on Capitol Hill that any action would be taken against the churchman."

It soon became evident that the shrewd and far-seeing Cannon had looked farther down the road than his enemies. He had coolly calculated that of the five members of the Lobby Committee, four were dry. One of the four was Walsh, who had shown that he was in favor of bringing Cannon to heel, but the other three were not only in the prohibitionist camp, but quite unlikely to take any action against the Bishop that the prohibitionists might find objectionable. These three men were Chairman Caraway and Senators William E. Borah, of Idaho, and Arthur R. Robinson, of Indiana. All had been absent from many sessions, especially those at which Cannon was being grilled, but when the time came to decide what action the committee would take concerning *l'affaire* Cannon, the full quota of five would cast their ballots — and nobody knew this better than the Bishop.

But before the matter came to a vote, Cannon issued a statement on June 6 in which he declared that his walkout the preceding day signified no discourtesy. Then on June 11 he strode back into the presence of the Senate Lobby Committee as abruptly as he had made his exit the week before. He answered questions on activities of the Southern Methodist Church, but persisted in his refusal to undergo examination on his own campaign against Al Smith. This time the Bishop's manner was highly deferential, contrasted with his hostile and contemptuous attitude of six days previously. He reiterated that he had intended no discourtesy on that occasion.

The proceedings were enlivened by the action of an elderly woman who stepped up to the committee table and proclaimed: "This is a Romanist hold-up of Protestant America, and I protest." Chairman Caraway rapped sharply for order, and she returned to her seat.

After the day's hearing had been completed the committee took a vote on whether it had authority to question Cannon specifically concerning his anti-Smith activities two years previously, and the members stood four to one in the negative, with Blaine the only committeeman voting aye. Walsh said he still thought the committee had the right to pursue the inquiry, but explained that since the group was divided on the point, he deemed it "unwise to go further."

There remained the possibility that Walsh would push his move to submit the problem to the Senate and request wider investigative authority. It soon became evident, however, that he would not. Senators Borah and Robinson, of the committee, were openly opposed to his doing so. It was understood that Borah took this position because of the explosive character of the debate that could be expected on such a motion, involving, as it might, the whole matter of Catholicism, anti-Catholicism, and the Ku Klux Klan. Senator J. Thomas Heflin, of Alabama, the notorious spokesman for kluxery, whose tirades against the Vatican for years had emptied the floor and the galleries, announced that he would have much to say if the move was pressed to give the Lobby Committee increased authority.

So the entire effort to bring Bishop Cannon to book was abandoned by the committee. This astounding politico-cleric had executed a highly meaningful and difficult maneuver with a finesse and an éclat that Cardinal Richelieu might indeed have envied. He not only had won his own fight, but had forced the committee to confess, in effect, that it had exceeded its authority in various other inquiries made by it since the previous autumn. And this in the face of the fact that on the committee were two of the ablest lawyers in the Senate, Walsh and Borah.

But if the Bishop had won a resounding technical victory, the fact remained that he had refused to tell what he did with the $48,300 that Jameson had given him. His reticence, it was widely noted, contrasted with the frankness shown before the Caraway committee by Henry H. Curran, president of the Association Against the Prohibition Amendment. Curran, like Cannon, told the group that he did not believe it had the power to compel answers, but he answered all questions anyway.

It is noteworthy, too, that whereas Cannon was treated with great deference by the committee, that prohibitionist-dominated body went after Curran almost as though he were a criminal and his work against the Eighteenth Amendment in flagrant violation of the Constitution and the statutes. In the words of Walter Lippmann, writing in the *Forum:*

> Early this Spring a Senate committee presided over by Senator Caraway of Arkansas sent an agent to the offices of the Association Against the Prohibition Amendment, seized all the papers in the office of its president, Major Curran, took them off to Washington, read them, and then made public letters — private or otherwise — which it thought would damage Major Curran and his association . . . in short Senator Caraway brutally invaded the privacy of American citizens for malicious and partisan purposes.

Thus the man who answered all questions, despite his belief that he was not obligated to do so, was hounded in a gross and inexcusable manner, while the leader of the "moral forces" who flatly refused to answer numerous questions, and who never revealed what he did with $48,300, was allowed to make good his defiance. It was but another sample of the sort of partisanship that was shown by prohibition's votaries during the heyday of the "noble experiment."

Not only did Bishop Cannon win a famous victory over the Senate Lobby Committee, but it developed that he had got away with a violation of the Virginia election laws. Leon M. Bazile, Richmond lawyer who had served for ten years as Assistant Attorney General of Virginia, asserted immediately following the conclusion of the proceedings before the Lobby Committee that the prelate had admitted, in one of his statements to the press in connection with the Washington hearings, that he had taken steps that were contrary to the "pure elections law" of the Old Dominion. Bazile, who subsequently was elevated to the circuit bench in Virginia, directed attention to Cannon's declaration that he had used part of the Jameson fund to compensate "speakers" and "organizers" in the campaign of 1928. He quoted the statute and pointed out that whereas it permitted funds to be spent for such purposes as clerk hire, travel, advertising, postage, hiring halls, and transporting voters to the polls, there was no authorization of payments to "speakers" or "organizers." But Bazile also directed attention to the fact that although penalties of up to five hundred dollars or twelve months in jail or both were provided for violations, and that Cannon was clearly a violator, prosecution had to begin within one year after any breach. Consequently it was too late to institute proceedings against him.

So the cleric not only had backed the Senate and its Lobby Committee off the map, but had also broken the Virginia election laws with impunity. It was beginning to look as though no agency of the Southern Methodist Church, of the Federal government, or of the government of Virginia was smart enough and forehanded enough to win a joust with the "Best Brain in America."

But the Senate Lobby Committee had hardly written finis to the Cannon case when Representative Tinkham returned to the attack with a long speech to the House in which he flatly accused the Bishop of violating the Federal Corrupt Practices Act. The extremely wet Massachusetts Congressman was greeted by two minutes of sustained applause when he rose to address the overwhelmingly dry House, which listened with close attention throughout. He not only declared that Bishop Cannon had violated the Corrupt Practices Act, but added that until the ecclesiastic told in detail what he did with the $48,300 he received from Edwin C. Jameson, he would "stand convicted in the eyes of all honest men of having appropriated the money to his own uses." At the conclusion of his thirty-minute speech Tinkham told the press that he would demand prosecution of Cannon by the Department of Justice.

The Bishop thereupon assailed Tinkham as a "blustering cowardly Congressman" for attacking him on the floor of the House under immunity from prosecution for libel. He dared Tinkham to give to the press over his personal signature the statements he had made under congressional immunity. The answer of the lawmaker from New England was a chuckle and a remark that he did "not accept challenges from discredited persons."

Two days later, however, Tinkham decided to issue a declaration to the press, thus divesting himself of immunity in connection with it. This statement was much briefer than the address he delivered to the House, but it contained the charge that the Bishop was "a shameless violator of the Federal Corrupt Practices Act." It asserted that Cannon "illegally concealed . . . until February 15, 1929" the receipt of $65,300 from Edwin C. Jameson, and that the Bishop "has not yet accounted for $48,300 of this amount, refusing to do so before the Senate Lobby Investigating Committee." It was promptly noted that Tinkham had omitted the assertion he had previously made that Cannon would "stand convicted in the eyes of all honest men of having appropriated the [Jameson] money to his own uses."

These exchanges occurred in June 1930, shortly before the Bishop sailed for London with his bride-to-be, Mrs. McCallum. Since they left for Brazil soon after being wed and did not return to the United States until early autumn, at which time the groom was facing charges of gross immorality filed by four Methodist ministers, the Cannon-Tinkham feud remained quiescent for the time being.

The Bishop was confronted by the official inquiry into the

immorality charges and was ill with arthritis in a Washington hospital when Tinkham wrote to Attorney General Mitchell in November formally demanding that he be brought to trial for violation of the Corrupt Practices Act.

Then Senator Carter Glass introduced a resolution in the Senate designed to make Cannon go before the Select Committee on Senatorial Campaign Expenditures, headed by Senator Gerald P. Nye, of North Dakota, and answer the questions that he had refused to answer before the Caraway Lobby Committee. The resolution specifically empowered the Nye committee to investigate violations of the Corrupt Practices Act and the "fraudulent conversion to private uses . . . of campaign funds." It was promptly adopted.

Two weeks later the Bishop appeared before twelve ministers of his own church, charged with adultery, bucketshop gambling, lying, and other grave offenses. The elders found "no trial necessary" on February 7, 1931. On February 9 Senator Nye announced that his committee would investigate Cannon's campaign expenditures.

A few weeks later, when the Bishop had recovered sufficiently from the strain of the ecclesiastical inquiry into his sex life and related matters, he wrote to Senator Nye from Los Angeles that the Glass resolution was unconstitutional, since it conferred purely "judicial powers" upon a legislative committee. The resolution attempted to have the committee "assume the functions of a grand jury," and the Supreme Court has held, the Bishop went on, that investigation of such matters is "for the courts and not for Congress." Senator Nye said he would take this under advisement.

Some weeks later he accused Cannon of "making sport of the committee," in that the Bishop had pleaded that he was too ill to appear and tell the committee what he did with the $48,300 given him by Jameson, although there were press reports of his appearances before various church organizations. In reply the cleric reiterated that his strength was insufficient to cope with a senatorial investigation and its resultant "world-wide newspaper publicity," but he said he could "preach a short sermon every Sunday or give a prohibition talk every night in the week." These latter forms of activity involved "practically no nervous strain," he asserted.

The unedifying spectacle of a Methodist Bishop dodging one trial after another, on technical or other grounds, and leaving many things unanswered and unexplained in so far as members of his church and the public at large were concerned, naturally caused enormous repercussions in the ranks of Methodism.

Feeling against the Bishop crystallized in the spring of 1931 in petitions signed by many Southern Methodist laymen declaring that "the Cannon case" had given rise to "a condition unparalleled in the history of our church." The signers, who came from all over the South, expressed the conviction that Cannon had not been vindicated, and said: "The least that could be asked of Bishop Cannon . . . is that for the good and peace of the church he resign his office." The petitions were filed with the College of Bishops at Nashville. The documents declared that "thousands of laymen throughout our church are much exercised," and "a great many laymen are refusing to contribute to any of our causes except the local church expense." It was stated further that "some of our best people who know something of the story have had their confidence in the standards of our church severely shaken." Although "reports that gravely reflect on the moral character of Bishop Cannon have been published throughout the country," said the petitioners, "he has made no public statement that would vindicate himself or that would relieve the church of embarrassment." The College of Bishops was besought by the laymen to "take such action for the relief of the church as your godly judgment may dictate."

Personal letters also were written by certain Methodist laymen to individual bishops requesting action, and specifically urging that Cannon be not elevated to the post of presiding bishop, an honor for which he appeared to be next in line.

When the College of Bishops met on May 2, it considered the petitions, seventeen in number, and eight letters and telegrams from individuals, but took no action. It was explained that the college was without authority to remove a bishop from office. Cannon himself asked that he not be considered for the senior episcopal rank.

The Bishop Wins Again

It developed ten days later that the college had met informally prior to May 2 and had voted not to make Cannon the presiding bishop.[5] Naturally, then, when he requested on May 2 that he not be elevated, his request was granted. In all likelihood he knew of the college's prior decision when he presented the request.

Actually Cannon had been scheduled to be named presiding bishop the previous December, but he was ill and was awaiting his church's investigation of the immorality charges against him. Consequently Bishop W. B. Beauchamp, who was next in seniority, was chosen. Then in May Cannon again was passed by. That was his last chance to preside over the college.

The average man, and especially the average clergyman, who had been under fire from many different directions, and whose garments had been badly singed, would have sought to avoid the spotlight where possible. Certainly he would not have raised an unnecessary clamor in the press about matters concerning which the least said the better. But such was not Cannon's way.

At the height of the uproar over his financial dealings, and just when laymen in his own church were seeking to oust him from the bishopric, this gentleman of the cloth with the "rhinoceros hide" published an open letter in the *Richmond Christian Advocate* demanding that the Federal Council of Churches of Christ in America explain why his name had been omitted from the council's recently published report on birth control. This report was made by the council's Committee on Marriage and the Home, a committee (oh, ironic fact!) set up in 1926 at Bishop Cannon's suggestion. He had served as its chairman from that time until February 15, 1931. On the latter date the Bishop had resigned as chairman "on account of ill health."

It is sufficiently extraordinary, surely, that Dr. Cannon, of all people, had served as chairman of that particular committee throughout that particular period. For it will be recalled that his romance with Mrs. McCallum began in 1928, before his first wife's death, and that it continued until their marriage in 1930. Cannon's retirement from the chairmanship of this remarkable Committee on Marriage and the Home came only one week after he faced the twelve Methodist elders on charges of adultery.

His retirement as chairman of the committee did not remove him as a member, however. That is why he looked for his name when the committee's report on birth control was released. When he failed to find it, he took the matter to the press instead of keeping quiet, as almost anybody else would have done under similar circumstances. His protest was particularly out of place in that he had refused to sign both the majority and the minority report of the committee, and had he been listed at all in the publicity, it would have been with three other members who likewise signed neither document. Yet he chose to demand an explanation. None seems to have been forthcoming. Perhaps the Federal Council felt that the explanation was obvious.

Not content with creating this unnecessary stir, the Bishop went out of his way to cause another a few months later.

Obviously taking full cognizance of the intense feeling against Cannon in Methodist circles, Bishop Edwin D. Mouzon had sent him a telegram asking him not to attend the Baltimore Methodist Conference at Roanoke, Virginia, over which Mouzon was to preside. Cannon attended anyway. Not only so, but when Bishop Mouzon failed to invite him to the platform, Bishop Cannon delivered a speech from the floor expressing his "amazement" that any bishop of his church "should be so unaware or intentionally unmindful of the courtesy so uniform under such circumstances." Mouzon did not change his expression while Cannon was speaking. When the latter concluded, Mouzon rose and said: "Are there any further announcements?" [6]

There was no mystery in the fact that Mouzon had telegraphed Cannon not to come to the conference. Although the two men had fought side by side against Al Smith in 1928, the subsequent revelations concerning Cannon's extramarital and fiscal behavior were too much for Bishop Mouzon. He realized, furthermore, that they were too much for thousands of other Methodists. Yet instead of heeding the request that he not come to the Baltimore conference and protesting quietly, if he wished to protest at all, Cannon chose to express himself brazenly and with a maximum of fanfare. He had behaved similarly on other occasions over a long period of years.

But his fondness for the limelight was at least partially satisfied by another inquiry into his anti-Smith financing, that of the Nye committee, which began in the spring of 1931 and continued off and on for months.

As he had done with so many other investigations of his record, Cannon sought to block this one by a resort to technicalities. He contended, for example, that the Federal Corrupt Practices Act, which he was suspected of violating, was unconstitutional. He argued that the committee had no right to delve into his affairs, and claimed, as we have seen, that the Glass resolution extending the powers of that body was also unconstitutional.

Senator Nye disregarded these arguments and summoned Miss Ada L. Burroughs, treasurer of the Anti-Smith Headquarters Democratic Committee, as the first witness. She appeared on May 7. Bishop Cannon sat near by, resting his chin on one of his crutches, as she took the stand and flatly refused to give any testimony whatever to the committee. Miss Burroughs read a prepared statement protesting the committee's authority on grounds identical with those already advanced by the Bishop. Senator Nye stated that he expected to cite her for contempt.

That ended the hearings for the time being. Later in the month Cannon asked Nye to postpone the rest of the inquiry until September 20, since he would probably be out of the country until then. Nye refused, saying that if he did so, the statute of limitations against prosecution in the case would apply on September 18. He pointed out that the first of the Jameson contributions had been made on September 18, 1928. Cannon retorted two days later that the statute of limitations would not apply, in his opinion, and that even if it did, contributions made by Jameson after September 20 would "give ample margin for hearings" begun on that date. The Bishop took occasion in his letter to the Senator to drag in the usual references to the wets and the Roman Catholics and the usual denunciation of the efforts of "certain Virginia Democrats to secure, if possible, the list of names of those who worked in Virginia cities, districts and precincts to defeat Alfred E. Smith, in order that, if possible, they may be so intimidated and harassed that they will fear to do such work again." "That list will certainly not be furnished by me," he asserted categorically.

Following this exchange, the Bishop bounced back into the public prints by filing a $500,000 libel suit against Representative Tinkham for having termed him a "shameless violator of the Federal Corrupt Practices Act." Cannon said: "I have brought suit so that these charges may be investigated and tried, not by a Senate committee, but by the courts, which will determine whether I am a shameless violator of the Federal Corrupt Practices Act and whether I have illegally concealed receipt or disposition of the Jameson contributions as Congressman Tinkham declared."

This flamboyant play to the galleries was so much sound and fury. In actual fact, Cannon offered through his attorney to withdraw his $500,000 action upon payment by Tinkham of $2,500.[7] Tinkham refused to pay one dollar and insisted that the case go to trial. The result was that the issue dragged through the courts for years. The final outcome, as we shall see, was far from creditable to Cannon.

During the summer of 1931 the Bishop was on a suit-filing spree. Actions for libel totaling $2,500,000 were instituted against various Hearst papers, and since he had sued several of these papers and Hearst personally the preceding year for $5,000,000, that brought the total to $7,500,000. His $500,000 suit against the *Philadelphia Record* also was filed at this time. The following year he filed suits for $200,000 each against the Macon, Georgia, *Telegraph* and the *Atlanta Constitution*. The *Telegraph* had published an editorial comparing Cannon to Al Capone, the Chicago gangster, and the *Constitution* had reproduced it.

The Bishop's technique in these matters was clear. It was to slap a tremendous suit on a newspaper or a chain of papers and then try to settle it for a small sum without going to trial, the amount of the settlement being less than it would cost the paper to defend the suit. In none of the foregoing libel actions, nearly all of which involved his relations with Mrs. McCallum, did he so much as attempt to have a hearing on the facts in open court. In the Hearst suit, or series of suits, he accepted an over-all settlement, understood to have been approximately $5,000. In the *Philadelphia Record* case, as we have seen, the *Record* refused to pay a cent and showed that it was ready to go to trial. The suit was withdrawn. The Macon and Atlanta papers each settled out of court for $1,000. And when the Bishop announced that he intended to sue the *Catholic Union and Times*, of Buffalo, only to have that journal throw him back on his heels with a ringing challenge to him to do his worst, he dropped the matter like a hot brick. He also failed to sue any of the other Catholic papers, despite the amount of time he spent talking about suing them.

As for the Nye committee investigation, which had been recessed in May, Cannon called into play every available legal device in an effort to prevent its resumption. He filed suit in the District of Columbia Supreme Court for a writ of prohibition, taking the case out of the committee's hands and directing that testimony already heard be destroyed. The petition was promptly denied. The committee accordingly resumed its hearings late in August. Cannon, meanwhile, had gone abroad, where he was addressing himself to matters of a moral and religious character. As the Nye committee began taking testimony, the Bishop cabled from London terming the entire procedure a personal attack.

A large crowd of interested spectators was on hand for the opening day and throughout the hearing. Great interest was shown as extended testimony was offered concerning the Bishop's juggling of bank accounts, together with certain strange financial transactions having to do with the estate of a widow, Mrs. Mary C. Moore, and the affairs of a concern known as the Newspaper Supply Company. As a consequence of this day's revelations Senator Clarence C. Dill, of Washington, a member of the committee, declared that Cannon had "deposited political contributions to his personal accounts," and Chairman Nye asserted that the Bishop had diverted campaign funds to his own use.

For several days witnesses adduced evidence of a similar nature, as the large audience that filled the committee room sat on the edge of their chairs. Basil Manly, who had been retained as an expert by the Nye committee and who had made a comprehensive and thorough study of the Bishop's complicated fiscal dealings, testified at length. He traced Cannon's intricate financial transactions by means of diagrams and charts. Manly declared that Cannon opened six new bank accounts during the presidential campaign of 1928, and that political funds were found in all but two of the ten accounts that he opened or used during this period. Manly also declared that only $22,544 of $68,717 held by Cannon in those accounts had been turned over to the anti-Smith organization.

The trusting Edwin C. Jameson, who had given the Bishop $65,300, nearly all of it in cash, and $7,300 of it after the campaign ended, was on hand.

"That's news to me!" he shouted in marked surprise when a letter was read that Cannon had written to "fellow-workers" under date of January 26, 1929, asking for contributions to cover what was described in the letter as a campaign deficit. Jameson said he had understood that his $7,300, given considerably prior to that date, was sufficient to cover the deficit. Such, he stated, was the information he had received from the Bishop himself at the time Jameson agreed to make the donation. But here was written evidence that Cannon had gone out into the vineyard again, without his knowledge, and had implored the brethren to make further contributions. Poor Jameson must have left the hearing a sadly disillusioned man.

Miss Ada L. Burroughs refused once more to testify before the Nye committee, and so did the Rev. J. Sidney Peters, secretary of the Anti-Smith Democratic Headquarters Committee, of which Miss Burroughs was treasurer.

Throughout these hearings the committee room was packed to the doors with an eager crowd of spectators. Especial interest was manifested in the testimony of two Virginians who were active in the anti-Smith fight in 1928, but who failed to substantiate some of the Bishop's basic contentions.

It will be recalled that during the Caraway committee hearing in 1930, Bishop Cannon finally released a largely meaningless statement of how he had spent the unreported $48,300 given him by Jameson. This statement listed the total amounts that he said had been disbursed in each of the Virginia congressional districts. The sum of $4,500 was listed for the Second District, and $4,000 for the Fifth District.

But at the Nye committee hearing H. G. Luhring, of Norfolk, treasurer of the Greater Norfolk Anti-Smith Democratic Committee for the Second District, testified that he received only $200 from Bishop Cannon during the entire campaign. He himself raised $2,293, he said, and as far as he knew this, plus the $200, was all that was spent there by the anti-Smith organization. He added that he found it "rather hard . . . to believe" that $4,500 was spent in the district, since he "organized thirty-five Anti-Smith Clubs" there with the money he raised. He understood that his was the only anti-Smith organization operating in the district. Luhring also testified that he had never heard of a Virginia Anti-Smith Committee, but only of the Virginia Headquarters Committee.[8]

Dr. S. E. Hughes, of Danville, chairman of the Anti-Smith Democratic Committee for that city, much the largest urban community in the Fifth Congressional District, said he had received no funds whatever from Bishop Cannon throughout the campaign. Dr. Hughes said the Bishop told him when he dined at the Hughes home during the campaign that he hoped Danville would be able to finance its own fight against Smith. The physician had seen no part of the $4,000 that Cannon listed for the Fifth District. He too had never heard of any Virginia Anti-Smith Committee.[9]

Following this testimony the committee adjourned until October.

It should perhaps be reiterated that Cannon based his contention that he did not have to give the Federal government an itemized accounting of how he spent Jameson's $48,300, on the ground that this sum was expended by an agency called the Virginia Anti-Smith Committee, which, he said, operated wholly within the State of Virginia, and hence was not required to account to Washington for its expenditures.

At this juncture Bishop Cannon sent a cable from London demanding to know why Senator Glass had not sought an investigation of either the Democratic or the Republican state committees in Virginia. Glass replied that the answer was simple: "No such investigation has been demanded because nobody has accused either the Democratic or the Republican chairman of stealing campaign funds or diverting them to his own private use." The acid-tongued Virginia Senator then went on to declare that if the Bishop were to "bring any such accusation against Republican Chairman Angell or Democratic Chairman Hooker, I will promptly demand that the accusation be thoroughly investigated and will give my personal bond that each of these gentlemen will also demand investigation and not run away to Europe or seek to hide his culpability behind the skirts of a woman secretary."

The Bishop denied hotly that he had "run away" or that he was hiding behind anyone's skirts. He also charged the Nye committee by cable with "deliberately" holding the hearings in his absence, since he had informed the committee in May that "official church duties required my presence in Europe from August 10 to September 20." He stated further that since the hearings had now adjourned until October, this action "flatly contradicts the previous statement made by the committee that the statute of limitations made an August committee meeting necessary."

The Nye committee had not formulated its report, but the United States District Attorney requested a transcript of the testimony and access to the exhibits that had been filed, with a view to possible criminal action. The committee made the material available, as requested.

When news of this development was flashed overseas, the Bishop issued a statement to the Associated Press in which he declared, bewilderingly, that he had never opposed a grand-jury investigation of his financial operations in the 1928 campaign "if the Department of Justice decided that the law and the facts warranted such a procedure." It was promptly pointed out by the *Richmond News Leader* that Cannon had been complaining loudly shortly before that the Nye committee was holding an ex parte hearing at which he had no opportunity to present or to cross-examine witnesses, but that he now was professing himself willing to have grand-jury action, which would be similarly ex parte, with no opportunity for his side to be heard. Two weeks later the Bishop returned to the United States and declared that he was not only willing but anxious for a grand-jury inquiry.

The mounting difficulties that faced him did not seem to have injured his health, for the Associated Press reported from New York: "As he walked down the gangplank of the Mauretania, he

appeared not at all the invalid he was when he sailed seven weeks
ago. Then he carried a crutch. He lost it in a Paris taxicab, he
explained, but he insisted that he had no need for it anyway.
. . . He was in a modest tourist cabin he had occupied with
three young men."

The Federal authorities decided on grand-jury action, and the
inquiry began on October 8. Counsel for Cannon promptly filed
a brief contending that the Bishop was not subject to indictment
and prosecution by a Federal grand jury and the Federal courts,
since his campaign had concerned only the choice of presidential electors in Virginia. It was argued that presidential electors
had been held by the courts to be state officials, and it was
asked therefore that the whole proceeding be dismissed. Thus
Bishop Cannon's "desire" for a grand-jury investigation lasted
only a few weeks. As soon as the matter was put to the test, he
was trying, as usual, to dodge an inquiry.

On October 16 he and Miss Burroughs were indicted on
charges of violating and conspiring to violate the Federal Corrupt Practices Act. The penalty, upon conviction, was $1,000 fine
or one year in prison, or both, for technical violation, and the
same prison term or up to $10,000 fine, or both, for willful vio-
lation.

When advised of his indictment, the Bishop stated that he
was "not surprised at anything that Roman Catholic District Attorney [apparently Leo A. Rover] might do." He attributed the
true bill found by the grand jury to "religious persecution." Although he had said on his return from Europe a month previously that he no longer needed his crutch, he was using one when
interviewed by the press concerning the grand jury's action.

It was noted in his latter years that Cannon usually showed up
at, or walked out of, inquiries into his ecclesiastical, political, or
personal behavior hobbling on a crutch. Undoubtedly the crutch
was often necessary, but whether it was really needed every
time he used it remains to be proved. Certainly the crutch was a
psychological factor whose importance so shrewd a man as Cannon would never have overlooked.

Having tried unsuccessfully to prevent grand-jury action, after
saying that he wanted a grand-jury investigation, Cannon left

no stone unturned to have the indictment thrown out or otherwise to stop the inquiry. The first of his legal maneuvers, all of
which taken together staved off a trial for some two and a half
years, was to claim that the indictment was defective. This demurrer was sustained in the lower court, but was lost in the
United States Supreme Court in May 1933, a year and a half
after the indictment was brought by the grand jury. But that
was only one of the various steps that Cannon took, through his
counsel, to block a trial. Others will be noted later.

Meanwhile the Bishop's admirers — for quite a few remained,
in spite of everything — began passing the hat for funds "to secure competent counsel for him in defense of the Corrupt Practices Act charges, and to assist in meeting similar attacks upon
him and to restore his influence as a prohibition leader." The
hat-passers, who solicited funds in letters sent out over their
signatures, were five Virginians. Following publication of the fact
that they were initiating this activity, Cannon expressed "hearty
approval" and "deep appreciation." He added that he did not
think it was the public's business how much had been collected.

Further evidence that there were those who had faith in the
Bishop's protestations of innocence was seen in the action of
nearly three hundred prohibitionists assembled in Richmond on
the night of December 10. When Thomas Whitehead, veteran
attorney of Amherst Courthouse, Virginia, proclaimed to the
gathering that "Bishop Cannon is the greatest martyr that Virginia has ever produced since the Apostles," the audience cheered
and applauded vigorously. Some weeks later the Anti-Saloon
League of America executive committee, meeting in Washington, D.C., eulogized the Bishop in formal resolutions.

The findings of the Nye committee were released on December 21, and there was no hint in them of a belief on the part of
the four signers that the Bishop was eligible for martyrdom or
that he was in any wise comparable to the Apostles. The signers,
all Protestants, were Chairman Nye and Senators Porter H. Dale,
of Vermont, Clarence C. Dill, of Washington, and Robert F.
Wagner, of New York. Their official report found that Cannon
had committed "numerous apparent violations of the Federal
Corrupt Practices Act." It declared that the total amount of

political funds handled by him or Miss Burroughs during the campaign of 1928, or in connection with deficits alleged to have been created during that campaign, was in excess of $130,000. The committee declared "that of this total only $58,558.62 was accounted for in statements filed with the Clerk of the House of Representatives in accordance with the provisions of the Federal Corrupt Practices Act of 1925." Among the unreported contributions was a $20,000 item from former Senator J. S. Frelinghuysen, of New Jersey.

Chairman Nye and his associates noted that all this money should have been accounted for in the reports to the House. They expressed the view that there was, in fact, no such agency as the Virginia Committee of the Anti-Smith Democrats, and stated that even if the committee had existed, it "was clearly a subsidiary of the Headquarters Committee, Anti-Smith Democrats, and any funds received or expended in its behalf should, therefore, have been reported." It will be recalled that whereas Cannon had testified to the existence of a Virginia Committee, two of his former associates in the campaign of 1928, Dr. Hughes and Mr. Luhring, said they had never heard of it. Furthermore, representatives of the Guardian Publishing Company, which issued almost all the printed matter used by the anti-Smith Democrats during the campaign, "stated that they had no knowledge of any committee except the Headquarters Committee, and that all printing, including sample ballots for the State of Virginia, was ordered through the Headquarters Committee," the Nye report declared. The report also directed attention to the fact that a large number of items which related exclusively to the conduct of the Virginia campaign, and which would properly have been charged to and paid by the Virginia Committee if that agency had actually existed as a separate entity, appeared on the accounts of the Headquarters Committee.

The Nye report went on to say that "none of the $62,300 contributed by E. C. Jameson prior to January 1, 1929 was accounted for in any of the reports required to be filed by that date under the Federal Corrupt Practices Act. It asserted that when Miss Burroughs accounted for $17,000 of this amount under date of February 11, 1929, this "was not a compliance with the requirements of the law or a disclosure of the total amount of the Jameson money." Furthermore, this report was not "a voluntary attempt to rectify errors or omissions," but was made only "as a result of inquiries by the Senate committee, headed by Senator Steiwer." Although Miss Burroughs was the "nominal treasurer of the Headquarters Committee," the report added, Bishop Cannon, who actually handled most of the money and who deposited it in accounts "upon which he alone was able to draw checks," bore a "peculiar responsibility to see that the statements filed in accordance with the Federal Corrupt Practices Act were accurate and complete." The Nye committee did not feel that the Bishop had measured up to his obligation.

It also directed attention to a neat scheme by which the leader of the moral and religious forces was able to camouflage political contributions. The committee quoted from a letter Cannon wrote on September 15, 1928 to W. C. Gregg, of Hackensack, New Jersey, in which Gregg was solicited for a contribution. The Bishop pointed out that "all funds which are used under the auspices of the Anti-Smith Democrats must be reported by our treasurer as used for political purposes," but he said if Gregg preferred that his gift "should not appear in the report of the committee, it can be utilized in the literature campaign of the Board of Temperance and Social Service of the Methodist Episcopal Church, South, which can concentrate to that extent to the amount of $500 especially in Tennessee." Dr. Cannon advised Gregg that this literature "emphasizes very strongly the prohibition issue without calling the names of the candidates, but making, in my judgment, equally as effective an appeal for Mr. Hoover and against Smith as the literature which backs up the personal candidacy." The Nye report comments: "This letter, which was written early in the campaign, would appear to indicate the existence of a plan by which funds contributed to influence the result of the election would not appear in the official reports of the organization." No light was shed in the report on the extent to which this device was used.

Taking up the question whether there had been any "fraudulent conversion to private uses . . . of any campaign funds contributed for use in any election as defined in the Federal

The Bishop Wins Again

Corrupt Practices Act," the Nye committee declared: "Funds aggregating $18,300 representing moneys contributed for political purposes were placed on deposit to the credit of James Cannon, Jr., executor, prior to the date of the general election in 1928 and remained on deposit to the credit of such accounts for considerable periods subsequent to that election."

The bewildering complexity of Cannon's ten bank accounts was such that it took long and intensive study on the part of Basil Manly, the committee's able special assistant, to make head or tail of the intricate juggling that had gone on. It would serve no useful purpose to repeat any large portion of Manly's testimony here. Details may be found in the published reports of the Nye committee's proceedings, with much documentation, as well as charts and diagrams.

Samples of the sort of thing that Manly uncovered are cited in the committee's final report. For instance, in late October 1928 Cannon placed a total of $16,000 on time certificates of deposit in two banks at Blackstone, Virginia, and represented the money to be trust funds of the Newspaper Supply Company. But the committee declared that the company was "a defunct corporation" whose charter had been revoked seven years previously. It also stated that of the $16,000 in question, "$8,000 was a political contribution made by E. C. Jameson, of New York; $5,000 was a withdrawal of political funds deposited to the credit of James Cannon, Jr., chairman, in the Continental Trust Company, of Washington; and $2,433.78 represented proceeds of the sale of property of an estate [that of Mrs. Mary C. Moore] of which Bishop Cannon was executor. The balance, amounting to $566.22 was withdrawn from Bishop Cannon's personal account in the Citizens Bank to round out the total of $16,000."

The committee also noted that the above-mentioned $8,000 that was contributed by Jameson for political purposes on October 19, 1928 "was held intact for more than three months after the end of the campaign in the form of a time certificate of deposit in the name of James Cannon, Jr., and was then merged with other funds in a savings account standing in the name of James Cannon, Jr., executor." All this despite the fact that the

281

$8,000 was represented to be funds of the defunct Newspaper Supply Company.

When the Nye report was published, Cannon was irate in his comment. "Amazing misstatements of fact . . . unwarranted conclusions . . . unwarranted reflections upon other innocent parties besides myself," he said. But the Bishop provided scarcely any answers to the specific allegations in the report. With regard to the committee's statement that he and Miss Burroughs had handled in excess of $130,000, but had reported only $58,558.62, Cannon said merely that "the total amount was much less than $130,000." He did not say how much less, nor did he claim that they had handled no more than the sum named in their official declaration. The public could hardly avoid the conclusion, therefore, that the Bishop had tacitly admitted reporting to the government less than he and Miss Burroughs had received.

Cannon did make two general complaints. First, "the Nye Committee has been unfair and unjust to me from the beginning of the hearings . . . all three hearings were fixed without reference to my convenience or official engagements." The Bishop said the first hearing was held when it was known that he was ill in the hospital; the second was fixed for a date when he was known to have another engagement, and the third was arranged for a time when the committee well knew he had to go to Europe.

"Finally and pre-eminently," he went on, "notwithstanding the committee's positive guarantee given to me in February of opportunity to file sworn statement, if necessary, 'to prove that no criminal or dishonorable act has been committed by me,' before my return from Europe, without giving me an opportunity to present such sworn statement, the transcript of the testimony was turned over to the United States District Attorney for investigation by the grand jury, which District Attorney and grand jury flatly refused me permission to file such sworn statement."

Chairman Nye made no comment on the foregoing allegations. It may be remarked, in passing, that since Cannon expressed a strong desire for a grand-jury investigation on September 18, the very day he returned from Europe, it is a bit difficult to see wherein an injustice was done him when the committee and the grand jury sought to gratify that desire. If the committee did, in fact, agree to allow him to file a sworn statement with it, that agency should have kept its promise, but the Bishop presented no proof of such an agreement. As for the filing of a statement with the grand jury, so astute a man as Cannon must have known that this would have been a most irregular, if not unprecedented procedure, since it is common knowledge that grand juries hear only the prosecution's side of the case.

Another aspect of the controversy was noted by the *Richmond News Leader,* which pointed to Cannon's admission that he made advances "for political purposes, partly out of my personal funds, partly out of funds of which I was executor or trustee, and for which I was personally responsible." The newspaper observed: "It is enough to say on this point . . . that if the laws of Virginia are such that a trustee or executor can borrow from trust funds for political purposes, even though he is personally responsible for settlement in the end, there is something fundamentally wrong with those laws."

The Nye committee had found heavily against the Bishop, but no penalty was involved, and unless he could be convicted in court, none would be. Public opinion was turning more and more against this bellicose ecclesiastic who had never hesitated to condemn others for any dereliction, however petty or trivial, and who himself was now under a deep cloud of suspicion. But as yet he had received no specific punishment from any tribunal, whether clerical or lay, before which he had appeared. Furthermore, he was still engaged in desperate efforts to have the indictment brought against him by the Federal grand jury declared null and void in the courts.

The United States Supreme Court pronounced the indictment valid, as has been noted, but another point was carried up to that tribunal, involving the jurisdiction of the District of Columbia Court of Appeals. The highest court ruled against that demurrer in April 1933. Then Cannon appealed to the Supreme Court to hold that he would not have to be tried. The court held on January 9, 1934 that he would have to stand trial, but it ruled out eight of the ten counts in the indictment. Only the two conspiracy counts were held valid, which meant that the government would have to prove "conspiracy" between Bishop Cannon and Miss Burroughs. Conspiracy is usually an extremely difficult thing to prove. Under the other eight counts, however, it would have been necessary to convict Miss Burroughs as well as Cannon, since she was charged as the principal and he as the accessory.

About a month after the Supreme Court ruled that Cannon must stand trial on conspiracy charges, his dwindling group of admirers sent out another appeal for funds "to several hundred persons and the religious press." This circular set forth that it had been prepared — evidently by Cannon himself — at the request of his friends, "who have been greatly concerned about the persecution he has undergone for several years." It said he was without funds for his defense.

The amount thus collected was never made known. At all events, the Bishop, who had been indicted on October 16, 1931, finally went on trial April 9, 1934 before a jury of eleven men and one woman in the District of Columbia Supreme Court. So much time had elapsed since the Hoover-Smith presidential campaign that public interest in the Cannon case had waned. Franklin D. Roosevelt had succeeded Herbert Hoover in the White House thirteen months before, and national prohibition had been repealed. All these circumstances combined to dull the edge of popular concern.

Justice Peyton Gordon asked each prospective juror as the jury box was being filled: "Would you be prevented from giving a fair and impartial trial on the ground that the said [Alfred E.] Smith was a member of the Roman Catholic Church or that he sought repeal of the National Prohibition Law?" The twelve who were chosen answered in the negative.

Bishop Cannon and Miss Burroughs went on trial together, and both pleaded "Not guilty."

The Bishop seemed bored by the proceedings. He dozed at frequent intervals while he was being accused of a "mutual and corrupt understanding."

Robert H. McNeill, of Washington, his counsel in this case as in several others over a period of years, told the jury that his client had kept several bank accounts, but he said this was done in an effort to protect the Bishop's followers from the wrath of Virginia's Democratic machine.

Prosecutor John J. Wilson quoted Cannon as having said before he sailed for the Mediterranean in February 1929 (on the trip awarded him for his contributions to religious progress) that he "destroyed all the correspondence I could lay my hands on so that anyone who delved into my affairs would find nothing. . . . I know that bunch down in Virginia."

Wilson declared that the high point in the case at bar was "the incident of February 11, 1929, which points to the guilt of these defendants — the incident which reeks with their partnership in crime." He stated that the Steiwer committee had asked Cannon on that date for information concerning his anti-Smith campaign. "A disclosure was about to come out," said the prosecutor. "Congress was about to hear of the Jameson contribution. So Cannon and Miss Burroughs got up their report, while they were still asking for contributions to make up their phony deficit."

Lee P. Oliver, special agent of the Department of Justice, said on the stand that Cannon told him in 1931 that he carried "four or five thousand dollars in his pocket" during the Hoover-Smith campaign to "pay individuals whom he approached." Oliver also quoted A. J. Dunning, of Norfolk, an anti-Smith worker, as having told him in 1933 that his committee or club at Norfolk "was not part of any State committee," and that he had never heard of the so-called Virginia Committee of Anti-Smith Democrats.

The slight and quiet-mannered Edwin C. Jameson was a witness, of course. He opened his testimony in a voice so low that the court had to urge him to speak louder. Jameson and various other witnesses gave testimony similar to that which they had given before the Caraway and Nye committees.

A motion by Attorney McNeill for a directed verdict of acquittal was denied by Justice Gordon. McNeill had shouted in support of his motion: "I wouldn't want to convict the mangiest yellow dog on the worst street in Washington on such evidence."

Finally, on April 19, Bishop Cannon took the stand in his own defense. Walking slowly, and with a slight limp, he went to the witness chair. Mrs. Cannon, storm center of the inquiry by the

Southern Methodist Church into her husband's private morality, watched from the well inside the courtroom, as did one of the Bishop's sons.

It was the first time that the Bishop had testified in public concerning the disposition he had made of the anti-Smith funds in 1928. Always calm and collected, he spoke slowly, drumming with his fingers on the chair rail, or looking up at the ceiling as he sought to recall events that had occurred nearly six years before. He testified that the battle against Smith was a fight to stop the election of a "wet cocktail President of the United States."

The prosecution had introduced his campaign stationery in evidence, with letter-heads showing the Headquarters Committee, but never mentioning a Virginia Committee. The Bishop answered that "to cut down expenses, only one letter-head was used."

The crux of his testimony was reached when he declared that conspiracy between himself and Miss Burroughs was impossible. He asserted that they "could not have conspired to violate the Federal Corrupt Practices Act" in failing to report $48,300 received from Edwin C. Jameson, since Miss Burroughs "never knew" Jameson had given the money. The prosecution was unable to shake the Bishop on this vital point.

Part of the funds entrusted to his care were used, he said, for publication and distribution of the pamphlet *Is Southern Protestantism More Intolerant than Romanism?* Cannon stated that 380,000 copies of this violent tract were turned out, and that about 148,000 were distributed in Virginia. As was pointed out in a previous chapter, the pamphlet appeared so late in the campaign that scarcely any opportunity to answer it was afforded.

As the case neared the jury, Cannon evidently realized that conspiracy had not been proved against him, for when his counsel indicated to the judge an intention to move for a mistrial, the Bishop said in a loud voice: "No! No!" The motion was not made.

Miss Burroughs took the stand near the close to say that until long after the campaign was over she knew nothing of any Jameson contribution except the $17,300 which she had reported to the government. It was when Jameson told a Senate investigating committee that he had provided the Bishop with $65,300, and she read about his testimony in the press, that she first became aware of his munificence, she said.

If the jury believed this, it would have to acquit both Miss Burroughs and Cannon, since conspiracy requires a criminal plan between two or more persons to violate the law.

Prosecution and defense each had a maximum of four hours for summing up. While John J. Wilson stated the case for the government, Cannon sat listening impassively, leaning back in his chair. Miss Burroughs continued to take notes in the book where she had been jotting down memoranda ever since the trial began.

Mrs. Cannon, who had been present throughout the proceedings, wept silently as McNeill referred directly to her husband in presenting the argument for the defense. The Bishop showed no trace of emotion while his wife was wiping away her tears.

Justice Gordon repeatedly warned the jury as it prepared to take the case: "You can't find one guilty without finding the other guilty. If one is not guilty, the other is not guilty." This meant that although Cannon was obviously the brains behind the conspiracy, if there was a conspiracy, and Miss Burroughs merely carried out his instructions, the verdict had to be the same for both.

Shortly after noon on April 27 the jurors retired to begin their deliberations. Three hours later they indicated that a verdict had been reached. The courtroom was jammed as Justice Gordon ascended the bench. A moment later the jury filed in.

For the first time Bishop Cannon seemed tense. He sat on the edge of his chair, leaning foward to hear the verdict. Miss Burroughs stood stiffly, grasping a table.

The foreman announced that the two defendants had been found not guilty on both counts.

Cannon smiled and settled back in his chair. Miss Burroughs remained standing for a moment and then sat down. Mrs. Cannon wiped away more tears.

Owing to the lack of evidence against Miss Burroughs, acquittal had been almost inevitable from the first. Unanimity was not achieved, however, until four ballots had been taken. The jury voted on the first ballot as follows: nine for acquittal, one for conviction of willfully violating the Corrupt Practices Act, and two for unwillful but unlawful violation. On the second ballot the vote stood ten for acquittal, with the other two for unwillful violation. Another vote was taken, and eleven were for acquittal. On the fourth ballot all twelve decided to find the Bishop and his co-worker not guilty.[10]

There was only a mild demonstration when the verdict was announced. Officials shut off the slight wave of handclapping that rippled through the courtroom.

Friends and newspapermen crowded around the Bishop as court adjourned. He declined immediate comment, saying he would have some observations to make "after I take a nap." Miss Burroughs refused to be quoted.

At this juncture a woman fought her way through the crowd to Cannon's side.

"Bishop, I said I'd hug you if you were acquitted," said she.

"Hug away!" said the Bishop smiling.

She accepted the invitation.

"We still love you," said the effusive lady. "We know you are not a criminal. This is a victory for Protestantism."

Her name was given in the press as Ada Pairecy, of Parkersburg, West Virginia.

After these amenities had been concluded, the courtroom emptied and Cannon retired for the "nap" of which he had spoken. Having rested briefly from the ordeal of the trial, which had begun nearly three weeks before, he issued a characteristic blast. Much of it was a repetitive rehash of things he had often said. He devoted especial attention to the "attacks" that had been made on him over a period of years. He did not overlook the opportunity to thank those still loyal admirers who had made up a defense fund for him during the preceding months, and expressed "high appreciation of the very many friends who, out of straitened circumstances, have sent contributions to assist me." The Bishop also took note of his greatly improved health. "My physical condition is far better than in 1930 when I was suffering from the effects of African fever," he declared. In other words, the long series of inquiries into his public life and his private morals had not weakened his physique. Many men would have been mental and physical wrecks at the end of a succession of such investigations as Cannon had faced. But not he. On the contrary, he went out of his way to declare that he was in much better health than before.

Once again he had foiled his enemies and emerged from an ecclesiastical or a legal proceeding with the verdict that he sought. During the almost six years that had passed since the hectic campaign of 1928, Dr. Cannon had successfully run the gantlet of the Caraway committee, the Nye committee, and the Department of Justice. During the same period he had also managed to sidestep two church trials. It was beginning to look as though this man bore a charmed existence. Some of the keenest minds in Southern Methodism, both clerical and lay, had sought earnestly to prove him guilty of crimes against the church or the state, against religion or morality. He had checkmated them all.

An ironic fact needs to be noted, however. For although Cannon managed to avoid conviction by a jury in the District of Columbia Supreme Court on charges of conspiracy to violate the Corrupt Practices Act, a judge of that same court held three years later, in 1937, as we shall see, that he himself had admitted violating the act in a deposition filed by him prior to the 1937 trial. The court therefore dismissed Cannon's $500,000 libel suit against Representative Tinkham, who had termed him a "shameless violator" of the act. The Bishop carried this case up to the United States Supreme Court, but without avail. Both the Circuit Court of Appeals and the Supreme Court refused to upset the directed verdict of the lower court for Tinkham. This was, of course, a setback for the Bishop, but it imposed no punishment or penalty upon him, except the negative one of preventing him from getting damages from the Massachusetts Congressman. This caused many to conclude that only technicalities had prevented his conviction three years previously.

One further aspect of the matter should be emphasized. Bishop Cannon based his refusal over a long period of years to tell what he did with the $48,300 of Jameson money, on the ground that he had to protect the anti-Smith Democrats of Virginia from re-

Dry Messiah

prisals at the hands of a vindictive state political machine. In resolutions adopted by the directors of the Anti-Saloon League of America in 1932, Cannon, who was one of those directors, was praised fulsomely for his refusal to divulge the names of these anti-Smith Democrats. "Only his resolution and sacrifice stands between thousands of independent voters and social ostracism, financial ruin, serious physical harm," said the resolution.

This is nonsense. In the first place, there was no real mystery as to the identities of the Virginia anti-Smith leaders or voters. They attended scores of political rallies without inhibitions during the campaign and applauded wildly when this or that spellbinder virtually declared that Al Smith's election would mean the end of religion, sobriety, and family life in the nation, and it was hinted that the Pope might be expected to take up his residence in the East Wing of the White House. The anti-Smith leaders for the state were known to everyone, and there was no particular secret concerning the names of the leaders in the districts and the localities. Similarly, the anti-Smith rank and file were not operating under cover.[11]

But even if this had not been true, there was the striking gesture of conciliation that the "vindictive" Democratic machine made in the direction of all these anti-Smith voters during the gubernatorial campaign of 1929. Instead of announcing that every Democrat who had voted for Herbert Hoover in 1928 was ineligible, under the law and the Democratic "party plan," to participate in the Democratic primary of 1929, the machine's Attorney General, John R. Saunders, came up with a ruling that they were all welcome to return to the party fold. Some felt this to be contrary to the statutes as well as the "party plan," but the ruling stood. In other words, the machine went out of its way to conciliate the anti-Smith Democrats. Not only so, but they later came back into the party in droves in 1929, contrary to the exhortations of Bishop Cannon, and elected Cannon's long-time enemy, John Garland Pollard, to the governorship.

All of which means that the reasons given by Bishop Cannon for his remarkable reticence concerning the disposition of Jameson's $48,300 were specious. The statement of the professional drys that "social ostracism, financial ruin, serious physical harm" would come to any Virginia anti-Smith Democrats who might be identified was absolute balderdash. Yet Cannon gave no other reason for his repeated refusals to tell what he did with the Jameson money.

Those refusals had sufficient technical validity for the Bishop to escape conviction and possible imprisonment. Since it was subsequently held by a Federal judge, however, that Cannon himself had inadvertently admitted violating the Corrupt Practices Act, he failed once more to convince the public of his innocence.

CHAPTER *xviii*

Demise of the Noble Experiment

Dᴜʀɪɴɢ the years when Bishop Cannon's name was emblazoned across the front pages, he became one of the most fervently attacked and defended individuals in the world. The spectacle of a "moral leader" who was under heavy fire from members of his own church, and who was investigated by Senate committees and tried in the Federal courts, was sufficiently strange. Millions of Americans, including many who had previously admired and defended him, went over to the opposition. They were unable to accept such scanty and dubious explanations as he was willing to give in extenuation of his conduct.

Yet Cannon retained his high place in the hierarchy of the Anti-Saloon League of America. The "church in action," which had not gagged at the methods of which "Pussyfoot" Johnson boasted, took the revelations concerning the Bishop in its stride. Cannon remained a member of its executive committee and its administrative committee, as well as chairman of its national legislative committee. Reference has been made to the fearful and wonderful resolutions passed by the league's executive committee in 1932, lauding the Bishop as a hero for his refusal to reveal how he spent the missing $48,300 of Jameson funds. In 1935 Louis La Coss reported to the *New York Times* from St. Louis, concerning the league's annual convention there, that Bishop Cannon, "despite everything, remains the most potent leader within the organization."

This was one reason why the cause of prohibition, which seemed to have won a signal victory in the presidential election of 1928, gradually found itself forced on the defensive. It was difficult to dissociate the Eighteenth Amendment and the Volstead Act in the popular mind from the agency that had done most to secure their adoption. That agency was becoming increasingly vulnerable in the eyes of the public.

There was, for example, the case of S. S. Kresge, the chainstore magnate, who was one of the Anti-Saloon League's most lavish supporters. Kresge made it a point not to give money to any church whose pastor used tobacco. He announced to the league convention in Washington late in 1927 that he was a prohibitionist not only because of the economic benefits that flowed from the Eighteenth Amendment, but because he believed it "to be a righteous law, contributing to the moral and social good of the people." He announced that he would give the league $500,000 for its newly projected "educational campaign."

Two months later Kresge was convicted by a New York jury of misconduct on seven different occasions with a stenographer, and his wife was granted a divorce.[1] Asked whether the Anti-Saloon League would return the Kresge gift of $500,000, Dr. F. Scott McBride, general superintendent, said it would not. Since Bishop Cannon had inveighed in earlier years against any church that accepted money from sources that he regarded as tainted, it might have been supposed that he would lift up his voice against the Anti-Saloon League for its attitude in this matter. But if Cannon protested, his protest was inaudible to the public ear. Certainly the league salted the $500,000 gratefully away.

For a time after President Hoover took office, there were scant indications that prohibition was on the way out. Very much to the contrary, it appeared to be riding high, and the Protestant prelates who had delivered so many votes in the campaign seemed to be potent at the White House. The Anti-Saloon League and the two Methodist boards, all of which maintained offices virtually within the shadow of the Capitol, impressed observers as more powerful than before.

In his inaugural Hoover had delivered the famous pronouncement: "Our country has deliberately undertaken a great social and economic experiment, noble in motive and farreaching in purpose. It must be worked out constructively." Irving Fisher, one of the foremost advocates of what was to be known ever afterward as the "noble experiment," declared that the President, in the above quoted words, had made "plain his faith in prohibition." Mrs. Ella Boole, president of the Woman's Christian Temperance Union, asserted that "in less than ten minutes from the time he had taken the oath of office the whole world knew that prohibition was safe in his hands."

That was the interpretation which the drys chose to put upon the language of the presidential inaugural. Actually the words were highly ambiguous, with the result that even the beaten and bedraggled wets drew from them some slight meed of comfort.

A few months after he had taken office President Hoover evoked further doxologies from the prohibitionists by announcing his intention of drying up the District of Columbia and making it "a model for this country." Bishop Cannon considered this declaration "the most important statement which has been made on the subject of prohibition since the inauguration." He also opined that "the number of drinking Senators and Congressmen is comparatively small, and that the amount of bootlegging around the Capitol Building is exaggerated." This despite the fact that former Assistant Attorney General Mabel Walker Willebrandt, who had had charge of prohibition cases for the government over a period of eight years, declared in 1929 that "bootleggers infest the halls of Congress and ply their trade there." [2]

Indeed, persistent reports were heard of deliveries in case lots to parched-throated statesmen, many of whom continued to hiccup loudly while proclaiming the virtues of prohibition. A shadowy figure called "the Man in the Green Hat" was commonly said to be the congressional bootlegger-in-chief.

It was during this period that Bishop Cannon sought to sit in the House press gallery in order more closely to observe the happenings on the floor below. He accordingly took a bag of sandwiches to the gallery and posted himself there, with paper and pencil. Soon he was informed that it was not permissible for him to use those precincts unless he could produce the credentials of a correspondent. Since he had none, he departed. The

Bishop was photographed leaving the sanctum of the press with his bag of sandwiches.

As the debate over prohibition proceeded, Henry Ford proclaimed to all and sundry: "If booze ever comes back to the United States I am through with manufacturing. I would not be bothered with the problem of handling over 200,000 men and trying to pay them wages which the saloons would take away from them. I wouldn't be interested in putting automobiles into the hands of a generation soggy with drink." [3] A few years afterward many recalled this extraordinary pronunciamento with bewilderment. Ford gave no tangible evidence in the middle and late 1930's of being "through with manufacturing."

Despite the apparent confidence of the drys following the Hoover landslide, there were a few happenings that made them wonder. As early as 1926 both Illinois and New York had urged Congress overwhelmingly by referendum to modify the Volstead Law. Nevada in the same year had appealed to Congress by referendum to amend the Eighteenth Amendment, Montana repealed its state enforcement act, and Wisconsin voted heavily for 2.75 per cent beer. Another event in 1926 was the straw vote held by 326 newspapers, under the auspices of the Newspaper Enterprise Association. It brought in nearly 1,750,000 ballots, only 18.9 per cent of which registered satisfaction with the existing law, whereas 49.8 per cent favored modification, and 31.3 per cent repeal.

Then in 1928 Massachusetts instructed its senators to seek repeal of the Eighteenth Amendment, and Montana refused to re-enact its state dry law. The following year Wisconsin repealed its state law by a huge majority.

President Calvin Coolidge had signed the drastic Jones "Five-and-Ten" Law the day before President Hoover's inauguration. Passage of this legislation by Congress was evidence that the lawmaking body was still under the spell of the prohibition lobby. The Jones Act amended the Volstead Act by increasing possible maximum penalties for violations to five years or $10,000 fine, or both, and making all violations of the Volstead Act felonies. It had passed the Senate 65 to 18 and the House 284 to 90.

Yet despite the lopsided congressional majorities returned for this law only a few weeks before Hoover took office, the sharp evidences of revolt in such states as Illinois, New York, Massachusetts, Montana, Nevada, and Wisconsin were not to be overlooked. The cloud on the horizon seemed hardly bigger than the scriptural "man's hand," but it was there.

Bishop Cannon was fond of saying that he had "seen more drunken men and women on the Strand and Fleet Street, and at the midnight closing of the cafes of Geneva in one night than I have seen in the United States in five years." St. John Ervine, the distinguished British dramatic critic, provided a counterblast when he declared: "I saw more drunken women in New York in several months than I saw in England in seven years, and just before the elections thirty-one men were found dead on Broadway."

The Bishop favored larger appropriations and bigger engines of enforcement. In 1926 he had urged sterner penalties for drunkenness and the passage of legislation that would compel the purchaser of intoxicants to divulge the source of his supply. In 1929 he urged amendment of the Volstead Law to make the buyer of liquor equally guilty with the seller. The United States Circuit Court of Appeals at Philadelphia had just rendered an opinion holding that the purchase of liquor was not an offense under the Eighteenth Amendment and the Volstead Act. Senator Morris Sheppard, of Texas, accordingly introduced a bill to make the buyer subject to penalties. Little was heard of it thereafter, chiefly because some of the leading drys disagreed with Bishop Cannon on the desirability of such a law.

One of Bishop Cannon's objectives in 1929 and for several years thereafter was to secure the adoption of a constitutional amendment excluding aliens from the population count on which congressional apportionment is based. The Bishop had obtained endorsement for this "Stop Alien Representation" amendment from the Virginia anti-Smith Democratic convention of 1929. On this subject he wrote: "I hold the position that the great mass of aliens who are in this country without any naturalization and who are herded very largely in urban centers are a great menace to our national life. I am in sympathy with the law to prevent these unnaturalized aliens from having a quasi-representation in the halls of Congress." Various other Methodist potentates endorsed the plan. They estimated that 7,500,000 unnaturalized aliens who could not themselves vote legally in any election in the United States would be affected, and that the areas in which they lived would have their congressional representation reduced through the amendment, while the states with scarcely any aliens would have theirs increased.

The amendment had been first introduced in 1927 by Representative Gale H. Stalker, of New York State, likewise co-patron of the Jones "Five-and-Ten" Law. Two years later steam was generated behind the movement by a former superintendent of the New York Anti-Saloon League, William H. Anderson, who had emerged shortly before from Sing Sing. Anderson was convicted in 1924 by a New York City jury and given from one to two years on a charge of third-degree forgery.

On the eve of Anderson's trial, the executive committee of the Anti-Saloon League of America had adopted a resolution by a five-to-three vote reaffirming "its confidence in the integrity, ability, and efficiency" of the indicted New York superintendent. Cannon was one of the five who favored the resolution. The jury took another view of the matter and found Anderson guilty.

After serving nine months and being paroled, Anderson organized something called the American Protestant Alliance, its purpose being to fight for the "Stop Alien Representation" amendment. Anderson began publishing the *Allied Protestant American,* which changed its name to the *American Citizen.* In this elevating journal he appealed for the support of the Ku Klux Klan, urged his readers to subscribe to the *New Menace,* the notorious anti-Catholic publication, and frequently lauded Bishop Cannon. Anderson also sold leaflets along with subscriptions to his magazine. One of these was entitled *How Political Romanism Started the American Protestant Alliance by Railroading William H. Anderson, Innocent, to Prison to Help Make Al Smith President.*

In 1930 Bishop Cannon declared that adoption of the proposed constitutional amendment was "the most important legislative proposition before the country." The amendment was approved subsequently by the House Judiciary Committee, but it got no farther. Cannon assailed President Franklin D. Roosevelt some years later for his failure to back the amendment, charging that he was greatly influenced in his attitude by "alien political Romanism."

Throughout these years the cartoonists of the metropolitan press, the overwhelming bulk of which was implacably opposed to prohibition, dedicated their pens to the task of ridiculing the drys. "Prohibition" was usually depicted as a long-faced, long-nosed, cadaverous-looking individual with a battered high silk hat and a black umbrella. His facial expression was sour, if not cruel, and his demeanor repulsive. The most devastating of all these pen-and-ink assaults were those of Rollin Kirby in the *New York World*. Kirby's quill was a javelin that impaled the Anti-Saloon League leaders and their cohorts relentlessly. Yet the drys became hardened to this ridicule and even joked about it in a grim sort of way. For example, Bishop Cannon remarked to a newspaperman as he looked at one of the *World's* cartoons: "I wonder what's the matter today; his nose isn't as long as usual."

Before his election to the presidency Hoover had announced that, in the event of a Republican victory, there would be "an organized investigation of fact and cause" with respect to prohibition for the purpose of correcting "grave abuses." The anti-prohibitionists had seized upon this in the campaign as a hopeful omen.

But after the new President was safely installed, he broadened the projected inquiry and announced that there would be "a searching investigation of the whole structure of our jurisprudence, to include the method of enforcement of the Eighteenth Amendment and the causes of abuse under it." There was nothing in the prospectus to indicate that study would be given to the enforceability of the prohibition laws, which impressed many persons as the principal question at issue. Thus the campaign commitment to an intensive inquiry into the working of the Eighteenth Amendment in order to correct abuses was drastically amended, and the promised probe was metamorphosed into a much more inclusive study, in which the dry law was to be only one aspect of the entire law-enforcement problem.

Bishop Cannon issued a statement approving the broadened scope of the inquiry, but expressing the view that "the country has understood that there will be a special investigation, consideration and recommendations concerning the efficient enforcement of the Eighteenth Amendment, and the wisest course to follow to secure the best results." He commended President Hoover strongly for his declaration that the lawlessness current in the country at the time was not due to the prohibition law. "Any proper study of conditions," said the Bishop, "will show that for the last forty years there has been a steady increase of general lawlessness."

Cannon telegraphed George W. Wickersham, former Attorney General of the United States, that he hoped reports were correct that Hoover would name him chairman of the proposed Law Enforcement Commission. Later Wickersham, after his acceptance, issued a statement that Cannon attacked as highly inappropriate and "defeatist." This, as we have seen in Chapter xv, was Wickersham's assertion that both "national and state laws might be modified so as to become reasonably enforceable."

Cannon still professed complete confidence in President Hoover's zeal for prohibition, however, and he urged that "multitudinous private letters and public resolutions" be dispatched to the White House, informing the occupant that "we do stand squarely behind him in his purpose to uphold the majesty of the law."

The Bishop also suggested the establishing "in suitable centers of the nation a chain of daily newspapers which will place the truth and the moral betterment of the people above the cash box." He urged the substitution "for the sewage which pours into our homes almost daily from the columns of many of the present-day secular dailies, weeklies and monthlies a stream of clean, properly filtered news." The projected newspapers would concern themselves with "the incontestable benefits which have come to the great mass of our people from the closing of the saloons and the prohibition of the legalized traffic," in contrast to the greater part of the press, which, he said, preferred "to picture all the boys and girls with hip flasks, daring bootleggers outwitting enforcement officers, or tyrannical officers murdering innocent law violators."

Presumably the "clean, properly filtered news" that the Bishop sought to offer the American public through his projected chain of unsullied and immaculate dailies would be comparable to that served up through his *Richmond Virginian* of fragrant memory. The *Virginian*, it will be recalled, employed numerous hard-drinking practitioners who managed, between bouts at the near-by saloons, to turn out a reasonable quantity of copy dedicated to the prohibitionist cause. The paper involved itself in various inconsistencies and contradictions, among which was a lamentable failure to live up to its own chaste professions. If the *Virginian* was to serve as a model for the Bishop's white knights of journalism, observers could be pardoned for raising a skeptical eyebrow. Actually his plan came to nothing.

In an effort to co-ordinate the organizations throughout the nation that were dedicated to the furtherance of the dry cause, a central clearing-house was established in the autumn of 1929. A score of prohibition's leaders met in Washington, and out of their deliberations came the Cooperative Committee for Prohibition Enforcement, with headquarters in the national capital. Patrick H. Callahan, a Louisville businessman and an official of the Association of Catholics Favoring Prohibition, was named chairman of the newly formed organization. Bishop Cannon was one of those present at the Washington conclave that chose Callahan to the post. If he questioned the wisdom of electing a Roman Catholic as chairman of the committee, he did not share his apprehension with the public.

A few months later the Bishop let go a torrid blast in the press, charging that the country was experiencing another "whiskey rebellion." He blamed "Catholic ecclesiastical leaders" and others. It had become a question of "the Constitution or anarchy," said Cannon.

"No other outstanding spokesman of the drys during the whole ten-year period that the Eighteenth Amendment has been in effect has candidly conceded so wide a degree of prohibition failure," wrote J. Fred Essary, in the *Baltimore Sun.*

In addition to belaboring Archbishop Curley, of Baltimore, Cardinal O'Connell, of Boston, and the Vatican, Cannon vigorously assailed President Nicholas Murray Butler, of Columbia University, former Governor Alfred E. Smith, of New York, and Mrs. Charles H. Sabin, former Republican National Committeewoman from New York. Dr. Butler was described by the Bishop as "the apostle of selfish individualism as opposed to the general welfare." The president of Columbia had made deprecatory remarks concerning the Wickersham Commission's recent report, terming it "pathetic evidence that Washington, like the Emperor Nero, fiddled while Rome is burning." Cannon called this "egotistical arrogance" and went on:

> Mr. Butler clamors "to clear out of the House of Representatives November next those wretched creatures who sit there to cheer and to laugh when murder is extolled in their presence."
> What condemnation is severe enough for the president of a great university who deliberately misrepresents and perverts the attitude of patriotic Congressmen who declared their intention to support the officers and men of the Coast Guard in the performance of their duty, rather than to make martyrs of smugglers?

Mrs. Sabin was assailed by the Bishop as "the leader of a group of society women opposed to prohibition." He asserted that "there is morally no distinction between those whom she contemptuously brands as 'prohibition's criminal offspring, the bootlegger, smuggler and the racketeer,' and those who she declared 'in their resentment of the law's invasion of their personal liberties will continue in their everyday lives deliberately and completely to disregard the law's very existence.'"

Bishop Cannon loosed his broadside on the eve of his departure for Europe and Africa. When his ship touched at Spain, he dispatched a cable denouncing a bill pending in Congress to legalize 2.75 per cent beer and demanding again that the buyer of intoxicants be made equally guilty with the seller. Formal pleas for repeal of the Eighteenth Amendment were being heard by Congress for the first time since the enactment of prohibition. Cannon's recipe for dealing with all these manifestations of revolt against the Eighteenth Amendment and the Volstead Act was Congressional action to "provide whatever money and men are necessary to convince the present rebels against prohibition that the government will suppress rebellion wherever found, even though incited and supported as their whiskey rebellion has been, by a section of the metropolitan press."

On his arrival in London some months later the Bishop fired another blast in opposition to those who had been seeking to bring about changes in the prohibition laws. They had made out no case, said he. "Why not try education and strict enforcement and see what results will follow?" he asked. Referring to those who had appeared before the House committee in opposition to the dry law, Cannon said that they "openly justify social flaunting [*sic*] of the law, exalt as martyrs, smugglers or bootleggers shot while resisting arrest, and they criticize or denounce government officials for enforcing the law, and characterize the friends or advocates of prohibition as bigoted Puritans, fanatics or hypocrites." The Bishop observed that prohibition is "neither hypocrisy, Puritanism nor fanaticism; it is benevolent common sense."

Shortly after Cannon got back to the United States, the drys began reeling under the impact of returns from the *Literary Digest* poll on prohibition. This magazine had taken various nation-wide polls, including two presidential straw votes that had been almost supernaturally accurate (in the elections of 1924 and 1928). Now, in the spring of 1930, it set out to get a cross-section of national sentiment on the dry law.

When the results came in, they jarred the prohibitionists from head to toe. More than 4,800,000 ballots were returned to the *Digest*, and of these fewer than 1,500,000 were for retention of the Eighteenth Amendment. Outright repeal got nearly 2,000,000, and beer and wine nearly 1,400,000 more. The dry vote exceeded the combined total for repeal and modification in only five states. Newspaper polls were taken in various sections with a view to checking the accuracy of the *Digest* figures, and in all of them the returns were wetter than those of the magazine for the same territory. Chief among these was the poll of the twenty-five Scripps-Howard papers from coast to coast, which brought in an avalanche of anti-prohibitionist ballots.

Spokesmen for the Anti-Saloon League and kindred agencies were kept busy trying to explain away these evidences of dislike for the existing dispensation. Bishop Cannon said there were two salient reasons why the *Digest* poll and similar straw votes were inaccurate and unrepresentative: first, "millions of dry voters decline to participate in such polls, believing that it is not a proper or accurate method to obtain the sentiment of the people"; second, "because great masses of people, especially clerks and so-called labor classes (men and especially women) and the rural voters are not reached by such polls, and yet a great majority of these very people will vote against any repeal or weakening of the prohibition law."

But if Cannon and his fellow defenders of the status quo professed to see no significance in the results obtained by the *Digest*, the opposition was jubilant. What the Bishop had several times termed the "whiskey rebellion" mounted in a new crescendo.

For years the making of home-brew in cellars and attics had been a major occupation of thirsty souls, as had the manufacture of bathtub gin and divers varieties of homemade wine. These beverages were sometimes good and sometimes bad, but they were drunk in huge quantities. Salesmen peddled the best ingredients from house to house, together with efficient apparatus for transmuting them into the desired decoctions. Yeast, hops, wine bricks, grain alcohol, oil of juniper and other similar essentials to the manufacture of alcoholic potables were purchasable with a minimum of trouble, and virtually no risk.

Prohibition Director Amos W. W. Woodcock declared officially in 1930 that the makers of homemade and home-consumed wine and beer were immune from prosecution under Federal law. He pointed out that those who made beer or wine in their residences were safe from intrusions by Federal prohibition agents, since a private dwelling could not be searched without a warrant. The Volstead Law forbade the issuance of a warrant unless there was positive evidence that alcoholic beverages were being sold. So long as they were brewed and consumed under one roof, the Federal authorities were powerless, he asserted.

This declaration brought a snort of dissent from Bishop Cannon. "All I can say," he declared, "is that there is no question of the meaning of the prohibition amendment — I was one of seven who wrote it." He quoted the amendment as providing that "the manufacture, sale, importation, exportation, etc., of intoxicating liquor is prohibited," and added: "That means anywhere — in the home or anywhere else." He was not "criticizing anyone," but he asserted that "Colonel Woodcock's statement cannot change the

law." Nor did the Bishop's declaration change Colonel Woodcock. Yeasty odors and vinous exhalations continued to issue from
thousands of cellars and garrets, and the Federal agents did nothing to stop it.

One reason why the homemade-wine business mounted to new
peaks lay in the assistance rendered its promoters by Mrs. Mabel
Walker Willebrandt. After serving for eight years as Assistant
Attorney General in charge of prohibition enforcement, Mrs.
Willebrandt resigned in 1929 and returned to the private prac-
tice of law. She had taken an active part in the campaign for
Hoover during the preceding year, but one of her speeches had
brought such a storm of criticism that it was rumored to have
been responsible for her leaving the Federal service soon after
Hoover's inauguration.

At all events, the former legal spearhead of Federal prohibition enforcement acquired the California Fruit Industries as a
client. This concern manufactured a wine brick that, when subjected to the proper incantations, was quickly metamorphosed
into wine with an alcoholic content of up to twelve per cent.

Al Smith, who had been attacked by Mrs. Willebrandt in the
campaign of 1928, was zestful in delivering a riposte. Speaking
at Newark, New Jersey, he said:

> I congratulate the Fruit Industries in securing the services of
> so competent a person as Mabel. She did two things for them, two
> wonderful things. She convinced the Department of Justice that
> this 12 per cent wine was not intoxicating. That was some stunt
> when you figure that old Andy Volstead fixed it at half of one per
> cent, and she jumped it up 11½ per cent and still robbed it of ev-
> ery intoxicating character. But she did something else for them
> that was equally important. She got the Farm Board to lend them
> $20,000,000.
>
> So when all is said and done, Mabel collected a beautiful fee
> for making the Volstead Act look like thirty cents.[4]

In addition to home-fermented vintages and domestically
brewed beers that were being manufactured throughout the land,
and the well-systematized moonshine-bootleg trade, which functioned practically everywhere, there was the vast number of
speakeasies that flourished in the great cities.

Demise of the Noble Experiment

"Carry Nations by the thousands should rise up and smash the speakeasies of New York City and other places where officers refuse to enforce the prohibition law," Cannon told a prohibitionist mass meeting in Atlanta. At the same time he expressed strong opposition to the resolution that the American Federation of Labor had adopted shortly before at its Vancouver convention, demanding 2.75 per cent beer.

Mrs. Ella Boole, the ubiquitous president of the W.C.T.U., leaped into the breach with the dictum that "unfermented fruit juices make delectable puddings" and with a list of "delicious non-acoholic drinks," including "orange tea," "cherry shrub," "raspberry freeze," "spiced grape juice," "oriental punch," and, incredible as it may appear, something called "mint julep." The ingredients of this last were lemons, sugar, water, ginger ale — and mint.

In an interview that he granted to H. L. Mencken for the *Baltimore Evening Sun,* Bishop Cannon set forth his views concerning the prohibition situation. He expressed dismay that the "Christian people" of Baltimore did not insist upon enforcement of the dry law in that sinful city, devoted as it was to gustatory delights, many of which revolved about libations of Maryland rye, or seafood washed down with lager.

"The Bishop looks more amiable than his photographs," wrote Mencken following his séance with Cannon in the latter's office at the headquarters of the Southern Methodist Board of Temperance and Social Service in Washington.

> When he sits for a photographer he puts on an episcopal frown, and as a result his portraits give him a certain resemblance to the Methodist dervish of the cartoonists. In reality he is too well-fed for the role, and his toothbrush mustache is in the way.
>
> What he would look like in the mitre, amice, alb, girdle, stole, maniple, tunicle, chamble, and pastoral staff of his ghostly office I do not know [wrote Mencken], and neither does anyone else, for he never wears them. He assured me, indeed, that he had no mitre, nor even a shovel hat. He spoke of wearing gaiters, but I gathered that he had reference to ordinary spats.

The interviewer went on to declare that the Bishop's "private apartments in the Methodist Vatican are wholly devoid of that rococo voluptuousness which one associates with the dens of Bishops." He added that "there is no stained glass in the windows, there are no tiger-skins on the floor, and there is no display whatever of ecclesiastical tassels, badges and pompoms."

His Grace works at an old-time roll-top desk — an antique of the late McKinley period, probably worth $7.75 at auction. It groans under two huge piles of letters — one consisting of encomiums from the saved and the other of anathemas from the damned. . . .

The rest of the furnishings are extremely meagre — in fact, the audience chamber looks a great deal more like the office of a lawyer in insufficient practice than the quarters of one of the most puissant ecclesiastical dignitaries of modern times, whose word is gospel to millions and whose merest wink can make a President of the United States leap like a bullfrog.

It is an interesting fact that, although Cannon and Mencken were often at opposite poles in their views of public issues, and pre-eminently so where prohibition was concerned, they were at this period on wholly amicable terms. Mr. and Mrs. Mencken entertained Bishop and Mrs. Cannon at luncheon in their Baltimore apartment, and the Bishop was to consult Mencken from time to time thereafter concerning the preparation of his memoirs. When the Baltimore libertarian wrote of the Bishop, he did so in a vein of ironic adulation. The above-quoted interview, published in the autumn of 1931, was typical of his gently satiric approach.

It was also in the fall of 1931 that the Rev. Dr. Rembert G. Smith, who had assailed the Bishop in 1929 for the activities of his Board of Temperance and Social Service in the Hoover-Smith campaign, was made to feel the wrath of the church. Dr. Smith, a Georgia Methodist, was summoned before a committee of thirteen North Carolina Methodists to answer charges of "gross imprudence and unministerial conduct." No further specifications were given to the public concerning the nature of these allegations. The committee recommended a one-year suspension from the ministry. Smith appealed, and the church court of last resort, meeting at Nashville, concurred in the recommendation of the North Carolinians. Smith thereupon issued the following comment:

Demise of the Noble Experiment

The active agents in my prosecution were all aggressive Cannonites and Hoovercrats, who were guilty in 1928 of using pulpits and church offices and church papers for the support of the party of pseudo-prohibition and of predatory wealth. . . . I do not regret having made the fight which I have made against the degradation of my church, and will continue to fight.

It became increasingly probable in 1931 that a definite showdown on the Eighteenth Amendment was coming. As early as 1926 there had been stirrings among a wealthy group of industrialists in opposition to prohibition. The Association Against the Prohibition Amendment had been formed, and these financial "angels," among whom the du Ponts were conspicuous, became the leading factors in the organization. They were opposed to the dry law because of the manifest evils that had sprung up since its enactment, and they also pointed out that the income from liquor, wine, and beer taxes would lighten the tax burden for both individuals and corporations.

Further impetus was given the cause of repeal when the Voluntary Committee of Lawyers, Inc., was formed in 1929. Leading members of the bar from coast to coast enlisted in the fight, with the result that in 1930 the American Bar Association called for the death-knell of prohibition.

The Wickersham Commission's final report on the dry law was made public in 1931, and it caused a furore. The prohibitionists interpreted it as signifying agreement on the part of all the commissioners that "the liquor traffic was a social and political menace, that there must be no relaxation in the struggle for its suppression, that the saloon must not return, that the Eighteenth Amendment must be neither nullified nor repealed, and that, if it were revised, Congress should be given power to control or entirely suppress the liquor traffic, and that there should be honest and vigorous enforcement of the law."

The wets, on the other hand, speaking through the Voluntary Committee of Lawyers, Inc., arrived at conclusions almost the reverse. They said:

These findings of fact, concurred in by all the members of the [Wickersham] commission, fully support the conclusions of the board of managers of the Voluntary Committee of Lawyers: (1)

307

that the Eighteenth Amendment, being a police regulation, has no proper place in the Constitution of the United States; (2) that it is unenforceable because it has not the support of law-abiding citizens; (3) that it does not tend to bring about temperance; (4) that it tends to increase crime and corruption; and (5) that it impairs the due administration of justice and causes disrespect for law.

The committee added that the commissioners "are practically unanimous in agreeing that the Eighteenth Amendment should be repealed or that some other plan should be adopted."

The average citizen was naturally bewildered by the foregoing contradictory statements. The explanation for the obviously irreconcilable interpretations of the report would seem to lie in the extraordinary way in which it was prepared and the manner in which the conclusions apparently were forced into a predetermined mold by Chairman Wickersham. It was strongly suspected that the White House put pressure on him to that end. Although eight of the eleven functioning members favored change in the law and only three preferred the status quo, the "conclusions" were presented in such a way as to create an entirely different impression.[5] While the Wickersham report, therefore, was deemed to be something of a farce, it added to the general ferment over repeal.

That ferment was well under way by 1932. An agency that added much impetus to the movement was the Women's Organization for National Prohibition Reform, of which Mrs. Charles H. Sabin was president. It was an innovation to have an aggressive group of women working for elimination of the dry law, since the weight of organized womanhood had previously been thrown into the scales on the side of prohibition. The W.O.N.P.R. differed from the W.C.T.U., however, in several respects. Chief among them, perhaps, was the fact that its members were often affiliated with so-called "high society" and some were wealthy.

Mrs. Sabin had been a supporter of the Eighteenth Amendment and had backed Hoover for the presidency. Although by 1928 she had become skeptical of prohibition's beneficent effects, she counted on the incoming Republican President to conduct a searching inquiry into the workings of the law. But when he announced in his inaugural that the whole system of jurisprudence would be examined, she concluded that she had been misled. She accordingly resigned as Republican National Committeewoman from New York. Upon the entry of the personable Mrs. Sabin into the ranks of the active repealists, a United States Senator exclaimed: "Thank God, a pretty woman in politics at last!"

Clarence True Wilson, on the other hand, commented scathingly upon the activity of W.O.N.P.R. and declared that "the little group of wine-drinking society women who are uncomfortable under prohibition will have as much influence in assaulting the Constitution of their country as they would have blowing soap-bubbles at Gibraltar." To Dr. D. Leigh Colvin, chairman of the National Prohibition Committee, the members of the organization were "Bacchanalian maidens, parching for wine — wet women who, like the drunkards whom their program will produce, would take pennies off the eyes of the dead for the sake of legalizing booze." Dr. Mary Armor, president of the Georgia W.C.T.U., said on the same general subject: "As to Mrs. Sabin and her cocktail-drinking women, we will out-live them, out-fight them, out-love them, out-talk them, out-pray them, and out-vote them."

A fair percentage of the W.O.N.P.R. members belonged to the Episcopal and Catholic churches. The light in which these workers in the vineyard were regarded by orthodox W.C.T.U.'s was seen in the observation of a dry lady from Kentucky that she did "not consider that Episcopalians and Catholics are Christians."

The *American Independent,* a prohibitionist organ published in Kentucky, remarked that "you cannot find two dozen women in the state who openly advocate the repeal of the Eighteenth Amendment who is [sic] not either a drunkard, or whose home life is not immoral, or who does not expect to get into the liquor business when and if it is again legalized."

Such was the reception that greeted W.O.N.P.R. when it threw itself wholeheartedly into the repeal movement.

The drys were still pretending that this movement had no prospect of success. Their attitude was typified by Senator Morris Sheppard, of Texas, who had proclaimed that "there is as much chance of repealing the Eighteenth Amendment as there is for a humming-bird to fly to the planet Mars with the Washington Monument tied to its tail." Yet the country was seething with revolt against the law.

This became plainer as the presidential campaign of 1932 neared. Early in the year Bishop Cannon began uttering warnings to both parties. As had been his wont in 1920, 1924, and 1928, he called for the nomination and election of candidates for president and vice-president who were favorable to prohibition, and for a law-enforcement plank in the platform. He preferred this last to a dry plank.

As one who had been affiliated with the Democratic Party practically all his life, Cannon addressed himself more particularly to that party. If the Democrats should name a wet candidate on a wet platform, said he, "then the same group which repudiated the wet-Tammany-Smith leadership in 1928 will repudiate vigorously, and I believe effectively, similar leadership in 1932." As for President Hoover, who was expected to run for re-election, the Bishop exhorted him to demand a plank calling for law enforcement.

But the country was in the depths of the Great Depression, and the terrific shrinkage in Federal revenues lent weight to the argument of many Democrats that legal liquor, beer, and wine would bring in substantial revenues and help to finance the essential activities of the government.

The leading Democratic candidate was Governor Franklin D. Roosevelt, of New York, but Roosevelt was accounted more dry than wet by some observers. President Hoover was considered certain to be renominated by the Republicans; yet the people were in no mood to keep the Republicans in office.

About a week before the Republican National Convention and two weeks before the Democratic National Convention, a political blockbuster was tossed by John D. Rockefeller, Jr. He and his father had contributed $350,000 to the Anti-Saloon League at one time or another, and he was accounted the most prominent individual in the ranks of prohibition's supporters. On June 7 the press carried the news that Rockefeller, a lifelong teetotaler, favored outright repeal of the Eighteenth Amendment. He pronounced prohibition a flat failure, saying that its evils greatly outweighed its benefits. The philanthropist expressed the hope that both major political parties would stand for repeal in their conventions.

Rockefeller's apostasy was a frightful blow to the dry cause. His change of front was ascribed to an "inferiority complex" by Bishop Cannon, who added that Rockefeller's attitude had been influenced by his residence in New York, "where literally Satan's seat is." [6]

The Bishop's chameleon-like shifts in his appraisal of the Rockefellers had long been well-nigh incredible. Back in 1905 Cannon had written that John D. Rockefeller, Sr., was the "representative of the greatest evil in public life," and that for the church to accept gifts from him would be to "padlock the lips of the pulpits." [7] Yet the following year Cannon was expressing heartfelt gratitude to the General Education Board, financed entirely with Rockefeller money, for its offer of ten thousand dollars to Randolph-Macon College.[8] By 1916 the Bishop had evolved a new theory of whether a church or a public institution could properly receive gifts from persons who had made their money in ways not condoned by it. This dictum was to the effect that if the church or institution "publicly states its opposition to the methods by which such money is made, and does not abate in any degree its denunciation of such methods because of such gifts, there is no shame or disgrace in accepting them." [9] In 1921 the Rockefellers were both termed "thoughtful, progressive Protestant Christians" by the Bishop.[10] But then in 1932 Cannon turned on the younger Rockefeller for his abandonment of prohibition.

At all events, Rockefeller's declaration that prohibition had failed added great impetus to the repeal movement. The Republicans were the last remaining hope of the prohibitionists, but this pronunciamento from a lifelong dry leader of that party was sensational in its impact. When the national convention of the party met, the Anti-Saloon League and kindred bodies were still hopeful that they could rally under Hoover's tattered banner for a last stand to save the Eighteenth Amendment. But the convention's prohibition plank turned out to be a magnificent straddle, satisfactory to nobody. It took no stand for or against repeal, but proposed that the question be submitted to state conventions.

This gave the Democrats their opportunity. They were leaning already toward a more forthright position than that of the Republicans, and when they convened at Chicago, the wets were quick to take advantage of the opening.

Bishop Cannon was on hand. He hoped to get the law-enforcement plank that he had been seeking, and he also wanted to influence the choice of the nominee. But the tide was running so heavily against the prohibitionist cause that he was like a straw man caught in a cyclone.

When the Bishop appeared at a tumultuous session of the platform committee to urge a law-enforcement plank, there was a great uproar from the floor and the galleries, which had been quite adequately packed by Mayor Anton J. Cermak, of Chicago. The wets howled with derision when Cannon began his remarks. Furthermore, Senator Carter Glass ostentatiously left the hall, saying that he would not listen to the arguments of "such a man."

Cannon, imperturbable as ever, delivered his warning to the committeemen amid a great din from the anti-prohibitionist camp. The chairman, Senator Hitchcock, was unable to maintain order, and when the Bishop concluded, the deafening hostile demonstration continued for five minutes. When the yells and boos finally subsided, Representative Michael Igoe, of Illinois, a member of the committee, rose from his seat in the second row and called to Cannon:

"Your broker wants you!"

This sally was greeted with a chorus of hisses from the dry ladies who occupied half of the gallery. The Bishop retorted icily:

"I thought I was addressing gentlemen. You apparently do not want facts."

"We don't like traitors!" a man sitting next to Igoe shouted at Cannon, with considerable irrelevance.

The Bishop was treated with a similar lack of respect at other points in the convention proceedings. He reported that several newspapers were hurled at him.

On top of everything, the convention adopted a dripping, sopping plank on prohibition, calling for outright repeal, and for the legalization of beer pending repeal. Nominee Roosevelt flew to

Chicago and proclaimed his acceptance of the platform "100 per cent." It was a debacle, nothing less, for Cannon and the other professional drys.

The Bishop was not slow in letting his views be known. He blasted Senator Thomas J. Walsh, of Montana, the convention's permanent chairman, because Walsh, a dry, had complimented the huge gathering on its behavior during the debate on prohibition. "The conduct of the convention was most reprehensible," said Cannon. "It indicated very clearly that repeal supporters did not believe in fair play."

Next day he declared that "there is not the slightest idea of yielding to this present-day whiskey rebellion." He went on to say that the Southern delegates to the convention had been guilty of a "double betrayal," since they had sat "dumbly, impotently or indifferently" while the dry cause was being sold out. Recalling the "stinging rebuke" of 1928, he appealed to "the moral forces of the South" to find "another leadership, which will not betray them as in 1928 and 1932."

In August came Hoover's acceptance speech, and in it the President went well beyond his party's platform. He called for repeal of the Eighteenth Amendment and for the return of control to the states. By that time the Bishop was in Geneva, but he assailed Hoover by cable as having surrendered "to the speakeasies, bootleggers and nullifiers of the Constitution."

President Hoover's position, and that of his party, was still much less unequivocal than the outright stand for repeal taken by Roosevelt and the Democrats, but it was now clear that the professional drys had nowhere to go. None could doubt, after the Hoover acceptance speech, that prohibition was doomed. Many prohibitionists felt that they had been double-crossed — by Hoover, or Roosevelt, or both.

On his return to the United States, Cannon denounced Hoover again for surrendering to the wets. He called on both Roosevelt and Hoover in almost identical letters to explain how they proposed to avoid the return of the saloon. He found a measure of comfort in the fact that Hoover had not mentioned modification of the Volstead Law in his acceptance speech, and the further fact that the Republican platform omitted any such reference. But with both candidates on record as favoring repeal, this was a clear case of grasping at straws.

Prohibition was about to be blitzed, no matter who won, and everything pointed to a Democratic victory in the presidential election. The repealists had massed their forces behind Roosevelt.

Late in October Bishop Cannon hinted strongly that he would support Hoover, but he didn't quite commit himself. "If I vote for Mr. Hoover," he told a Richmond audience, "it will have to be with the understanding that I disagree with the statements made in his acceptance speech, and because I believe he is sincere and will have more sympathy with prohibition enforcement than any other candidate who has a chance." Then in Birmingham he stated publicly that he would vote for Hoover as the only way to defeat Roosevelt.

But the Bishop did not vote on election day in his home precinct at Blackstone, Virginia, either in person or by mail.[11]

Roosevelt carried the state and nation by a landslide. It appeared, in the words of the bitterly disillusioned drys, that the United States was about to "go off the God standard." Such was the phrase used by State Senator George W. Layman, leader of the Virginia prohibitionists, on the floor of the legislature when it was evident that modification of the Layman Act, the state dry law, was imminent.

The Roosevelt victory was the signal for a relentless drive to get rid of the Eighteenth Amendment. First it was decided to bring back 3.2 per cent beer at once, in accordance with the beer plank in the Democratic platform. Bishop Cannon had warned that congressmen supporting any such measure would violate their oaths of office, since legislation of this character "attempts to legalize intoxicating liquor."

There was a measure of justice in the Bishop's contention, but the country was in no mood to listen. President Roosevelt sent Congress a special message on March 13, 1933, recommending modification of the Volstead Act to legalize the manufacture and sale of beer and other beverages "of such alcoholic content as is permissible under the Constitution; and to provide through such manufacture and sale, by substantial taxes, a proper and much needed revenue for the government." This became law on March 22, nine days after the message was delivered. The country now was moving at a furious pace toward the elimination of the regime that had long been dominant in Washington and most of the states.

Beer became legal under the new Federal dispensation on April 7, and it was freely consumed on that date in nineteen states and the District of Columbia. The brew was drunk joyfully, but there were complaints that the supply was inadequate. On Broadway, New Yorkers paraded behind a hearse bearing the legend "Near Beer is Dead," while a band in gaudy Bavarian uniforms played dirges and drinking songs. In Milwaukee, steins were raised to the gladsome strains of *Ach, du lieber Augustin.*

A leading dry who regarded the beer bill as "a palpable violation of the Constitution" wrote with respect to the results which flowed from its adoption:

> The passage of this act produced the intended effect. The fighting drys were scattered and dazed, and millions of men and women who had always voted dry became discouraged and decided that, since the liquor traffic was actually back and they could not help it, they might as well legalize it so that it could be taxed. On the other hand, the wet hordes were fired with hope and courage and thus prepared for the last great battle in the war for repeal.

The battle began promptly. The strategy of the repealists was to hold referendums in the various states and, where repeal was voted, to summon a state convention shortly thereafter which would cast the ballot of that state for the Twenty-first Amendment, eliminating the Eighteenth Amendment from the Constitution.

President Roosevelt threw his weight into the scales on behalf of repeal, and Postmaster General James A. Farley devoted his quite notable political virtuosity to the crusade. The President made it clear that higher taxes then under consideration would be made unnecessary by the revenue anticipated from liquor. He argued that recovery from the depression would thus be promoted.

Half a dozen states fell in line for repeal during the spring of 1933, all by huge majorities. Bishop Cannon became badly worried. He had said during the preceding February that "it now seems evident that the Eighteenth Amendment will not be repealed at an early date, and probably not at all." But with the approach of summer he was obviously perturbed. Indiana was to vote on June 6 and Cannon declared that "if we can win in Indiana, we can prevent repeal." Indiana went wet by nearly two to one.

Cannon then attended a dry rally in Birmingham in the once arid state of Alabama, but he declined to predict the outcome in the referendum there, set for July 18. Alabama voted for repeal on that date by almost three to two. Arkansas, once considered equally amenable to the ukases of the Anti-Saloon League, went for repeal on the same day by a similar majority. Tennessee went wet two days later. The jig was obviously up for the prohibitionist cause.

On the eve of the balloting in the once dry state of Texas, Cannon said in a letter to the *Richmond Times-Dispatch:*

> The present mad stampede for repeal, stimulated and lashed on by unprecedented and indefensible methods, may succeed, but there are still millions of people in the United States, including the leadership of the great Protestant bodics, with the country preachers, at whom the *Times-Dispatch* sneers (whose shoe-latchets the *Times-Dispatch* writers are not worthy to unloose), whose convictions are unchanged as to the necessity for the national law. . . . Repeal may come now, as a result of the ignorance of the younger generation or of forgetfulness of past evils, but . . . the nation . . . will return to national prohibition.

Texas went for repeal by a huge majority.

Robert M. Smith, author of the "Daily Mirror of Washington" column in the *Philadelphia Public Ledger* and the *New York Evening Post,* wrote apropos of Bishop Cannon: " 'Pussyfoot' Johnson apparently is a better philosopher than the Bishop. He saw that the more speeches he made the wetter the country became; so he retired to his farm, conceding that 'the devil often gets the best of it.' "

Al Smith said in his monthly editorial for the *New Outlook* that "nothing could go further to show the moral rout of the 'dry' forces in the recent convention campaigns than the use by them of old discredited hacks such as Bishop Cannon." The Bishop retorted by asking Al why he did not "take his medicine like a man" instead of "showing the yellow streak, as he did when he rushed away from Chicago [during the convention of 1932] without waiting for the nominee's arrival, and when he sulked pouting for three months, until the Newark speech in October."

Since Cannon made no addresses in Virginia prior to the referendum there on October 3, he may finally have taken a leaf from "Pussyfoot" Johnson's book. At all events, he could not have stemmed the tide, for what he termed "the mad stampede for repeal" was going merrily forward. The Virginia electorate supported the Twenty-first Amendment by better than three to two. The Bishop, curiously enough, did not even vote at Blackstone, either in person or by mail.[12]

The thirty-sixth state, Utah, ratified repeal on December 5, and on that date the Eighteenth Amendment was superseded by the Twenty-first. In the nineteen states whose laws permitted the sale of hard liquor there were celebrations, but the revelry was more restrained than had been anticipated. Supplies of non-bootleg stuff were scarce, since repeal had arrived with such speed that many hotels and restaurants were caught flatfooted. Some hotels had extensive supplies of "medicinal" liquor, and these were useful in the crisis.

A piquant item came over the wires from Annapolis. This special dispatch to the *New York Times* said: "Wet legislators here will patriotically support legal liquor. The State House bootlegger received formal notice today to discontinue his trade. The notice was served by a policeman on duty at the Capitol."

On this ironic note repeal became a fact. The long reign of the Anti-Saloon League had come to an end. December 5, 1933 was to become a milestone in the social history of the United States.

Was the achievement of repeal principally attributable to any single individual?

Robert M. Smith, the Washington columnist quoted above, expressed the view in the Philadelphia and New York papers for which he wrote that the credit for repeal was mainly due to Captain William H. Stayton, founder and first president of the Association Against the Prohibition Amendment and chairman of its board until the dissolution of the organization.

But when later he reiterated this opinion in person to the "sturdy old seadog," Captain Stayton modestly disclaimed the accolade.

"To whom then would you award the honor?" asked Smith.

"To Bishop Cannon," the captain answered without hesitation.[13]

CHAPTER *xix*

His Soul Goes Marching On

Bishop Cannon, and the whole coterie of like-minded exemplars of the "Thou Shalt Not" philosophy who had been dominant in American life for at least a decade and a half, were suddenly reduced to semi-obscurity by the repeal of prohibition. It was a cataclysmic fall for these men. Long accustomed to telling Presidents, congressmen, and state legislators what they wanted, and getting it, they found themselves thrust aside and treated with scant consideration.

Cannon's involuntary role in helping to bring about repeal was emphasized by more than one official of the Association Against the Prohibition Amendment. Jouett Shouse, executive secretary of the organization headed by Captain Stayton, was wont to term the Bishop "God's gift to the repeal cause." [1] Senator Glass had called Cannon "the Methodist Pope" in the days of the cleric's political ascendancy, but the phrase, always ironically employed by the Senator, now had a hollow ring. Aside from the doctor's loss of prestige with the general public, he appeared to be in danger of superannuation, or enforced retirement as Bishop, at the hands of his own church.

In April 1934, just prior to his trial in Washington on charges of violating the Federal Corrupt Practices Act, Cannon published in the *Nashville Christian Advocate* the statement that he had no intention of asking for retirement at the General Conference that was to meet later in the month. He confessed that his superannuation four years ahead of schedule "would greatly delight my enemies."

Immediately following his acquittal by a jury in United States District Court, he left for Jackson, Mississippi, where the General

319

Conference was in session and where the issue of his retirement was boiling hot. His "enemies" were actively seeking his forcible removal as an active Bishop. Just as this storm center of a hundred controversies arrived at the gathering to receive what the Associated Press described as "a great ovation . . . on the floor," members of the Committee on Episcopacy disclosed that they had voted 43 to 28 for his superannuation. The Associated Press reported that Bishop Cannon received the news "with an expression of surprise." He declined to comment.

His friends went to work immediately with a view to overriding the recommendation of the Committee on Episcopacy. The pattern was that of the 1930 Dallas conference all over again. This great and good man was being "crucified," said his supporters. If so noble a martyr should be forcibly retired, it would play directly into the hands of the "wet press and the Roman Catholics." The buttonholing and lobbying by both sides went on intensively for forty-eight hours. At the end of that time the cause of righteousness was seen to have emerged triumphant once more. The conference voted, 269 to 170, to override its own committee and to keep the Bishop on active service for four more years. He was assigned to conferences on the Pacific coast and in Arizona and Mexico.

By midsummer 1934 Bishop Cannon was convinced that the saloon had returned and that conditions in the country at large were "the most distressing this writer has ever known." He declared that the barroom had come back "not only with its former evil accompaniments but with the addition of barmaids and with indiscriminate patronage by women." By early 1935 Cannon was predicting the re-enactment of both national and state prohibition.

In October of that year he openly denounced President Roosevelt for having broken numerous pledges, notably his promise that "the 'old time' saloon under any guise" would not return. Other pledges that Cannon said the White House had "tossed aside with such recklessness and callousness" had to do with "the gold standard, deflation of the dollar, reduction of governmental expenditures, balancing of the budget, and the fundamental necessity for the rights of the states to be preserved unimpaired." The

His Soul Goes Marching On

Bishop made these pointed accusations in a letter to the President, written in response to a request from Roosevelt to the nation's clergymen for information concerning conditions in their communities.

When the Anti-Saloon League of America held its annual convention at St. Louis in December, it served fair warning that every effort would be made to bring back national prohibition. The league fixed 1945, ten years in the future, as the date when it believed the policy would once again be written into the Constitution. Definite instructions were given to workers from all sections of the country by National Superintendent F. Scott McBride to pursue the same methods that had brought the enactment of the Eighteenth Amendment. Bishop Cannon was the dominant figure in the convention and perhaps most influential in mapping the campaign.

The presidential contest of 1936 between President Roosevelt and former Governor Alfred M. Landon, of Kansas, evoked Cannon's interest, although prohibition was not regarded by most observers as an issue. The Bishop by that time was extremely hostile to F. D. R., not only because of what he considered to be the President's broken promises concerning the saloon, but also because he believed practically the entire New Deal to be outrageous and indefensible. The Bishop expressed amazement that he found himself in the same political bed with Al Smith, whom he had fought so furiously eight years before. He even praised his old enemy for "putting political principles above party loyalty," an attitude which he interpreted as being precisely similar to that adopted by his own anti-Smith Democrats in 1928. At the same time Cannon denounced the Democratic leaders of Virginia as traitorous, in that they professed Jeffersonian principles and then proceeded to endorse President Roosevelt for a second term. His conclusion was that they believed it was better to be "office-holding Senators and Congressmen than jobless heroes." The Bishop was especially bitter in his denunciation of Senator Glass, whom he accused of "self-glorification" in an address on Patrick Henry. Glass commented that he would not reply, since he did not "intend to make any contribution whatsoever to the resurrection of this discredited cleric."

A left-handed slap at Cannon came almost simultaneously from another direction. Bishop Edwin D. Mouzon told the Virginia annual conference of the Methodist Church, South: "We used to have a Board of Temperance and Social Service. It paid mighty little attention to social service. Its attention was devoted principally to devising political methods to get rid of liquor." The board had been abolished two years previously by the General Conference at Jackson, Mississippi, as part of an "economy program." Cannon had not been made happy by this action, and now his direction of the board's activities in past years was being criticized by a Bishop of his own church.

Nor were Bishop Cannon's drooping spirits cheered a few weeks later when President Roosevelt defeated Alf Landon by a landslide in the presidential election.

Cannon's $500,000 libel suit against Representative George H. Tinkham, of Massachusetts, went to trial in January 1937, some five and a half years after it had been filed. It will be recalled that in 1930 Tinkham had called Cannon "a shameless violator of the Corrupt Practices Act." Public interest in the suit, as well as in Cannon himself, had largely disappeared by the time the hearing began before Justice Jennings Bailey in the United States District Court for the District of Columbia. Illness prevented the Bishop from being present. A long deposition that he had given six months previously while a patient in Sibley Hospital was crucially important in the case.

It was brought out in the deposition that Cannon had refused to say, under cross-examination by Roger J. Whiteford, counsel for Tinkham, whether he had kept his promise to the Dallas General Conference not to gamble in any more bucketshops. The Bishop said he considered the question a reflection on his veracity and "an invasion of my rights." Repeated efforts by opposing counsel failed to elicit any information from him on the point.

The trial occupied about a week, and Justice Bailey finally announced to the jury:

> I find from testimony of the plaintiff and of his own witnesses that he was guilty of violating the corrupt practices act, and that the charges made against him are substantially true.
>
> I therefore direct you to return a verdict for the defendant.

Justice Bailey did not indicate which testimony of Cannon and Cannon's witnesses seemed to him proof of guilt. When Cannon appealed unsuccessfully from the directed verdict to the United States Court of Appeals, counsel for Tinkham filed a brief discussing these "admissions" by the Bishop. Whiteford stated therein that Cannon's own testimony showed that he had violated the Corrupt Practices Act in "not treating his committee, entitled 'Headquarters Committee, Anti-Smith Democrats,' as a political committee," "by failing to account for contributions received," and "in failing to account, under Section 245 of the act," which requires persons who spend fifty dollars or more "for the purpose of influencing in two or more states the election of candidates" to file with the clerk of the House of Representatives an "itemized detailed statement."

Late in 1938 the United States Supreme Court ended Cannon's last hope of collecting from Tinkham when it refused to review the directed verdict for the plaintiff handed down in the District Court by Justice Bailey.

Aside from the fact that the Bishop suffered a loss of prestige in this matter, it was a heavy financial blow to him. His automatic retirement as Bishop had taken place at the General Conference of 1938, and his salary had been cut to two thousand dollars. A substantial verdict against Tinkham would have gone far to rehabilitate his sinking fiscal fortunes. Not only was he hard-pressed for funds, but his health was not good, and neither was Mrs. Cannon's. His medical expenses were a burden. In 1936 he estimated that his hospital bills for the preceding six years had totaled two or three thousand dollars, not counting what he had paid to doctors. At that time he was being treated for bad circulation and nervousness, as well as arthritis, and the preceding year he had been in a Los Angeles hospital three weeks for a prostate operation. There had been other illnesses in hospitals in Los Angeles and Washington and at Duke and Vanderbilt universities, as well as in Bradenton, Florida.

As for the cost of defending himself in the corrupt-practices case, he estimated that this totaled around ten thousand dollars. He did not say what part of that sum was covered by contributions from his admirers.

No evidence has been found that Cannon took any fliers in the stock market after the promise to abstain that he gave the General Conference of 1930. If he did any more plunging, he had little or no luck, but the probabilities are that he kept his pledge, despite his refusal to be cross-examined on the point.

Various friends and acquaintances testify that he lived a life of almost Spartan simplicity after his retirement as Bishop. He had always traveled economically, even in the days of his greatest fame and affluence. On journeys to the Pacific coast he had often gone by day-coach all the way across the continent, and when sailing to Europe he invariably had modest, even third-class accommodations. The same was true of his hotel arrangements, for he frequently ordered a room without bath.

From 1937 on he maintained his residence in Richmond. In March 1937 he took a room in one of the cheaper hotels, the Capitol, and remained there until well into the following year. Mrs. Cannon was in California during this period. She returned to Richmond when Cannon bought the small dwelling at 24 North Allen Avenue with part of the money collected some nine years before by friends who sought to provide a "home" for him in Washington. This latter deal, it will be recalled, netted the doctor $9,500 — after he had expressed a desire for a residence in Washington that was well known to be slated for early condemnation. By 1938 he still had enough left to buy the Richmond house for $4,800. What had happened to the remainder was not disclosed.

During his sojourn at the Capitol Hotel in 1937–8, the Bishop was interviewed twice by feature writers for the *Richmond Times-Dispatch,* and on both occasions he exuded a mellow geniality and a tolerance for his erstwhile foes that contrasted sharply with the bellicosity of earlier days. There are those, indeed, who have always contended that the Bishop had a sense of humor, and that the grim, unsmiling Torquemada who fought the saloon and waged bitter warfare on Al Smith could be a responsive, almost genial companion when relaxing in his private capacity. But this side of his nature was almost never shown to the public, so that nearly everybody, including various persons who were thrown into close contact with him in the prohibition movement, failed to recognize that he had any human qualities. In fact, when he posed for a photograph during one of the above-mentioned newspaper interviews in Richmond, his features cast themselves in the same hard and flinty lines with which the public long had been familiar, and his almost truculent gaze seemed to belie the soft and conciliatory words he had spoken to the interviewer. Perhaps an explanation for these seemingly contradictory manifestations is to be found in the fact that during nearly all Cannon's long life he drove himself at so furious a pace, and he was engaged in so many violent controversies, that he had virtually no time for relaxation. From force of habit he found it well-nigh impossible to smile for a photographer. He could unbend when he had the proper environment and the time, but he seldom had either. Furthermore, the longer he lived, the fewer friends he had left with whom to relax, for more and more dropped away from him as he alienated them in this way or that. Those who remained faithful to him were fanatically loyal, but they were not numerous.

A group of these last were to be found on the Pacific coast. Shortly before Cannon's retirement the Pacific annual conference adopted resolutions that spoke of him as "one of the greatest spirits, wisest minds and most heroic hearts that this generation has produced." The conference went on to "rejoice in the fact that those evil forces which he has unflinchingly faced throughout his active and meaningful life have been unable to bow his head or stifle his spirit" and to "express to him our love and loyal admiration and proclaim him a brother, a patriot, a statesman, a leader, a citizen, and a Christian, and a man of whom we are profoundly proud."

Such was the view of the still faithful few. But there were many who were more intimately familiar with the Bishop's record from longer acquaintance and greater proximity than the Methodists of the Far West had been able to enjoy, except for a brief period, and who viewed his pretensions with the most profound skepticism, if not complete disgust.

Their opinions were expressed, in a measure, by Senator William Cabell Bruce, of Maryland, on the Senate floor in 1929, when he said:

325

Dry Messiah

God forbid that any clergyman of this kind should ever come near me for the purpose of exercising any office that appertains to his profession. If he were to sprinkle baptismal water upon the head of a child, I should expect its scalp to be scalded rather than hallowed. If he solemnized the marriage of a maid, I should not be surprised to see the orange blossoms that encircled her brow immediately wither and die under the scorching effect of his abusive breath. So far as I am concerned, just as soon would I have a raven perched upon the head of my bed as to have such a clergyman approach me in my last agony. If he were to preach a funeral sermon over my corpse, I believe that like Lazarus, I would throw aside the cerements of the grave and come back to life in indignant resurrection.

In the face of such widely held sentiments, and despite wholesale desertion by former idolators, the Bishop declared unctuously to one of the above-mentioned *Times-Dispatch* interviewers: "Sincerity is the touchstone. I have been sincere. I have adhered to that which I believed sincerely. More than that no man can say."

The interviewer forbore to make any comment upon this pronouncement. He did say in his article that talking to Cannon "was very much like being in the presence of an extinct volcano," and that "one sensed the litany-like repetition of the pattern of his ideas, the unwillingness to revise them. . . ."

The Bishop was working in Richmond during 1937–8 on his memoirs. He seemed confident of completing them by the end of 1938, but he was far from finishing them when he died six years later.

Perhaps his interest in public affairs and his active participation in efforts to revive prohibition consumed so much of his energy that he was never able to find the time to complete his reminiscences. Certainly he bombarded the secular and religious press with letters at frequent intervals, and he likewise made a great many speeches inside and outside Virginia on "Prohibition's Inevitable Return" and similar topics. During one or two of these years the circulation in his feet was so inadequate that he could not stand on them for any length of time, with the result that he delivered addresses almost invariably sitting.

His Soul Goes Marching On

The impregnability of a moral leader from the assaults of the ungodly was demonstrated again at this time by the action of the Federal Council of Churches of Christ in America. The council elected Cannon as a Methodist representative on its executive committee. Indeed, the Bishop served as chairman of the Methodist delegation at the council's convention.

When in his Richmond hotel room, Cannon spent much of his time in bed. His secretary came daily at noon, and they worked on his papers, correspondence, or memoirs until five. She returned at seven and remained until ten. Cannon then proceeded alone until he became sleepy. His diet was monastic in its simplicity and consisted largely of milk, fruit, hard-boiled eggs, and nuts, with an occasional ham sandwich, all brought to his room by the bellboy.

It was in 1937 that Cannon was said to have tasted alcohol for the first time. His doctor ordered him to take wine in thirty-drop doses. He took the doses, but said he didn't like them.

During his closing years the Bishop made frequent excursions into the state for the purpose of occupying Methodist pulpits in the interests of the dry cause. Sometimes he was invited by the pastor; sometimes he simply wrote or wired the pastor that he was coming on such-and-such a day and that he would preach at the morning or the evening service. Even when the minister wanted to object, he was usually afraid to do so. On these occasions Cannon spoke at great length, took up a collection for the Anti-Saloon League, and departed. After June 1942 the Virginia league had no active superintendent, and the organization consisted of the Bishop and a secretary. All funds seem to have been handled by the Bishop, with no accounting to anyone.

In his numerous sermons and speeches on prohibition Dr. Cannon made predictions of the return of state and Federal dry laws, which did not materialize. In 1937 he predicted that the Virginia legislature would abolish the state's ABC system of liquor sales through state stores either that winter or two years thereafter. The system is still intact. Cannon pronounced the ABC a flat failure on the basis of a three-year trial, although he contended vigorously that fourteen years' experience with national prohibition did not furnish adequate grounds for the judgment that it had failed. He made various wholly erroneous forecasts of the return of Federal prohibition. One was that it would be back "before I die," and another, made in 1939, that "within ten years" Congress would be empowered through a constitutional amendment to prohibit the sale of liquor.

Although some of the officials of the Anti-Saloon League of America regarded the Bishop as a heavy liability, he retained his hold on the organization and was chairman of its national legislative committee and a member of its executive and administrative committees until the end. Those who valued his services to the league agreed with Dr. Alexander Copeland Millar, of Little Rock, who said in addressing the league's annual Southeastern convention in 1937 that Cannon was "the worst persecuted preacher in America since colonial days." The Bishop sat in the front row and listened to the loud applause that greeted this declaration. He was always on hand for the Anti-Saloon League's Southeastern conventions, except when illness prevented, and was usually a speaker. At the 1938 conclave, for instance, he declared that repeal came because "we never had a President in the White House who put on an efficient program of law enforcement." He even charged that his onetime idol President Hoover "was more responsible for repeal of the Eighteenth Amendment than anyone else."

By 1940 the Bishop seemed to be making occasional slips as to facts — something that had been unknown theretofore. For example, early in that year he published the extraordinary declaration that the Virginia dry law had been abolished in 1933 "without any vote of the people." Cannon was then seventy-five years old and entitled to an occasional lapse. Such a mistake on his part would have been inconceivable a decade earlier.

But if there were a few such instances, the aging cleric appeared on most occasions to be in full command of his mental powers. Certainly the volume of his correspondence with sundry officials and newspapers indicated no lack of vigor. He was no longer on the front pages and he appeared but seldom in the news, but he kept up a veritable barrage of letters to President Roosevelt, Secretaries Cordell Hull and Henry L. Stimson, and the editors of the two Richmond newspapers

His Soul Goes Marching On

When Japan stepped up her warfare against China in 1937, Cannon wrote urging Secretary Hull to demand an immediate cessation of hostilities. If this was refused, said the Bishop, we should sever diplomatic and commercial relations with Japan. These ideas were reiterated several times in long communications to Washington officials prior to Pearl Harbor. Similarly, when Germany overran Norway, the Low Countries, and France in 1940, Cannon appealed for an immediate declaration of war. He found himself in the same bed on this issue with his ancient foe Senator Glass, who was calling on the United States to "shoot hell out of Hitler."

Passage of the Conscription Act in September 1940 caused Cannon to begin immediate efforts to obtain the adoption of "protective legislation for the soldiers against the liquor and vice traffics" similar to that passed in 1917. In several communications to the press in 1941 and 1942 the Bishop quoted General John J. Pershing as having said to him, when he was overseas in 1918: "I shall not go slow on prohibition, for I know what is the greatest foe to my men, greater even than the bullets of the enemy." Cannon cited this supposed declaration of Pershing in support of the Josh Lee bone-dry liquor bill, then pending in Congress, which forbade the sale of light wines and beer as well as whisky on all military or naval reservations and empowered the Secretaries of War and Navy to extend the prohibition to adjacent areas, including entire cities.

The editor of the *Richmond Times-Dispatch* wrote to General Pershing to inquire whether he had, in fact, said what Cannon quoted him as having said about prohibition and "the greatest foe to my men." The reply came from his military secretary, Colonel Adamson, who said the general had directed him to send an extract from Pershing's memoirs, *My Experiences in the World War.* This extract declared that the commander-in-chief of the A.E.F. had been impressed with the necessity "for controlling the use of strong drink among our troops" in France. He went on to state that he had to declare "every bar and restaurant where the heavy liquor was sold as 'off limits' for our troops." Although he deemed this "limited prohibition" to be necessary, he said: "Even though it had been possible of enforcement, I should not have issued orders to our armies prohibiting use of light wines and beer."

The above-quoted sentence effectively disposed of the Bishop's clear implication that General Pershing was in sympathy with the Lee bill then pending, a bill that banned light wines and beer as well as whisky. Publication of an editorial in the *Times-Dispatch* setting forth Pershing's true position brought a characteristically windy letter to the editor from the doctor. It merely rehashed stale material at enormous length and proved nothing.

After Japan struck in the Hawaiian Islands, Cannon strongly urged "equality of sacrifice" and conscription "of all manpower and all capital resources." He contended that the tax bill passed by Congress was "very unfair in its treatment of men and women in the lower brackets." He mentioned that in the Virginia Methodist Conference "there are around 200 preachers who receive from $1,000 to $1,800 per year, and most of them have families to support." The bill, he said, was grievously unjust to them and to others like them.

For his "Appeal to the Industrial Leaders of the South," made in 1927, the Bishop had been denounced as a radical, and his criticism of the tax bill put him once more on the side of those with small incomes. But he objected strongly to the labor legislation adopted by Congress during the Roosevelt Administration and was violently critical of the "closed shop." He also was openly against a Federal anti-lynching bill as an invasion of states' rights and as offering no prospect of improvement over existing laws.

At about this period the Bishop filed the last suit of his career. It was against Time, Inc., publishers of the magazines *Time* and *Life*. *Time* had referred to Cannon as "reactionary"; *Life* had termed him "bigoted" and had classified him erroneously among the opponents of Methodist unification. It was noteworthy that, in this narrowly defined legal action, which was for $30,000 damages, there was no possibility of the defendant's dragging in the old charges of adultery or bucketshop gambling. Consequently the Bishop could safely press the suit in the hope of collecting. But Time, Inc., unlike some of the other publishing concerns which paid Cannon a few thousand dollars, rather than go to court, fought back. Not only so, but it won a ruling in the United

States District Court that the court lacked jurisdiction to hear the case. This was upheld unanimously by the Circuit Court of Appeals, and the action was dropped.

In 1939 Bishop Cannon had become deeply moved by the plight of the German Jews and he flamed with indignation when the steamship *St. Louis* was refused permission by Cuban authorities to land its cargo of more than nine hundred of these hounded and persecuted human beings. Although he had been quoted during the presidential campaign of 1928 as having said highly critical things of the Jews in New York City, his sympathies were touched by the homeless refugees on board the *St. Louis.* When the American government joined the Cuban government in refusing to give them a haven, he pronounced the action "one of the most disgraceful things which has happened in American history." In July 1943, when an "Emergency Conference to Save the Jews of Europe" was called in New York City, Bishop Cannon was one of the sponsors, and he was chosen chairman of the conference's panel on religion. That panel called on the Christian church to demand immediate action to save the Jews under Nazi domination. Unfortunately, Hitler's extermination camps and gas chambers were going full blast at the time and it was too late to save more than a pitiful remnant.

During the year 1942 the Bishop became involved in a couple of rather absurd controversies. The first was with the late Thomas Lomax Hunter, columnist for the *Richmond Times-Dispatch.* "The Cavalier," as he was known, dearly loved to tweak the noses of professional prohibitionists and similar gentry, whom he was fond of describing as "moral mercenaries" and "Hessian soldiers of the cross." In one of his numerous dissertations upon the dry laws Hunter declared that those statutes "succeeded in making the largest army of law violators ever mobilized on this footstool of God." He went on to declare that "prohibition never stopped me from taking a drink" and "I never encountered a man whom it stopped from taking a drink."

"The Cavalier" then proceeded to compliment Bishop Cannon a bit ironically on the fact that, unlike those who were prohibitionists for purely political reasons, the Bishop "has never faltered; he has never flinched . . . it is an undaunted heart that beats under his chasuble." "It thrills us," Hunter went on, "like the memory of Leonidas at the Pass, Horatius at the Bridge, Casey at the Bat, and Charley at the Cat-hole."

To which Cannon replied at immense length and with immense solemnity in a letter to the editor. "Mr. Hunter speaks of the 'encyclical of His Right Reverence, Bishop James Cannon, Jr.,'" quoth the Bishop. "He uses the words 'hierarchy,' 'ex cathedra,' 'infallibility,' and issuance of 'a bull.' Mr. Hunter well knows that no Methodist Bishop is called 'His Right Reverence . . . Methodist Bishops are general superintendents, and make no claim to any apostolical succession. His comparison of myself with 'Leonidas,' 'Horatius,' 'Casey' and 'Charley at the Cat-hole' are a species of ridicule, indicating an utter lack of any concern because of the tremendous tragic results of the traffic in intoxicating liquors. . . . Attempted humor is sadly out of place concerning such horrible facts. Indeed, it seems almost sacrilegious to me to wind up such an article with those sacred words *Ora pro nobis* (Pray for us). . . ."

From extensive observation it was apparent to "the Cavalier" that he could rouse the Bishop to long and ponderous retorts with his well-directed barbs, so he returned to the assault. He wrote:

> Fruit juices fermented will still produce alcohol, just as they did when Noah became a husbandman and planted a vineyard. That is a fact which gives the guzzler hope. He will discover a way to make the stuff which he so delights in. . . . It was not for nothing that God saved Noah. He was the father of us all. He showed us what could be done.
>
> Cheer up Reuben, don't you cry,
> Nature's winepress never runs dry.

To which Bishop Cannon replied:

> What a statement! He attributes to God the saving of Noah, that he might plant a vineyard, grow grapes, make and drink wine, lose all control of himself, and sink to the floor of his tent with his clothes falling from him, lying uncovered in a drunken stupor. . . . Genesis, Hebrews and Peter all state that God saved Noah because he was "righteous," and not that he might plant a vineyard, make wine and become drunken. . . .

His Soul Goes Marching On

At this point Mrs. Florence Dickinson Stearns, Richmond poet, intervened in the discussion to say that "Mr. Hunter is wrong to stir up Bishop Cannon." She went on to inquire whether Hunter did not know that "the Bishop is the very apex of the literal . . . and that his sense of humor could be lightly balanced on the back of a gnat." This brought from the doctor another long and heavy blast, in which he referred, among other things, to "the time, when as a boy of eight years old, he [Cannon] saw a beloved uncle die from hydrophobia, caused by the bite of a dog, set upon him by a drunken man." Mrs. Stearns felt that this justified her assumption that the Bishop "sees through a glass darkly where humor is concerned," since "he comes back at me with something about a mad dog biting his favorite uncle." She added that the long article from him which her letter had evoked "was about as relevant as my asking for a recipe for baking a ham, and being given a formula for the extermination of the boll weevil." As for Noah, said she, "he probably was so fed up on water he wanted to establish an average, when he got on dry land."

During these years the Bishop revealed, surprisingly enough, that he was an avid reader of certain comic strips. In a letter to the *Richmond Times-Dispatch* protesting a reduction in the size of the Sunday comics from standard measurement to tabloid Cannon declared, with special reference to "Prince Valiant," a strip having to do with the knights of King Arthur's time, that he read the comics when away from home on Sundays. This confession that he made a habit of reading not only Sunday newspapers but even Sunday comics was a far cry from his early diatribes against all Sunday papers.

About a year later the Bishop wrote the *Times-Dispatch* again, this time to protest the omission of "The Phantom" from the daily paper. This strip, depicting the deeds of a tough and resourceful fellow in the "Superman" tradition, was described by Cannon as his favorite among all the comics carried by the paper.

That "Prince Valiant" and "The Phantom," with their essentially juvenile appeal, should have been Bishop Cannon's preferred comic strips is indicative of the quality of his mind and of a certain lack of subtlety and maturity in his mental processes. These strips are pure "adventure," without a trace of humor.

"Prince Valiant," with its superior draftsmanship and coloring, is perhaps the best of all those having a historical flavor, but both strips, and especially "The Phantom," appeal strongly to boys and girls. Neither, be it said to the Bishop's credit, is in the "Wham!" "Sock!" and "Zowie!" tradition.

The Bishop was in his late seventies when he wrote the letters concerning these comics, but it would be far from accurate to say that he was in his second childhood. His mind, except for occasional slips as to facts, was keen and strong. Yet despite the razor-sharpness of his intellect, his shrewd and eel-like capacity for eluding the grasp of those who sought to convict him of various derelictions, and his ability to hold his own with anybody in debate on the limited group of subjects in which he was interested, Cannon's thought processes were neither profound nor highly discriminating.

He was likewise a thoroughly unimaginative person. This was illustrated in various ways, notably in his discussion of a mural entitled *The Burning of Richmond,* painted by Julien Binford, distinguished Virginia artist, for one of Richmond's branch post offices. "The probability that two white women, one of them practically nude, were lying around in the street, one on her back, and the nude woman in a semi-recumbent position, and that a man on a horse, without saddle or bridle, was sitting bolt upright, seemingly quite complacent, without struggling to restrain the horse, is too small to justify what is almost a grotesque scene," the Bishop wrote in a letter to the *Times-Dispatch.* "The writer has been in all the great galleries of Europe, and of this country, and has seen many nudes and horses in sculpture and in painting, and to him the legs of the horse, and the woman's back and hips are poorly portrayed. . . ."

This brought a tart rejoinder from Binford:

> "The woman's back and hips," says the Bishop, "are poorly portrayed." There is no question of this phase of the Bishop's like or dislike of nudes in general, of nudes in certain historic scenes, or nudes in certain attitudes. The Bishop makes it plain that it is the shape of this particular nude woman which offends the expert knowledge of his eye, and at that, not her arms, her head, her legs, nor her neck, but specifically her back and hips.

His Soul Goes Marching On

When and how did this Bishop become an authority on the "back and hips" of nude women?

Binford went on to discuss the "boast of this priest" that he had "visited 'all' the great galleries of Europe and of this country, contemplating nudes." He concluded that "most of us have visited not 'all' but a great many of the great churches of both continents, yet this has not given us the front to set ourselves up as qualified theologians who could permit themselves to seek out this man's priest hole and advise him on the temporal dexterities of his craft.

"So go on; scat! Bishop, and get off my scaffold," concluded the painter, "I am not trying to swarm your pulpit."

Cannon's reply was couched in his customarily solemn and pious vein. He spoke of the "discourteous and sidestepping communication of Julien Binford" and added: "It is a pity that he seems to let his temper get away with him." As was his wont, the Bishop explained laboriously that he was "not a priest," since "no Methodist preacher is a priest."

The old Bishop was nearing the end of his pilgrimage, but there seemed to be no serious diminution of his faculties. His polemical writings retained their pristine vigor, albeit they usually belabored the same dreary round of facts, or supposed facts, having to do with what he customarily termed "the body and soul-destroying liquor traffic." Cannon's last years were decidedly anticlimactic. He was no longer the national figure that he had been in earlier days; his political influence had shrunk to almost nothing on both the national and the state level, and his finances were in deplorable condition. For a former arbiter of the South's political destiny to be reduced to writing querulous letters to editors, letters that most people ignored, must have been depressing. So, no doubt, must have been the chilly reception that both he and Mrs. Cannon got in many Methodist circles. And while Cannon's tastes had never been expensive, in so far as his personal mode of living was concerned, the shabbiness of his wardrobe in his final years seemed symbolic of the over-all decline in his fortunes.

After his retirement from the episcopacy in 1938, his income was insufficient to meet necessary expenses. A four months' illness in 1940 cost approximately $2,000 for nursing, medicine, and medical care, and he estimated that thereafter average monthly medical expenses for himself and Mrs. Cannon amounted to over $50, or nearly $700 annually. This drain on his resources was met by sales of property and by borrowing from banks. In 1944 he said that he had sold the last property he owned and had borrowed on his life insurance to meet the notes.[2]

Then, too, the realization must have been painful to him that some of the mightiest men-at-arms in the long struggle for prohibition, men who had battled beside him for decades against whisky and its attendant devils, were either dead or in retirement. Dr. Clarence True Wilson and Dr. Arthur J. Barton, who had mobilized the Methodists and Baptists in battalions, regiments, and divisions on behalf of the dry cause, had gone to their reward. "Pussyfoot" Johnson had laid aside his shield and buckler.

Yet the Bishop was outwardly undismayed. In the last year of his life he seized the initiative, despite counsels of caution from less aggressive drys, and sought to obtain a referendum on the return of state-wide prohibition to Virginia. In a circular letter to members of the Virginia legislature he again pronounced the ABC system a failure and requested an opportunity for the people to express themselves on its abolition. Nearly four weeks later he announced that no bill had been introduced because insufficient time remained during the session "to deliver the sentiment of voters to their representatives in the General Assembly in support of such a measure." He failed to mention that he had tried unsuccessfully to persuade several members of the General Assembly to sponsor his legislation. Some months later he returned to the attack and urged a referendum before a legislative commission that was studying the ABC system.

All this was without effect, but there is no mystery surrounding Bishop Cannon's belief that the state's lawmakers were susceptible to pressure from the Anti-Saloon League and the W.C.T.U. Six years previously those weak-kneed gentlemen had ordered one thousand copies of a scientific study of alcohol's effects on the human system shoveled into the Capitol furnace at Richmond unread — and all because the professional drys demanded it. The legislature itself had directed that the treatise be prepared for use in the public schools, and the State Board of Education had pronounced it "a most valuable contribution . . . scientifically sound and very scholarly." But the "temperance" forces learned that, although the report emphatically affirmed and reiterated the dangers of overindulgence, it also declared that small quantities of alcohol "may favor digestive activities" and "small quantities . . . do not directly affect the heart or the blood vessels." The two authors stated, furthermore, that "we cannot abolish drinking by legislation." Such heresies were altogether too much for the professional prohibitionists. They asserted that the report must be burned forthwith before the lawmakers who had ordered it had so much as read it. The legislators complied at once.

Remembering this astounding performance, it is easy to see why Bishop Cannon thought the legislature could be "persuaded" again. He found that he was mistaken. For one thing, many of the prohibitionists felt that his move for a referendum was premature and they did not co-operate. For another, the assemblymen apparently concluded that they had made an unholy spectacle of themselves six years before and were determined not to do so again.

Cannon's advocacy of a Virginia referendum in the course of his appearance before the legislative commission investigating the ABC system took place on July 19, 1944 and was recorded in the public prints of the Old Dominion the following day. Then the Bishop dropped out of sight.

The next thing the people of the state and nation read of him was the unexpected news of his death in Chicago. He had gone there for a meeting of the Anti-Saloon League and had suffered a heart attack in his hotel. Removed thence to the Wesley Memorial Hospital, he died of a cerebral hemorrhage on Wednesday morning, September 6. The public knew nothing of his illness until it was advised of his passing. He was almost eighty years old.

In Virginia, where the Bishop had long maintained his residence, and where he had always been before the public to a greater or lesser degree, his death caused a mild stir. In the country at large it was received with something approaching a yawn.

Most people probably thought he had died years before, so much time had passed since they had heard his name.

"It is hard to believe that a man so obscure and harmless at his death ever could have been the object of such wide and hearty hatred," wrote Westbrook Pegler in his newspaper column. "How curious to recall that Bishop James Cannon, Jr., who died yesterday, for a considerable period was one of the most powerful figures on the national stage!" mused the *Baltimore Sun*. And the *Washington Post*, discussing the furious zeal with which Cannon had pursued his objectives, quoted George Santayana as having said that "fanaticism consists in redoubling your effort after you have forgotten your aims!"

Most newspapers carried no editorial on the passing of the Bishop. Such a thing would have seemed incredible a decade and a half previously, when Cannon was constantly on the nation's front pages, but by 1944 he seemed almost a ghost out of the past.

Aside from the fact that prohibition had been repealed a decade before, there was the preoccupation of the American people with the second World War, then rising to a terrific climax both in Europe and in the Pacific. James Cannon, Jr., had come into the world as Sherman was marching through Georgia, and he went out of it as Patton's Third Army lunged across France to Verdun and as the American land, sea, and air forces were preparing the final crushing blows against the Philippines, the Ryukyus, and Japan itself. Such events necessarily distracted attention from the passing of a man whose role in the affairs of the state and the nation no longer was deemed significant.

Cannon's body was brought to Richmond, and the casket, with lid closed, was placed on view in the Sunday-school auditorium of Broad Street Methodist Church, across the street from the City Hall and one block from Capitol Square. It remained there all day Monday, September 10, and until three p.m. the following day. An estimated thousand persons filed past it. On the afternoon of September 11 the coffin was removed to the main church auditorium for the funeral service.

Mrs. Cannon walked just behind the casket, on the arm of the Bishop's eldest son, James Cannon III, as it was carried by the pallbearers up the front steps of the church, while trolley cars clanged past, clouds gathered, and a faint summer haze settled over the city. Most of the seats in the large auditorium, with a capacity of about a thousand, were filled. The pallbearers, prominent figures in Virginia Methodism, bore the body down the aisle and placed it below the chancel. Honorary pallbearers were the active and retired ministers of the Virginia Methodist Conference.

The funeral sermon was preached by the Rev. Dr. J. W. Moore, a classmate of Cannon's at Randolph-Macon College sixty-three years before. Cannon had chosen Moore to perform this rite. The sermon was, of course, a panegyric of the deceased. It reviewed his manifold controversies and concluded that he was right in all of them. The Bishop's widow sat in one of the front pews and dabbed at her eyes several times during the service.

After these ceremonies, the body of Bishop Cannon was carried to beautiful Hollywood Cemetery, overlooking the James, and laid, at his request, beside that of his first wife. At the graveside the large group of Methodist ministers united in singing "A Charge to Keep I Have." Members of the W.C.T.U. and wives of the clergy were flower-bearers.

A few days later the Bishop's will was admitted to probate in Richmond chancery court. The once affluent and financially successful investor in real estate, stocks, bonds, and other commodities died leaving property of all kinds worth only $3,600. The official court papers listed no real estate, although official records of the city board of real-estate assessors have it that the dwelling at 24 North Allen Avenue was not sold by Mrs. Cannon until December 18, more than three months after the Bishop's death. Yet in a codicil to his will, dated some three months before he died, he said that he had found it necessary to sell the last of his property. Whatever the explanation for this discrepancy, the estate that he left was an extremely small one and in rather pathetic contrast to what must have been his expectations during the years when his fortunes were prospering. The man who at one time operated simultaneously ten bank accounts had been owner of a weekly church paper and part owner of a daily paper, had organized and directed a college, owned a summer-resort hotel, and plunged to his neck in bucket-shops, had died with only a small handful of property. It was clear that the succession of investigations, trials, and illnesses that Cannon encountered during the final decade and a half of his life had undermined his fiscal position and brought him close to penury.

His widow was the chief beneficiary of his modest estate. His children and one grandchild were left twenty-five dollars each, and he directed that if a balance remained in "any bank to the credit of 'James Cannon, Jr., Special,'" it be paid to James Cannon III, to assist in the publication of the Bishop's autobiographical work, *Life As I have Seen It.* This volume has not made its appearance, although plans for publication are said to be under way.

After the Bishop's death and the sale of their Richmond home, Mrs. Cannon moved to California. She, of course, went on the pension roll of the church to receive the small stipend allotted the widow of every Methodist Bishop. Many Methodists were made distinctly unhappy by the thought of her being a permanent pensioner of their church, but they were powerless to prevent it.

The passing of James Cannon, Jr., removed one of the most brilliantly militant drys from the American scene, but it did not lessen the determination of his surviving confreres to bring back some form of Federal prohibition. True, there were occasional efforts to quiet the apprehensions of those who feared that such was their objective, just as nearly four decades previously the Anti-Saloon League denied publicly that the movement in which it was then engaged was intended "to enforce total abstinence by law." But the camouflage this time was a bit more transparent, and those who remembered what happened in the early years of the century seemed less likely to be taken in again by the soothing assurances of the need for "education" and "local option."

There was also the fact that millions recalled the farcical and and tragic results of national prohibition and were determined to prevent a repetition. Yet a generation was growing up that knew of these things only by hearsay, and there were factors in the existing situation that gave no cause for satisfaction to the opponents of sumptuary legislation.

Bishop Cannon would have blinked, for example, to read in

the columns of his inveterate critic, the *Chicago Tribune,* an editorial published in 1948 that said:

> If ever there was a time to be against the saloon, it is the present. The old time saloon was certainly no beacon light of virtue. It was engaged in selling whiskey and its customers indubitably got drunk on occasion. But the old time saloon keeper, and the police captain who took graft to let him open on Sunday, would both have recoiled in horror from the modern cave of love, with its secluded booths and lights so low that gentlemen can't find their drinks, and ladies, in the course of an evening, sometimes can't find their gentlemen.
>
> Neither can the present roadhouse with teen agers and bobby-soxers playing slot machines and preparing to kill themselves in automobile wrecks, be compared favorably with its predecessor, which got a good share of its trade from the pallbearers and mourners who stopped in to warm their feet on the way home from the cemetery.

Recognizing that such dubious and lethal happenings were building up sentiment slowly but surely for some sort of corrective action, the professional advocates of drastic solutions were moving cautiously, but with one ultimate objective in mind: Federal prohibition. Such spellbinders as the Rev. Sam Morris — termed by a brewing executive "easily the most valuable man who has entered into the service of the 'dry' cause in generations" — were exhorting the faithful on the radio and in mass assemblages to outlaw alcohol in all its forms.

Significant after the close of the second World War was the revival of the weekly "Clipsheet" of the Methodist Board of Temperance, formerly the Board of Temperance, Prohibition and Public Morals. This organ of a large and aggressive segment of prohibitionist opinion had faded out in 1933, with the advent of repeal, but thirteen years later it came lustily to life, with Deets Pickett at the helm. Dr. Pickett, who is described by a fellow Methodist clergyman, the Rev. Alson J. Smith, as "the brains of the 'dry' movement in the United States today," operates from the same handsome five-story building opposite the Capitol in Washington that served as headquarters for Dr. Clarence True Wilson. Smith also terms Pickett — "and this is not meant as a

sneer," he says — "the personification of Protestant Jesuitism."
Pickett's objective, according to the same authority, is "legal dry-
ness not only for the United States but for the whole world." [3]
Now that the Northern and Southern branches of the Methodist
Church have merged, Dr. Pickett's organization is comparable in
potency to a combination of those mighty engines of morality
which were commanded by Dr. Wilson and Dr. Cannon in the
days before unification.

The Anti-Saloon League's decision in 1948 to change its name
to the Temperance League of America signified a new approach
on the part of that agency, but no basic change in its aims. The
Anti-Saloon League evidently concluded that its association in
the public mind with many of the more odious aspects of prohibition made a face-lifting operation desirable.

There is new leadership at the helm of the Temperance League
of America, but no informed person doubts that this organization,
as well as the Methodist Board of Temperance, the W.C.T.U.,
and numerous kindred bodies, are all working toward Federal
prohibition. Many parts of rural America seem ready to fall in
with the plan. Tens of thousands of local-option elections have
been held since repeal, and the drys have won most of them.
These elections are stepping-stones toward the ultimate objective,
just as they were more than a generation ago.

Few took Dr. Cannon and his compatriots seriously in the early
years of the first drive for national prohibition, and there is a
widespread inclination to be similarly apathetic today. Those who
live in our large cities are especially prone to minimize the danger, for they do not realize the depth and intensity of the feeling
against liquor in the more evangelical of the rural churches. "The
Best Brain in America" capitalized on this overconfidence when
he was a leader in riveting prohibition on Virginia and the nation
by methods that, however questionable and devious, were certainly devastatingly effective. It remains to be seen whether the
country will take warning and refuse to be deceived again.

The grass is green above the grave of Bishop Cannon, and his
stormy career has ended, but his soul goes marching on.

Notes

CHAPTER I

1. Letter to the author from a long-time acquaintance of Cannon who witnessed several of his refusals to "come to Jesus."

CHAPTER II

1. *Unspotted from the World*, p. 3, col. 1. The title of this leaflet, taken from that of a *Richmond News Leader* editorial, goes back to James, i, 27.
2. Ibid.
3. *Richmond News Leader*, July 24, August 10 and 18, 1908.
4. *Baltimore and Richmond Christian Advocate*, November 9, 1911.
5. Dated September 25, 1929. Copy made by author and in his files.
6. *Unspotted from the World*, p. 4, col. 2.

CHAPTER III

1. *Daily Advocate*, 1902, Minority Report of Committee on Publishing Interests on "war claim."

CHAPTER IV

1. Rev. Albert Richmond Bond, D.D.: *Southern Baptists and Illiteracy*. Published by Education Board, Southern Baptist Convention, March 26, 1928. An exhaustive statistical study, 31 pages.
2. Quoted in *Baltimore and Richmond Christian Advocate*, September 29, 1904.
3. Charles Stelzle: *Why Prohibition*, p. 202.
4. Ibid., pp. 145–6.

CHAPTER V

1. *Unspotted from the World*, p. 3, col. 1.
2. Virginia Edition, *American Issue*, December 11, 1909; *Baltimore and Richmond Christian Advocate*, January 27, 1916.

Notes

CHAPTER VI

1. In a conversation with the author.
2. *Baltimore and Richmond Christian Advocate,* August 17, 1905.
3. Ibid., February 1, 1906.
4. Ibid., September 5, 1907.
5. *Richmond Virginian,* March 18, 1912.
6. March 28, 1912.
7. May 22, 1915.
8. *Virginian,* July 30, 1917.
9. Letter in *Richmond News Leader,* June 6, 1941.
10. In a conversation with the author.

CHAPTER VIII

1. March 1, 1917. All quotations of Cannon in this chapter are from the *Baltimore and Richmond Christian Advocate.*

CHAPTER IX

1. *Richmond Times-Dispatch,* February 18, 1916.
2. August 7, 1917.
3. *Times-Dispatch,* November 6, 1928.

CHAPTER X

1. Charles Stelzle: *Why Prohibition,* p. 228.
2. *Statistics Concerning Intoxicating Liquors,* U. S. Treasury Department, 1930, p. 1, quoted in Merz: *The Dry Decade,* p. 315. Complete table giving date when each of forty-six states ratified, and the vote in each legislative branch.
3. Frederick Palmer: *Newton D. Baker,* Vol. II, p. 151.
4. Ibid., p. 253.

CHAPTER XI

1. In a conversation with the author.
2. *Baltimore and Richmond Christian Advocate,* July 4, 1912.
3. "James Cannon, Jr.," by Dixon Merritt, *Outlook,* September 12, 1928.

CHAPTER XII

1. This and the succeeding episodes involving Cannon and the lieutenant are vouched for by the lieutenant in a written memorandum furnished the author.
2. *New York Times,* September 13, 1926.

Notes

CHAPTER XIV

1. Mabel Walker Willebrandt: *The Inside of Prohibition*, p. 26.
2. Ibid., p. 144.
3. June 13, 1928.
4. *Baltimore and Richmond Christian Advocate*, December 17, 1908, January 26, 1911, February 16, 1911.
5. Ibid., January 30, 1913.
6. Owen P. White in *Collier's*, October 6, 1928.

CHAPTER XV

1. In a conversation with the author.
2. Documents in files of the late Senator Carter Glass, quoting testimony of J. W. Hough, member of the solicitation group.
3. *New York Times*, August 7, 1929.
4. Official records, Richmond Board of Real Estate Assessors.
5. Letter to author, dated December 27, 1929, from J. A. Compton, registrar Blackstone Precinct, says Cannon "did not vote by mail or otherwise in the recent gubernatorial election, November 5, 1929."
6. *Baltimore Sun*, May 19, 1930, dispatch by W. A. S. Douglas. On the following day Douglas reported that the vote had been 56 to 24. The *Southern Methodist*, of Memphis, for May 28, 1930, gave the vote as 44 to 29.
7. Associated Press dispatch from Savannah, Georgia, dated May 26, 1930, in *Richmond News Leader* of that date.
8. Associated Press dispatch from Macon, Georgia, dated May 31, 1930, in *Richmond News Leader* of that date.
9. The correspondence was published almost in full in the *New York Times*, *New York World*, *Chicago Tribune*, and *Baltimore Sun* for June 13, 1930. The *Times* article also appeared in the *Congressional Record* for July 3, 1930.
10. This will be dealt with in Chapter xvii.
11. Letter to the author from Rev. Edward J. Ferger, editor of the *Union and Times* in 1930. The paper is now the *Union and Echo*.

CHAPTER XVI

1. *New York World* News Service dispatch in *Washington Post*, September 23, 1930.
2. George H. Manning in *Richmond Times-Dispatch*, October 17, 1930.

3. Associated Press dispatch in *Richmond Times-Dispatch,* October 18, 1930.
4. *Time,* February 16, 1931.
5. The twelve men who conducted the inquiry were later announced to have been: Revs. H. B. Porter, North Carolina Conference; T. G. Herbert, South Carolina Conference; R. D. Stockhouse, Upper South Carolina Conference; A. M. Hughlett, Florida Conference; W. L. Duran, North Georgia Conference; E. M. Overby, South Georgia Conference; W. E. Arnold, Kentucky Conference; B. P. Taylor, West Virginia Conference; A. T. McIlwain, North Mississippi Conference; R. N. Harper, Louisiana Conference; W. P. Whaley, North Arkansas Conference; J. S. Bacus, North Texas Conference.
6. Photostat of the original obtained from the late Senator Carter Glass.
7. Copy obtained from the late Senator Glass. Both this document and the one mentioned in note 6 have been verified as identical with those presented by Bishop Cannon's accusers at the church investigation in Washington.
8. Deposition taken at Sibley Hospital, Washington, June 15, 1936, by Robert H. McNeill, counsel to Bishop Cannon, and filed in the United States District Court for the District of Columbia.

CHAPTER XVII

1. *New York Herald Tribune,* May 7, 1930.
2. Ibid.
3. Franklyn Waltman, Jr., in the *Baltimore Sun,* June 6, 1930.
4. There is an unexplained discrepancy here of $300 between the $48,000, contained in his telegram to Jameson on February 12, 1929, and the $48,300 that he now mentions.
5. *Richmond Times-Dispatch,* May 14, 1931.
6. Associated Press dispatch from Roanoke, Virginia, published in *Richmond Times-Dispatch,* October 3, 1931.
7. Statement to the author by Roger J. Whiteford, of Washington, D.C., counsel for Tinkham in the case.
8. Report of the Select Committee on Senatorial Campaign Expenditures, Senator Gerald P. Nye, chairman. Seventy-Second Congress, First Session, Report No. 24, pp. 11–12.
9. Ibid., p. 11.
10. Associated Press dispatch published in *New York Times,* April 28, 1934.

Notes

11. Statements in this paragraph are based on personal, first-hand observation by the author, who was chief political reporter for the *Richmond Times-Dispatch* during the Hoover-Smith campaign, and who reported various anti-Smith rallies. The statements are reinforced, furthermore, by declarations to the author from Virginia Democrats who led the fight for Smith in 1928.

CHAPTER XVIII

1. *New York Times,* October 25 and December 17, 1927, and February 7 and 8, 1928.
2. Mabel Walker Willebrandt: *The Inside of Prohibition,* p. 144.
3. *Pictorial Review,* September 1929.
4. Stanley Walker: *Mrs. Astor's Horse,* p. 195.
5. J. Fred Essary in *Baltimore Sun,* March 5, 1931. Most of his article was republished in *Richmond Times-Dispatch,* March 22, 1931.
6. *New York Times,* June 9, 1932.
7. *Baltimore and Richmond Christian Advocate,* April 20, 1905.
8. Ibid., October 25, 1906.
9. Ibid., October 5, 1916.
10. Ibid., August 18, 1921.
11. *Richmond Times-Dispatch,* November 9, 1932.
12. Associated Press dispatch from Petersburg, Virginia, published in *Richmond Times-Dispatch,* October 4, 1933.
13. Washington dispatch from Robert M. Smith to *Philadelphia Public Ledger* and *New York Evening Post,* dated July 24, 1933.

CHAPTER XIX

1. Ibid.
2. Last will and testament of Bishop Cannon, on file at Chancery Court, Richmond, Virginia.
3. Rev. Alson J. Smith: "Inside Prohibition Headquarters," *American Mercury,* January 1948.

Bibliography

Most of the material relative to the career of Bishop James Cannon, Jr., is of a fugitive nature. It is to be found mainly in religious periodicals, in secular newspapers and magazines, and in the publications of the Anti-Saloon League and various Methodist bodies. Very little of it is between book covers.

The most valuable single source is the *Baltimore and Richmond Christian Advocate*, from 1904 to 1918, inclusive, during which period Dr. Cannon was editor of this Methodist weekly. The *Richmond Christian Advocate*, which succeeded it, also contains much material, and its files from 1919 to 1929 have been carefully examined.

The files of the Richmond newspapers since the beginning of the present century have been freely consulted. Considerable use likewise has been made of the *New York Times* and of its excellent *Index*.

I have likewise gained insight into the character and career of Bishop Cannon through conversations with scores, if not hundreds, of persons who had been thrown into close contact with him, many of whom are now dead. Some of these conversations were with the Bishop's admirers, some with his detractors. I have pursued the study of Cannon's career intermittently since 1929, and am extremely grateful to all those who have aided me. I wish especially to thank my wife for valuable criticism and for help in reading the proofs.

I sought access to the unpublished memoirs of the Bishop and the voluminous supporting papers, in order, among other things, that Cannon's side in all controversies might be fully reviewed. Access was not granted, for the stated reason that plans for publication of the work might be adversely affected if portions appeared elsewhere.

The complete list of authorities follows:

BOOKS

ASBURY, HERBERT: *Carry Nation*. New York, 1929.
BEER, THOMAS: *The Mauve Decade*. New York, 1926.

Bibliography

BOOLE, ELLA A.: *Give Prohibition Its Chance.* Evanston, Ill., 1929.

BROCK, H. I.: *Meddlers.* New York, 1930.

BROUN, HEYWOOD, and LEECH, MARGARET: *Anthony Comstock, Roundsman of the Lord.* New York, 1927.

CHERRINGTON, E. H., ed.: *Standard Encyclopedia of the Alcohol Problem.* Westerville, Ohio, 1925.

COLVIN, D. LEIGH: *Prohibition in the United States.* New York, 1926.

DOBYNS, FLETCHER: *The Amazing Story of Repeal.* Chicago and New York, 1940.

FARISH, HUNTER DICKINSON: *The Circuit Rider Dismounts: A Social History of Southern Methodism.* Richmond, 1938.

FISHER, IRVING, assisted by H. BRUCE BROUGHAM: *Prohibition Still at Its Worst.* New York, 1928.

IRBY, RICHARD: *History of Randolph-Macon College, Virginia.* Richmond, no date (1898?).

MERZ, CHARLES: *The Dry Decade.* Garden City, 1931.

MONAHAN, M., ed.: *A Text Book of True Temperance,* published by United States Brewers' Association, second edition. New York, 1911.

MOSKOWITZ, HENRY, ed.: *Progressive Democracy, Addresses and State Papers of Alfred E. Smith.* New York, 1928.

NEVINS, ALLAN: *The American States during and after the Revolution, 1775–1779.* New York, 1924.

ODEGARD, PETER: *Pressure Politics, the Story of the Anti-Saloon League.* New York, 1928.

PALMER, FREDERICK: *Newton D. Baker: America at War.* 2 vols., New York, 1931.

ROOT, GRACE C.: *Women and Repeal.* New York, 1934.

SHAY, FRANK, and HELD, JOHN, JR.: *Drawn from the Wood.* New York, 1929.

STELZLE, CHARLES: *Why Prohibition.* New York, 1918.

STEUART, JUSTIN: *Wayne Wheeler, Dry Boss.* New York, 1928.

STOUT, CHARLES TABER: *The Eighteenth Amendment and the Part Played by Organized Medicine.* New York, 1921.

SULLIVAN, MARK: *Our Times,* Vols. I–VI, New York, 1926, 1927, 1930, 1932, 1933, 1935.

WALKER, STANLEY: *Mrs. Astor's Horse.* New York, 1935.

WASSON, REV. E. A.: *Religion and Drink.* New York, 1914.

WEST, WILLIS MASON: *American History and Government.* New York, 1913.

Bibliography

WILLEBRANDT, MABEL WALKER: *The Inside of Prohibition.* Indianapolis, 1929.

YOUNG, HUGH: *A Surgeon's Autobiography.* New York, 1940.

PAMPHLETS, PERIODICALS, MINUTES, PROCEEDINGS, NEWSPAPERS, *etc.*

American Issue, Virginia Edition, 1908, 1909, 1925–9, inclusive.

Anti-Prohibition Manual, The, 1915–17, published by the National Wholesale Liquor Dealers' Association of America.

Anti-Prohibition Manual, The, 1918, published by the National Association of Distillers and Wholesale Dealers.

ASBURY, HERBERT: "The Drys Try Again," *Collier's,* June 8, 1946.

Baltimore and Richmond Christian Advocate, 1904–18, inclusive (1914 and 1915 files incomplete).

BIVENS, IRENE: "Bishop Cannon Works," *Richmond Times-Dispatch* Sunday Magazine, February 20, 1938.

BOND, REV. ALBERT RICHMOND, D.D.: *Southern Baptists and Illiteracy,* published by Southern Baptist Education Board, March 26, 1928.

Bonfort's Wine and Spirit Circular, 1909–19, inclusive.

BROWNELL, FREDERICK G.: "Is Prohibition Coming Back?" *American Magazine,* September 1947.

Catalogue, Blackstone Female Institute, 1909–10, and *Catalogue, Blackstone College for Girls,* 1919–20.

Catalogue, Princeton Theological Seminary, 1885–8, inclusive.

Catalogue, State Female Normal School, Farmville, Va., 1894–5, 1910–11, 1915–16.

CANNON, JAMES, JR.: sketch of, in *Men of Mark in Virginia,* Washington, D.C., 1907.

——: *Farewell Address to Class of 1906,* Blackstone Female Institute.

——: *Farewell Address to Class of 1908,* Blackstone Female Institute.

——: "Prohibition in the United States," *Current History,* March 1923.

——: "We're Going to Stay Dry," *Collier's,* July 31, 1926.

——: "The Militant Prohibition Stand," *Review of Reviews,* March 1928.

——: "Al Smith, Catholic, Tammany, Wet," *Nation,* July 4, 1928.

——: *Unspotted from the World,* leaflet published by Cannon, dated August 3, 1929.

CHERRINGTON, E. H., ed.: *Anti-Saloon League Year Book,* 1909–14, inclusive, 1918, 1923–8, inclusive.

Bibliography

CHERRINGTON, E. H., ed.: *Proceedings, Fifteenth International Congress against Alcoholism,* Washington, D.C., September 21–6, 1920.

CLARKE, ALAN BURTON: "Seventeen Years in the Desert," series of twenty articles in *Richmond Times-Dispatch,* October 30–November 30, 1933, a history of the prohibition movement in Virginia.

Cyclopedia of Temperance and Prohibition, New York, 1891. Articles on "Bible and Drink," "Bible Wines," and "Communion Wine."

DABNEY, VIRGINIUS: "Bishop Cannon Wins an Award," *Nation,* April 17, 1929.

Daily Advocate (published during each General Conference of the M.E. Church, South), 1902, 1922, 1938.

DAVENPORT, WALTER: "The Virginia Reel," *Collier's,* November 2, 1929.

Discipline, M.E. Church, South, 1926.

Encyclopædia Britannica, 13th ed., article on "Prohibition." 11th ed., article on "Liquor Laws."

Hearings before a Select Committee on Senatorial Campaign Expenditures, United States Senate, Seventy-first Congress, Virginia, Parts I and II.

HENNING, ARTHUR SEARS: "The Lobby of the Churches," *Liberty,* April 6, 1929.

HIGH, STANLEY: "The Drys Return to the Wars," *Saturday Evening Post,* November 25, 1939.

HUNTINGTON, ELLSWORTH, and WHITNEY, LEON F.: "Religion and Who's Who," *American Mercury,* August 1927.

IRWIN, WILL: "The Resurrection of Mr. Volstead," *Scribner's,* February 1939.

Journals, General Conferences, M.E. Church, South, 1902, 1906, 1910, 1914, 1918, 1922, 1926.

Manufacturer's Record, April 21 and 28, May 12, 1927; February 16, 1928.

McNEILL, ROBERT H., attorney for James Cannon, Jr., in his suit against Representative George H. Tinkham for $500,000. Deposition taken by him from Cannon at Sibley Hospital, Washington, June 15, 1936, and filed thereafter in United States District Court, District of Columbia.

MERRITT, DIXON: "James Cannon, Jr.," *Outlook,* September 12, 1928.

Mida's Criterion, 1914.

Minority Report, Committee on Publishing Interests, M.E. Church, South, on the "War Claim," to General Conference of 1902.

352

Bibliography

Minority Report, Unification Commission, M.E. Church, South, and M.E. Church, Chattanooga, Tenn., July 3, 1924.

Minutes, Washington Literary Society, Randolph-Macon College, 1881–5, inclusive.

Normal Record, The, State Female Normal School, Farmville, Va., November 1897.

Periscope, The, 1926–8, inclusive.

PEZET, WASHINGTON: "The Temporal Power of Evangelism," *Forum,* October 1926.

Proceedings, Annual Conventions, Anti-Saloon League of America, 1898–1911, inclusive.

Proceedings, International Congress against Alcoholism, Winona Lake, Ind., August 17–23, 1927.

Proceedings, National Retail Liquor League of America, 1911–13, inclusive, and *National Retail Liquor Dealers' Association,* 1914–16, inclusive.

Proceedings, United States Brewers' Association, 1907–10, inclusive.

Randolph-Macon Monthly, Semi-Centennial Edition, April 1882.

Report, Select Committee on Senatorial Campaign Expenditures (Report No. 24).

Richmond Christian Advocate, 1919–29, inclusive.

RYAN, JOHN A., D.D.: "A Catholic View of the Election," *Current History,* December 1928.

SMITH, REV. ALSON, J.: "Inside Prohibition Headquarters," *American Mercury,* January 1948.

——: "Is Prohibition Coming Back?", *American Mercury,* October 1948.

Statement of the Book Agents and Report of the Book Committee to the General Conference, M.E. Church, South, 1902.

Virginia Conference Annual, published by Virginia Conference, M.E. Church, South, 1888–1918, inclusive.

WHITE, OWEN P.: "Workers in the Vineyard," *Collier's,* October 6, 1928.

WOOD, JUNIUS B.: "Is Prohibition Coming Back?" *Nation's Business,* September 1946.

Year Book, United States Brewers' Association, 1909–21, inclusive.

INDEX

Index

Index

Index

Index

Index

Index

Index